UNDERSTANDING JOINT OPERATING AGREEMENTS

UNDERSTANDING JOINT OPERATING AGREEMENTS

Edited by
Eduardo G. Pereira

intersentia
Cambridge – Antwerp – Portland

Intersentia Ltd
Sheraton House | Castle Park
Cambridge | CB3 0AX | United Kingdom
Tel.: +44 1223 370 170 | Fax: +44 1223 370 169
Email: mail@intersentia.co.uk
www.intersentia.com | www.intersentia.co.uk

Distribution for the UK and Ireland:
NBN International
Airport Business Centre, 10 Thornbury Road
Plymouth, PL6 7 PP
United Kingdom
Tel.: +44 1752 202 301 | Fax: +44 1752 202 331
Email: orders@nbninternational.com

Distribution for Europe and all other countries:
Intersentia Publishing nv
Groenstraat 31
2640 Mortsel
Belgium
Tel.: +32 3 680 15 50 | Fax: +32 3 658 71 21
Email: mail@intersentia.be

Distribution for the USA and Canada:
International Specialized Book Services
920 NE 58th Ave. Suite 300
Portland, OR 97213
USA
Tel.: +1 800 944 6190 (toll free) | Fax: +1 503 280 8832
Email: info@isbs.com

ISBN: 978-1-78068-411-6
Depot no.: D/2016/7849/88
NUR: 820

GPRC
Guaranteed
Peer Reviewed
Content

British Library Cataloguing in Publication Data. A catalogue record for this book is available from the British Library.

CONTENTS

LIST OF ABBREVIATIONS

AAPL	American Association of Professional Landmen
ABC	anti-bribery and corruption
AFE	authorisation for expenditure
AIPN	Association of International Petroleum Negotiators
ALARP	'as low as reasonably practicable'
AMIA	area of mutual interest agreement
AO	authorised officer
API	American Petroleum Institute
capex	capital expenditures
CAPL	Canadian Association of Petroleum Landmen
CAR	Construction All Risk
DOJ	US Department of Justice
DPA	deferred prosecution agreement
DSA	Decommissioning Security Agreement
E&P	exploration and production
EITI	Extractive Industries Transparency Initiative
FOA	farm-out agreement
FCPA	US Foreign Corrupt Practices Act
GBMP	Greenland's Bureau of Minerals and Petroleum
HGI	Host Government Instrument
HSE	health, safety and environment
IMO	International Maritime Organization
IOC	international oil company
JBA	joint bidding agreement
JOA	joint operating agreement
JSBA	Joint Study and Bid Agreement
JV	joint venture
JVA	joint venture agreement
NOC	national oil company
NPA	non-prosecution agreement
NPD	Norwegian Petroleum Directorate
OEE	Operators' Extra Expenses
OGA	Oil and Gas Authority
OGUK	Oil & Gas UK
OpCom	Operating Committee
opex	operating expenses

OPOL	Offshore Pollution Liability Agreement
OSPAR Convention	Convention on the Protection of the Marine Environment of the North-East Atlantic
PAA	partial amendment agreement
PSA	production sharing agreement
PSC	production sharing contract
RMMLF	Rocky Mountain Mineral Law Foundation
SEC	US Securities and Exchange Commission
SFO	Serious Fraud Office
SPA	sale and purchase agreement
SPV	special purpose vehicle
UKCS	United Kingdom Continental Shelf
UNCLOS	United Nations Convention on the Law of the Sea 1982
WPB	work programme and budget

LIST OF AUTHORS

Jen Ackroyd
Senior Associate, Ashurst LLP

Giulia Carloni
Senior Consultant, LXL LLP

Yanal Abul Failat
Associate, LXL LLP

Anaïs Harlé
Associate, White & Case LLP

Birgitte Jensen
Senior Consultant, LXL LLP

Ole Kirkvaag
Head of the international petroleum and natural resources advisory group of Arntzen de Besche

Aaron Murphy
International corruption attorney

Dyfan Owen
Head of Dispute Resolution in the Middle East, Ashurst LLP

Eduardo G. Pereira
Adjunct Professor of Energy Law, University of Eastern Finland Law School; attorney/international energy consultant

Michael Polkinghorne
Partner, White & Case LLP

Craig Purdie
International oil and gas attorney

Peter Roberts
Partner, Orrick LLP, Head of Oil and Gas

Harry J. Sullivan, Jr.
Kosmos Energy

David Sweeney
Partner, K&L Gates LLP

Tuuli Timonen
Senior Associate, White & Case LLP

Wei Wei Wang
Associate, Ashurst LLP

Katie Winterbourne
BSc, LLB, LLM; Director, Lantegy Legal Pty Ltd

Leslie Weihua Zhang
Director, Project Management Division, Legal Dept., China National Offshore Oil Corporation

Syed Marzidy Syed Marzuki
General Counsel, PETRONAS Chemicals Group

INTRODUCTION

Eduardo G. Pereira

Typically oil and gas resources belong to the relevant host government and private investors should obtain permission from that government to conduct oil and gas exploration and production activities. This permission is commonly granted through a concession contract, production sharing contract, service contract or a variation on any of the above (host government contracts). Private parties tend to regulate their own relationship in a private document known as a joint operating agreement (JOA). The JOA is one of the most important instruments in the upstream industry, along with the host government contracts.

The JOA is widely used in the petroleum industry across different continents and standards. Several regions prefer to issue a standard model form to speed up the negotiation process and to indicate the accepted practices in that region. Although different regions might have individual particularities, they tend to use similar structures and key provisions in regulating joint ventures.

There are a few publications available that explain what a JOA is, what the main provisions, the views of Non-Operators, and the consequences of a sole risk project. But there is no single publication that analyses and explains key practical concerns related to all JOAs. This book focuses on key practical issues that oil and gas companies might face in different parts of the world whenever they negotiate or implement a JOA.

The first part of this book deals with the enforceability of JOAs and practical issues related to regulatory challenges. This is a critical issue in any JOA, as all parties hope and expect to sign an enforceable agreement. It would be an unpleasant surprise to find out later in court or from the host government that the signed JOA is not enforceable or that it is not fit for purpose. For these reasons the first part of this book will address a variety of issues including but not limited to the challenges in signing a JOA in civil law countries, the considerations and concerns in negotiating a JOA for unconventional operations, the consequences and concerns arising from the interaction between JOAs and host government contracts, and compliance with bribery laws and decommissioning obligations.

The second part of the book deals with key clauses for any JOA. We place greater emphasis on the control of operations and expenditures as they lie at the heart of any consortium. From a non-operator's point of view, this might be the most important concern in the consortium, as the non-operator often cannot control or decide the pace of operations. The key issues in control of operations and expenditures will be addressed in this book including but not limited to the enforceability of the default mechanisms, the liabilities of the parties, the procedures and concerns arising from an assignment, and the financial procedures to control the expenses in the consortium.

This book addresses key topical issues and is written by leading experts from key oil and gas jurisdictions around the world, including Australia, Brazil, China, Malaysia, Norway, the United Kingdom and United States of America, among others.

In short, this book provides valuable practical knowledge on JOAs for lawyers, consultants, academics and business people interested in upstream contracts and regulations.

PART I

CONSIDERATIONS PRIOR TO ENTERING INTO A JOA

Participants in the oil and gas industry often operate on a global scale, with each region and each petroleum province having a clearly defined set of requirements and obligations. That being said, the challenges faced by these requirements are similar, and as a result it is straightforward for participants to agree upon and implement similar contracts and avoid lengthy contractual negotiations.[1] This makes it simple to use standard JOA model forms to facilitate the negotiation of that agreement.

While most of oil and gas regions have developed their own JOA model form over time and through experience that addresses their individual needs. Different provinces and regions carry out their activities in different contexts (e.g. onshore or offshore) and are constrained by different legal systems (e.g. civil or common law), so it is thus important to note that, regardless of common threads within JOA model forms, they need to be adapted to the specific characteristics of the region. Nonetheless, all JOA model forms are based on similar principles.[2] Standardised JOA model forms are important; they are a valuable resource for the advancement of oil and gas transactions. However, they often cannot comprehensively address the specific demands and factors of each negotiation and therefore a flexible approach to adjustment is key.[3]

Since the introduction of JOAs, the world has changed. The oil and gas industry now has to face ever-increasing costs, more environmental regulation, reduced accessibility of 'easy resources', and a greater number of competing companies. JOAs are now more frequently revised and added to because of the increased number of participants, all of whom agree on the variables that need to be addressed. This tends to benefit operations as the greater pool of knowledge and experience creates JOAs that are relevant, practical and enforceable in a given jurisdiction. The original models had few environmental constraints and were not limited by costs, and companies were much freer to explore and exploit

1. C. Malaquias Miles, 'AIPN 2002 Model Form Joint Operating Agreement in Oil and Gas Joint Ventures' (2003) 22 *Australian Resources & Energy L.J.* 153-160.
2. Ibid.
3. A. Timothy Martin, 'Model Contracts: a Survey of the Global Petroleum Industry' (2004) 22 *J. Energy & Nat. Resources L.* 284.

oil and gas. The increased regulations have allowed for the progressive and welcome development of the JOA model.[4]

In conclusion, there are a variety of issues that oil and gas companies should be aware of before signing a JOA, including civil law issues, anti-bribery laws, unitisation, unconventional resources, decommissioning, HSE, and host government contracts.

[4] G.B. Conine, 'Property Provisions of the Operating Agreement, Interpretation, Validity, and Enforceability' (1988) 19 *Tex. Tech L. Rev.* 1265.

BRIBERY LAWS AND COMPLIANCE

Dyfan OWEN, Wei Wei WANG and Aaron MURPHY

1. INTRODUCTION

The oil and gas sector is recognised as being at risk of corrupt practices. Some of the largest fines for bribery and corruption globally have related to the activities of oil and gas companies.[1]

This chapter provides an overview of key anti-bribery and corruption (ABC) legislation and conventions that affect the oil and gas sector. It analyses the primary challenges and concerns affecting risk profiles of companies entering into JOAs, and provides guidance and practical advice on putting in place adequate ABC measures to deal with these risks.[2]

2. KEY LEGISLATION AND INSTRUMENTS

2.1. UK: BRIBERY ACT 2010

The UK Bribery Act 2010 (Bribery Act) came into force on 1 July 2011. It criminalises the giving[3] and receiving[4] of bribes, bribery of foreign public officials[5] and, significantly for companies, includes an offence of failing to prevent bribery by persons performing services for or on their behalf

1 In July 2010, it was announced that Italian multinational Eni and its Dutch subsidiary would pay US$365 million in penalties and disgorgement to settle FCPA charges in relation to contracts for the construction of LNG facilities on Bonny Island, Nigeria. In May 2013, French oil giant Total agreed to pay US$398 million in penalties and disgorgement to settle FCPA charges in relation to bribes paid to win oil and gas contracts in Iran.

2 This chapter is not intended to be a comprehensive review of all developments in the law and practice, or to cover all aspects of those referred to. Each company will have its own unique risks and the guidance set out in this chapter will not necessarily deal with each such risk. Readers should take legal advice before applying the information contained in this chapter to their specific issues or transactions.

3 Bribery Act 2010, s. 1.

4 *Ibid.*, s. 2.

5 *Ibid.*, s. 6.

(associated persons) (Section 7 Offence).[6] Such an association can arise from a company's relationship with contractors, suppliers, distributors or, as tends to be more common in the energy sector, joint venture partners. A company can be criminally liable for bribery committed by an associated person even if the company was unaware of the bribe. However, the company has a full defence if it can demonstrate that, despite a particular case of bribery, it nevertheless had 'adequate procedures' in place to prevent persons associated with it from committing bribery.[7]

The Bribery Act provides the most comprehensive anti-bribery legislation to date with a wide territorial reach. For an offence to come within the scope of the Bribery Act, it must have been committed in the UK or, if committed outside the UK, the offender must have a close connection with the UK. Specifically, the Bribery Act applies if the offence was committed by a UK citizen, a person usually resident in the UK, or a company incorporated under the laws of the UK. Senior officers of a company that has engaged in bribery can also be prosecuted for the offence. International energy companies that carry on a business or part of a business in the UK, wherever in the world they may be incorporated or formed, will likely be caught by the Bribery Act.

2.2. US: FOREIGN CORRUPT PRACTICES ACT

The US Foreign Corrupt Practices Act (FCPA) contains two distinct sets of provisions:

(a) *Anti-bribery provisions*: These make it a crime to offer, promise or provide anything of value to a foreign official for the purpose of obtaining or retaining business or securing an improper business advantage.[8] They apply to any US citizen or resident, any US chartered business or any company traded on a US exchange anywhere in the world.[9] They also apply to anyone else who carries out any part of a violation on US soil or through the use of any means of interstate commerce. The anti-bribery provisions are aggressively pursued by the US Department of Justice (DOJ).

(b) *Record-keeping and internal controls provisions*: These apply to companies required to file periodic reports with the US Securities and Exchange Commission (SEC) and any company traded on a US exchange.[10] These provisions require companies to maintain records that, in 'reasonable

6 *Ibid.*, s. 7.
7 *Ibid.*, s. 7(2).
8 15 U.S.C. §§78dd-l(a), 78dd-2(a), 78dd-3(a).
9 15 U.S.C. §§78dd-l(a), 15 U.S.C. §78dd-2(h).
10 15 U.S.C. §78m(b)(2).

detail', accurately reflect the disposition of the company's assets and to institute a system of internal controls designed to ensure proper use of the company's assets. 'Reasonable detail' means a level sufficient to 'satisfy prudent officials in the management of their own affairs.'[11] These provisions are subject to broad interpretation.

US companies can obtain substantial credit for robust compliance programmes, including complete declinations to pursue any charges. Under US law, the measure of what constitutes an effective compliance programme is derived from the US Sentencing Guidelines[12] and the Principles of Federal Prosecution of Business Organizations[13] (Federal Principles) contained in the US Attorney's Manual.

The plain language of the Bribery Act is broader than the FCPA in three significant respects:

- the Bribery Act applies to both the giver of the bribe ('active' bribery) and the recipient of the bribe ('passive' bribery);
- the Bribery Act governs both public corruption and private bribery. On its face, the FCPA applies only to public corruption. However, in practice, both the DOJ and SEC have pursued private bribery in recent years using different legislative regimes;[14] and
- the Bribery Act does not include an exception for facilitation payments. The FCPA permits small payments given to foreign officials to induce them to perform a non-discretionary function that they are already obligated to perform (for example, a small payment to a recalcitrant immigration official who refuses to stamp a passport despite it having a properly issued visa). However, the exception is interpreted by the DOJ and SEC in the narrowest possible light.

Finally, in practice, provisions similar to the Bribery Act's 'adequate procedures' defence[15] are available in the US, although they are not formally prescribed

---

11 15 U.S.C. §78m(b)(7).

12 United States Sentencing Guidelines §§8B2.1, 8C1.1, 8C2.5, 8D1.4.

13 United States Attorney's Manual §9-28.800.

14 Whether a bribe is considered by the authorities to be 'public' or 'private' is determined based on whether the recipient is a public official or an employee at a private company. This distinction is blurred in situations involving state-owned, or state-controlled, companies that operate like private entities. However, both UK and US laws are drafted widely and consider employees of such entities as public officials even if they are not members of management. Therefore, US and UK authorities are likely to consider, and pursue, as a public corruption case the bribery of an employee of a national oil company (for example, at Petrobras, a publicly traded corporation with the Government of Brazil as its majority shareholder) in the same manner as the bribery of a public official at a national ministry of oil.

15 Bribery Act 2010, s. 7(2).

in the legislation. The central difference between what qualifies as 'adequate procedures' under the two acts is that a company subject to the Bribery Act will have to address active private bribery as well as bribery of foreign public officials as part of its compliance programme. This is because the adequate procedures defence in respect of the Section 7 Offence is aimed directly at compliance with the active anti-bribery provisions of the Bribery Act. A failure properly to address in its compliance programme active bribery and bribery of foreign public officials will automatically disqualify a company from being able to claim benefit from the adequate procedures defence.

2.3. OECD CONVENTION ON COMBATING BRIBERY OF FOREIGN PUBLIC OFFICIALS IN INTERNATIONAL BUSINESS TRANSACTIONS

First adopted in 1997, the OECD Convention on Combating Bribery of Foreign Public Officials in International Business Transactions (OECD Anti-Bribery Convention) has had a significant impact on global anti-corruption legislation. It requires each nation to implement laws against foreign and domestic corruption, to provide mutual legal assistance to signatory states, to make corruption offences extraditable and to ensure that there are proportionate civil sanctions against companies in countries that do not recognise corporate criminal liability (such as Germany and Japan). The adoption of the OECD Anti-Bribery Convention kicked off a wave of new and amended legislation around the world and signalled the rise of ABC enforcement as an issue of lasting and global significance. As at 21 May 2014, 41 countries had adopted the OECD Anti-Bribery Convention.[16]

2.4. WORLD BANK ANTI-CORRUPTION STRATEGIES

From the mid-1990s, the World Bank began adopting anti-corruption regulations to govern its lending programmes. World Bank enforcement has global reach and impact, particularly in the developing world where its lending programmes are focused. Many companies are subject to World Bank regulations without necessarily being aware of it. For example, products or services delivered to a World Bank-funded project are typically covered by World Bank anti-corruption and fraud rules. The World Bank takes a very wide view of what constitutes corruption and fraud, and debarment is virtually automatic once action is initiated against a violator. The consequences can be severe because the World

[16] <www.oecd.org/daf/anti-bribery/WGBRatificationStatus.pdf> accessed 29.02.2016.

Bank is party to a cross-debarment treaty with the other four major multilateral development banks. This means that once any company is debarred for more than one year by any of the five treaty members, they are automatically also debarred by the other four.[17]

2.5. UNITED NATIONS CONVENTION AGAINST CORRUPTION

Effective in 2005, the United Nations Convention against Corruption is the most widely adopted ABC convention (at the time of writing 178 nations have adopted it). The UN Convention contains a mix of mandatory and optional provisions, which has resulted in continued non-uniformity around the world on issues such as corporate criminal liability, passive bribery of foreign officials and commercial bribery.

Most important are the UN Convention's provisions on international cooperation, which have contributed greatly to the rise of large, multi-jurisdictional investigations. The UN Convention requires parties to assist each other in combating corruption in the form of mutual legal assistance, extradition, law enforcement cooperation and asset recovery. This has made prosecution and evidence gathering through cross-border investigations much easier in recent years.

2.6. ENACTMENTS AND INITIATIVES TARGETING TRANSPARENCY IN THE OIL AND GAS SECTOR

As well as general ABC legislation, there are a number of enactments and initiatives which specifically target financial transparency in the oil and gas sector.

Set up in 2002, the Extractive Industries Transparency Initiative[18] (EITI) was one of the first such initiatives. These countries agree to implement the EITI standard to ensure full disclosure of taxes and other payments made by oil, gas and mining companies to governments. These payments are published in an annual report, allowing citizens to see how much their government is receiving from their country's natural resources. Currently, 49 countries are implementing the EITI standard.

---

17 The parties to the agreement are the African Development Bank, the Asian Development Bank, the European Bank for Reconstruction and Development, the Inter-American Development Bank Group and the World Bank Group <http://siteresources.worldbank.org/NEWS/Resources/AgreementForMutualEnforcementofDebarmentDecisions.pdf> accessed 29.02.2016.

18 <http://eiti.org/eiti> accessed 29.02.2016.

The EU Accounting Directive was enacted in June 2013.[19] Chapter 10 of the Directive requires companies active in the extractives industry to report on payments made to governments worldwide on a country and project basis. Member States had until July 2015 to implement the EU Accounting Directive into national legislation. The UK, like a number of others, committed to expedited implementation and its implementing legislation came into force on 1 December 2014.[20] Under this legislation, UK incorporated companies above a certain size are required to make disclosures for financial years commencing on or after 1 January 2015 (one year earlier than required by the EU Directive).

3. CONSEQUENCES

Bribery cases are typically subject to a broad range of penalties, including criminal and civil fines, disgorgement of profits, imprisonment for individuals and various regulatory sanctions. Countries vary on how severely they treat different types of infractions, but the trend in recent years has been to increase and broaden the penalties available.

3.1. FINES

In the US, financial penalties are set out in the FCPA itself. However, in corporate prosecutions the more common means of calculating the fine is through one of the three methods set out in the US Sentencing Guidelines. The methods employed are complex and require the calculation of an 'offence level' and 'culpability score' that are then used to compute a fine amount, which, depending on factors such as the level of cooperation, is further increased or decreased by applying a multiplier. Even in cases involving deferred or non-prosecution agreements (see below), or SEC cease and desist orders, where the US Sentencing Guidelines would not technically apply, their calculations will typically be the starting point for any discussion of fine or restitution amounts. In 2014, a total of US$1.56 billion was reportedly paid by ten companies to settle FCPA charges, compared to US$731.1 million paid by twelve companies in 2013,[21] indicating a trend towards larger fines for corruption offences.

The UK Sentencing Council, following the lead of the US, has introduced guidelines for sentencing companies convicted of offences that are caught by the

---

19 Directive 2013/34/EU of 26 June 2013 on the annual financial statements, consolidated financial statements and related reports of certain types of undertakings [2013] OJ L182/19.

20 Reports on Payments to Governments Regulations 2014/3209.

21 FCPA Blog, *The 2014 Enforcement Index* by Richard L. Cassin, 05.01.2015.

Bribery Act.[22] Under the guidelines, which follow the US approach, courts in England and Wales will assess:

- the offender's culpability, determined, by reference to factors such as its role and motivation, to be either 'high', 'medium' or 'lesser' (for example, a sustained period of offending, abuse of a dominant market position or wilful failure to put in place effective systems are factors indicative of a higher level of culpability); and
- the harm caused (that is, the amount of the gain or the amount of loss avoided).

Once the levels of culpability and harm have been established, the courts will then apply the relevant multiplier and may impose fines of up to 400% of the company's gross profit from the contract obtained, retained or sought as a result of the offence. Alternatively, the fine may reflect the likely cost avoided by failing to put in place appropriate measures to prevent the bribery. Where there is insufficient evidence of the amount that was likely to be obtained, the court may instead impose a fine of between 10 and 20% of the company's worldwide revenue derived from the product or business area to which the offence related for the period of the offence.

On 19 February 2016, UK construction company Sweett Group plc became the first corporate to be convicted under the Bribery Act. It had pleaded guilty to a charge under the Section 7 Offence for failing to prevent £680,000 in bribes from being paid through a subsidiary in order to win a contract related to the construction of a luxury hotel in Dubai. On sentencing, it was ordered to pay £1.4 million in fines as well as a confiscation order of £851,000 and costs of £95,000 to the Serious Fraud Office (SFO), the relevant UK prosecuting authority. The case demonstrates the SFO's appetite for securing the highest possible fines against corporate offenders.

It is expected that other countries will adopt penalty regimes that borrow heavily from those discussed above. However, the impact of any penalty regime will ultimately depend on the country's appetite for taking enforcement action.

3.2. IMPRISONMENT

Prison sentences vary widely from country to country but the trend is towards longer sentences among countries that have recently updated their ABC legislation. The threat of prison time is very real for any member of senior management who consents to, or participates in, corrupt activity. In August

[22] Fraud, bribery and money laundering offences: Definitive Guideline; *Sentencing Council*, pp. 47–53 <http://www.sentencingcouncil.org.uk/wp-content/uploads/Fraud_bribery_and_money_laundering_offences_-_Definitive_guideline.pdf> accessed 29.02.2016.

2014, four executives of global chemicals company Innospec were sentenced for bribing state officials in Indonesia and Iraq. Three received prison sentences, the longest being four years in respect of former chief executive Dennis Kerrison.[23] On sentencing, the judge said: 'Corruption in this company was endemic, institutionalised and ingrained ... but despite being a separate legal entity it is not an automated machine; decisions are made my human minds.'[24]

3.3. DEFERRED PROSECUTION AGREEMENTS AND NON-PROSECUTION AGREEMENTS

A deferred prosecution agreement (DPA) is an agreement reached under judicial supervision between the prosecutor and an offending company that allows a prosecution to be suspended for a defined period provided the organisation meets certain specified conditions. The conditions can include payment of penalties and/or compensation and the appointment of a monitor to oversee the implementation of an ABC programme. If the conditions of the DPA are satisfied, the case is dismissed and the company is never prosecuted.

In the US, DPAs have a long history and are widely used, particularly in corruption prosecutions. In addition, the DOJ uses non-prosecution agreements (NPAs), which offer even more flexibility. These are essentially an agreement between the DOJ and the accused whereby the accused agrees to waive any applicable limitation periods and fulfil certain specified requirements in exchange for the DOJ agreeing not to pursue a criminal case during the period of the agreement. NPAs typically last for three years and require companies to implement very specific compliance programmes, to report any additional instances of wrongdoing to the DOJ and to cooperate in any ongoing investigations of other companies or company employees. They are private agreements that are not subject to judicial oversight.

UK prosecutors were granted additional powers in the fight against fraud and economic crime and are now able to enter into US-style DPAs following provisions that came into force on 24 February 2014. At present, DPAs in the UK only apply to companies in cases of economic crime. However, DPAs will not be offered to companies where the alleged offence is an established and systemic part of its business practices or where such conduct is carried out with the knowledge of the company's senior management. DPAs in the UK are subject to judicial oversight.[25]

---

23 Kerrison's sentence was reduced on appeal to three years.

24 SFO press release, *Four sentenced for role in Innospec corruption*, 04.8.2014.

25 DPAs in the US are filed with a court and remain active cases on the court's docket for the duration of the deferment. As such, they are subject to court oversight although, in practice, judges in the US typically do not become highly involved in setting the terms of the agreement.

On 30 November 2015, the first UK DPA in relation to the Section 7 Offence received judicial approval. Entered into between the Serious Fraud Office and ICBC Standard Bank plc (Standard Bank), it related to payments made by Standard Bank's sister company, Stanbic Bank Tanzania Ltd (Stanbic), to a local partner in Tanzania which was in fact a conduit for bribes to government officials in order to secure a joint mandate for Standard Bank and Stanbic.[26] It was held that Stanbic and the Stanbic employees who had paid the bribes were associated persons of Standard Bank, since the latter stood to benefit from the award of the mandate. Despite there being obvious 'red flags' (see below), Standard Bank relied on Stanbic to carry out the necessary due diligence, meaning that its own ABC procedures were held to be inadequate. The case highlights the importance of early self-reporting and full and genuine cooperation with the SFO in obtaining a DPA and thereby avoiding prosecution.

3.4. DEBARMENT FROM PUBLIC PROCUREMENT

As mentioned above, the default sanction under the World Bank's compliance programme is debarment from World Bank and other multilateral development bank projects. But debarment as a sanction is also widely used by individual jurisdictions. Of particular relevance to the oil and gas sector is the EU Public Sector Procurement Directive,[27] under which companies face debarment from tendering for public sector contracts if they are convicted of certain offences including bribery and corruption (for example, under the UK Public Contracts Regulations 2015, companies face mandatory debarment if convicted of any of the offences of giving or receiving a bribe, or bribery of foreign public officials, under the Bribery Act).[28] Debarment is also particularly relevant in developing countries where many of the major projects – again, especially in the energy sector – have a high degree of government involvement. Most nations do not want companies known for corruption to continue to participate in public projects, often because elected officials do not want to be seen to be associated with such entities. Being frozen out of lucrative markets for a period of years

---

26 Under its DPA, Standard Bank was ordered to pay a financial penalty of US$16.8 million, pay back the bribe (US$6 million plus interest), disgorge the profit made (USS$8.4 million), cooperate in further investigations, undergo a compliance review and pay the SFO's legal costs (£330,000). It is interesting to note that, despite Standard Bank's early self-reporting and cooperation with the prosecuting authority, the fine levied is at the higher end of the scale in recognition of the seriousness of the bank's failings and the level of harm caused to the public (being the diversion of government funds).

27 Directive 2014/24/EU of 26 February 2014 on public procurement [2014] OJ L94/65. This came into force on 17.04.2014 and repealed Directive 2004/18/EC. Member States have two years to implement the new directive.

28 Regulation 57(1)(d) of the Public Contracts Regulations 2015/102.

(or permanently in severe cases) can effectively destroy a business until the debarment period ends.

3.5. NEGATIVE PUBLICITY AND RISK OF CROSS-BORDER INVESTIGATIONS

Corruption scandals make good press and being at the centre of a negative media storm can do long-lasting damage to a company's reputation and share price, and not just in the jurisdiction where the problem originated. For example, Walmart's share price fell 8.2% in the three days after details of its alleged bribery were publicised, wiping approximately US$17 billion off its market value.[29] Additionally, bad press in one part of the world may even prompt inquiries from enforcement agencies in other jurisdictions.

4. MANAGING RISK

The OECD Foreign Bribery Report published on 2 December 2014[30] revealed that out of over 400 cases of bribery of foreign public officials occurring over the last 15 years the highest percentage (19%) originated in the extractives sector. The oil and gas sector also ranked towards the bottom of Transparency International's Bribe Payers Index,[31] which analysed the likelihood of companies from 28 leading economies winning business abroad by paying bribes.

The following are factors which contribute to the apparent high propensity for corruption in the oil and gas sector:

- Many of the world's oil reserves are located in countries where corruption is considered to be widespread. For example, in Transparency International's Corruption Perceptions Index of 2015, Kazakhstan ranked 123rd out of 168 countries, Nigeria 136th, Venezuela 158th and Libya 161st.[32] Whether due to political instability, cultural dynamic or lack of infrastructure, many of these countries struggle to effectively combat corruption;

---

29 <www.reuters.com/article/2014/05/09/us-walmart-mexico-lawsuit-idUSBREA480F620140509> accessed 29.02.2016.

30 The OECD Foreign Bribery Report <http://www.oecd.org/corruption/oecd-foreign-bribery-report-9789264226616-en.htm> accessed 29.02.2016, analysed data from the 427 transnational cases of bribery of foreign public officials that have been concluded since the Convention on Anti-Bribery came into force in 1999.

31 <www.transparency.org/whatwedo/publication/bpi_2011> accessed 29.02.2016.

32 <http://www.transparency.org/cpi2015/#results-table> accessed 29.02.2016.

- Market conditions such as volatility in commodity prices are pushing oil and gas companies to venture into markets which may traditionally have been regarded as too high-risk. Advances in extraction technology is allowing them to do so. Entering into new, rapid-growth markets places stress on ethical standards;
- Oil and gas projects are characterised by high-value investment and significant government interaction and regulation, both of which provide opportunities and incentives for corruption. A common form of bribery in the oil and gas sector is perceived to be companies using improper contributions to high-ranking public officials with the intention of securing influence over policy and regulatory and/or legislative decisions; and
- Oil and gas projects also involve complex contractual and working arrangements with joint venture partners and third-parties, making the detection of bribery more difficult and exposing companies to the possibility of being held responsible for bribery committed by others.

For a company, a strong compliance programme is the best defence in any enforcement action or investigation. Companies in the oil and gas sector should consider adopting the measures recommended below in order to strengthen their ABC procedures and manage the risks identified above.

4.1. COMMITMENT FROM TOP-LEVEL MANAGEMENT

The UK Ministry of Justice's guidance on the Bribery Act[33] (MoJ Guidance) states that top-level management (i.e. board members and owners) should be at the forefront of fostering a culture in which bribery is never acceptable. Without that top-level commitment, there is a risk that any company's procedures will be perceived as inadequate. Most importantly of all, top-level management is expected to practise what it preaches. This is of even greater significant in light of the OECD Foreign Bribery Report, which found that 53% of foreign bribery cases involved corporate management or CEOs.[34]

To facilitate public awareness of their corporate governance standards, companies should also consider joining, and actively participating in, collective ABC initiatives and multi-stakeholder processes at a sectoral level such as EITI (see section 2.6 above).

---

33 <https://www.gov.uk/government/publications/bribery-act-2010-guidance> accessed 29.02.2016.

34 <http://www.oecd.org/corruption/oecd-foreign-bribery-report-9789264226616-en.htm> accessed 29.02.2016.

Companies traded on a US stock exchange are typically required to have a code of conduct that sets out high-level corporate ethics and legal standards. This code will often be introduced by the CEO or a corporate officer of similar status, making a clear statement that the code requires similar standards of all employees, from the highest officers and board members to entry-level employees. The code will then touch on a broad range of subjects, only one of which will usually be corruption.

A company's ABC policy (see below) should also be prefaced with a clear and unequivocal statement from the CEO (or other member of senior management) to employees regarding the company's zero tolerance approach to bribery.

4.2. ENSURING ADEQUATE PROCEDURES

As noted above, the only defence that is available to a company under the Bribery Act for failing to prevent bribery is to demonstrate that it had implemented adequate procedures to prevent such incidents. Therefore, an ABC policy should be supported by appropriate underlying procedures that give effect to the guidance within the policy and provide the tools by which bribery risks can be managed.

4.2.1. Risk Assessment Procedures

The MoJ Guidance makes clear that companies are expected to adopt a risk-based approach to managing bribery risks. Adopting a risk-based approach is likely to help companies focus their efforts where they are needed and ensure that procedures are proportionate to the risks faced. The guidance also emphasises the need for proportionality – what is proportionate will depend on the bribery risks faced and the nature, size and complexity of the company.

Although the US Sentencing Guidelines and the Federal Principles do not speak in the same proportionality terms, the concepts embedded in what they consider to be adequate compliance programmes are largely similar to the MoJ Guidance. However, there are certain instances where the US Sentencing Guidelines are highly specific or technical in ways that the UK guidance is not.

A company should carry out a risk assessment in respect of each new project or associated person and should renew its risk assessments on any material change of circumstances or climate. Where necessary, a company's ABC policy should be updated to address newly identified risks. However, as bribery risks can vary from one jurisdiction to another, or one company to another, a company should ensure that its decision making is tailored to the specific local risks.

4.2.2. *Red Flags*

Following the corruption allegations made against BAE Systems plc in relation to the Al Yamamah UK–Saudi Arabia arms deal,[35] the Woolf Committee's report on ethical policies and processes included a list of 'red flags'[36] to alert companies to areas of risk in relation to engaging associated persons. Certain facts and background information relating to an associated person can indicate a higher risk of exposure to bribery and corruption, which may require a greater level of due diligence.

The red flags identified by the Woolf Committee were the following:

- there is a history of corruption in the territory;
- the associated person lacks experience in the sector and/or in the jurisdiction in question;
- the associated person does not reside in the country where the customer or the project is located;
- the associated person's business has no significant presence within the country;
- the associated person represents companies with questionable reputation;
- the associated person refuses to sign an agreement to the effect that it has not and will not make a prohibited payment;
- the associated person states that money is needed to 'get the business';
- the associated person requests 'urgent' payments or unusually high commissions;
- the associated person requests payments to be made in cash, via a corporate vehicle (including in the form of equity), to a third country, to a numbered bank account or to some other person or entity;
- the associated person requires payment of the commission, or a significant proportion thereof, before or immediately upon award of the contract by the customer to the company;
- the associated person claims it can help secure the contract because it knows the right people;
- the associated person has a close personal/professional relationship with the government or a customer that could improperly influence the customer's decision;
- the associated person is recommended by a government official or customer;
- the associated person arrives on the scene just prior to the contract being awarded;

---

35 See Woolf Committee Report, '*Ethical Business in BAE Systems plc – the way forward*', May 2008 <https://www.icaew.com/~/media/corporate/files/technical/ethics/woolf%20report%202008.ashx> accessed 29.02.2016.

36 *Ibid.*, p. 26.

- the associated person indicates that a payment made to it will be set aside for a government official; and
- there are insufficient bona fide business reasons for retaining the associated person.

Following its consideration of red flags such as those listed above, a company will need to assess whether it is satisfied that there is a low risk of bribery. In certain instances, the risk identified may be so significant that it will not be possible to mitigate or manage the risk. In these circumstances the appointment of the proposed associated person should be rejected and recorded. If the company intends to continue with the appointment of that associated person despite the existence of red flags, it should obtain board-level approval and record the reasons in the board minutes.

However, the existence of a red flag does not always mean that a company cannot engage with the proposed third party. Appropriate additional investigation or diligence may clear the red flag by demonstrating that an initial concern was misplaced or inaccurate. Obtaining robust contractual protections such as warranties and indemnities may help in mitigating risks, although companies should bear in mind that proceeding in the face of red flags means enforcement authorities will be more aggressive if an issue arises later.

4.2.3. Due Diligence

Where the risk assessment indicates that there is a substantial risk of bribery, appropriate due diligence should be undertaken to evaluate that risk. Companies that are involved in joint ventures, regularly appoint intermediaries or agents, or operate in jurisdictions where facilitation payments are commonplace are at greater risk of being liable for bribery offences, and should take into account the following considerations:

(a) *Joint ventures*: When entering into a new joint venture, companies should consider having representation on the board of the joint venture company; ensure that the joint venture itself has adequate ABC procedures in place; establish an audit committee; and include adequate contractual protections. These controls are particularly critical where a company exercises control over the joint venture (either by contractual relationship, through equity investment, or in fact).[37]

[37] It is well settled under US law that a company with a majority stake will generally be held responsible for the corrupt activities of the joint venture. When a company holds a minority stake, the SC and DOJ will look to the level of control the company had over the corrupt activity. Under UK law, the position is similar, both legal entity and contractual joint ventures are covered by the Bribery Act. In case of bribery by contractual joint venture partners, a

The MoJ Guidance on the Section 7 Offence states that whether one joint venture party can be held liable for bribery committed by an employee of another joint venture party will depend on the level of control that that joint venture party has over the project.[38] In the case of JOAs, each party to the JOA will be represented on the operating committee and non-operators will exert a certain amount of control over the operator. This may count as sufficient 'control' for the purposes of the Section 7 Offence.

Companies entering into JOAs should conduct both initial and ongoing due diligence in respect of their joint venture partners and third parties:

(i) Initial due diligence should be conducted in respect of the award of the production licence and any governmental/regulatory approvals required for the project. A company should ensure that no such licence or approvals are procured through bribery and corruption, the risk of which is high due to the necessary involvement of government officials; and

(ii) Ongoing due diligence should be conducted throughout the life of the JOA. Whilst contractual provisions can afford some protection as against JOA partners (see below), particular attention should be paid to relationships and working arrangements with agents and third parties.

(b) *Agreements with agents*: These can involve exposing companies to high risks as it is often difficult for a company to closely monitor the agent's activities. Measures that may assist a company in mitigating the risks associated with appointing agents include establishing at the outset a clear statement of the precise nature of the agent's services, costs and commission (or other remuneration), with particular focus on success fees; conducting due diligence and reviewing any red flags; communicating the company's ABC procedures and delivering training where appropriate; asking the agent about its own ABC strategies; and reviewing the agreement annually and including contractual ABC protections (see below).

(c) Depending on the company's assessment of the risks associated with a particular transaction, it may be necessary to undertake detailed due diligence. In high-risk situations, it may be prudent for companies to instruct specialist due diligence providers through their legal teams to provide further detailed information in respect of new markets and/or new

company's liability will turn on the degree of its control over the joint venture – a question of fact, which will be decided by the courts on a case-by-case basis. For separate legal entity joint ventures, a company will only be liable if the joint venture was performing services on its behalf and the bribe is paid with the intention of benefiting the company. Ultimately, however, a company will need to fall back on whether it had in place 'adequate procedures' in order to prevent bribery by the joint venture from occurring.

[38] <https://www.gov.uk/government/publications/bribery-act-2010-guidance> accessed 29.02.2016, paragraph 41.

business partners. Such reports can vary in scope and range from simple, desktop-based searches across proprietary compliance databases and a negative media check on subjects to more detailed background studies informed by local language media searches, on-the-ground business intelligence and multiple source interviews.

4.2.4. Contractual Protections

Companies should consider including precedent ABC clauses for employees to use in contracts with third parties.

The Association of International Petroleum Negotiators published a new model form joint operating agreement (Model JOA) in 2012. Whilst the previous 2002 version of the Model JOA contained basic ABC protections, the 2012 version introduces more stringent provisions in an effort to address the increase in ABC enforcement activity worldwide and the coming into force of the Bribery Act. The 2012 Model JOA is expected to take over as the benchmark for joint operating arrangements in the international upstream oil and gas industry. The additional ABC protections afforded by the 2012 version of the Model JOA include the following:

- parties have the option to select a definition of 'Anti-Bribery Laws and Obligations' which is wide enough to ensure compliance with the Bribery Act by all parties;
- enhanced warranties as to past compliance with applicable ABC regulations and parties may include a right to request certification of such compliance for the preceding twelve-month period;
- parties have the right to make requests for information in order to verify compliance with applicable ABC regulations by other parties;
- an obligation on each party to the JOA to notify the other parties of any investigation or proceeding initiated by any government authority relating to an alleged violation of applicable ABC regulations;
- each party will indemnify the other parties for any damages and costs arising from that party's admission of bribery allegations or the final adjudication that bribery has taken place;
- an optional provision that, where a party that is withdrawing from the JOA for the sole reason that another party has breached its undertaking not to breach applicable ABC regulations, that party will have included in its calculation of damages the amount of its investment that is lost as a result of its withdrawal; and
- an option to include a right for non-operators to remove an operator that has admitted breach of applicable ABC regulations or that has been finally adjudicated as being guilty of such violations.

4.2.5. *Adequate Books and Records*

The procedures should include guidance on maintaining adequate records and books of accounts that accurately reflect each transaction entered into by the company. Employees should be prohibited from making false or misleading entries for any reason. All contractual agreements should also accurately describe the transactions and services to which they relate. No payment should be approved without adequate supporting documentation, and no payment should be made with the intention or understanding that all or part of any such payment is to be used for any purpose other than that described by the documents supporting the payment.

4.2.6. *Gifts and Hospitality*

Although the Bribery Act does not prescribe a particular limit, the MoJ Guidance recommends that hospitality should be 'commensurate with the reasonable and proportionate norms for the particular industry'. The FCPA contains an affirmative defence for promotional activities, which would include meals, gifts and entertainment, and it is generally understood that the value of any such gifts or hospitality should be modest and reasonable. Given the recognition that reasonable and proportionate hospitality, which seeks to improve a company's image, is an established and important part of doing business, bona fide hospitality that falls within the standards or norms for the particular sector is in itself unlikely to trigger the bribery offence. However, companies should take into account any applicable limits under local laws or under the rules of the proposed recipient/donor company or public organisation regarding the value of gifts and hospitality that may be given or received. Companies should provide clear guidance in their ABC procedures to prevent bribery from occurring under the guise of corporate hospitality.

4.2.7. *Facilitation Payments*

Although technically permitted under US law (and in a few other countries) these should be prohibited as they are prohibited by the Bribery Act and by the laws of virtually every other jurisdiction.[39] Employees should be required to report and record any demands for, or payments of, facilitation payments. Companies should also carry out a tailored risk assessment for all jurisdictions in which facilitation payments are regularly demanded with a view to dealing with bribery risks in jurisdictions where such demands are commonplace.

---

39 However, it should be noted that payments made under duress or in circumstances involving extortion, for example, where an individual's life or liberty is threatened, are typically not considered bribes or facilitation payments under UK or US laws.

4.2.8. *Training*

Companies should deliver training on their ABC policy and procedures to all employees (in the local language if necessary). Bespoke training should be rolled out to employees in senior and/or sensitive positions such as marketing, government relations, contracting, procurement and sales. Policies should indicate that employees are required to attend ABC training and existing training programmes should be reviewed to ensure that the desired corporate culture is understood by employees in all jurisdictions. In addition, companies should consider providing their associated persons with similar anti-bribery training or contractually requiring them to undertake the training themselves. Procedures should be implemented to record all training given.[40] This record should be reviewed periodically to ensure that refresher training can be provided where necessary and, in any event, following any new risk assessment or changes to the company's ABC policy.

4.2.9. *Reporting*

Companies should implement robust reporting procedures to empower and protect whistle-blowers who experience or witness bribery. These may consist of direct internal reporting procedures (for use by employees) or the use of whistleblowing hotlines that are resourced internally or through external providers (for use by employees and/or third parties such as associated persons). However, companies should obtain local legal advice to ensure that such reporting facilities do not breach their obligations under relevant data protection and employment laws.

4.2.10. *Monitoring compliance*

The ABC policy should include a procedure for monitoring and reviewing employees' compliance with it, ideally in conjunction with performance reviews. Such monitoring should include spot-checking employees' compliance with ABC procedures (for example, whether gifts and hospitality registers are being maintained, and whether training is being delivered and attended by employees) and the internal audit teams' performance of regular and comprehensive reviews. Non-compliance with the ABC policy should be a disciplinary offence.

---

40 This is especially important as the ability to prove that specific individuals received training is often a critical part of a company's defence.

4.3. ABC POLICY – OTHER PRACTICAL CONSIDERATIONS

It is important for an ABC policy to be capable of, and subject to, effective implementation and uptake by the business. A policy that is too complex to implement is a serious risk to the availability of the adequate procedures defence. In addition, an excessive administrative burden is also likely to be counterproductive.

4.3.1. Scope

The scope of the ABC policy should extend to all company personnel and any entities over which the company has control, and, where possible, to its associated persons. They should be asked to sign and return acknowledgement forms certifying that they have read and understood the policy.

4.3.2. Bribery and ABC Legislation to be Captured in Broadest Terms

The ABC policy should capture bribery and ABC legislation in their widest terms. 'ABC legislation' should be defined widely and should encompass any ABC laws and related rules, regulations and guidance applicable to the company's business operations, including, but not limited to, the laws and regulations of the US and UK (even where there is no direct link with either jurisdiction). This is because UK and US legislation are considered as setting the gold standard in ABC compliance, and collectively include several important provisions (such as prohibiting private- and public-sector bribery and facilitation payments) that may not be prohibited by local ABC laws.

4.3.3. Structure

The ABC policy should be structured so that headline guidance, of global application, is included in the ABC policy, while details of the underlying procedures can be set out in appendices. The practical advantages of this approach are:

(a) *Ease of amendment*: An ABC policy that contains guidance that is of common application to each of the company's offices will not need to be amended frequently to take into account changes in local laws. Procedures tailored to local risks and based on local laws can be set out in an appendix and updated as necessary.
(b) *Accessibility*: The ABC policy is ultimately intended to be read and digested by employees on the ground. Limiting the content of the ABC policy to

basic principles will enable the company to circulate a clear, brief document that is likely to be read and understood by a higher number of employees. Those who require information on particular procedures (for example, the company's protocol on gifts and hospitality) can turn to the relevant appendix for more detail.

(c) *Selectivity*: Where the company requires an associated person to comply contractually with certain ABC procedures, these can be isolated from the ABC pack and circulated individually and expressly referenced in any contractual warranties being obtained.

4.3.4. *Consistency with Other Policies*

The ABC policy should be consistent with other company policies. Where the company has other stand-alone policies that relate to topics covered by the ABC policy, such as a code of ethics or a whistle-blowing policy, these should be reviewed to check that the message is consistent with the guidance in the ABC policy.

4.3.5. *Availability*

The ABC policy should be easily available, for example, on the company's intranet, including, where its operations are based in multiple countries, in the language(s) of those countries. It is also good practice to make the policy available on the company's external website so that third parties can inform themselves of the company's stance on bribery.

5. CONCLUSION

Organisations that are involved in oil and gas projects need to be hands-on in implementing anti-bribery measures. Well-drafted agreements with associated persons, as well as robust ABC programmes, can make the difference between being the target of detailed international enforcement scrutiny or simply being a witness testifying to bribery committed by an associated person. All companies should therefore review their risk profiles, contracts and ABC programmes to ensure these are fit for purpose.

A compliance programme will only be fit for purpose if it addresses the risks the business faces. A proper risk analysis is essential. Top-level commitment is critical if a compliance programme is to meet the good faith requirement. Regular monitoring, reporting to the board and example-setting is an absolute must if any defence of 'adequate procedures' is to succeed.

A compliance programme will only work if it is user friendly and easy to implement. Keeping it simple, clear, and easy to follow, together with proper training, where appropriate, is key, as is monitoring its use and effectiveness. The case involving the Switzerland-based oil services firm Weatherford provides a salutary lesson. The company paid US$252 million in penalties and fines for FCPA and trade sanction violations in November 2013. Leslie Caldwell, chief of the DOJ's criminal division, noted that Weatherford 'had little more than a weak paper compliance program.'[41] In their plea agreements, the subsidiaries admitted that Weatherford did not have a dedicated compliance officer or compliance personnel, did not conduct anti-corruption training, and lacked an effective system for investigating employee reports of ethics and compliance violations.

International cooperation and intelligence sharing in order to prevent bribery and corruption is expected to increase. The implications of this renewed global focus on anti-bribery enforcement are challenging for many companies in the energy sector. The penalties are severe. Fines are increasing (the highest combined fine amounting to €1.8 billion), and lengthy prison sentences are being handed down. That, together with the negative impact the taint of corruption can have on a company's reputation and business, means companies cannot afford to let their compliance guard slip.

---

[41] <http://www.justice.gov/opa/speech/remarks-assistant-attorney-general-criminal-division-leslie-r-caldwell-22nd-annual-ethics> accessed 29.02.2016.

THE RELATIONSHIP WITH OTHER JOINT VENTURE AGREEMENTS

Jen Ackroyd

1. INTRODUCTION

Success in the international oil and gas industry has always required cooperation with other parties, whether they be contractors, governments or competitors.[1] Historically, oil and gas companies have formed joint venture groups or consortia as vehicles to conduct exploration, development and production activities. This is done primarily to reduce risk, share expertise and in part to diversify the production portfolio of a single company.[2] Such cooperation has become a dominant and unique feature of upstream petroleum operations.

[1] A. Timothy Martin and J. Jay Park, QC, 'Global petroleum industry model contracts revisited: Higher, faster, stronger' (2010) 3(1) *Journal of World Energy Law & Business* 4.

[2] K. Talus, S. Looper and S Otillar, 'Lex Petrolea and the Internationalization of Petroleum Agreements: Focus on Host Government Contracts' (2012) 5 *Journal of World Energy Law & Business* 181-193.

The JOA is undoubtedly the most prominent and familiar cooperation agreement seen in the international upstream petroleum industry. However, prior to any JOA coming into force (or in parallel to the JOA) the regulation of various activities involving some or all participants for which the JOA does not cater may require the execution of additional agreements dealing with joint venture or cooperation issues.

This chapter will explore, in brief, certain other joint venture agreements born out of a commercial need for competitors (and sometimes other stake holders) to collaborate in the exploration and development of hydrocarbons, and how such joint venture agreements interact with the JOA.

This chapter does not discuss considerations relating to, among others, competition, taxation and insurance. Such matters may need to be taken into account when entering into the arrangements described below.

2. AREA OF MUTUAL INTEREST AGREEMENTS

2.1. OVERVIEW

An area of mutual interest agreement (AMIA) is an agreement commonly used in the upstream oil and gas industry when two or more parties have identified, usually at the exploration stage, that the same area of acreage (whether it be offshore or onshore) is of interest to them both.

The AMIA is a form of joint venture agreement brought about by the commercial need for parties to work together to explore and exploit an area of mutual interest and its purpose is to establish the rights and obligations of the parties regarding the relevant acreage.

As with other joint venture instruments the AMIA is a cooperation agreement aimed at achieving a shared commercial objective. The basis for entry into an AMIA may include the sharing of financial risks, expertise and data and the pooling of knowledge of the co-venturing parties with respect to a block or in anticipation of bidding rounds.[3]

Generally, AMIAs will be structured to govern the rights and obligations of the parties in relation to the sharing of newly identified opportunities or in relation to existing opportunities.

---

3 K.C. Mildwaters, 'Joint Operating Agreement: A Consideration of Legal Aspects Relevant to Joint Operating Agreements Used in Great Britain and Australia by Participants thereto to Regulate the Joint Undertaking of Exploration for Petroleum in Offshore Areas, with Particular Reference to Rights and Duties', 1990, Vol. 3.

2.2. SCOPE AND KEY FEATURES

Most AMIAs seek to identify and record the acreage which is of mutual interest to the parties and confirm the rights and obligations of the parties in relation to the evaluation and joint development of such acreage.

It is not uncommon for parties to approach the AMIA as a basic framework arrangement which simply documents the parties' intention to jointly conduct petroleum activities within the designated area rather than contain fully enforceable provisions.[4] Some parties, however, seek to adopt a more detailed and definitive form of agreement to safeguard their interests in the designated area.

Regardless of the form of AMIA adopted, there are certain key provisions of an AMIA that will feature in even the most basic form. For example, an AMIA will always include a description of the designated area which is the subject of the AMIA, most commonly by reference to an area defined in a schedule.

The parties' participating interests in relation to the designated area are also usually specified in the AMIA. This not only sets out the parties' respective shares in any applications made or future interests or petroleum rights in the acreage to be developed, but may also be used as a basis for sharing the costs incurred in any evaluation of the designated area or the submission of bids or applications.

The AMIA, like many other joint venture agreements, typically appoints a party as the operator or manager, whose role is to essentially coordinate the other parties with respect to the decisions and applications made under the AMIA. The operator's role may also extend to evaluating and reporting on the designated area where a work programme and budget have been pre-agreed.

Additionally, parties may be expected to agree to conduct all activities jointly in the designated area. Such an undertaking is commonly drafted restrictively, preventing the parties from conducting an activity or making an application in relation to the designated area independently from the other parties to the AMIA or in association with a third party. However, it should be noted that these restrictions are not always absolute and, as explained below, there are circumstances which may allow a party to acquire an interest or right in the designated area either independently or together with a third party.

Given that an AMIA is generally not directly linked to acreage offered in a government licensing round or tender process, the AMIA may not provide procedures to determine how the parties might apply for future petroleum rights. Instead, such mechanisms are often the subject of a supplementary joint bidding agreement (discussed in detail later in this chapter). However, nothing prevents the parties to an AMIA from incorporating specific procedures for

---

4 A. Jennings, *Oil and Gas Exploration Contracts*, Sweet and Maxwell, London 2002, p. 58.

making an application within the area of mutual interest should there be a future desire to do so.[5]

Where parties do decide to incorporate specific procedures, they should be set out in a clear manner and address how the parties will decide on which applications to make, how commercial terms are decided and the votes required to carry a decision (this will often require unanimity). There will also be a process whereby an individual party may propose to acquire an interest or right in the designated area, in which case it must notify the other parties who may subsequently elect to participate alongside the notifying party, or elect not to participate.

Ideally, the AMIA should stipulate a mechanism in the event that unanimity between the parties is not achieved or if no party elects to participate alongside a notifying party in an application. Where this is the case, the AMIA may allow such a party to pursue applications independently or invite third parties to participate in certain circumstances, or it may allow the interested participants to proceed whilst preventing any non-participating party from competing.

The AMIA will typically include various covenants intended to maintain the objective of collaboration between the parties. For instance, it is important for the parties to agree not to compete or apply for an interest in the designated area other than in accordance with the terms of the AMIA. Such covenants are often regarded as the most fundamental feature of the AMIA and generally underpin the decision to enter into such an arrangement in the first place.

Parties to an AMIA may have previously entered into a confidentiality agreement to protect information or data which has been or will be disclosed in contemplation of the AMIA. If this is not the case, the AMIA should contain appropriate confidentiality provisions in relation to the information and data obtained or developed for the purposes of the AMIA or the designated area.

AMIAs tend to be long-term agreements, and given that the AMIA does not tend to be linked to a particular licensing round or other concession offer the parties will normally stipulate the required term for which it should remain in force. However, AMIAs may also provide for early termination events, such as when there is a unanimous written decision by the parties not to make an application to develop acreage in the designated area, or alternatively upon the execution of a JOA in respect of a permit or interest granted over the designated area.

At the time of writing, there is no industry standard form of AMIA in circulation. However, the AIPN is currently in the process of developing a model AMIA. It is expected that the AMIA will adopt the usual AIPN format providing alternative drafting options to reflect different approaches to AMIAs in common use in the international upstream oil and gas industry. In the experience of the

5 *Ibid.*, p. 42.

author, parties tend to place less importance on the negotiation and drafting of an AMIA than that which they invest in the preparation of other joint venture agreements such as the JOA. Maybe this is due in part to the lack of a standard form of AMIA which can be readily tabled for discussion or perhaps because AMIAs are signed at such an early stage and therefore the risk exposure to the parties is not as significant.

The absence of a standardised AMIA means that the form of an AMIA varies hugely depending on the circumstances of the proposed commercial objective. Some AMIAs are drafted in broad and general terms, more as statements of principle, whereas others contain far more detail and fully termed operative provisions, so as to try to make them as binding and enforceable as possible.

2.3. RELATIONSHIP WITH JOA

The AMIA tends to be ancillary to the JOA and depending on the particular area of mutual interest there may or may not already be a JOA in existence which relates to the relevant acreage. Prior to entering into an AMIA, parties should undertake appropriate due diligence to determine whether a JOA relating to the acreage in question already exists.

Where there is no existing JOA, and depending on the underlying commercial objective, the parties may wish to include express provisions in the AMIA to oblige the parties to negotiate and enter into a JOA in respect of the award of any future petroleum rights in the area of mutual interest. In such circumstances, the parties may agree certain principles upon which to base a JOA to govern future operations in respect of the area of mutual interest and append such principles to the AMIA. Typically the parties will agree to be bound by the JOA principles until such time as the parties execute the relevant JOA.

Where the area of mutual interest is covered by an existing JOA, this can create complications in relation to rights of first refusal or exclusivity under the AMIA depending on the underlying commercial objective. If a party has already acquired an interest in the acreage that is the subject of the AMIA and wishes to dispose of an interest, any rights of first refusal which the other party (or parties) have may be impacted by the terms of the existing JOA. For example, an existing JOA which covers the area of mutual interest may provide for pre-emption provisions requiring the relevant party to first offer such interest to its JOA co-venturers. A conflict between the terms of the AMIA and the relevant JOA could result in a party being unable to comply with the terms of the AMIA or breaching the terms of the JOA and potentially forfeiting the sale of its interest if challenged by co-venturers under the JOA.

Equally, when preparing a joint bidding agreement, JOA or other such upstream joint venture agreements parties should undertake appropriate due diligence to determine whether there are any AMIAs in existence in relation to the relevant acreage.

Ideally, rights in relation to the regulation of petroleum activities and the designation of the relevant acreage in an AMIA should be aligned as much as possible between ancillary agreements such as a JOA to avoid conflicts and uncertainty.

3. JOINT BIDDING AGREEMENTS

3.1. OVERVIEW

A joint bidding agreement (JBA) is another form of joint venture agreement usually entered into in the contemplation of entry into the bidding process for acreage for the purpose of making a joint bid for petroleum rights. The JBA sets out the terms on which the parties will submit their joint bid and the rights and obligations of the parties that follow should they be successful in being awarded rights.

JBAs are commonly used in the international upstream petroleum industry in order to lower the financial cost, spread the risk and allow the pooling together of technical expertise, experience and knowledge at the bidding stage in the most optimal way. The strategic alliance formed under a JBA also has the effect of grouping together parties which would otherwise be competing bidders, thus pooling resources and reducing competition for the petroleum rights.

3.2. SCOPE AND KEY FEATURES

When parties approach each other to engage in a joint bid, typically the first step is to negotiate a confidentiality (or non-disclosure) agreement to govern the dissemination of commercially sensitive information between them. Commercially sensitive information will inevitably be disclosed during the course of preliminary discussions between the parties when identifying what strengths and worth each party will bring to the joint venture arrangement. A confidentiality agreement will provide the parties with a certain degree of comfort prior to engaging in the negotiation and preparation of the JBA.

A JBA may be entered into to supplement an existing AMIA. It is important that the parties are aware of any prior AMIAs which relate to the acreage the subject of the joint application. A suitable representation and warranty that the acreage the subject of the joint application does not conflict with any pre-existing AMIAs may be incorporated into the JBA to deal with this issue.

The scope of a JBA will typically cover how the joint application process will be managed by the parties, delineate the particular acreage being applied for and provide general direction as to how the parties will conduct themselves following the successful award of petroleum rights.

The form of the JBA will generally be dictated by the requirements of the particular bidding process and time available to the parties. Ideally, the JBA will be drafted in sufficient detail to govern the rights and the obligations of the parties in the interim period up to the implementation of a definitive JOA. However, given potential time restraints imposed by a formal bid or tender process this may not always be practical for the parties to achieve.

There are a number of key terms and conditions which commonly feature in a JBA and are intended to facilitate a successful coordinated joint approach. First, the duration of a JBA is usually linked to the success of the application. If the application results in the award of petroleum rights, the JBA typically continues to apply until the effectiveness of a JOA. If no petroleum rights are awarded, then the JBA will usually terminate upon receipt of notice from the body administering the bid or tender process that the application has been unsuccessful and subject to the final accounting and settlement under the JBA.[6]

Additionally parties will be expected to covenant or enter into an exclusivity provision which operates to prevent a party from making an application or bid for the particular acreage the subject of the JBA outside of the group. Such restriction may also extend to prevent a party from making an application for any other acreage offered in the same bidding round or tender process. It is important to note, however, that such exclusions may have competition law implications depending on how the exclusivity provision is presented in the JBA. As mentioned previously, the analysis of competition law that may apply in this context is outside the scope of this chapter.

A clause setting out the percentage interests of the parties and their respective voting rights is usually included in the JBA. Each party will typically have a share of the vote equal to its participating interest. A well-drafted voting procedure will be fundamental to the decision making process of the parties and careful consideration should be given as to how dissenting parties are managed.

A suitable procedure should be included in the JBA to facilitate the parties reaching agreement on the form of joint application to be submitted. The application procedure should provide for how the financial costs of the application will be allocated between the parties and a mechanism for ensuring that the proposed application complies with the requirements of the bid process.

A well-structured JBA will also deal with what happens in the event that the parties fail to reach agreement on the application to be submitted or if a party elects not to proceed with the application and wishes to withdraw from the group. Most JBAs will provide for the interests of the dissenting or withdrawing party to be absorbed by the remaining party (or parties) or for a new third party

---

6 *Ibid.*, p. 63.

to be brought in. Alternatively, some JBAs may provide that if the parties fail to reach agreement on the application by a certain deadline that the parties may apply separately.

If a JBA envisages the introduction of a third party, then it should contain sufficient clarity as to how the new party will accede to the JBA (including how approval and consent of the existing parties will be dealt with) and the fiscal terms on which the new party will be expected to join. Of particular interest (to both the new party and the existing participants) will be whether the new party will be liable to contribute to the group's past costs.

The appointment and role of the operator together with the establishment of a management committee are key terms that should feature in a JBA. The provisions relating to the management committee are largely similar to those adopted in a JOA.

The sharing of costs is a fundamental issue for the parties to a JBA. The JBA should clearly express how costs are to be apportioned between the parties, as well as addressing budget and approval of the work programme, the thresholds for approvals for expenditure and the implications for a party which fails to make payment of monies due.

Consideration should also be given to certain other key administrative issues which are likely to arise during the course of the arrangement, including appropriate default provisions to deal with the consequences of a party defaulting in the performance of its obligations, transfer rights and relinquishment, accounting procedure, warranties and indemnities, the sharing and acquisition of data (if not covered by a confidentiality agreement) and force majeure provisions.

The AIPN Model Form International Study and Bid Group Agreement (2006) is a common starting point for companies looking to commit to a joint bid. This model contract has been revised to reflect increased bid rounds around the world and the need for alignment with other AIPN model contracts, in particular the JOA.

Clearly the context, including the joint commercial objective of the parties and the requirements of any formal bid or tender process, will guide the scope and content of a JBA, and as such bespoke arrangements may need to be incorporated to manage unique circumstances.

3.3. RELATIONSHIP WITH JOA

The JBA acts as a precursor to the JOA and is often the first major cooperation agreement entered into in the context of an upstream petroleum project. By comparison the JOA, a more detailed and enduring instrument, operates subsequent to the award of exploration and production rights, whereas a JBA functions to regulate the activities of the parties prior to the award of such hydrocarbon rights.

The JBA and the JOA share common characteristics: both forms are used by co-venturing companies with a common commercial interest, and they function to regulate the joint venture relationship and seek to mitigate the risks and liabilities associated with the relevant undertaking.

The scope of the JBA will typically contain an undertaking by the parties to enter into a JOA in the event the parties are successful in achieving the award of acreage and normally acknowledge that the JBA will remain in force and will apply until a JOA is executed. However, such duration will vary if the parties have applied for and are successfully awarded multiple blocks and if separate JOAs are required to manage acreage awards.

Parties to a JBA will ideally seek to agree the scope, content and structure of the JOA during negotiation of the JBA. The agreed form of JOA will then be appended to the JBA to avoid needless re-negotiation further down the line. However, this desired approach may not always be possible due to time constraints imposed by the particular bidding procedure or simply because the negotiation of a JOA can often be a very involved and laborious process.

If the parties are unable to achieve an agreed form of JOA during the negotiation of the JBA, the parties will need to rely on the JBA to do the job of the JOA until a definitive JOA is agreed and becomes effective. In such circumstances, the JBA should be detailed enough to support operations and provide a suitable framework as to the parties' rights and obligations following the successful award of petroleum rights.

Despite the JBA and JOA sharing certain thematic similarities in terms of content, the parties may wish certain terms or obligations to apply differently in the context of the JOA. For instance terms such as operatorship (including appointment and removal) should be carefully considered; the operator under the JBA may not necessarily be the same operator to be appointed under the JOA. However, the procedures relating to the operation of the management committee will often share similarities with those adopted by the operating committee established under a JOA.

In addition it is typical for parties to have differing views on the technical and commercial aspects of the bid. This creates complications where the parties are not aligned on the approach to be taken in creating and managing the bid. Further, a potential conflict of interests can also mean that a more experienced player may take advantage of a junior bidding partner who may be inclined to defer to a greater financial or technical strength. This can be further complicated if the JOA reflects this imbalance at the time it is negotiated and there is little or no scope to rebalance the interests of the parties later on.

While JBAs are a popular and useful cooperation tool, there are some practical drawbacks which should be taken into consideration prior to committing to a joint bid. A JBA will often represent the first major collaborative agreement between co-venturers, but attention should be given to the relationship of the parties following the successful award of petroleum rights. While the JOA should be the definitive governing instrument of the parties, co-venturers should ensure that sufficient detail and foresight be given to allow the JBA to function as intended until the JOA is effective.

4. FARM-OUT AGREEMENTS

4.1. OVERVIEW

A farm-out agreement (FOA) is a transactional instrument commonly used in the upstream petroleum industry. In general terms, an FOA is a form of asset acquisition agreement where a party acquires an interest in a licence or concession in return for performing certain work obligations or paying certain costs in relation to the licence or concession. For the purposes of this chapter we will refer to the party disposing of the relevant interest as the 'farmor' and the party obtaining the interest as the 'farmee'.

FOAs have become a permanent and unique feature of upstream development. There are a variety of drivers behind a decision to adopt a farm-out approach to divesting of an interest ranging from financial incentives to technical and operational motivations. A FOA allows parties to share financial responsibility and risk. From the perspective of a farmor, such apportionment of risk enables the farmor to reduce its financial exposure for meeting work commitments or to alleviate a funding gap. In return for sharing risk, the farmee has the opportunity to obtain an interest in a licence or concession. As discussed in more detail below, it is pertinent to discuss FOAs in the context of joint venture arrangements because unlike a traditional asset sale which upon completion results in a revision of participating interests under the JOA, the FOA will give rise to a further layer of joint venture relationships which will, for some time at least, coexist with a JOA.

Combining technical expertise and capabilities is often at the heart of upstream joint ventures. A shortage of expertise and skills allows a farmor to bring in a co-venturer who has the relevant capabilities to expedite exploration and development of the interest. On the other hand, a farmee may be seeking to invest in a prospect which is currently operated by a party with intimate working knowledge of the contract area and as such is best placed to exploit and develop the prospect.

From an operational point of view, parties engaging in a farm-out have the opportunity to participate in a greater number of projects. In particular, it provides farmors with the ability to devote more time and resources to existing core projects or to seek new investment opportunities.

FOAs are also used as a method by which companies can acquire or diversify their oil and gas interests outside formal bid or licensing rounds.[7]

4.2. SCOPE AND KEY FEATURES

The structure of an FOA and its terms are defined by the commercial objectives of the parties and the particular stage of development of the petroleum asset in question. A farm-out arrangement occurs post-award of petroleum rights and is typically undertaken during exploration, appraisal or development.

The structure of an FOA is similar to that of a conventional sale and purchase agreement; it is a transactional document to effect the transfer of interest in a particular asset in return for consideration. However, certain key characteristics of farm-out arrangements are unique to an FOA and distinguish the structure of an FOA from that of a conventional sale and purchase agreement. Most notable of these characteristics is the form of consideration and the timing of transfer of interest in the asset.

Under a conventional asset sale and purchase agreement, consideration is normally in the form of cash, whereas under an FOA the form of consideration can include the performance of a particular work obligation, the payment of a cash sum or a combination of both. Transfer of interest in the asset under a conventional sale and purchase agreement will generally be triggered upon the payment of consideration, whereas under an FOA structure the transfer of interest in the asset commonly takes place following execution of the FOA and upon satisfaction or waiver of certain conditions precedent.

The FOA will generally identify the interest to be assigned and state that the farmor is obliged to transfer such interest to the farmee. The FOA will typically specify the interests held by the existing parties in relation to the licence or concession and what the interests in the licence or concession will be once the interest has been transferred.

The conditions precedent which parties may seek to include in an FOA will vary depending on the structure of the transaction (e.g. the form of consideration), the stage of development of the petroleum asset, the regulatory and legal framework of the jurisdiction in which the petroleum asset is located and the provisions of any existing JOA. For example, such conditions may include the procurement of governmental consent to effect the transfer of a legal interest in the licence or concession, or if there is a JOA in place, procurement of the consent of the other joint venture participants and possibly procurement of a waiver of any rights of pre-emption. The FOA will usually include a long-stop

---

7 A. Berkley, *Farm-ins and Farm-Outs,* Petroleum Law Seminar Proceedings, Churchill College, Cambridge, England, 08.01.2013, 1978, p. 17.2.

date by which time the conditions precedent must be satisfied or waived or the FOA will terminate.

The form of consideration underpins the FOA and will drive the drafting of many key provisions. Generally, consideration under an FOA will be the performance of a work obligation or the payment of certain costs by the farmee or a combination of both. The form of consideration will also be linked to the stage of development of the petroleum asset. At the exploration stage, consideration is typically linked to the minimum work obligations of the licence or concession. For example, the farmee may agree to perform certain exploration activities which are required to be completed in accordance with the minimum work programme (such as seismic work or drilling exploration wells) and/or contribute to the cost of such activities. Similarly, should a farm-out occur during the appraisal stage, the farmee may conduct and/or contribute to the cost of conducting appraisal activities (e.g. such as drilling appraisal wells).

During the development stage, the farmee will typically be bound to contribute its share of costs in accordance with the existing JOA and/or cover the farmor's costs of development up to a certain trigger point (typically being commencement of commercial production). The farmee will also be required to comply with its joint venture obligations attaching to the particular licence or concession.

The point at which transfer of the farm-out interest takes place is of fundamental importance and is a key provision of the FOA. Generally, the transfer of interest will occur either following execution of the FOA by the parties (and upon satisfaction or waiver of certain conditions precedent) or upon completion of the work obligation the farmee has agreed to carry out. For obvious reasons, a farmor will usually try to negotiate the interest to be transferred upon fulfilment of the relevant work obligation, whereas a farmee will generally prefer the interest to be transferred 'up-front' upon execution of the FOA.

Timing of the transfer of the farm-out interest will be relevant in the context of any default provisions to be included in the FOA. When the farm-out interest is transferred 'up-front' the farmor takes the inherent risk that the farmee may not complete the work obligation within the agreed completion period or that the farmee will breach its payment obligations. In such circumstances, the farmor will typically seek to charge interest on late payments or apply the more uncompromising measure of requiring the farmee to reassign the interest back to the farmor. Reassignment provisions require careful consideration given that there may be the same practical constraints which applied to the initial transfer of interest. For example, governmental approval together with joint venture party consent and/or waiver of pre-emption rights may be necessary to legally effect the reassignment of interest. Implementation of such reassignment will to an extent depend on the cooperation of the farmee, unless there are strong enforcement provisions, as the farmee will be required to consent to the reassignment of interest and execute the relevant transfer instruments.

Certain other key terms which typically feature in a conventional sale and purchase agreement should be incorporated into the FOA, such as interim period provisions to manage the rights and obligations of the parties in respect of the farm-out interest until such interest is transferred, confidentiality provisions, appropriate representations and warranties, force majeure provisions and an appropriate dispute resolution mechanism.

At the time of writing, the AIPN has established a drafting committee to review and update the current AIPN model form FOA which was produced in 2004. Although a useful starting point, the AIPN model form FOA will often require careful modification to ensure that it adequately reflects the commercial farm-out arrangement. Ideally, a bespoke approach which takes into consideration the applicable regulatory and legal regime together with the requirements of the underlying licence or concession and the JOA will ensure that the FOA is fit for purpose.

4.3. RELATIONSHIP WITH JOA

A farmee takes his interest subject to the terms and conditions of the underlying licence or concession and usually the existing JOA.

If the farmor is the single holder of the underlying concession or licence there will be no JOA in existence. In this situation, there will be a need for the farmor and the farmee to enter into a JOA to govern the new relationship. The parties to the FOA typically seek to agree the scope of the JOA during negotiation of the FOA and append the agreed form of JOA to the FOA. The parties then normally agree to execute the JOA contemporaneously with the execution and delivery of the instrument which effects the assignment of interest or at an agreed future date.

Certain fundamental terms of the FOA will need to be reflected in the JOA, such as the ownership interests in the underlying concession or licence once the farm-out interest has been transferred to the farmee and which party will be appointed as operator.

If there is a JOA already in existence, the FOA will need to be tailored to ensure that it is consistent with the JOA. A primary and key concern for both the farmor and farmee is whether the existing JOA will act to prevent the assignment of interest contemplated by the FOA.

The existing JOA will invariably contain a requirement that any assignment of interest in the underlying licence or concession must be done with the consent of the existing parties to the JOA. In addition, the existing JOA may also contain pre-emption rights. This means that completion under the FOA will require the waiver of any pre-emption rights and the consent of the existing parties to the

JOA (together with any applicable governmental consents). Such waiver and consent is normally dealt with under the FOA by way of condition precedent.

Together with a formal assignment of the underlying licence or concession, the farmee will need to be brought in as a party to any existing JOA when the FOA interest is transferred. This is typically done by way of a novation of the JOA, to which all the parties to the JOA and the farmee will join so as to give full legal effect to the assumption by the farmee of rights and obligations under the JOA.[8]

Another consideration to be taken into account where there is an existing JOA is how the parties to the FOA deal with the fact that the farmee will not become a party to the JOA until the interest under the FOA has been transferred (and the JOA has been amended and novated to reflect the state of affairs following the transfer). To manage this issue the FOA will typically include appropriate provisions dealing with the period between the execution of the FOA and the transfer of interest to the farmee. Such interim period obligations may include the farmor agreeing not to do anything under the existing JOA (and/or licence or concession) in the interim period which may adversely impact the interest being transferred to the farmee.

In addition, during such interim period the farmee will not have the ability to actively participate in the joint venture under the existing JOA. The parties can manage this to an extent by including specific interim period obligations which oblige the farmor to provide the farmee with information in relation to the interest. In particular, the farmee may seek a covenant from the farmor that it will consult with the farmee before making any decisions or taking certain actions under the JOA. Such covenants will need to be carefully considered in light of any confidentiality restrictions under the JOA which may prevent the operation of such provisions under the FOA.

Given that the FOA and JOA are separate and distinct joint venture instruments it is unlikely that a conflict should arise between the terms of the two agreements. However, in the event of such a conflict, the terms of the FOA will generally prevail and this is normally expressly provided for in the FOA.

5. CONCLUSION

AMIAs, JBAs and FOAs are arrangements commonly used by the international upstream petroleum industry to manage the interaction of collaborating parties at different stages of joint venture relationships. Over the years it has become clear that for various reasons the form and content of these documents are often

8 M. Roberts, 'Contract and the Legal Framework of Petroleum Interests in the United Kingdom in the context of farm-ins' (1983) 2 *Oil and Gas Law and Taxation Review* 21.

overlooked and their relative complexity underestimated when compared with the time, expense and resources often allocated to the negotiation and preparation of a JOA (for which the industry has over the years also developed a far more detailed and sophisticated set of precedents). As this chapter has demonstrated, these documents often underpin the relationships between parties at an early stage of a joint venture and can remain in place well into the exploration and production stages of an asset.

For this reason time spent planning and documenting processes to manage the parties' interaction in the context of possible future operations is seldom wasted. In addition, the objectives of these arrangements are often inextricably linked and a lack of alignment or clarity in one can have unwanted consequences in administering the objectives of another. As with all critical project documents, careful consideration and attention should be given to the preparation and negotiation phase to reduce unwanted risk and to allow parties to achieve the commercial objective which underpins the nature of the joint venture arrangement.

UNITISATION AND UNIT OPERATING AGREEMENTS

Eduardo G. Pereira and Giulia Carloni

1. INTRODUCTION

Petroleum resources are typically owned by the host government of the country where these natural resources are located.[1] If an investor has an interest in searching for and producing oil and gas, it is required for them to obtain

[1] Most jurisdictions provide that natural resources located in the subsoil belong to the government and that it may only be explored if authorised by the respective government.

permission from the relevant host government.[2] Petroleum licences, production sharing agreements (PSAs), service agreements or combinations all exist as established ways to grant this permission, and without them the contracting party has no authority to conduct exploration and production operations.[3]

The host government typically prefers to divest their portfolio of assets/ blocks within different companies and contracts. This is done by way of allocating different contract licence areas and licences to different licence holders. The licence holders then each enter into a separate agreement (i.e. a joint operating agreement) to regulate the relationship between them with respect to how they wish to jointly undertake exploration, development and production activities for that particular licence. However, as is often the case, nature does not easily fit within man-made rules. In the petroleum industry, this can be illustrated by oil and gas fields not always conforming to pre-defined property boundaries commonly referred as 'contract area'. This is because hydrocarbon reserves can often 'straddle' two or more licences that would have no connection with each other otherwise.

The issue then arises as to how parties to different licences can extract hydrocarbons from these fields, having a commonality of purpose in the sense of maximising their potential and not unnecessarily depleting the field, as well as how they are then to split any revenues arising out of these operations that are to be undertaken under two (or more) different licences, how they are to manage these operations, and how they are to determine the respective licence holders' interests. To address this issue, the oil and gas industry has developed the concept of the 'unitisation and unit operating agreement'.

This chapter will look at some of the main features of a typical unitisation agreement, its main purpose, and its interaction with JOAs. It will focus in particular on intra-border unitisation (that is, unitisation of a field straddling two or more licences within the same national boundaries)[4] and not deal with

However, there are exceptions to this rule, such as in the United States. See: B.G. Taverne, *Petroluem, Industry and Governments: A Study of the Involvement of Industry and Government with the Production and Use of Petroleum*, 2nd edn, Kluwer Law International, Alphen aan den Rijn 2008, p. 380..

2 'The JOA does not operate in isolation: It has to be viewed on the background of the production licence (PL), to which it is made a formal condition. And further: The PL is based on the Petroleum Act, and has to be viewed in this context.' J. Knut Kaasen, 'Scope of Joint Operating Agreements in Norway', Petroleum Law Seminar, St. Raphael, 2000, p. 8.

3 For the purposes of this chapter, the terms 'licence', 'PSA' or 'service agreement' might be used individually but they always refer to the petroleum title signed between the private party and the host government.

4 For further information see: A. Derman, 'Unitization and Unit Operating Agreement', in E.G. Pereira, *Encyclopaedia of Oil and Gas Law*, Vol 1 (Globe Law and Business, London 2014); J. Lang Weaver and D.F. Asmus, 'Unitizing Oil and Gas Fields Around the World: A Comparative Analysis of National Laws and Private Contracts' (2006) 28(1) *Houston Journal of International Law* 12; A. Derman and K. Vollus, 'Unitization' (2002) 215 *ADVISOR, Association of International Petroleum Negotiators* 5.

cross-border unitisation (i.e. the unitisation of a field which straddles licences within two or more different countries).[5]

2. THE CONCEPT OF 'UNITISATION': PARTICIPATING INTEREST, TRACK PARTICIPATION AND UNIT INTEREST

Unitisation in the oil and gas industry is historically a US concept and is commonly defined as 'the joint, coordinated operation of a petroleum reservoir by all the owners of rights in the separate tracts overlying the reservoir'.[6] The United States' policy on ownership of minerals – which effectively translates into private landowners owning the minerals which are located underneath their land – has meant that ownership of an oil and gas common reservoir is divided amongst tens, hundreds and sometimes thousands of private landowners who lease their 'tracts' in exchange for royalty interests, and with their lessees (as working-interest owners) having interests in the same reservoirs.[7]

A corollary of the US 'rule of capture'[8] is that all the landowners are incentivised to compete in terms of both drilling and production, and this has led to inefficiency and misuse of the underlying assets. This is the reason why the United States has led the way in the concept of unitisation, which has then been adopted by a large variety of other jurisdictions, including Brazil, Norway, the United Kingdom, and so on.

In the UK, the Secretary of State for Energy and Climate Change has powers to impose unitisation between licensees if it is in the national interest for the purposes of ensuring maximum recovery of petroleum and avoiding competitive

5 For further information see: P.C. Reid, 'Joint Development Zones Between Countries' (1987) 6(1) *AMPLA Bulletin* 4-13; D.M. Ong, 'Joint Development of Common Offshore Oil and Gas Deposits, "Mere" State Practice or Customary International Law?' (1999) 93 *American Journal of International Law* 771; D.M. Ong, 'The 1979 and 1990 Malaysia-Thailand Joint Development Agreements: A Model for International Legal Co-operation in Common Offshore Petroleum Deposits?' (1999) 14(2) *International Journal of Marine and Coastal Law* 207, 245; E.E. Smith, 'Joint Development of Offshore Oil and Gas: A Model Agreement for States for Joint Development With Explanatory Commentary' (1992) 86 *American Journal of International Law* 241; M. Miyoshi, 'The Joint Development of Offshore Oil and Gas in Relation to Maritime Boundary Delimitation' (1999) 2(5) *International Boundary Research Unit Maritime Briefing* 41; M. Miyoshi, 'Some Comments on Legal Aspects of Precedents for Joint Development' (1981) 6(11) *Energy* 1359; C.B. Okafor, 'Model Agreements for Joint Development, a Case Study' (2007) 25 *J. Energy Nat. Resources L.* 102.

6 See H.R. Williams et al., *Williams & Meyers Manual of Oil and Gas Terms* (12th edn, 2003), p. 850.

7 This concept does not apply to federal lands and offshore areas.

8 *Westmoreland and Cambria Natural Gas v. DeWitt*, 1889 Supreme Court of Pennsylvania.

drilling.[9] Typically the host government has powers to enforce an unitisation as it is in the public interest to make sure the contractors or licensee maximises the recovery of their fields rather than causes early depletion.

Unitisations have become increasingly common for a number of reasons. First, as oil and gas fields mature, exploration blocks become smaller, making it more likely that two or more licences may relate to one field. Secondly, geophysical studies have become more sophisticated, leading to earlier identification of common fields. Thirdly, governments are also becoming more involved in the management of their national oil and gas resources and consequently are starting to prompt producers to unitise these common hydrocarbon reservoirs.[10]

Effectively, this concept allows for separate leases/licences to be merged into one single lease/licence, with a single unit operator appointed to manage the development of the field. Nevertheless, this might not represent a complete merger of both licences or of the totality of the contract area. This has a number of benefits in that:

- it preserves the unit of the reservoir;
- it avoids the economic waste of unnecessary well drilling and construction of related facilities;
- it allows sharing of the infrastructure and information, therefore lowering the costs of production through economies of scale;
- it maximises the ultimate recovery of petroleum from a field according to the best technical/engineering information; and
- it gives all owners of rights in the common reservoir a fair share of the production.[11]

2.1. UK LEGAL FRAMEWORK

In light of the fact that there has not been any case on the point or any statement by the UK government to clarify this, it is not known whether the 'rule of capture' as it applies to hydrocarbons is applicable in the UK.

Looking at the relevant legislation, it will be seen that 'property in petroleum, existing in its natural condition in strata in Great Britain' is vested in the Crown.[12] At a first and somewhat hasty glance, this would seem to suggest therefore that – because licence holders do not have first ownership – the rule

---

9 Paragraph 2.5.1 of DECC's Guidance on the content of offshore oil and gas field development plans.

10 D. Beggs and J. Bremen, *Oil and Gas: a practical handbook – Unitisation and Unitisation Agreements*, p. 58.

11 Lang Weaver and Asmus, *supra* n. 4.

12 See section 1(1) of the Petroleum (Production) Act 1934.

of capture has no application in the UK Continental Shelf (UKCS). However, Model Clause 2 states further that the licensee is granted an 'exclusive licence and liberty during the continuance of this licence and subject to the provisions hereof to search and bore for, and get, Petroleum under [the licensed area]'. Some commentators have read this and argued that licensees had a vested right to such petroleum as lies below their licensed area.[13] However, this contention does not seem very compelling and has been challenged since. In addition, in the UKCS outside the territorial sea the Crown has only a sovereign right to exploit resources, not a full right of ownership.[14] The licensees obtain original title upon extraction – which is a clear exemplification of the rule of capture.[15] In any event, well-established primary legislation – in the form of the Petroleum Act 1934 and consistently since then – has effectively ensured that competitive drilling and its unwanted consequences are unlikely to take place in the UK. Such legislation has granted the Secretary of State the power to impose schemes to unitise production between licence holders if he/she considers it to be in the national interest to secure maximum recovery of petroleum and in order to avoid unnecessary competitive drilling.

Clause 27 of the Model Clauses for Seaward Production Licences[16] gives the Secretary of State the power to give licensees notice requiring them to prepare a development scheme for the development of the petroleum field as a unit. In addition, the Secretary of State also has the authority to develop such a scheme on behalf of the licensees if they fail to do so. The Guidance Notes of the Department of Energy and Climate Change (DECC) further set out that in circumstances where a field straddles into another licence, the DECC will have to be satisfied that the development plan for that area is the one most likely fully to exploit the recovery of economic reserves before any approval will be given. To this end, licensees will be expected to 'discuss their plans with their neighbours at an early stage and propose an agreed Field Development Plan'.[17] The Guidance Notes further stipulate that it should allow 'an optimum Field Development Programme and demonstrate that there would be no risk of unnecessary competitive drilling'.

2.2. PRE-UNITISATION AGREEMENT

Prior to entering into the unitisation agreement, parties may decide to enter into a pre-unitisation agreement. This is a useful preliminary agreement because

13 See Daintith, Willoughby and Hill, para. 5-2732.

14 P. Cameron, *Property rights and sovereign rights: the case of North Sea Oil* (1983), pp. 46–50.

15 Gordon et al., *Oil and Gas Law — Current Practice and Emerging Trends*, 2nd edn, Dundee University Press, Dundee, p. 417.

16 See Schedule 1 of Petroleum Licensing (Production) (Seawards Areas) Regulations 2008/225.

17 Paragraph 2.5.1 of DECC's Offshore Field Development Guidelines.

negotiating a full unitisation agreement may take a significant amount of time. This typically happens when a discovery is made but parties possess little information about the reservoir. In addition, the execution of a pre-unitisation agreement will allow licensees to undertake initial unitisation evaluation work, with each party committing to (and funding) certain exploration and appraisal works which will be necessary to better be able to define the petroleum reservoir to be unitised.[18] In essence, a pre-unitisation agreement is akin to a joint study and bid agreement – it will set the terms upon which the different licensees to a common hydrocarbon reservoir will jointly evaluate it with a view to submitting a common field development plan, including a plan for unitisation.

The typical matters which are dealt with in a pre-unitisation agreement are as follows:

- determination of initial unit interest of the parties;
- appointment of an operator for conduct of the pre-unit operations – typically preparation of the unit work programme and budget;
- appointment of an operating committee to review/approve all pre-unitisation operations;
- data exchange to allow each licensee to receive copies of all data with respect to the other licence (subject to confidentiality obligations with any third parties);
- preparation of a development plan for submission to the government;
- provision governing the negotiation of a unitisation agreement within defined period of time;
- ownership and disposal of the petroleum produced;
- sole risk and non-unit operations;
- default and assignment provisions;
- decommissioning;
- public announcements;
- governmental approvals; and
- termination event provisions e.g. (i) upon the decision of a licensee not to participate in the development or (ii) upon execution of a unitisation agreement.[19]

One of the features which is worth bearing in mind in respect of a pre-unitisation agreement is that the interests of the parties will not necessarily stay the same in the subsequent unitisation agreement. The reason for this is that the parties will learn more about the reservoir through the geological evaluation activities and studies undertaken and as a result of these one or more 'redeterminations' can take place.

---

18 *Joint Operating Agreements – A practical guide: Appendix F: Unitisation and the JOA*, p. 319.

19 Chooramun, *Notes from the Field – An English Law Perspective on the Oil & Gas Market – Unitisation – The Oil and Gas Industry's Solution to One of Geology's Many Conundrums*, August 2014.

Data exchange between the licence groups can be problematic, as licence groups are looking to preserve the confidentiality of their own data acquired in respect of their licence. In practice, negotiation of a confidentiality agreement between the licence groups can be a lengthy process particularly where parties fail to agree the precise purpose for the use of confidential data and subsequently request to see data which is beyond the scope of the confidentiality agreement in place.

Unitisation should take place before any development activities are commenced in respect of the unit area, so that the basis for sharing the costs and outcome of those works between all parties is set out in advance.[20]

If the unitisation exercise happens after any exploration or appraisal (or even development/production) activities have taken place in respect of any of the concession areas, the costs and outcome of those activities may need to be the subject of a post-unitisation reconciliation so that they are allocated retrospectively between all the unitised parties according to the agreed unit interests. Although this sounds straightforward, it can in reality be quite a complex exercise and can lead to some animosity where a party that is required to make a contribution is dissatisfied with the level of those costs or the manner in which they were incurred by the relevant party. This is also why the unitisation exercise should be undertaken at the earliest possible opportunity.[21] If unitisation takes place later on (e.g. at the production stage), the parties who were responsible for that production could feel that they should be compensated for the development risk which they originally took – this could take the form of granting those parties a greater unit interest. However in practice it can be very difficult to quantify the equation between sunk costs and assumed risks on the one hand and the corresponding level of unit interest on the other. As a result, any compensation that is agreed to be due could instead be payable through a share of the petroleum produced from the unit, a cash payment or both.[22]

2.3. UNITISATION AND UNIT OPERATING AGREEMENT

When parties to different licences wish to amalgamate the management of their respective JOAs in relation to the exploration and production of a straddling field – or alternatively where the unitisation process may be called for by the relevant underlying mineral laws or concessions/licensing terms – they will negotiate and enter into a unitisation and unit operating agreement (UUOA).

---

20 *Joint Operating Agreements – A practical guide: Appendix F: Unitisation and the JOA*, p. 319.
21 *Ibid.*, p. 319.
22 *Ibid.*, p. 319.

The UUOA is therefore effectively set up to address two distinct stages, namely (i) the mechanics of the unitisation of the relevant licence areas; and (ii) the subsequent operation of that unitised area.[23]

To achieve the primary goal, the UUOA will provide for 'unit operations' to be undertaken by the various licensees in the 'unit area'. This in essence will be the total joint area of the parties' respective portions of the gas/oil reservoir which lies below each of their respective licences, ignoring the artificial licence boundaries which would otherwise exist between them.

That portion of the unit area which belongs to one licence area is usually known as a 'tract', so that for example it is common to have 'Tract A' (with licence holders from Licence A) and 'Tract B' (with licence holders from Licence B).

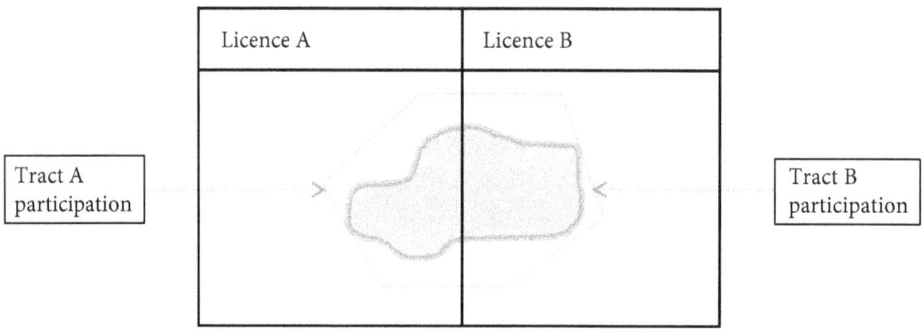

All rights and obligation of the parties will be shared in proportion to their individual 'unit equity' – also often referred to as the 'tract participation'. A typical clause regarding tract participation would read as follows:

> 'All rights and interests of the Parties under the Licences are hereby unitised in accordance with the provisions of this Agreement insofar as such rights and interests pertain to the Unitised Area and each of the Parties shall own all Unit Property and Unitised Petroleum in undivided shares in proportion to its Unit Equity'.[24]

This clause therefore prescribes that the different licence holders will have a claim to production in proportion to their unitised interest, regardless of where in the field the oil and gas is coming from.

It should be mentioned that it is possible to enter into two separate agreements, a unit agreement and a unit operating agreement – this is for example the approach taken in the US and Canada.[25] However, in most other jurisdictions it is commonplace to enter into a single agreement (the UUOA) which achieves

---

23 *Ibid.*, p. 317.

24 English, 'Unitisation Agreements', p. 97.

25 E.E. Smith et al., *International Petroleum Transactions*, 3rd edn, Rocky Mountain Mineral Law Foundation, Denver 2010, 'Unitized Operations', pp. 628 and 629.

these two objectives at the same time. This is also the approach which AIPN took in its model form International Unitization and Unit Operating Agreement in 2006.

A typical UUOA will include provisions dealing with the following:

- duration;
- creation of the unit (area, depths and substances being unitised);
- supremacy of UUOA over underlying JOAs where inconsistent;
- tract and unit interests (including detailed provisions dealing with 'determination' and 'redetermination');
- non-unit and unit operation provisions;
- appointment, removal, rights and duties of the unit operator;
- appointment and responsibilities of the unit operating committee;
- submission and approval of work programme and budgets;
- default and withdrawal provisions;
- abandonment and decommissioning;
- assignment; and
- applicable law and dispute resolution process.

3. THE INTER-RELATION BETWEEN THE JOA AND UUOA

In many ways, the UUOA is similar to the JOA. It has been said that, in practice, a UUOA is a 'super JOA' – this is because it will be largely based on the same language, provisions and structure of a typical JOA.[26] Kenneth Barnhill explains the similarity between a JOA and a UUOA as follows:

> '"Joint operations" is the term generally used to refer to the procedure whereby co-owners of mineral properties agree upon the development and operations of such properties by one or more of the co-owners for the benefit of the other co-owners. "Unitized operations" denote a similar arrangement, but generally on a larger scale, such as for the exploration, development, and operation of an entire pool, structure or field, or a substantial portion thereof.'[27]

The UUOA is effectively the JOA for the unit and will take the place of many of the provisions of the underlying JOAs. However, that is not to say that the respective JOAs will cease to apply – they will exist side by side with the UUOA

26 Chooramun, *supra* n. 19.

27 K.E. Barnhill Jr., 'Taxation of Oil and Gas Operating Agreements. The Scope and Application of I. T. 3930' (1953–1954) 26 *Rocky Mountain Law Review* 133.

and, whilst the UUOA will contain provisions to the effect that its terms will prevail over any terms in any JOAs which are inconsistent with it, the respective JOAs will still be valid and in full force and will still be used by the parties to regulate operations which are undertaken outside the unit area[28] – see figure below:

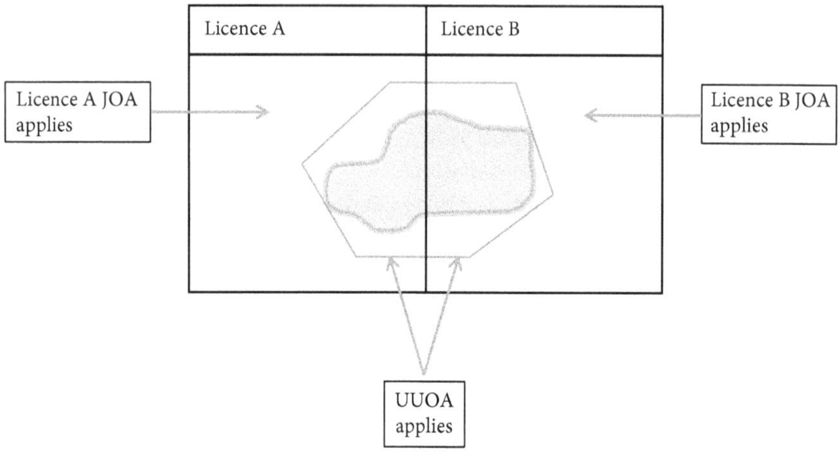

It is also possible for the JOAs to cover only certain substances or certain depths and in those cases the JOAs will continue to govern with respect to those substances/depths that are not unitised. The JOAs generally also continue to apply between the parties of each licence group in respect of issues such as withdrawal, assignment and default. If a party wants to assign its unit share, that party will in practice usually have to comply with the assignment requirements in both the UUOA and its own licence group's JOA.[29]

4. DISTINCTIONS AND CLASHES BETWEEN THE JOA AND UUOA

A JOA is the vehicle used in the international oil and gas arena to regulate the relationship between two or more parties who hold the rights to explore, develop or produce hydrocarbons in respect of a defined contract area from the host government, and will for example include the appointment of a single operator to carry out the exploration/development/production activities on behalf of all the parties. All these agreements generally deal with the conduct of joint petroleum operations on the relevant block/licence, appointment of a single operator to

28 'Joint Operating Agreements – A practical guide: Appendix F: Unitisation and the JOA', p. 323.
29 Gordon et al., *supra* n. 15, p. 421.

conduct such operation and collective decision-making. The single operator is usually one of the consortium parties but it might also be a third party operator or even a special purposes vehicle incorporated by the consortium parties.

Whilst a UUOA will mirror in many respects many of the provisions contained in the underlying JOAs (as seen above), it will also contain a number of provisions which encapsulate concepts which are only typical of a unitisation. The typical effects of a UUOA are as follows:

- unitised shares of production and costs are allocated to each block;
- cost recovery, profit oil and royalties continue to be calculated on a block basis, using the share of production and costs allocated to each block;
- taxes, if ring-fenced by block, continue to be ring-fenced but will use the shares of production and costs allocated to each block for purposes of determining income and expenditures; and
- any remaining minimum work obligations continue to be calculated on a block basis.

There are also very important practical considerations to keep in mind in relation to issues such as the provisions of any existing contracts which the parties may have entered into prior to the unitisation having taken place. These may include, for example, project finance agreements which may contain very stringent provisions which would require the signatories to obtain prior approval from the various lenders and project sponsors.

4.1. DETERMINATION

A key difference from a standard JOA also relates to how the unit equity (tract participation) will be determined under the UUOA provisions. Whilst in a JOA each party's participation interest is usually predefined and agreed at the outset, taking into account the parties' financial contribution to the joint venture, and will not change (other than by virtue of a sale of part or all of the interest to a third party or in the case of a default), in a UUOA two (or more) groups of licensees will need to establish what interest each group will have in the unit. This is not entirely straightforward. Without going into too much detail, it is important to bear in mind that the process for determining each group licence's tract participations is incredibly lengthy and complex in terms of negotiations. Different methods can be used to calculate tract participations, the most common of which are as follows:

(1) 'stock tank oil originally in place' (STOOIP) – this looks at the total amount of oil in the reservoir before production – this has the advantage of generally being the easiest way to determine tract participation. Its drawback lies in

the fact that it may not be entirely fair, because some of the oil will never actually be produced.

(2) 'recoverable reserves' – this method simply looks at those reserves which are recovered. Arguably this is the most equitable method but naturally it has the disadvantage that it can never be final until the field has been fully depleted and then there will be no reserves left for making final equitable adjustments.

(3) 'moveable oil originally in place' (MOOIP) – this is based on the oil originally in place and which is capable of movement within a reservoir. This method is no more equitable than STOOIP and has more uncertainties.

The majority of unitisations in the UKCS have been based on the STOOIP method.[30]

Each group of licensees will wish its unit equity to be based on the percentage of total hydrocarbons in that portion of the field which lies below its tract. The interest held by each individual party will then be that proportion of the unit equity that the party is entitled to under that group's JOA.[31] Putting it in simple mathematical terms, once the tract participation has been determined, each party's unit interest will be determined by multiplying that party's percentage interest under the relevant JOA by the initial tract participation for that licence.

Below is a worked example of how the unit equities are determined applying the above principles:[32]

Party	Licence Group	JOA P.I.	Tract Participation	Unit Equity
A Ltd	A	60%	45%	27%
B Ltd	A	30%	45%	13.5%
C Ltd	A	10%	45%	4.5%
		100%		**45%**
Party	**Licence Group**	**JOA P.I.**	**Tract Participation**	**Unit Equity**
D Ltd	B	70%	35%	24.5%
E Ltd	B	20%	35%	7%
F Ltd	B	10%	35%	3.5%
		100%		**35%**

30 Daintith, Willoughby and Hill, *supra* n. 13, para. 1-742.

31 D. Beggs and J. Stockdate, 'Unitisation and Unitisation Agreements', in G. Picton-Turbervill (ed.), *Oil and Gas: A Practical Handbook*,, 2nd edn, Globe Law and Business, London 2014, p. 63.

32 It is common for a typical UUOA to contain an appendix setting out the parties' respective unit equities in the same – or very similar – form to the one set out in this worked example.

Party	Licence Group	JOA P.I.	Tract Participation	Unit Equity
G Ltd	C	40%	20%	8%
H Ltd	C	25%	20%	5%
B Ltd	C	35%	20%	7%
		100%		**20%**
				= **100%**

4.2. REDETERMINATION

Another feature exclusive of the UUOA relates to 'redetermination'. It would seem at first somewhat counterintuitive that the parties, having undertaken the determination process – which as explained is rather complex and likely to take considerable amount of time – would later on want to 'redetermine' their unit interests. The explanation lies on the basic fact that the original calculation of hydrocarbons attributable to each tract will only be a good estimate until the time these hydrocarbons are actually being produced. At this time, the parties will have a far better idea of the extent to which the oil reservoir lies below each of the blocks. Therefore, the UUOA will contain provisions to ensure that there is an agreed mechanism pursuant to which the parties may adjust their original unit equity. Such mechanism is known as 'redetermination' and it effectively will entail re-calculating each licence group's tract participation in light of this newly acquired field data (which will in turn affect all the individual parties' respective unit equity, either increasing or decreasing their respective unit equity).

The key issues which a standard redetermination provision should cover are the following.

4.2.1. *When will Redetermination Take Place?*

Redetermination may be undertaken at certain regular intervals during the term of the UUOA, or alternatively it could be triggered on reaching a certain amount of production; or it may be instigated by one party.[33] Some UUOAs will only allow this to happen after all development drilling has taken place or where significant new geological data is available.[34] Redetermination can be a lengthy process and also expensive – therefore it is usual to place some limits and restrictions regarding when this can be triggered. For example, there may be a maximum number of redeterminations allowed during the term of a UUOA. There may

33 Beggs and Stockdate, *supra* n. 31, p. 64.
34 Deemer, 'Unitisation Agreements', at 7.

also be provisions which address the possibility that a redetermination process is found to be 'frivolous', for example if it results in less than an agreed percentage change in the tract participations – in which circumstances the licence group who requested it may be liable to meet all or part of the other licence group's incurred costs.[35] It is also usual to confine redeterminations to the first few years of production.[36]

4.2.2. *How is the Redetermination Administered?*

The redetermination process may be carried out in some instances by the unit operator, though it is more usual for the operating committee to do this. Any changes to the tract participations usually need to be unanimously approved by all the parties or at least to a substantial majority of them, including some from each licence/block.[37] Alternatively, if the parties fail to agree this on a voluntary basis, this may be referred to dispute resolution and be done by a third party.

In most cases, the terms of reference for the redetermination will be included as an exhibit to the UUOA. These would usually follow the procedure which was adopted at the time of calculating the determination of unit equities.

4.2.3. *What are the Consequences of the Redetermination?*

Firstly, there are substantial financial implications associated with any redetermination. This is because it affects all the parties' unit equity from the beginning, i.e. acting retrospectively – therefore the UUOA will also need to include provisions dealing with adjustments to petroleum which has already been lifted. In the end, each party will as a result of it receive a revised entitlement to production. If a licence group's tract participation has increased, the relevant licence holders will be entitled to lift a share of production each year and in addition lift a percentage of their deficient amount.[38] This is normally done over the life of the field and, in the unlikely event that it is not possible to make up this deficit over its life, the UUOA may contain provisions to the effect that the other licence group parties will have to make a cash payment to the aggrieved licence group.

In addition, the redetermination will also deal with adjustments in respect of each party's financial inputs, re-allocating capital expenditures, operating costs and past production of oil and gas. Therefore it is hardly surprising that the

[35] Weaver et al, 'International Unitisation', at 63.
[36] Beggs and Stockdate, *supra* n. 31, p. 64.
[37] Lang Weaver and Asmus, *supra* n. 4.
[38] Gordon et al., *supra* n. 15, p. 426.

calculation involved in this process tends to be very complex in light of the fact that it also needs to account for the larger expenditure such a party should have made.

In light of its lengthy and complex nature, naturally an unwanted consequence of redetermination can be disagreement between the parties on the adjustments to be made and therefore this may trigger the dispute resolution process – which is usually dealt with by expert determination due to the technical nature of the process.

Despite being hugely expensive and time-consuming, redeterminations are still seen as necessary in the UK by oil and gas companies. The reason for this is that both determination and redetermination have a direct bearing on the value of the underlying assets.

5. JOINT OPERATIONS, EXCLUSIVE OPERATIONS, UNIT OPERATIONS AND NON-UNIT OPERATIONS

The UUOA will contain provisions for the proposal and approval of a work programme and budget which will be akin to those provided for in the JOA. Petroleum produced will be shared by each licence group holder in proportion to their respective tract participation and it will then be further allocated within that individual licence group pursuant to the terms of the applicable JOA.[39]

In terms of non-unit operations, the UUOA will cater for operations which may be undertaken by a certain licence group in relation to an area which falls outside the unit area (but is within their licence) – it may include provisions which allow these licence group to make use of the unit property or even within the unit area under specific procedures. It is important that such operations do not disrupt the unit operations. This is a principle which also applies to exclusive operations, which are therefore not to become frequent as they may otherwise devalue the production from the unit area and be detrimental to all other unit owners.

Pursuant to the AIPN model UUOA, non-unit operations can be carried out in two different ways by the parties: (i) they may be carried out by the unit operator; or (ii) they could be undertaken by the relevant JOA operator. Whichever way they are ultimately carried out, they will be at the sole costs of the relevant parties who wish to carry these out.

[39] 'Joint Operating Agreements – A practical guide: Appendix F: Unitisation and the JOA', p. 327.

6. OPERATOR AND UNIT OPERATOR

The unit operator will have very similar rights and responsibilities to the JOA operator, such as:

- a duty to prepare work programme and budgets for the unit area and to provide copies of relevant reports and any relevant information to the parties;
- a duty to consult and inform with the other parties in relation to the unit property and unit operations;
- a duty to undertake all oil and gas unit operations in accordance with good oil (or gas) industry practice and in a manner which ensures that the licences are maintained in full force;
- a duty to obtain and maintain insurance in respect of the unit property and unit operations;
- a duty to follow the decision-making carried out by the Unit Opcom;
- a duty to obtain all governmental consents relating to the unitisation and unit operations;
- a right to conduct the unit operation by itself, its agents and sub-contractors; and
- a duty to pay and discharge all costs incurred by the unit parties and to keep accounts pursuant to the accounting procedure set out in the UUOA.

There may be instances where the unit operator could be in a situation of potential conflict of interests in the performance of that role as opposed to its additional and separate role as a party to, and possibly also the operator of, one of the underlying JOAs. In these circumstances one would have to consider the fiduciary duties which might be owed.[40]

7. OPCOM AND UNIT OPCOM

The UUOA will contain specific provisions prescribing the setting up and operation of a unit operating committee – this will largely mirror the provisions in the underlying JOAs. The party with the largest interest will usually become the operator and will not want their proposals being vetoed by owners with smaller interests. Equally, the smallest interest holders will want to resist being forced into approving a decision which they do not agree with. This is often a hotly debated issue and may usually be resolved by including a provision in the UUOA to the effect that no licence group can be pressured into agreeing a decision by the vote of others unless that licensee's share is minimal.[41]

40 'Joint Operating Agreements – A practical guide: Appendix F: Unitisation and the JOA', p. 325.
41 English, *supra* n. 24, p. 103.

In terms of voting, this may be done based on an agreed pass rate; however, given that it is possible and often happens that one party is a licence holder under two (or more) licence groups, there may also be provisions to the effect that there must be at least one different party as a representative of each licence.

8. DEFAULT

As for JOAs, the main parties' obligation under the UUOA will entail the payment of the relevant cash call issued by the unit operator pursuant to the provisions of the UUOA. Similarly then, if a party fails to pay the cash call within the prescribed terms of the agreement, a default situation will arise. The key issue to keep in mind when analysing a default situation relates to establishing what would be the appropriate remedy pursuant to the UUOA vis-à-vis its relationship with the underlying JOAs. This is particularly the case in the event of forfeiture because, in the event of a party defaulting under a JOA, it is not desirable or indeed appropriate for its participating interest to be transferred to all the non-defaulting parties under the unit area. One solution may involve the UUOA prescribing that a default situation which is remedied by the other parties of that licence group will be dealt with at the JOA level, whereas in the case of a default which is made in respect of the unit area and by all the licence group, the forfeiture provisions of the UUOA may apply to the interests of that licence group as a whole.[42] It has also been noted that a solution may otherwise simply be to include in the UUOA a default provision which provides for suspension of rights only of the defaulting party.[43]

9. ASSIGNMENT

Usually, the transfer of a party's interest in its licence/JOA will be regulated by the said JOA and the UUOA will have a provision to clarify this, although it is common for such provision to also state that such assignment should be accompanied by a corresponding transfer of the transferor's interests in the UUOA. Naturally, this also applies in the opposite scenario, i.e. if a party wishes to transfer its interest under the UUOA it should also assign its underlying licence interest pursuant to the relevant JOA. It is also important to consider whether there may be express provisions regarding any pre-emption rights applying pursuant to the UUOA, which will mirror pre-emption rights provisions under a JOA.

---

42 'Joint Operating Agreements – A practical guide: Appendix F: Unitisation and the JOA', p. 327.

43 M. Taylor and S. Tyne, *Taylor and Winsor on Joint Operating Agreements*, 2nd edn, Sweet & Maxwell, London 1992, p. 121.

10. DECOMMISSIONING

The parties will usually be responsible for decommissioning costs pursuant to the UUOA in proportion to their individual unit equity. Similar concerns as applying to the JOAs will also apply so that there will be relevant provisions for security arrangements in relation to anticipated decommissioning expenses to be made by each unit owner.

If operations were to end in the context of a specific licence and JOA without affecting the continued operation of the unit as a whole, then the abandonment of any infrastructure would normally be undertaken pursuant to the provisions of the relevant licence/JOA and not the UUOA.[44]

11. CONCLUSION

A UUOA is in many respects a JOA in respect of the unit area but with a larger scope. Therefore many provisions will be very similar (if not in some instances virtually identical) to those contained in a JOA. Notwithstanding the familiarity of the language used in the various provisions contained therein, it is essential to bear in mind from the outset that negotiating the UUOA is likely to take considerable amount of time in light of the difficult decisions which need to be reached amongst the several parties regarding the determination of their individual tract participations (as well as concerning the redetermination procedures), which involves, *inter alia*, agreeing on very complex mathematical calculations. In addition, there will be a number of issues where there will be a degree of overlapping between the provisions in the UUOA and those in the underlying JOAs, which will inevitably add to the complexity and may also create a certain ambiguity as to which should apply when.

Notwithstanding the intricacies associated with negotiating this type of agreement, the UUOA agreement is widely recognised in the oil and gas industry as the most appropriate instrument to address the inherent issues which arise from the geological realities of hydrocarbon reservoirs which lie beneath separate licences.

---

44 'Joint Operating Agreements – A practical guide: Appendix F: Unitisation and the JOA', p. 327.

KEY ISSUES RELATING TO JOAs IN CIVIL LAW COUNTRIES

Eduardo G. Pereira and Yanal Abul Failat

1. INTRODUCTION[1]

Whilst each of these states in which the oil and gas industry operates has its own particular needs and requirements, they tend to share notable similarities

[1] This chapter is based on the book E.G. Pereira (ed.), *Joint Operating Agreements: Challenges and Concerns from Civil Law Jurisdictions*, Kluwer Law International, the Netherlands 2015.

deriving from the international nature of the oil and gas industry. Most of the major companies have assets in various jurisdictions,[2] and so influence national governance by applying international practices and sharing expertise under local content requirements. More often than not, national regulation takes into account regulatory models and experiences of other jurisdictions so they can improve their own regulatory regime.[3]

The same situation applies for JOAs, a well-established form of private agreement. Despite the fact that many of the oil and gas regions have their own JOA model form to address their specific needs, almost all of such models are based on similar principles and assumptions.[4]

Nevertheless, negotiating, executing and implementing a JOA in a civil law country may generate unexpected legal challenges unless such parties are aware of the differences between the common law and civil law systems. The main difference relates to the primary source of law. In civil law systems, the primary source of law derives from statutes and regulations, whereas in common law jurisdictions the primary source of law is case law (judicial precedents). Therefore, judges in civil law jurisdictions are not empowered to make law but rather to interpret statutory law and to an extent take on the role of an investigator.[5] Some civil law jurisdictions however are moving towards certain rules of legal precedents within their relevant courts (e.g. Brazil).[6] Whilst civil law judges are strictly bound by the country's constitution, the legal praxis and expert opinions of the scholars are gradually being given greater consideration.

Naturally, all countries have their own special features. In China, for example, judges are bound to the interests of the Chinese Communist Party. In federal countries such as in Russia and Argentina, the legislative power at the provincial level must be acknowledged. Moreover, when parties elect to agree that the JOA is governed by a common law jurisdiction (e.g. English law) in a civil law country,

---

2 C. Miles, 'AIPN 2002 Model Form Joint Operating Agreement in Oil and Gas Joint Ventures' (2003) 22 *Australian Resources & Energy Law Journal* 153–160.

3 A.T. Martin, 'Model Contracts: a Survey of the Global Petroleum Industry' (2004) 22 *Journal of Energy & Natural Resources Law* 284.

4 Miles, *supra* n. 2.

5 The basic principle of the civil law tradition is the separation of legislative and judicial powers. Initially, commonly statutes enacted by the legislative power could be considered as law. However, in many civil law countries custom can also be regarded as a source of law, even though this is inconsistent with the very fundamental idea that only the state can make law. In the civil law tradition, the sources of law are the constitution, statutes, regulations and custom. The order of authority is descending: in other words, statutory law always prevails over a customary law. For more information about the civil law tradition, see J.H. Merryman., *The Civil Law Tradition - An Introduction to the Legal Systems of Western Europe and Latin America*, Stanford University Press, Stanford 1969, pp. 20–26.

6 Brazilian Supreme Court Divisions available at: <http://www.stf.jus.br/portal/cms/verTexto.asp?servico=jurisprudenciaSumulaVinculante> accessed 23.04.2015.

the provisions of the JOA are subject to and therefore need to be harmonised with the host government agreement and any mandatory provisions applicable under local petroleum laws.

The differing rules, procedures and issues that exist among civil law jurisdictions 'do not permit a universal solution via standard form provisions or articles'.[7] Therefore, in order to avoid unlawful or unenforceable provisions, the contracting parties should be careful before using or adopting an international JOA standard form. Although a variety of model JOAs have been published and are available for use, the model JOA published by the Association of International Petroleum Negotiators (AIPN) is one of the most updated and preferred standard forms throughout most regions of the world. The AIPN JOA was last revised in 2012 and provides various provisions that allows JOAs to be tailored to suit civil jurisdictions. Guidance notes for operations governed by civil law also supplement the AIPN JOA. Although the guidance notes are short, they do pinpoint the key issues, which may require particular attention and serve as a helpful starting point in any transaction.[8]

The key issues that may be relevant when negotiating and drafting/tailoring a JOA that is governed by civil law rather than common law are summarised in what follows.

2. CONTRACTUAL CONCERNS AND CHALLENGES

2.1. GENERAL CONTRACT LAW PRINCIPLES

2.1.1. Freedom of Contract

In most civil law countries (e.g. Argentina, Brazil, France, Norway and Portugal) any contract is generally based on the principle of freedom of contract. The parties have the autonomy to freely agree on the terms and conditions in the contract that binds them. Nevertheless, there are restrictions to such a freedom; for example, contracts cannot be drafted to contravene a public order (e.g. Turkey and Venezuela). This is a common issue, as the notion of what constitutes public order is not definitively defined in many civil jurisdictions and is therefore subject to broad interpretation by the local courts when challenged (e.g. Kazakhstan).

[7] AIPN, 'Guidance Notes to AIPN 2012 Model Joint Operating Agreement', 2012, p. 4.
[8] *Ibid.*

2.1.2. Good Faith

The obligation to negotiate, execute and perform contractual obligations in good faith is another basic principle regulated in most civil law countries through their civil codes (e.g. Argentina, Brazil, France and Portugal). In some countries a different term may be used for this obligation, such as 'honesty' or 'fairness' (e.g. China), but the meaning of the principle is the same. As a natural consequence, in civil law countries drafters are less likely to regulate this issue on a contractual level, as it would ordinarily be addressed by the civil codes. However, in order to avoid any doubt or wider interpretation by a third party, it would be good practice for the obligation to act in good faith to be expressly set out in the JOA.

2.1.3. Best and Reasonable Efforts

The meaning and interpretation of 'best and reasonable efforts' is not regulated in many civil law countries and therefore there is uncertainty as to its meaning and extent. Nevertheless, it is still widely used in commercial contracts due to the requests of common law lawyers to include these terms in the relevant contracts, and it is good practice to carefully define such terms when drafting a JOA.

2.1.4. Representations and Warranties

Commercial contracts concluded in civil law countries have frequently adopted the concept of representations and warranties from common law contracts, but the concept is usually not regulated in their relevant legislation and the breach of such provisions may result in the entire contract becoming invalid (e.g. in Kazakhstan, a breach of warranty is treated as a material mistake or even fraud). Thus the term 'representations' and 'warranties' should be clearly defined in the JOA in order to prevent any unintended interpretation by the local courts.

2.2. RELATIONSHIP BETWEEN THE PARTIES

There are two types of parties to a JOA: the operator and the non-operators.[9] The operator is the leader of the consortium,[10] and is responsible for conducting

---

9 The operator is commonly a party of the JV, but there are existing cases in which the role of the operator is given to a contracted Operator or even a company in which the JOA parties are the shareholders. For further information see: P. Roberts, *Joint Operating Agreements: A Practical Guide*, 3rd edn, Globe Law Business, London 2015, p. 96; S. Shaw, 'Joint Operating Agreements', in M.R David, *Upstream Oil and Gas Agreements*, Sweet and Maxwell, London 1996, p. 17.

10 It is important to note that usually the operator is approved by the host government who issued the petroleum title, as the host government is keen to control the person who will

the daily operations in the name of the consortium.[11] The non-operators (which include the operator in its capacity as non-operator) make up all the remaining parties to the JV that are not going to conduct the operations, but are mainly involved in the decision-making process.[12]

The relationship of the parties is an extremely important issue for any JOA, as it might affect the rights and duties carefully negotiated and drafted by the contracting parties. Consequently, it is essential to establish, in clear terms, their relationship.

However, it is also very important to remember that the JOA does not exclusively dictate the relationship of the parties, as the general law might also determine specific issues in this area.[13] Lee Jones clearly recognises this fact as follows:

> 'The parties to operating agreements usually desire a relation other than mining partnership or general partnership, and operating agreements frequently expressly provide that the parties do not intend to form a partnership of any type. *Such a provision, while of value as indicating intention, is not legally controlling. If the relationship established by agreement essentially conforms to the partnership pattern partnership law will govern, at least as to strangers, whatever may be the expressed intention of the parties.* It is of extreme importance, therefore, that the operating agreement contains terms and provisions which establish rights and duties between the parties inconsistent with the partnership relation.'[14]

---

conduct the operations of the consortium. In this context, the host government shall also approve any modification of the operator. See: Model Clauses 40, 42 and 42 of the Petroleum Licensing (Production) (Seaward Areas) Regulations 2008 (UK).

11 See C. Gonvala, 'Upstream joint ventures – bidding and operating agreements', in G. Pircton-Turbervill (ed.), *Oil and Gas: A practical handbook*, Globe Law and Business, London 2009, p. 46; C. Duval et al., *International Petroleum and Exploration Agreements: Legal, Economic & Policy Aspects*, Barrows, New York 2009, pp. 289-291; A. Jennings, *Oil and Gas Exploration Contracts*, Sweet & Maxwell, London 2008, p. 23; LXL LLP, *A Guide to the Energy Industry for the In-House Lawyer, focusing in 2012 on LNG*, LXL LLP, London 2012; M. Taylor, T.P. Winsor and S. Tyne, *The Joint Operating Agreement – Oil and Gas Law*, 2nd edn, Longman, London 1992, pp. 1-5.

12 See T. Daintith, G. Willoughby and A. Hill (eds.), *United Kingdom Oil & Gas Law*, Sweet & Maxwell, London 2009, p. 1140, G.M.D. Bean, *Fiduciary Obligations and Joint Ventures: The Collaborative Fiduciary Relationship*, Oxford University Press, Oxford 1995, pp. 14-15.

13 For the purposes of this section, the United Kingdom's legislation and jurisprudence will be considered.

14 L. Jones, 'Problems Presented by Joint Ownership of Oil, Gas and Other Minerals' (1953–1954) 32 *Texas Law Review* 717.

The most important issues where the general law might establish connections between parties in the JOA provisions are the following:

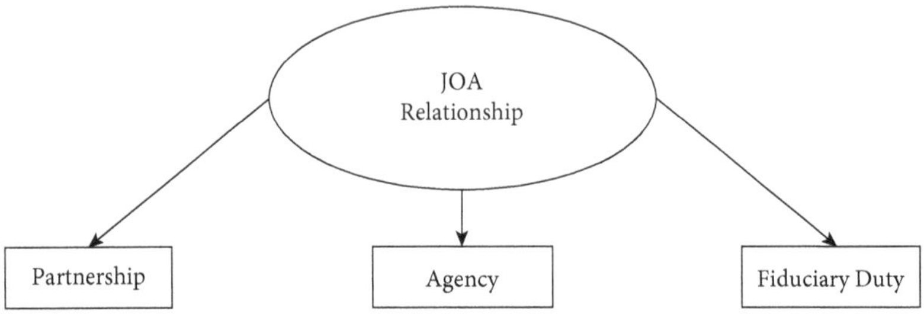

The establishment of any of the above-mentioned forms of partnership could add supplementary rights and duties to the JOA parties, as these issues are provided outside the body of the JOA but within a particular legal system. The majority of the duties (related to the forms of relationship presented above) only largely affect the operator, as the operator is responsible for conducting the joint operations. In these cases, the definition of the relationship between the parties is likely to increase the protection of the non-operators. Initially, from a legal standpoint, the possibility of a JOA being considered a partnership is potentially the most inconvenient for the contracting parties,[15] as it could increase their costs and responsibilities by reducing tax allowances and imposing further liabilities.[16]

Anita Himebaugh describes the 'real' impact that tax applications can exercise on certain oil and gas operations in the following terms:

> 'In 1981, the oil and gas industry paid in excess of $17 billion in federal income taxes and an additional $8 billion in windfall profits taxes. Obviously, any energy company's

15 It is important to note that recently another kind of partnership called 'Limited Liability Partnership' was incorporated into the UK's legislation. This partnership mainly separates the liabilities between this entity and its members. In other words, it is much more like a limited company than a partnership. However, this entity is outside the scope of this study. For further information see: J. Whittaker and J. Machell, *The Law of Limited Liability Partnerships*, Bloomsbury Professional, West Sussex 2009; S. Young, *Limited Liability Partnership Handbook*, Tottel Publishing, Haywards Heath 2007; Y. Land and P. Thorpe, *Accounts and Audit of Limited Liability Partnerships*, Smith & Williamson, London 2009.

16 For further information see T.P. Briggs and B. Lemons, 'Basic principles of tax partnerships for oil and gas operations' (1991) 39 *Oil & Gas Tax Quarterly* 428–484; D. Glusman and G. Ciociola, *Fiduciary Duties and Liabilities, Tax and Trust Accountant's Guide*, CCH, USA 2006; C. Nakhle, *Petroleum Taxation Sharing the Oil Wealth, a Study of Petroleum Taxation Yesterday, Today and Tomorrow*, Routledge, London 2008; J. Lewis, *Partnerships for Profit, Structuring and Managing Strategic Alliances*, The Free Press, London 1990.

great concern is the specific tax treatment accorded its exploration and development arrangements.'[17]

In this sense, it is very important for any party to think carefully before structuring the relevant arrangement; otherwise, the economics of the operation could be far from the initial expectations. However, tax is not the only concern for the JOA parties, as the way they structure their agreement might also increase their rights and obligations, which would have been carefully established in the JOA.

2.2.1. Partnership

In the AIPN 2012 JOA, it is clearly indicated that the relationship of the parties under a JOA cannot be considered a partnership.[18] The most common reason to avoid characterising the relationship as a partnership in common law countries is that of tax liabilities. However, in countries where the concept of partnership is regulated in legislation, it is often impossible to deny the existence of a partnership if the conditions for partnership under law are fulfilled. For example, in Brazil and Peru, the mandated form is a consortium and in Argentina through a form entitled 'Transitory Union of Companies'.[19] In such cases, a JOA provision stating that the JOA shall not form a partnership would be invalid under the local legislation. Therefore, when concluding a JOA, the parties should pay attention to the form of relationship that the JOA may create. Such form of cooperation can vary from an unincorporated partnership or joint venture with no legal personality to a compulsory incorporated joint venture. Besides the form of the partnership, the legislation of civil law countries differs, for example, as regards how liability is divided between the partners.

Despite specific legislation regulating such structures, the existence of a partnership or a joint venture may have to be evaluated on a case-by-case basis. In countries where there is no government control of the terms of the JOA, the parties are free to negotiate their type of association (e.g. US and Canada). In countries where the government requires the approval of the consortium agreement/shareholders agreement or certain parts of it (e.g. Brazil, Mexico, Russia and Venezuela), there is less room for discussion about what type of association the parties shall create. In such jurisdictions, drafters tend to recognise the application of the applicable legal form under local law rather than adopt the AIPN language, which negates the existence of a partnership or

---

17 A.G. Himebaugh, 'An Overview of Oil and Gas Contracts in the Williston Basin' (1983) 59 *North Dakota Law Review* 49.

18 AIPN JOA Articles 14 and 9.

19 AIPN Guidance Notes, *supra* n. 7, p. 8.

any other type of association. In countries where the host government offers the standard form JOA (e.g. Norway, Denmark and Mozambique), the parties have no choice in determining the legal form of the joint venture (i.e. incorporated or unincorporated).

2.2.2. *Agency/Fiduciary*

Another important issue is the agency status of the operator.[20] The recognition of such agency status could change the relationship between the parties, as further obligations would be imposed on the operator in its performance of the operations.[21] However, some JOAs seek to avoid such an effect, as they provide expressly for the exclusion of such agency characterisation.[22] The question then is whether the courts will recognise such a provision. The answer lies in the legal definition of agency and the context of the JOA, as will be analysed below.

The legal definition of agency was historically consolidated in English jurisprudence back in the 18th century.[23] However, Bowstead describes the essence of the definition as follows:

> '[T]he relationship, which exists between two persons, one of whom expressly or impliedly consents that the other should represent him or act on his behalf, and the other of whom similarly, consents to represent the former or so to act.'[24]

In other words, agency refers to '[a] person duly authorised to act on behalf of another; or one whose unauthorised act has been duly ratified.'[25] This concept

---

20 For further information about agency: F.R. Mechem, *A treatise on the Law of Agency V2, Part 1, Callaghan and Company 1914*, Kessinger, Whitefish, USA 2008; F.M.B. Reynolds, *Bowstead on Agency*, Sweet & Maxwell, London 1985; R.G. Woodyatt, *The Law of Agency*, Bibliolife, Charleston 1900.

21 See: Bean, *supra* n. 12; Taylor, Winsor and Tyne, *supra* n. 11, p. 10; Shaw, *supra* n. 9, pp. 16-17; Roberts, *supra* n. 9.

22 This situation is recognised as follows: 'Joint operating agreements might deny that an agency relationship exists between the operator and non-operators, or attempt to provide for a limited agency in the operator, or they might simply be silent on this issue.' J.G. Jackson, 'Agency in Joint Operating Agreements and Joint Ventures', Australian Mining and Petroleum Law Association Yearbook, 1986, p. 239.

23 E.g. *Nicholson v G. Juipman* (1793) 2. H. Bl. 254 & 3 R.R. 374; *Pickering v Busk* (1812) 15 East. 38, *Pole v Leask* (1863) 33 L. J. Ch. 162, *Kelner v Baxter* (1866–67) L.R. 2 C.P. 174; *Cole v London & North-Western Bank* (1875) L. K. 10 C. P. 354, *Markwick v Hardingham* (1880) 15 Ch. D. 339, *C.A.*, *Sagal (t/a Bunz UK) v Atelier Bunz GmbH* [2008] EWHC 789 (Comm); *Temple Legal Protection Ltd v QBE Insurance (Europe) Ltd* [2008] EWHC 843 (Comm); *Halifax Life Ltd v DLA Piper Scotland Ltd* [2009] CSOH 74; *Berry v Laytons* [2009] EWHC 1591 (QB); *National Trust for Places of Historic Interest v Birden* [2009] EWHC 2023 (Ch); *Garnac Grain Co Inc v HMF Faure & Fairclough Ltd* [1968] AC 1130.

24 Reynolds, *supra* n. 20, p. 1.

25 Woodyatt, *supra* n. 20; Reynolds, *supra* n. 20.

applies to any business and it is quite likely to apply to the most typical JOA relationship as the operator acts on the behalf of the consortium. Nevertheless, in a typical JOA the operator is the agent and principal at the same time, which is unique for an agency.

Most civil law jurisdictions are likely to recognise the existence of an agency relationship between the JOA parties to certain extent (e.g. France, Kazakhstan and Turkey). Sometimes a power of attorney might be required between the JOA parties. However, the industry players in those countries are less concerned with the potential fiduciary duties that could arise from this characterisation, as they have even stronger good faith obligations deriving from their civil codes (e.g. the Norwegian JOA model does not define or use the term 'fiduciary duties').

2.3. LIMITATION OF LIABILITY

The petroleum industry faces several types of risks and challenges.[26] Parties are fully aware that this is the nature of the industry and the operator is elected to conduct the operations on the pre-agreed basis of 'no gain, no loss'.[27] On the premise that the operator should not be penalised for any losses arising from the joint operations, most JOAs would limit the operator's liability in proportion to their respective share in the venture.[28] However, this principle becomes unreasonable if the operator commits serious mistakes that affect the operations. The provision of limitation of liability in a JOA addresses this issue. The exception to the exculpatory principle (i.e. no gain, no loss) applies whenever the operator conducts operations with gross negligence or wilful misconduct.[29]

---

26 See also G.K. Foster, 'Managing Expropriation Risks in the Energy Sector: Steps for Foreign Investors to Minimise their Exposure and Maximise Prospects for Recovery when Takings Occur' (2005) 23 *Journal of Energy and Natural Resources Law* 36–59; A.B. Derman and A. Melsheimer, 'Changing the Rules of the Game: Issues that arise under the 2002 AIPN JOA when a host government mandates a "replacement contract"' (2010) 8(4) *OGEL (Oil, Gas and Energy Law Journal)* 1–7<www.ogel.org> accessed 22.03.2016; V. Lowe, 'Recognition or Expropriation' (2004) 2(3) *OGEL* <www.ogel.org> accessed 22.03.2016.

27 C. Thorpe, *Fundamentals of Upstream Petroleum Agreements*, C.P. Thorpe, London 2008, p. 126.

28 'As a rule it is agreed that the operator shall make no profit nor suffer any loss as a result of acting as operator, but the party acting as operator carries a special liability for damage caused as a result of his conduct of the operations. Generally all liabilities and expenses are proportionally shared between the parties, but if damage is caused as a result of reckless behaviour or gross negligence on the part of the operator then the latter will be solely liable for the consequences, except for consequential or indirect damage or loss of production. The latter liability will in all circumstances be for the account of all parties and shared accordingly.' B. Taverne, *An Introduction to the Regulation of the Petroleum Industry: Law, Contracts and Conventions*, Graham & Trotman, London 1994, p. 136.

29 H. Dundas, 'Joint Operating Agreements: An Introduction', 1994 Summer Programme: UK Oil and Gas Law, CPMLP 09/09, 1994, p. 12.

In this case, the operator shall bear the costs independently, without the liability of the non-operators. Obviously, this is a highly debated provision during the negotiation of a JOA and the operator will be particularly concerned with how such liability may be limited in its favour. The operator on the one hand would want to limit any liability for an honest mistake, misjudgement, omission, a negligent act or any liability in the course of performing the joint operations, while the non-operators on the other hand would want to negotiate a wider clause.

The default position under Article 4.6.A of the AIPN JOA is set out as follows:

> '[N]either the Operator nor any other Operator Indemnitee shall bear (except as a Party to the extent of its Participating Interest share) any damage, loss, cost, expense or liability resulting from performing (of failing to perform) the duties and functions of Operator, and the Indemnitees are hereby released from Liability to Non-Operators for any and all damages, losses, costs, expenses and liabilities arising out of, incident to or resulting from such performance or failure to perform, even though caused in whole or in party by a pre-existing defect or the negligence (whether sole, joint or concurrent), gross negligence, wilful misconduct, strict liability or other legal fault of Operator (or any such Operator Indemnitee).'

Most JOAs will contain a provision whereby the non-operators indemnify the operator from any liability to third parties for any damages resulting from performing or failing to perform their duties and functions. Article 4.6.B of the AIPN JOA, provide that the 'parties shall (in proportion to their Participating Interests) defend and indemnify the Operator Indemnitees from any damages, losses, costs…and liability incident to claims, demands, or causes of action brought by or for any person or entity'.

This exclusion of liability may be subject to exceptions, for instance Article 4.6.D of the AIPN JOA, an optional clause, provides that, despite Articles 4.6.A and 4.6.B, if any 'Senior Supervisory Personnel' of the operator engages in gross negligence or wilful misconduct that causes the parties to the JOA damage, loss, cost or liability of claims then the operator will bear exclusively liability for certain losses and costs.

As explained in the Guidance Notes accompanying the AIPN JOA, two issues may arise, namely:

(1) the indemnity is subject to a causality test (i.e. for the indemnity to take effect, the injured party must show adequate causation and therefore remoteness) and any calculation of damages is calculated accordingly; and
(2) the indemnity may be construed as a guarantee analogous to third party liability insurance contracts.[30]

---

30 AIPN Guidance Notes, *supra* n. 7.

Such an analogy may be construed on the basis that in both the JOA and the third party insurance contract, the indemnity establishes that if a third party suffers damage or loss, it can request indemnification from the indemnitor.

Further limitations to the exceptions that are usually set out may arise.[31] The first limitation refers to the liability, as some JOAs allow the parties to define what type of losses should be compensated exclusively by the operator.[32] The second limitation refers to environmental damages and consequential losses, as the operator will not bear exclusive liability for environmental damages nor consequential losses regardless of the cause of the incident.[33] The rationale is that the operator should be punished only when an experienced person, completely under the control and responsibility of the operator, has made the error and will not cover all damage, but only certain types of damages, as otherwise it would be difficult to find any party interested in taking on the role of operator.

As reflected above, the definition of the operator's liabilities is a sensitive matter for all the parties involved. The liability shall be described carefully in the JOA, even though the JOA parties would be held jointly liable for the operations from a governmental perspective.[34] The provision of liability should also include the definitions of the relevant terms (i.e. gross negligence or wilful misconduct), as the law is not always consistent. It varies whether 'gross negligence' and 'wilful misconduct' is specifically regulated in the local legislation. In some cases, one of these terms may be regulated, but not both or not with the same definition and detail as the JOA parties might desire.[35] As there is no universal practice across civil jurisdictions, the best way to ensure the desired interpretation of the concepts is to define them clearly in the JOA.

Generally, civil law countries are less likely to interfere with the basic understanding of the JOA that the operator takes on this role on a no gain, no loss basis, except for restrictions related to indirect and environmental losses in some jurisdictions (e.g. Argentina and the Netherlands), but not all jurisdictions (e.g. Greenland). If a party carries out any activity with gross negligence or wilful misconduct, it is expected to bear the responsibility for all costs, regardless of the type of costs derived from such activities. In such cases, a provision in a JOA that limits the operator's liability under gross negligence and wilful misconduct may be deemed invalid by a local court in a civil law country. For example, Article 4.6.B of the AIPN JOA extends such indemnity to cover damages or loss arising from an 'existing defect, or the negligence (whether sole, joint or

31 Duval, *supra* n. 11, p. 294.

32 Roberts, *supra* n. 9, pp. 179–192.

33 'It is further provided that in neither case shall the operator be liable for 'any consequential loss, Taylor, Winsor and Tyne, *supra* n. 11, pp. 6–7.

34 See C. Wilkinson, *Joint Ventures & Shareholder's Agreements*, Bloomsbury Professional, London 2009, pp. 3-5; Bean, *supra* n. 12, p. 19.

35 Dundas, *supra* n. 29, p. 12.

concurrent), gross negligence, wilful misconduct, strict liability or other legal fault of Operator)'. Following the above analogy with insurance contracts, this must be evaluated in the context of the applicable insurance law, which may determine the extent of the indemnity. For example in Argentina, third party insurance contracts exclude coverage for liability arising from wilful misconduct and/or gross negligence by the insured party.[36]

Financial caps can be introduced in order to limit the amount of compensation. They also limit the risks between the parties and give a level of predictability, but they may be subject to similar restrictions by the legislation as general liability. Thus, the enforceability of financial caps should always be confirmed prior to concluding a JOA and one should bear in mind that in many countries the legislation allows the court to modify the amount of compensation if the financial cap can be deemed unreasonable, thus decreasing the security to some extent.

2.4. DEFAULT

The default provision is probably one the most critical in a JOA due to the extensive costs of oil and gas operations.[37] Each party must be able to ensure that they will make their contribution to the expenditures of the consortium.[38] If any party fails to provide its share, the consortium is put at risk, as the commitment to the government has to be honoured in order to keep the granting instrument in good standing.[39] Thus, JOAs commonly include heavy sanctions for default as a means of threatening all parties with severe consequences for any default. The options can be summarised as follows.[40]

2.4.1. Hydrocarbons Entitlement

The first option is taking the hydrocarbons of a defaulting party. For instance, under the AIPN JOA, Article 8.4.A provides that upon a default, the defaulting party shall not have a right to its hydrocarbon entitlement, which shall vest in and be the property of the non-defaulting parties. The clause also empowers the operator to sell such hydrocarbon entitlement, in an arm's length sale, on

---

36 D. Roizen, 'Certain Argentine Law Consideration Regarding the 2002 AIPN JOA Model Contract' (2012) 5(2) *Journal of World Energy Law and Business* 139, 141.

37 Taverne, *supra* n. 28, p. 138.

38 Bean, *supra* n. 12, p. 17.

39 S. Styles, 'Joint Operating Agreements', in G. Gordon, J. Paterson and E. Usenmez (eds.), *Oil and Gas Law: Current Practice and Emerging Trends*, Dundee University Press, Dundee 2007, p. 289.

40 Dundas, *supra* n. 29, pp. 14-15.

commercially reasonably terms, to be deposited into a reserve fund, following which any remaining surplus shall be paid to the defaulting party and any deficiency shall constitute a debt owed by the defaulting party to the non-defaulting parties.

In certain civil jurisdictions (e.g. Argentina), this provision may mean the non-defaulting parties acquire hydrocarbon entitlements as co-trustees of the defaulting party. Accordingly, such transfer is one that 'is not complete and unconditioned but fiduciary, where the defaulting party is the trustor, the non-defaulting parties are co-trustees and beneficiaries and the defaulting party is the final recipient for the remnant'.[41] This may be problematic in jurisdictions that restrict a trustor's creditor from seizing goods once transferred in trust. Diego Roizen explains that the trust acquisition of the hydrocarbon entitlement during the non-compliance period is nevertheless performed to the extent that these hydrocarbons are produced (rather than before) and therefore a defaulting party's creditor may impose an embargo on future hydrocarbon flow as they are produced, in which case the transfer in trust may not take place.[42]

2.4.2. Forfeiture and Withering Clauses

The second remedy is forfeiture.[43] In this case, the defaulting party shall lose all of its participation to the non-defaulting parties without any compensation. This is the most common in the petroleum industry.[44] Although this seems strict, it is necessary given the cost and risk involved in the industry. There is a variation to forfeiture called a withering provision.[45] It is the same concept as forfeiture with one key difference: the defaulting party will only lose a proportional share of its participation in relation to the amount of default.

The risks relating to the forfeiture (and withdrawal) clause are based on the nature of the forfeiture, which can be deemed a penalty clause. Penalty clauses are prohibited in most common law jurisdictions, while in others the case law is still unclear in this respect.[46] Civil law countries tend to allow the concept of punitive clauses (e.g.Angola, Argentina, Brazil, China, France, Kazakhstan, Portugal, Turkey and Venezuela). However, the key issue is the same as under common law; the default clause should be proportional and reasonable between the amount of default and investments occurred. Therefore, forfeiture clauses

---

41 Roizen, *supra* n. 36, p. 142: it is important to note that the whilst the operator is obliged to perform the sale of the defaulting party's entitlement, it will not be deemed a trustee: the non-operators are due to the wording of the Article 8.4.A, which makes it clear that the ownership of such entitlement is vested into the non-defaulting parties.

42 *Ibid.*

43 Thorpe, *supra* n. 27, pp. 139-140.

44 *Ibid.*

45 Dundas, *supra* n. 29, pp. 14-15.

46 Taylor, Winsor and Tyne, *supra* n. 11, p. 95.

should not be automatically omitted as a default provision, as some jurisdictions accept forfeiture or a similar mechanism without limits or with a requirement of proportionality (e.g. Greenland and Norway). The same rationale applies for the other types of sanctions and solutions imposed under the JOA, as the key issue is to define whether the measure/consequence (forfeiture, withering, buy-out, security, etc.) is proportional to the amount of default. Therefore, it is also important to note that the stage and the defaulting party's investment up to the default affect any evaluation of the proportionality of a forfeiture clause.

Whether such clauses are deemed punitive or not is often measured against the stage of the operations in which the default has occurred. It is arguable that, given that in the exploration stage the party will not have invested as much as by the time the operations are in the production stage, the earlier the default, the more likely the provision will be found enforceable. Nevertheless, the legal practice regarding the default provisions is still developing in many countries and the most suitable default provision should be evaluated in the context of individual jurisdictions, based on the current legal development and legislation in that country.

2.4.3. *Buy-Out Provisions*

A third remedy is the buy-out.[47] This option requires a mathematical formula to determine the valuation of the asset to be transferred, taking into account discounts, which reflect the situation of the sale. Such a formula would be either mutually agreed or determined by an expert. Generally speaking, the structure of a buy-out provision does not necessarily raise any issues in civil law jurisdictions except in some specific cases (e.g. when the discount is not proportional to the default and past investments). Accordingly, this option is considered an alternative to the forfeiture clause that generally allows negotiators and drafters to bypass the enforceability issue.

2.4.4. *Encumbrances/Securities*

A fourth option is the creation of encumbrances or securities over the participating interest of the other party and such collateral might be called to secure the default payments.[48] An alternative would be to exercise a lien and charge over the defaulting party's interests.[49] This option should be analysed in consistency with the applicable local law and granting instrument in order to be an enforceable option. For example, this could represent a variety challenges

47 *Ibid.*
48 *Ibid.*
49 Roberts, *supra* n. 9, p. 216.

in civil law countries like Brazil, as several provisions from the concession agreement and statutory requirements should be verified in such procedure as well as Brazilian law which prohibits the so-called *pacto comissório* (i.e. the beneficiary of a collateral cannot take over the asset as a payment but rather may sell it to a third party with the obligation to restitute payments in excess of the guaranteed amount to the non-defaulting parties).

2.5. EXCLUSIVE OPERATIONS

As a rule, all oil and gas activities are conducted as joint operations.[50] A sole risk project is a project conducted by fewer than all parties. The practicality of a sole risk project is that an activity proposed in the operating committee (OpCom) which does not achieve the required pass mark of approval as a joint operation can still be conducted. Even though the OpCom does not approve this proposal to be conducted as a joint operation, any party has the option to continue such an operation as a sole risk project (i.e. at their own risk and cost). The non-consent clause is less common. Whenever a proposal is approved in the OpCom and a party is not happy to proceed as a joint operation, then the non-consent clause allows such party to not participate in such operation. Nevertheless, the outcome for a sole risk or non-consent is the same, as it will lead to an operation by fewer than all parties.[51]

The concept of an exclusive operation is simple. However, the consequences are highly complex, as a typical model form JOA is not suitable for covering joint and exclusive operations. It becomes unclear which clauses apply to the exclusive operation and to what extent.[52] Ideally, a new JOA should be created for this exclusive area to tackle this issue, but instead of referring for the creation of a new JOA, the standard JOA models currently use to the term *mutatis mutandis*, which means that the other provisions of the JOA should apply as applicable. There are a number of other complexities regarding the conduct of operations, as in many jurisdictions only one operator is approved by the government to conduct operations in the licensed area. This can be problematic if the operator for the consortium is not a sole risk party. Protection of the non-participating parties from the risks and costs related to the exclusive operation is also an issue, as the sole risk participants could potentially cause severe damage to the entire consortium. In short, a sole risk provision is used to discourage exclusive operations and pressure the other parties to remain united, as the non-participating parties will be excluded from the results of these activities unless

---

[50] Dundas, *supra* n. 29, p. 10.

[51] Styles, *supra* n. 39, pp. 287-289.

[52] Daintith, Willoughby and Hill, *supra* n. 12, p. 1152.

the agreement allows a non-participating party to join at a later stage (however, the price could be prohibitive).[53]

Exclusive operations in civil law countries are possible in theory (e.g. Argentina, Denmark and Norway), but they are subject to specific restrictions or requirements in many jurisdictions. Firstly, several civil law jurisdictions do not recognise the distinction between 'legal interest' and 'beneficial interest' (e.g. Brazil, France and Portugal), which may lead to difficulties when interpreting the 2012 AIPN model JOA provisions. As an alternative, jurisdictions such as Poland make use of the distinction between the right to dispose and the right to benefit (e.g. legal interest and beneficial interest respectively).[54] For this reason, it is of the utmost importance that the parties draft and assess the enforceability of such a provision carefully, particularly when and if such operations are not expressly permitted under the applicable law. Secondly, exclusive operations may be subject to the approval of a competent authority. Furthermore, if the operator changes as a result of exclusive operations, an additional approval might be necessary. Other contractual changes resulting from exclusive operations are possible, and in some cases the parties to a JOA would benefit from restructuring the relationship under the JOA for the purposes of the exclusive operations. For example, in Uzbekistan, the parties tend to incorporate a separate legal entity and designate it as an operator when conducting exclusive operations. Such restructuring has benefits in a bureaucratic sense, and in certain countries, such as Russia, such restructuring would benefit the parties in the form of reduced taxation. Therefore, the JOA parties should carefully analyse the general definitions, legal system and consequences of an exclusive operation before implementing one in a civil law country.

2.6. ASSIGNMENT AND WITHDRAWAL

Assignment means a process whereby one party transfers its participating interest (partially or completely) to a third party or to another JOA party.[55] Withdrawal, on the other hand, refers to the desire by one or all of the JOA parties to leave the consortium and return it to the relevant governmental authorities, if none of the JOA parties remains within the area.[56] Unlike an assignment, withdrawal commonly does not involve any payment if the minimal work programme (i.e. the minimum commitment from the licensees towards the host government) has been completed.

53 Roberts, *supra* n. 9, p. 202.
54 AIPN, *supra* n. 7, p. 4.
55 See Taylor, Winsor and Tyne, *supra* n. 11, pp. 97–119.
56 *Ibid.*

The typical provision related to transfer or assignment is the right given to the other consortium parties to acquire the assets under a 'sale' prior to a third party (i.e. a party outside the consortium). This could be implemented as either a right of first refusal or as a pre-emptive right. The first allows the JOA parties to negotiate the sale prior to any other party. The second allows the transferor to negotiate with third parties first. Once a deal has been negotiated with such a third party, the JOA parties should have the opportunity to match the proposal. From the transferor's point of view, the pre-emptive right is undesirable as it decreases the attractiveness for third parties, who may negotiate for several months and ultimately lose the sale. From the other JOA parties' point of view, the pre-emptive right could be the best option as a third party completes the 'hard job' of negotiation, even though this could result in an overly high price for the other JOA parties. A JOA is a document that should remain valid for decades, so it is hard to anticipate which option is best during the negotiation period.

Assignment and withdrawal from the JOA usually require the consent of either the competent authority or all parties to the JOA.[57] This is understandable, because the whole or partial assignment of the rights and/or obligations of a party to a JOA may bring about significant changes to the operations. Furthermore, it will not be insignificant to whom the rights and/or obligations are assigned or who will replace the withdrawing party. Often, these industry-standard restrictions on the transfer of participation interest in the host government agreement and the JOA are drafted to cover both direct and indirect transfers. Other JOAs, more commonly in civil law countries, provide 'safe harbours' including exceptions for initial public offerings, indirect transfers that do not result in a change of control, or for package deals (i.e. where there is a simultaneous sale of interests in different blocks, where no individual block represents more than a certain percentage, e.g. 20% or 20% of the overall deal price).[58]

In the majority of civil law countries, the assignment and withdrawal rules are specifically limited and regulated in the legislation (e.g. Angola, Argentina, Brazil, China, Mozambique, Russia and Venezuela). However, the level of

---

57 Kenneth Mildwaters states that '[t]he Joint Operating Agreement usually provides that the Operator cannot assign the operatorship without the consent of the Participants. The right of the Participants to withhold their consent is usually absolute. In Great Britain the consent of the Secretary of State for Energy to a proposed assignee of the Operator would be required. The reason for this and the effect of failing to obtain the consent of the Secretary of State for Energy is discussed above. This is not the case in Australia.' K.C. Mildwaters, *Joint Operating Agreements. A Consideration of Legal Aspects Relevant to Joint Operating Agreements Used in Great Britain and Australia by Participants thereto to Regulate the Joint Undertaking of Exploration for Petroleum in Offshore Areas with Particular Reference to their Rights and Duties*, PhD Thesis, University of Dundee, 1990, p. 491.

58 J.V.L.E.L. Miranda, 'Joint Ventures', in E.G. Pereira, *Brazilian Upstream Oil and Gas: A Practical Guide to the Law and Regulation*, Globe Law and Business, London 2012, p. 88.

restriction and regulation vary. In some countries, such as in France and Russia, there are statutory pre-emption rights that need to be taken into account, as well as other special legislation that may be applied in cases of assignment or withdrawal.

2.7. FORCE MAJEURE

Force majeure is an act beyond the reasonable control of the parties such as a strike or a hurricane. Civil law countries tend to regulate force majeure within the relevant civil code (e.g. Argentina, Brazil, France, Portugal, etc.), while common law countries tend to provide a far more complex jurisprudence through a similar mechanism known as frustration. Despite such regulation, it has become common practice to adopt a contractual definition of force majeure. Care must be taken, however, when defining force majeure, as under the applicable law force majeure clauses may be deemed 'exculpatory clauses' and be subject to limitations and restrictions if drafted too broadly.

2.8. ECONOMIC EQUILIBRIUM

Economic equilibrium of the contract, commonly known as hardship, refers to unexpected events which could change the economic equilibrium of the contract by imposing an excessive burden on one party. Economic equilibrium is recognised in some civil law countries (e.g. the Netherlands) but is not widely recognised in most (e.g. Angola, Brazil, France and Portugal). The issue of lack of legislation on this matter arises again, as the concept does not have legislative support in many civil law countries. Thus, this principle should be clearly defined in the JOA if the parties would like it to apply to their consortium.

The main issue with a hardship clause in a JOA relates to the fact that the JOA is directly related to the host government contract. If the host government contract does not recognise such provision, then it is difficult to implement it at JOA level. In any case, the situations where such a provision would be applied at JOA level are fairly limited and unlikely to materialise, in contrast to what is the case with the host government contract.

3. CONCLUSION

JOA parties should be careful if they intend to use and sign a model form JOA that was not originally designed for a civil law country (e.g. the Norwegian and Greenlandic model form JOAs). If the JOA parties desire to use the AIPN JOA or another similar agreement, then they should understand the main principles and concepts acceptable by the relevant jurisdiction to make sure their JOA provisions and mechanisms are enforceable under the relevant jurisdiction. Unlike in North America, natural resources in civil law countries tend to be owned by the state. Therefore, a JOA is likely to be linked to a host government contract and several governmental permissions, and approval of the applicable JOA will be required.

THE RELATIONSHIP BETWEEN A JOA AND A HOST GOVERNMENT INSTRUMENT

Eduardo G. Pereira and Ole Kirkvaag

1. INTRODUCTION

A feature of most oil and gas operations is that they are conducted in a hostile environment subject to a number of risks, extending into geological, technical, financial and environmental, and also into political, to mention a few.[1] These risks can particularly affect the exploration phase and, as they can have a marked influence on each project, the oil and gas industry has become renowned for operating with a level of uncertainty.

Most host governments rely on sovereign ownership of the oil and gas reserves situated below their territory or continental shelf. However, they are not usually able to, or interested in, allocating public funds for a risk-laden business

---

1 See also: G.K. Foster, 'Managing Expropriation Risks in the Energy Sector: Steps for Foreign Investors to Minimise their Exposure and Maximise Prospects for Recovery when Takings Occur' (2005) 23 *J. Energy & Nat. Resources L.* 36–59; A.B. Derman and A. Melsheimer, 'Changing the Rules of the Game: Issues that arise under the 2002 AIPN JOA when a host government mandates a "replacement contract"' (2010) 8(4) *OGEL* 1–7; V. Lowe, 'Recognition or Expropriation' (2004) 2(3) *OGEL*.

such as oil and gas exploration.[2] For this reason most host governments tend to assign these risks by authorising investors to carry out the exploration and production activities.[3]

This authorisation can be granted through a Petroleum Licence, a Production Sharing Agreement (PSA), a Service Agreement or a hybrid form, collectively referred to in the following as Host Government Instruments (HGIs).These instruments serve to provide contracting parties with the necessary rights and duties for exploration and production of oil and gas in a determined location. Without the granting of these instruments, it would not be possible for the contracting party to consider any of these operations.[4]

Therefore, the HGI is the key document that regulates the relationship between the host government and the investors (i.e. licensees/contractors).

The investors in turn do not want to take all these risks alone. A joint venture (JV) is thus an answer to these risks. The uncertainty, in conjunction with the significant costs of each project, means that companies are encouraged and interested to spread these costs and risks.[5] A JV allows companies to have a share and interest in one or numerous different projects, rather than holding 100% of any particular project.[6] Consequently, if one particular area is not successful, the remaining assets could compensate the company for these other unforeseen losses.

Minimising risk and sharing costs are the fundamental purposes of the JV.[7] Typically a JOA is a private document, as it should serve to regulate the relationship of the JV members. As a natural consequence the JV parties normally are free[8] to negotiate and set up their own relationship.

---

2 B.G. Taverne, *Petroleum, Industry and Governments: A Study of the Involvement of Industry and Government with the Production and use of Petroleum*, 2nd edn, Kluwer Law International, Alphen aan den Rijn 2008, p. 380.

3 J. Knut Kaasen, 'Scope of Joint Operating Agreements in Norway', Petroleum Law Seminar, St. Raphael, 2000, p. 8.

4 For further information about the petroleum title see: E.V. Rostow, *A National Policy for the Oil Industry*, Yale University Press, London 1948, pp. 3–26, D. Barberis, *Negotiating Mining Agreements: Past, Present and Future Trends*, Kluwer Law International, London 1998, pp. 4–60, M. Bunter, 'The Iranian Buy Back Agreement' (2003) 1(2) *OGEL*.

5 *Supra* n. 1.

6 See B. Cooper and T.F. Gaskell, *North Sea Oil, The Great Gamble*, Heinemann, London 1966.

7 'Participants in the resource industry, while generally operating as competitors, will often form alliances to explore co-operatively in a particular area.' J. Tarrant, 'Agreements to Co-Operate at Common Law' (2006) 25(3) *Australian Resources and Energy Law Journal* 281.

8 In some jurisdictions the host government might offer its own standard version of JOA (e.g. Greenland, Mozambique, Morocco and Norway). In these cases, the JOA parties might have only limited leeway for negotiating the clauses of the JOA, as agreement to the standard form (or large parts of it) tends to be a condition for doing upstream business within these jurisdictions. It is outside of the scope of this chapter to analyse the peculiarity of these JOAs as there should not be any conflict between the HGI and JOA.

One of the main purposes of the JV agreement is to set up special rules regarding their relationship. Some agreements could set up different rules than the ones established in the relevant HGI. But to what extent should the JOA and the HGI be synchronised and to what extent do they differ from each other? To answer these questions the most critical provisions of these agreements will be analysed in the following sections.

2. LIABILITIES

One of the most critical issues for the investors in any HGI refers to the liabilities of the parties. When a host government accepts a bid proposal or direct negotiation from a consortium, the host government will commonly be likely to impose joint and several liabilities on all the JV contracting parties through the relevant HGI.[9]

Beneficially for the government granting such an instrument, protection increases, as all parties are liable for the obligations related to the HGI, regardless of the size of their participation.[10] The Brazilian Petroleum Law provides good examples as follows:

> 'Art. 38 - When the participation of companies in consortium is allowed, the bid announcement shall contain the following requirements:
>
> I - evidence of commitment, public or private, of formation of the consortium, signed by the consortium companies;
>
> II - appointment of the leader company responsible for the consortium and for conducting the operations, without excluding the joint responsibility of each one of the other participants in the consortium;
>
> III - presentation, by each one of the participants in the consortium, of the documents requested for evaluation of the technical capacity, and financial good standing qualification of the consortium;
>
> IV - no permission for a particular participant to participate in another consortium, nor individually, in the bidding for the same block;

---

9 'There is nothing to prevent an interested party from applying on its own. In so doing, such a party will be assuming 100% of the risk. The joint venture, on the other hand, represents a form of risk sharing and consequently risk reduction between the interested parties. It also offers an effective mechanism for the pooling of resources and provides the added security of being part of a group.' J. Wilkinson, *Introduction to Oil and Gas Joint Ventures*, OPL, Ledbury 1997, p. 11.

10 See C. Wilkinson, *Joint Ventures & Shareholder's Agreements*, 3rd edn, Bloomsbury Professional, West Sussex 2009, pp. 3-5 and G.M.D. Bean, *Fiduciary Obligations and Joint Ventures: The Collaborative Fiduciary Relationship*, Oxford University Press, Oxford 1995, p. 19.

V – the concession grant to a consortium winning bid shall be subject to the registration of the consortium's constitutive document, according to the provisions of art. 279, single paragraph, of Law no 6404, of December 15, 1976.'[11]

This, however, only shows the outwardly visible relationship between the JV and the host government (the vertical relationship).[12] As previously mentioned, the JOA is also vital in establishing the private parties' private relations and can determine different liabilities and responsibilities for each party (the horizontal relationship).

The JV parties are likely to modify this liability imposed by the host government. They are more likely to establish proportional liability for each JV party in accordance with their participating interests.[13] The AIPN 2012 Model JOA provides:

'Ownership, Obligations and Liabilities

3.3.A Unless otherwise provided in this Agreement, all the rights and interests in and under the Contract, all Joint Property, and any Hydrocarbons produced from the Contract Area shall, subject to the terms of the Contract, be owned by the Parties in proportion to their respective Participating Interests.

3.3.B Unless otherwise provided in this Agreement, the obligations of the Parties under the Contract and all costs and liabilities incurred by Operator (or by any Party on behalf of all Parties, as set out in this Agreement) in connection with Joint Operations shall be charged to the Joint Account and all credits to the Joint Account shall be shared by the Parties, in proportion to their respective Participating Interests.

3.3.C Each Party shall pay when due, in accordance with the Accounting Procedure, its Participating Interest share of Joint Account charges, including Cash Calls and interest, accrued under this Agreement. A Party's payment of any charge under this Agreement shall not prejudice its right to later contest the charge.'[14]

The general principle also applies to the operatorship. As a common rule the operator shall be liable for any payment or liability limited by its participating interest. This concept is based on the concept that the operator assumes this role under the principle of 'no gain, no loss'.[15]

---

11 Law No. 9478 of 6 August 1997, Article 38.

12 'The link between the PL and the JOA also implies a modification to the general rule that parties to a joint venture agreement (such as the JOA) may change the agreement by unanimous vote: Any amendment or addition to the JOA has to be approved by the state in order to be valid. Apart from the formal reason for this (i.e. the acceptance of the JOA being a condition for being granted the PL), the rationale for the provision presumably lies in the state's general wish for standardisation and for controlling "the rules of the game"'. Knut Kaasen, *supra* n. 3, p. 3.

13 E.g. OGUK JOA, clause 4 and AMPLA JOA, clause 3.

14 AIPN JOA 2012,– Article 3.3.

15 The above-mentioned concept and principle of pro rata liability is well recognised within the petroleum industry, as recognised by several academics and practitioners, such as: A. Jennings,

However, there are exceptions to the no gain, no loss principle.[16] If the operator performs its activities with gross negligence or wilful misconduct, then most JOAs state that the operator will be exclusively liable for those actions (i.e. it alone must pay all costs).

Some JOAs provide restrictions to this exception, as otherwise most operators would understandably be concerned about taking on this role without reasonable compensation.[17] The first restriction refers to the person involved in the action or activity performed by the operator: some JOAs require senior personnel to be involved in the action or activity to trigger this exception of exclusive liability for the operator. The second restriction refers to the amount of financial exposure: some JOAs establish a financial cap on the operator's liability. The third restriction refers to the type of liabilities: some JOAs restrict what kind of losses or damages should be excluded from this exception (e.g. environmental or indirect losses).

The AIPN 2012 Model JOA provides a practical example of these alternatives and options to be negotiated between the JOA parties:

1.1. 'Limitation on Liability of Operator

1.1.A [Except as set out in Articles 4.6.D], neither Operator nor any other Operator Indemnitee shall bear (except as a Party to the extent of its Participating Interest share) any damage, loss, cost, or liability resulting from performing (or failing to perform) the duties and functions of Operator, and the Operator Indemnitees are hereby released from liability to Non-Operators for any and all damages, losses, costs, and liabilities arising out of, incident to, or resulting from such performance or failure to perform, even though caused in whole or in part by a pre-existing defect, or the negligence (whether sole, joint or concurrent), gross negligence, willful misconduct, strict liability or other legal fault of Operator (or any other Operator Indemnitee).

Oil and Gas Exploration Contracts, 2nd edn, Sweet & Maxwell, London 2008, p. 24; Taverne, *supra* n. 2, p. 136; C. Thorpe, *Fundamentals of Upstream Petroleum Agreements,* 2008, p. 126; S. Shaw, 'Joint Operating Agreements', in M.R. David (ed.), *Upstream Oil and Gas Agreements,* Sweet and Maxwell, London 1996, p. 16; C. Golvala, 'Upstream joint ventures – bidding and operating agreements', in G. Picton-Tubervill (ed.), *Oil and Gas: A practical handbook,* Globe Law and Business, London 2009, p. 46; H. Dundas, 'Joint Operating Agreements: An Introduction', 1994 Summer Programme: UK Oil and Gas Law, CPMLP 09/09, 1994, p. 12.

16 For further information about exculpatory clause see: W. Woods, 'The Effect of Exculpatory Clauses in Joint Operating Agreements, What protections do operators really have in the oil patch?' (2005–2006) 38 *Texas Technology Law Review* 211; C. Feasby, 'Fiduciary Obligations and Exculpatory Clauses' (1997–1998) 36 *Alberta Law Review* 923; and J. Burrit McArthur, 'Judging Made Too Easy, The Judicial Exaggeration of Exculpatory and Liability-Limiting Clauses in the Oilfield's Operator Fiduciary Cases' (2003) 56 *S.M.U. L. Rev.* 925.

17 C. Duval et al., *International Petroleum and Exploration Agreements: Legal, Economic & Policy Aspects*, 2nd edn, Barrows, New York 2009, p. 294.

1.1.B [Except as set out in Articles 4.6.D], the Parties shall (in proportion to their Participating Interests) defend and indemnify Operator Indemnitees from any damages, losses, costs (including reasonable legal costs and attorneys' fees), and liabilities incident to claims, demands, or causes of action brought by or for any person or entity, which claims, demands or causes of action arise out of, are incident to or result from Joint Operations, even though caused in whole or in part by a pre-existing defect, or the negligence (whether sole, joint or concurrent), gross negligence, willful misconduct, strict liability or other legal fault of Operator (or any other Operator Indemnitee).

1.1.C Nothing in this Article 4.6 shall be deemed to relieve Operator from its obligation to perform its duties and functions under this Agreement, or from its Participating Interest share of any damage, loss, cost, or liability arising out of, incident to, or resulting from Joint Operations.

Optional Provision, Choose, if desired. Renumber following paragraph if Article 4.6.D is not chosen.

1.1.D Despite Article 4.6.A or 4.6.B, if

Optional Provision, Choose, if desired.

any Senior Supervisory Personnel of

Operator or its Affiliates engage in Gross Negligence/Willful Misconduct that proximately causes the Parties to incur damage, loss, cost, or liability for claims, demands or causes of action referred to in Article 4.6.A or 4.6.B, then, in addition to its Participating Interest share:

Alternative Provision, Choose one

Alternative#1 – No Limitation

Operator shall bear all such damages, losses, costs, and liabilities.

Alternative#2 – Joint Property Limitation

Operator shall bear only the actual damage, loss, cost, and liability to repair, replace and/or remove Joint Property so damaged or lost, if any.

Alternative#3 – Financial Limitation

Operator shall bear only the first [__________ U.S. dollars] of such damages, losses, costs, and liabilities.

Despite the foregoing, under no circumstances shall Operator (except as a Party to the extent of its Participating Interest) or any other Operator Indemnitee bear any Consequential Loss or Environmental Loss.'

Therefore, the JOA plays a key role by accurately regulating the liabilities of the JV parties, as the HGI will rarely address limitations of liability between the

JV partners. The licensees or contractors are likely to be jointly liable for any losses, damages or breaches related to the HGI. However, if the host government or any third party sues a JV member for any amount higher than this party's participating interest, then the JV member shall request reimbursement from the others.

3. SCOPE

The scope of the HGI is usually similar to that established in the JOA.[18] Both agreements regulate upstream oil and gas exploration and production activities.[19] In practical terms the scope of these agreements starts at the exploration phase and ends at the delivery point (i.e. when the oil or gas is ready to be exported).

The model production sharing contracts of Cyprus and Kenya, respectively, confirm this reality as they state that:

> 'This contract is a Production Sharing Contract, the scope of which is the exploration, appraisal, development and production of Hydrocarbons in the Contract Area and the supply of required infrastructure within and outside of the Contract Area up to the Delivery Point, all at the Contractor´s sole risk and expense.'[20]
>
> 'Delivery Point means the F.O.B. Hydrocarbons loading point at the export terminal or any other point in the Republic of Cyprus which may be agreed upon the Parties.'[21]
>
> 'The Contractor shall -
>
> (a) Be responsible to the Government for the execution of the petroleum operations contemplated hereunder in accordance with the provisions of this contract and is hereby appointed and constituted the exclusive legal entity to conduct petroleum operations in the contract area for the term hereof;
>
> ...
>
> "Petroleum Operations" means all or any of the operations, authorised under this Contract, related to the exploration for, finding, appraisal, development, extraction, production, separation and treatment, storage, transportation, and sale or disposal of, Petroleum up to the point of export or the agreed Delivery Point in Kenya or the point of entry into a refinery and includes natural gas processing operations but does not include petroleum refining operations...'[22]

---

18 *Ibid.*, p. 287.

19 Shaw, *supra* n. 15, p. 15.

20 PSA from Cyprus, Article 1.1.

21 PSA from Cyprus, Article 1.6.

22 PSA from Kenya, 1A and 1B.

The AIPN JOA Model Form provides the following details for the scope of its agreement:[23]

'The purpose of this Agreement is to establish the respective rights and obligations of the Parties concerning operations and activities under the Contract, including the joint exploration, appraisal, development, production of Hydrocarbons (including treatment, storage, and handling of produced Hydrocarbons upstream of the Delivery Point), the determination of Entitlements at the Delivery Point, and Decommissioning.

The Parties confirm that, except to the extent expressly included in the Contract, the following activities are outside of the scope of this Agreement:

Construction, operation, ownership, maintenance, repair, and removal of facilities downstream from the Delivery Point;

Transportation of the Parties' Entitlements downstream from the Delivery Point;

Marketing and sales of Hydrocarbons, except as expressly provided in Article 7.12.E, Article 8.4 and Article 9;

Acquisition of rights to explore for, appraise, develop or produce Hydrocarbons outside of the Contract Area (other than through unitization with an adjoining contract area under the Contract or Laws); and

Exploration, appraisal, development, or production of minerals other than Hydrocarbons, whether inside or outside the Contract Area.'[24]

The AMPLA model form JOA provides a similar approach to the one taken by the AIPN 2012 model form JOA as it focuses on the upstream activities:

'Objects and scope of the Joint Venture

(a) The objects of the Joint Venture are to undertake Joint Operations associated with the Title Area and, in particular, to:
  (i) maintain the Petroleum Titles and explore and evaluate the Title Area for reserves of Petroleum;
  (ii) conduct operations for the exploration, appraisal, development, production and offtake of Petroleum from the Title Area;
  (iii) if exploration and appraisal indicates the probable existence of a commercial reservoir of Petroleum in any part of the Title Area and, if the Operating Committee approves a Development Plan, develop, produce

---

23 It is relevant to note that the 2012 revision of the AIPN model extended the scope of the JOA to include decommissioning, storage, treatment and handing of produced petroleum from the delivery point.

24 AIPN model form JOA, §3.1.

and dispose of that Petroleum and, for such purpose, obtain all necessary further Petroleum Titles and other Authorisations;

(iv) do all things incidental to any of the objects as resolved by the Operating Committee; and

(v) undertake such other activities as the Participants unanimously agree from time to time,

upon the terms and conditions set out in this agreement.

(b) The following activities are outside of the scope of this agreement and are not included in Joint Operations:

(i) construction, operation, ownership, maintenance, repair and removal of facilities downstream from the Delivery Point;

(ii) transportation of the Entitlements of the Participants downstream from the Delivery Point;

(iii) marketing and sales of Petroleum, except as expressly provided for in this agreement;

(iv) acquisition of rights to explore for, appraise, develop or produce Petroleum outside of the Title Area (other than as a consequence of unitisation with an adjoining area under the terms of the Petroleum Titles); and

(v) exploration, appraisal, development or production of minerals other than Petroleum, whether inside or outside of the Title Area.'[25]

Several other model form JOAs follow a similar standard approach, such as the APEA,[26] OGUK[27] and Greenlandic model form JOAs.[28] Thus, it is reasonable to suggest that the petroleum industry tends to narrow the scope of the HGI and JOA to upstream activities.

As most JOAs represent private agreements, the JV parties should have more flexibility and room to negotiate an extension to the scope of such an agreement. Thus, the JOA parties could decide to include midstream and downstream activities or at least their principles within the JOA. Some standard models do, such as the AIPN and CAPL model form JOAs. If any additional activity goes beyond the scope of the relevant HGI, then further attention is required to define the duration or scope of the relevant JOA.[29]

---

25 AMPLA model form JOA, §3.2.

26 APEA model form JOA, §2.1 and 2.3.

27 OGUK model form JOA, §3.1.

28 Greenlandic model form JOA, §1.1.

29 K.C. Mildwaters, *Joint Operating Agreements. A Consideration of Legal Aspects Relevant to Joint Operating Agreements used in Great Britain and Australia by Participants thereto to Regulate the Joint Undertaking of Exploration for Petroleum in Offshore Areas with Particular Reference to their Rights and Duties*, PhD Thesis, University of Dundee, 1990, p. 76.

4. EXCLUSIVE OPERATIONS[30]

Typically, all the consortium parties are jointly engaged in any petroleum operation. An exception to this rule is the possibility of conducting operations by fewer than all parties. This is probably one of the key differences between the approach taken by the HGI and the JOA.

As previously mentioned, the HGI is likely to impose joint and several liability for all consortium parties. As a natural consequence it is unlikely to anticipate the possibility of conducting any exclusive operation at a host government level.

A JOA is likely to allow the possibility of conducting exclusive, or 'sole risk' operations.[31] The main rationale for allowing an exclusive operation is the fact that the JV members might have different views on how to conduct the relevant operations. Scott Styles and Hugh Dundas respectively explain this in the following terms:

> 'In an ideal world there would be unanimous agreement among the members on all significant decisions. In practice, there will from time to time be disagreements among the members and normally these disputes will be resolved within the Opcom by means of decisions taken which secure a pass mark.'[32]

> 'Joint ventures are seldom an association of equals. Since diverging opinions can arise among the participants, the Operating Committee passmark will be crucial and provisions are invariably incorporated in the JOA to alleviate such problems.'[33]

An exclusive operation is fairly complex and challenging as it changes the main principle of this agreement (i.e. sharing risks and costs in proportion to the participating interests in the HGI and the JOA).[34] But one of the main concerns and risks for any exclusive operation is the unknown 'attitude' of the relevant host government.

In general, from the host government perspective's all JV parties should always be working jointly on any petroleum operation, so exclusive operations are usually not allowed. As previously mentioned, the majority of JOAs are purely private instruments and the host government does not participate in the relevant JOA negotiations. So in most cases the host government might not be aware of any exclusive operation until a JOA party notifies them of this fact.

This potential information gap between the government and JOA parties creates several uncertainties for any exclusive operation. Firstly, when should

30 This phenomenon is often referred to in JOAs as 'sole risk' operations.

31 E.g. AIPN JOA, clause 7; OGUK, clause 15; AMPLA JOA, clause 13.

32 S. Styles, 'Joint Operating Agreements', in G. Gordon and J. Paterson (eds.), *Oil and Gas Law: Current Practice and Emerging Trends*, Dundee University Press, Dundee 2007, p. 288.

33 Dundas, *supra* n. 15, p. 10.

34 T. Daintith, G. Willoughby and A. Hill (eds.), *United Kingdom Oil & Gas Law*, 3rd edn, Sweet &Maxwell, London 2009, p. 1152.

the host government be notified of an exclusive operation? Should it be at its very beginning or only later if the sole risk project proves to be successful? Secondly, what should happen to the operatorship of an exclusive operation if the main operator for the joint operations refuses to conduct such operations? Thirdly, what happens to the liabilities of the non-participants towards the host government? How could a non-participating party be protected against any potential liability from the participating parties? Fourthly, if a sole risk project is successful, then should it create a sub-area within the existing JOA or should this area be segregated from the JOA and assigned to a new HGI covering only the exclusive operation parties and project?

There are no straightforward answers to those questions. The answers are likely to vary in accordance with the rules and procedures established in the relevant JOAs and HGIs. But the reality is that the main idea of an exclusive operation is to threaten the other parties with the possibility of conducting this complicated process and eventually taking all the benefits of it without sharing with the non-participating parties.[35]

5. DEFAULT

The main obligation of any JOA party is to pay its share of the related costs of the joint operations.[36] If any party fails to pay its share, then this might jeopardise the entire consortium.[37] For this reason, most JOAs tend to provide strict remedies to make sure that all JOA parties pay their participation in the joint operations.[38] The rationale for this is the same as that for exclusive operations (i.e. to pressure the parties to keep together and pay their costs).

Peter Roberts describes the psychology behind the perspective of the parties to the JOA as follows:

> 'The risk of a party's failure to meet its share of a cashcall or invoice request when due is ever-present within any JOA relationship. Historically, the greatest mitigant of this risk has been a combination of the operational sociology and the commercial logic of the JOA – that the parties to the JOA have been solvent and able to meet all of their cashcall or invoice request commitments; that the character of each party is such that it would do nothing to incur the reputational risk associated with becoming known as a defaulter; and that the parties have had an obvious commercial interest

35 'However, a sole risk clause still has its support because the use or threatened use of the clause gives the more aggressive parties the ability to provoke operations to the benefit of all co-venturers which might not otherwise have taken place.' *Ibid.*, pp. 1151–1153.

36 Taverne, *supra* n. 2, p. 138.

37 P. Roberts, *Joint Operating Agreements: A Practical Guide*, Globe Law Business, London 2010, p. 202.

38 E.g. AIPN JOA, clause 8; OGUK JOA, clause 17; AMPLA JOA, clause 15.

in maintaining their interest in a concession (and a JOA) which relates to a project which has significant prospectivity associated with it. Because of the existence of these factors, the remedies contained in the JOA, which would be applied to a party's default, while important to have in place, have typically played a secondary role in keeping the JOA relationship on track.

It has been an article of faith in operation of the JOA that the threat to a defaulting party of the loss by forfeiture (at least in part, and possibly completely) of its interests, and the reputational damage generally be sufficient to prevent the failure of a party to pay its share of a cashcall or of an invoice request when due. This has not been an unreasonable expectation, but any change for the worse in the character of the parties to the JOA should necessitate a re-evaluation of this assumption. It may be that a potentially defaulting party might be unconcerned by such a risk forfeiture, especially where the JOA (and particularly the implication of the attendant decommissioning costs liability) is proving to be more of a liability than an asset.'[39]

However, if a JOA party fails to pay its share within the defined schedule, then it shall be considered to be in default. A JOA typically provides a variety of sanctions and remedies to solve this critical situation. If the defaulting party does not manage to rectify its default within a specific time, then the natural consequences are likely to be the obligation to leave or lose part of its working interest in the consortium through one of these mechanisms: forfeiture, withdrawal, a withering provision, a buy-out, or security interest.[40]

From a host government's perspective it is not pertinent to know who is paying for the relevant petroleum operations and related obligations. Again, it is possible for a JOA party to be in default within the JV agreement and the host government not to be aware of this situation, as long the obligations and payments under the HGI are being fully met.

In this case, if the non-defaulting parties wish to fully implement the remedy under their JOA and remove the defaulting party from their consortium, then they should acquire the relevant host government's approval, as this will affect the contracting parties to the relevant HGI.

6. OTHER PROVISIONS

Assignment, force majeure, governing law and dispute mechanisms are typical provisions for any type of agreement. Thus, all of these provisions are likely

[39] Roberts, *supra* n. 37, p. 202.

[40] 'The forfeiture clause is not necessarily the only provision which can be made for default. Two other types, the "withering" and the "purchase price" clauses, proceed on the same assumption, ie that the defaulter should at least retain some benefit for the money he has expended on joint operations before default. … Another type of clause is the "cross charges" clause where parties to the JOA could create cross charges over each other's interests but this is arguably untenable.' Dundas, *supra* n. 15, pp. 14–15.

to be provided in the HGI and JOA. Ideally both instruments should use the same procedures and standards to avoid any mismatch or conflict between them. However, it is not uncommon to see different remedies for resolving conflicts in HGIs and JOAs in respect of the same licence or contract. While the predominant forum for conflict resolution in HGIs would be the law courts of the host country and governed by the law of the host country, the JV parties may still wish to settle issues between themselves by arbitration, even occasionally in accordance with a different jurisdictional framework (e.g. English law). Hence, we have seen cases of litigation in the host country in relation to one aspect of the conflict, while another aspect[41] of the conflict is the subject of arbitration following other sets of rules.

Some provisions of the JOA are unlikely to appear in the HGI. One such set of provisions regulates the decision-making processes in the JV. An HGI may to some extent rely on the fiction that the contractor (i.e. the JV) speaks with one voice, and will often nominate (or require the JV to elect) an operator to act on behalf of the collective. The JOA on the other hand must detail the decision-making processes of the JV, including how authority within the JV is exercised and distributed between the operator and the non-operators and how decisions are reached (voting rules) in the JV.

Therefore there will normally also be an asymmetry between the HGI and the JOA with respect to matters regulating the relationship between the operator and the non-operating partners.

Another set of clauses are those the subject matter of which appears in both types of instruments, yet is treated quite differently in the two. A previous chapter described work programmes and their budgets, as well as the AFE procedure. The former (work programmes) are central to both HGIs and JOAs, while the latter is an issue for the JOA only. The underlying reason is obvious: the HGI is focused on the JV financing and performing the work programme, while the JOA must be concerned with the mechanisms of what JV partners pay, what amounts and how to ensure that such funds are forthcoming at the right time. The internal dynamics of the joint venture direct the parties' attention to the financial aspects. But the fact that the HGI or the host country legislation normally stipulates joint and several liability on the JV partners further encourages those partners to develop a fairly detailed set of rules with an idea that such rules will provide more control of their partners' contributions and performance. Hence, financial provisions tend to be quite different in the HGI from those of the JOA. However, this seldom causes conflicts between the two types of instruments even in relation to the same licence or contract area.

[41] Clearly, the two judicial processes cannot be in relation the same subject matter as this would be *sub judice* in one forum once the process is started in the other.

7. CONCLUSION

In conclusion, the nature of these agreements provides the key answers to the potential conflict between them. Any HGI is likely to capture the nature of a public agreement and the JOA of a private agreement. As a natural consequence, the parties to the JOA might desire to stipulate different rules and procedures to govern their relationship. Although they have flexibility to regulate their private relationship, they should be aware of the relevant limitations and due process to avoid any illegal or void activity by their consortium.

DECOMMISSIONING OBLIGATIONS, PRACTICES AND PROCEDURES

Craig Purdie

The focus and approach of oil and gas sector participants in relation to decommissioning (or abandonment, as it was referred to historically) has notably evolved in some correlation with the general maturity of the sector. A consequence of some of the world's significant basins reaching maturity (characterised by flows from existing assets tailing off and new discoveries being few (or at least less significant)), is an increasing focus on decommissioning by concessionaires, governmental policy makers and those who see commercial opportunity in the business of decommissioning. Decommissioning security and costs have become key factors in oil and gas development, financing and asset transactions in the more mature oil and gas basins around the world. An as example of the scale of future decommissioning, on the United Kingdom Continental Shelf (UKCS) there are more than 600 offshore oil and gas installations, more than 10,000 km of pipelines, and around 5,000 wells and accumulations of drill cuttings. Associated with these are also 15 onshore terminals.[1] DECOM North Sea forecasts that decommissioning such North Sea oil and gas facilities is projected to cost between £30bn and £35bn between 2010 and 2040.

In comparison to oil and gas exploration, as a business, decommissioning in the oil and gas sector is relatively new. As a concern, however, the requirement to decommission has arguably always existed and was properly[2] enshrined in

1 Figures quoted by DECOM North Sea in February 2015 at <www.decomnorthsea.com/market.cfm>.

2 Note that the 1958 Geneva Convention on the Continental Shelf set out that installations which are abandoned or disused must be entirely removed, however, as a result of failure by most states to implement this rule, it has been argued that it has lost its binding force.

international law by the United Nations Convention on the Law of the Sea 1982 (UNCLOS). The burden of the requirement to decommission and of the issues associated therewith typically manifests when a basin reaches a level of maturity which results in a shift in the characteristics of the participants. From an analysis of mature basins, such as the UKCS, it is evident that maturity gives rise to a move away from large multinational companies holding a significant portfolio of producing assets with significant reserve profiles and strong financial covenant to the entry of smaller, independent, less creditworthy companies with small or single-asset portfolios in which the assets have limited time remaining in their respective lifecycles. The burden is also exacerbated by cost-cutting measures and increasing oil prices resulting in infrastructure remaining in use beyond the period for which it was originally intended, thus leading to the decommissioning of such infrastructure in a higher-cost environment.

A result of the above is that the obligation to decommission will likely crystallise when production, associated revenue and the creditworthiness of participants is low. The question of whether the smaller participants will even exist at the time of crystallisation is also valid. This backdrop has focused the minds of host governments and industry participants.

This chapter summarises the international legal obligations with respect to the decommissioning of offshore oil and gas assets and then focuses on the regime of the North-East Atlantic and the UK as an illustration of the potential reach of the liabilities which decommissioning can give rise to for a joint venture (although ultimately the decommissioning provisions in the JOA should be drafted to take into account the laws and regulations which govern decommissioning in the territory to which the JOA relates) and considers briefly the historical practice in relation to decommissioning in JOAs, followed by commentary in respect of the contemporary approach.

1. DECOMMISSIONING OBLIGATIONS

The international obligations in respect of the decommissioning of offshore oil and gas assets for most states are founded in UNCLOS, which has been ratified by 167 states as of 7 January 2015. Article 60(3) sets out that 'any installations or structures which are abandoned or disused shall be removed to ensure safety of navigation, taking into account any generally accepted international standards established in this regard by the competent international organization'.

The 'competent international organization' is a reference to the International Maritime Organization (IMO) which in 1989 produced international standards in this regard. IMO Resolution A.672(16) sets out 'Guidelines and Standards for the Removal of Offshore Installations and Structures on the Continental Shelf and in the Exclusive Economic Zone' (IMO Guidelines) which require the removal of: all installations standing in less than 75 metres of water and weighing less than 4,000 tonnes; all installations placed on the seabed after 1 January 1998 standing in less than 100 metres of water and weighing less than 4,000 tonnes; and installations located in primary navigational routes.

The next tier of regulation for many states stems from an action plan or convention which is a consequence of the Regional Seas Programme, an initiative launched by the United Nations Environment Programme in 1974. The Regional Seas Programme aims to address the accelerating degradation of the world's oceans and coastal areas through the sustainable management and use of the marine and coastal environment, by engaging neighbouring countries in comprehensive and specific actions to protect their shared marine environment. It has accomplished this by stimulating the creation of regional programmes to be coordinated and implemented by countries sharing a common body of water. There are eighteen such programmes in which more than 140 countries participate: Black Sea, Wider Caribbean, East Asia Seas, Eastern Africa, South Asian Seas, ROPME Sea Area, Mediterranean, North-East Pacific, Northwest Pacific, Red Sea and Gulf of Aden, South-East Pacific, Pacific, Western Africa, Antarctic, Arctic, Baltic Sea, Caspian Sea, and North-East Atlantic. All programmes reflect a similar approach but are tailored by their own governments and institutions to the particular challenges of that region. The programmes function through an Action Plan. In most cases the Action Plan is underpinned by a strong legal framework in the form of a regional convention and associated protocols on specific problems.

Given the focus of this book, it would not be appropriate and nor would it be an efficient use of the permitted quantum of words for this chapter to examine each regional programme, the decommissioning obligations arising from it and the domestic-level obligations of each country the subject thereof. The remainder of this chapter will therefore engage in discussion in respect of the joint venture issues arising from decommissioning with reference to the North-East Atlantic region and the UKCS – a mature basin in which decommissioning is very much in contemplation and in which contemporary approaches to decommissioning are significantly developed.

Neither UNCLOS nor the IMO Guidelines deal properly with the *dumping* of offshore installations but rather deal primarily with their *removal.* Absent any further international legislation, the problematic[3] option of deep sea disposal of installations remained and thus, with regard to the North-East Atlantic region, this issue was accordingly dealt with by the Convention on the Protection of the Marine Environment of the North-East Atlantic (OSPAR Convention) of 1992. OSPAR Decision 98/3 sets out requirements for the disposal of disused offshore

[3] See issues associated with the Brent Spar deep sea disposal: <http://en.wikipedia.org/wiki/Brent_Spar#Disposal_options>.

installations and is binding on all parties to the OSPAR Convention, including the United Kingdom. In effect, it provides that: the top sides of all installations must be returned to shore; all installations with a jacket weight of less than 10,000 tonnes must be completely removed for reuse, recycling or final disposal on land; and the footings of large steel installations weighing more than 10,000 tonnes and concrete installations may be subject to a derogation where their removal presents exceptional difficulties, but the installation must have been in place prior to 9 February 1999. In practice, this leads to the conclusion that most offshore installations will have to be returned to shore in their entirety.

How this is all transposed at a domestic level will be a question for each state to which the law applies, and it is this domestic legislation which will substantially shape the content of the JOA with respect to decommissioning. The UK has passed its liability under the OSPAR Convention to participants through primary domestic legislation, with the objective of the regime being to shield the state from decommissioning costs. The decommissioning of offshore installations is regulated domestically in the UK through the Petroleum Act 1998 as amended by the Energy Act 2008 (Petroleum Act) and through the vehicle for the concession by the Crown of its rights to petroleum to a third party; the petroleum production licence.

Section 29 of the Petroleum Act empowers the Secretary of State to serve a notice (Section 29 Notice) on persons who are required to submit a costed decommissioning programme for approval at such time as the Secretary of State may direct, which then gives rise to a decommissioning obligation. The infrastructure to which the Section 29 Notice and the decommissioning programme relate is set out in the Section 29 Notice. The Section 29 Notice may be issued to a wide range of persons:

- the person having the management of the installation or of its main structure (i.e. the operator or potentially a third-party contractor if it is performing the operator's role);
- persons with a right to exploit or explore mineral resources, or to store gas and to recover gas so stored, in the licence area, where such exploitation, exploration, storage and transportation are, or are intended to be, carried on from, by means of or on the installation (i.e. usually the licensees);
- any party to the JOA relating to such rights (i.e. usually the licensees);
- persons who own any interest in the installation otherwise than as security for a loan (i.e. usually the licensees); and
- any company outside of the above but which is associated with a company within any of the above (i.e. usually affiliates and parent companies).

Once the decommissioning programme is approved, the Section 29 Notice-holders are legally obliged to carry it out on a joint and several liability basis.

If a programme is not carried out or its conditions are not complied with, the Secretary of State may, by written notice, require remedial action to be taken. Failure to comply with any such notice is an offence and the Secretary of State can carry out the remedial action and recover the costs from a person to whom the notice was given.

As set out above, as the objective of the regime is to shield the government from decommissioning costs, the Section 29 Notice may be served on a wider group of parties, not just the current licensees, including any person having an ownership interest in the installation, and a parent or associated companies of a licensee. Typically, a Section 29 Notice will be served on this wider class of parties if the Secretary of State finds the decommissioning arrangements proposed by the licensees to be unsatisfactory. Additionally, section 34 of the Petroleum Act extends the right to issue a Section 29 Notice to anyone who, at any time since the issue of the first Section 29 Notice for the installation, was liable to have a Section 29 Notice served on it (i.e. former licensees).

The licensees remain liable for decommissioning obligations until the Section 29 Notice is withdrawn. When an interest in a field is sold, the Secretary of State may release a former licensee from its section 29 obligations. In most cases, the Section 29 Notice is withdrawn once the Secretary of State is satisfied that adequate financial security arrangements are in place in relation to the decommissioning liabilities. Such security arrangements are usually in the form of a Decommissioning Security Deed to which the Secretary of State may be a party, which ensures that the new incoming licensees can discharge the decommissioning liabilities. However, even if a former licensee is discharged from its section 29 obligations, in some circumstances the Secretary of State may use its claw-back power under section 34 to impose liability on that party.

The UK example of the potential extent of the reach of decommissioning liabilities highlights why oil and gas field participants should ensure that their JOA partners are allocated a fair share of the decommissioning liabilities and that they have sufficient financial resources to meet such liabilities, particularly where liability is allocated on a joint and several basis, which is typically the case where concessions are held by several participants. It is important that the JOA addresses such liabilities and related issues.

2. APPROACHES TO DECOMMISSIONING IN JOAs

2.1. THE HISTORICAL APPROACH

The historic practice to addressing decommissioning in JOAs has largely been light-touch and unsatisfactory, having been paid a lack of attention by participants. The historical brevity was perhaps the result of a number of factors:

- *The timing of entry into the JOA*: It is common practice that the JOA will be entered into by the partners at the earliest time the requirement arises to define their relationship – usually at the first occurrence of more than one participant holding an interest in the concession.[4] This may be at the time of issuance of the concession by the host government or perhaps upon the completion of a farm-in/out during the exploration stage (pre-discovery) or post-discovery. Pre-discovery, the partners may not find the negotiation of decommissioning provisions in the JOA an economically efficient allocation of resources; such negotiations will require the use of time and money and the benefit of this may not be realised should a discovery not be made under the concession.
- *The status of the local petroleum law*: Historically, the legal framework underpinning petroleum exploration and production activities may be under-developed or non-existent. In the absence of developed law, it is difficult to agree detailed requirements for decommissioning in the JOA. Given the increased focus on decommissioning in now-mature basins and the development of the law related thereto, coupled with increased experience of decommissioning and of the associated costs, it is perhaps easier now than it was historically to include detail in the JOA where the host state's law is underdeveloped. This is discussed in more detail below.
- *Focus on profit*: JOA parties were perhaps typically more concerned about extracting maximum commercial value from the project rather than focusing fully on the requirements of the decommissioning phase. Some JOAs set out in some detail provisions pursuing the maximum disposal of joint property and the crediting of its proceeds to the joint account but would disregard the requirement to plan for and provide funding for the proper decommissioning of the asset in a detailed manner.[5]
- *Dismissive mindset*: Success has been measured on making a discovery and monetising it rather than bringing the project to an end. There is much less glamour associated with the end-point than the start-point of a project and this could lead to procrastination. A dismissive mindset may also be evident in jurisdictions where the legal system is underdeveloped, the government is unstable or less dynamic and the participants are smaller entities. In such circumstances, there may be a prevalent hope that the decommissioning liabilities may never crystallise, either as a result of the host government having not fully considered the issue or due to the flight of the participating entities when the production profiles are in decline.

---

4 Note that well-organised and well-resourced partners may have agreed the JOA provisions at the time of negotiation and entry into a Joint Study and Bid Agreement or Area of Mutual Interest Agreement, albeit this pro-active housekeeping is a rare occurrence in practice.

5 As an example, see the model form JOA contained in *Taylor and Winsor on Joint Operating Agreements*, 2nd edn, Sweet & Maxwell, London 1992.

It was (and to some extent still is depending on the nature of the participants and the host state) common practice for the JOA to contain only simple, limited provisions in respect of decommissioning. In this case, the liability to decommission would typically be divided such that the joint and several liabilities owing to the government (if any) are divided amongst the partners on a several but not joint basis by reference to the partners' respective participating interests in the field.

In many JOAs, including the 1995 and 2002 versions of the AIPN Model Form International Operating Agreement, there was typically a requirement that the partners at a future date (usually following when a discovery is made but before the development plan is submitted to the host government) will negotiate, agree and execute a decommissioning agreement in respect of the ceasing of operations. Such an agreement will deal with the allocation of liability between the partners (should it not already be allocated in the JOA)[6] and the provision of security in respect of the decommissioning liability.

As an example, the 1995 and 2002 versions of the AIPN Model International Operating Agreement provide for the partners to agree to negotiate a security agreement prior to the submission of the field development plan to the host government should they be or become obliged to pay or contribute to the cost of ceasing operations under the concession or the host country's laws. The security agreement is to incorporate principles relating to the provision of security at a future date when the remaining value of the project equals an agreed percentage of the cost of ceasing operations.[7] It is noteworthy that in the 1995 and 2002 versions of the AIPN Model Form International Operating Agreement, such provisions are flagged as being optional, meaning the JOA partners could easily omit this requirement entirely. In the current climate, this optionality would seem an unlikely proposition. Such optionality may be reflective of the historical unimportance attached to decommissioning by JOA partners.

Under English law, a further concern with this historical approach is whether the provisions requiring the JOA partners to enter into a decommissioning agreement at a later date are enforceable. There is potential for the provisions to be considered to be an 'agreement to agree'. Under English law, there is a well-established position that unless all the key terms of a contract are agreed, there can be no binding contract – agreements to agree do not generally fulfil this requirement and are rendered unenforceable. These provisions therefore run the risk that they will not be legally binding on the JOA partners.

---

6 As an example, see the model form JOA in *Taylor and Winsor on Joint Operating Agreements*, *supra* n. 5.

7 See Article 10.3 in the 1995 and 2002 versions of the AIPN Model Form International Operating Agreement.

In the absence of such an agreement or of provisions sufficiently dealing with the securitisation of decommissioning, the liability to decommission would ordinarily fall under the standard liability regime set out in the JOA, and accordingly non-performance in respect of decommissioning would be referred to the default provisions in the JOA. This approach is not without problems as the default provisions in the JOA will be of little value to the non-defaulting partners at the end of the life of the asset and will not act to incentivise performance. The remaining value in the asset may be less than the cost to decommission.

2.2. THE CONTEMPORARY APPROACH

It remains difficult to draft fully detailed decommissioning provisions in advance of a discovery being made due to the inherent uncertainty around the properties of any potential discovery, the developmental infrastructure that it might require and the approach and costs associated with its decommissioning. This difficulty is further exacerbated where the host state does not have in place developed legislation and/or regulations in respect of the decommissioning of petroleum assets. There is however a practice developing of drafting increasingly detailed decommissioning provisions at the earlier stages of a joint venture.

Decommissioning is now recognised as a distinct phase in the lifecycle of a discovery and is accordingly paid greater attention by joint venture partners. It is recommendable that decommissioning is considered to be a material part of the scope of the joint venture arrangements at the outset of the joint venture and that the potential future costs of decommissioning are taken into account. Such costs could be significant.

Translating this into practice, detailed decommissioning provisions may be memorialised as follows:

- *Appended to/included in the Joint Study and Bid Agreement (JSBA)/Area of Mutual Interest Agreement ('AMIA')*: Well-organised and well-resourced partners may find themselves able to agree JOA provisions (or at least the key terms) at the time of negotiation and entry into a Joint Study and Bid Agreement. Given the potent scale of decommissioning costs, it is beneficial to the partners to establish certainty at the earliest stage of the joint venture. In practice, the JSBA/AMIA stage would likely be the earliest stage at which the decommissioning provisions can be agreed. The provisions may be included within the JSBA/AMIA itself, included within a draft JOA which is appended to the JSBA/AMIA, or included in a fully-developed draft decommissioning agreement which is appended to the JSBA/AMIA.
- *Incorporated within the JOA/annexed to the JOA*: the reality is that most joint ventures will not be in a position to achieve the inclusion of the

decommissioning provisions at the JSBA/AMIA stage. Such a pursuit requires time and resource commitment and the view may be that agreeing the decommissioning provisions at that stage is not the most economically efficient allocation of resources because ultimately a discovery may never be made. Given this, it is more common practice to include the decommissioning provisions as part of the JOA. This is usually done using one of two formats; either the substantive provisions will be included in the JOA[8] or a form of stand-alone decommissioning agreement will be appended to the JOA[9] for execution at the time of a later event – typically upon the making of a discovery and a development plan being submitted to the host government.

- *As a stand-alone decommissioning agreement*: modern practice also sees some joint ventures opting to enter into a dedicated stand-alone decommissioning agreement. This fully termed agreement may be entered into simultaneously to the JOA or at the time of a later event – typically upon the making of a discovery and a development plan being submitted to the host government. Where the latter approach is preferred, it is advisable to lock down the substantive form of the decommissioning agreement between the parties prior to such later event being triggered. Appending the form to the AMIA/JSBA or JOA as described above will provide the parties with a degree of certainty in advance of a discovery as to the standpoint of the partners and the treatment of decommissioning liabilities, which should assist in a harmonised transition of the discovery from the exploration and appraisal stage to the development stage.

Where the method of memorialisation of the decommissioning provisions involves the execution of an agreement at a later date, the partners should consider the risks associated with agreements to agree under English law. Partners should consider whether the problems associated with agreements to agree can be avoided by the use of more innovative methods of execution. For example, immediate execution coupled with the use of either escrow or conditionality around the agreement's effectiveness may be useful in allowing the agreement to be executed but also effectively putting it 'on ice' until its effectiveness is required.

The issues which the decommissioning provisions address are likely to be consistent regardless of the form which they take. It is important that the decommissioning provisions are drafted such that they address and reflect the

[8] See AIPN 2012 Model Form International Operating Agreement, Articles 6.5, 10.4 and exhibit E.

[9] See OGUK 2009 Model Form Joint Operating Agreement, clause 2.3 and schedule C and the OGUK 2009 Model Form Decommissioning Security Agreement.

complexity of the detail of the law and regulations relevant to decommissioning in the host state, the relationships between the past and present parties to the licence and the requirement for credit support. Particular consideration should be given to the following:

- *Sharing of liabilities*: The liabilities of the partners should be defined and should take account of the plugging of wells, demolition and removal of structures, disposal, clean-up, as well as potential ongoing liabilities in respect of partially-decommissioned assets and future environmental issues. The standard approach is that partners should be liable for decommissioning costs in proportion to their participating interests.
- *Decision to decommission*: The decision to decommission should be subject to the approval of the operating committee. Where a party has a significant participating interest such that it itself can satisfy the voting pass-mark (thus rendering the other parties with no control (or illusory control) over operating committee votes), it could be prudent to consider including an ability for non-consenting partners to take over the asset as an exclusive operation/sole risk project. The likelihood of a partner opting to continue production operations on an exclusive basis owing to a premature decommissioning decision will likely be conditioned by how the burden of future decommissioning liabilities is treated amongst the partners.
- *Decommissioning work programme and budget*: There should be a requirement in the JOA for the production and approval of a programme of joint operations and an associated budget for the purposes of the decommissioning of the asset. This will be the formal procedure for determining the conduct of decommissioning. The provisions relating to the decommissioning work programme and budget should set out:
  - *Responsibility*: The operator will typically have the duty to prepare the decommissioning work programme and budget and will be responsible for the implementation of the work programme. In order for them to become effective, their approval by the operating committee should be required.
  - *Timing*: As mentioned above, it is likely impossible that a decommissioning work programme and budget are able to be produced in advance of a discovery being made due to the inherent uncertainty around the properties of any potential discovery, the developmental infrastructure that it might require and the approach and costs associated with its decommissioning. The requirement to produce a decommissioning work programme and budget is typically triggered in the JOA when a discovery has been made and a development plan is being prepared by the operator for submission to the host government. The degree of detail included in the decommissioning work programme at this stage may however be light-touch and will likely evolve over time. The AIPN 2012 Model Form International Operating Agreement, for example, requires the partners to make a *preliminary* plan

and to make financial provision for decommissioning whilst preparing the development plan.[10] It is also prudent that decommissioning is considered annually and the programme and budget are updated with revised cost details in order for the partners to keep abreast of the extent of the financial liability. Some JOAs may however delay the requirement to consider the decommissioning work programme annually until a later trigger point.[11]

  - *Approval*: The operating committee will normally be required to approve the decommissioning work programme and budget and associated authorisations for expenditure. The JOA should also make provision for the operator to be able to submit a decommissioning work programme to the host government without operating committee approval where such approval has not been achieved by the date required under the concession.
- *Security*: The partners may find that they are subject to a joint and several liability regime under the host state's legislation.[12] Consequentially, it is in the best interests of each partner to protect itself as soon as possible in the lifecycle of the joint venture from the event of another partner defaulting in respect of decommissioning liability arising to the host government. Additionally, the host government may be concerned that there is a risk that the partners may not be able to pay for the costs of decommissioning when they crystallise and may therefore require security to be maintained to guard against this risk. Serious consideration should be given by the partners to the requirement for security. Accordingly, it is now common that security provisions are included in the JOA[13] with reference to the following:
  - *Timing*: The JOA should set out a time at which the parties should put in place sufficient security. Although it is recommendable to put security for decommissioning costs in place as soon as possible in the lifecycle of the joint venture, partners will be keen to avoid putting security in place too early in order to avoid tying up cash flow or paying a third party for the provision of the security. A trigger point is ordinarily used which is based on the value of the remaining reserves in the field falling below a certain defined percentage of the costs of decommissioning.
  - *Form:* The acceptable forms of security should be defined in the JOA. Typical forms are cash deposits, letters of credit, performance bonds and parent company guarantees. It may also be recognised that a partner may be of sufficient financial status in order for it to meet its liabilities

---

10 See AIPN 2012 Model Form International Operating Agreement, Article 10.4.

11 See AIPN 2012 Model Form International Operating Agreement, Article 6.5.A and annex E, section 3.1.

12 As an example, see clause 1(2) of a UK Seaward Production Licence.

13 Some JOAs may require the partners to enter into a separate supplemental agreement dealing specifically with decommissioning security. See the OGUK model form Decommissioning Security Agreement which is used for UKCS fields.

without it having to provide security, subject to re-assessment should its creditworthiness change.

  - *Value:* The security should cover the full forecasted costs of decommissioning. It is common for parties to provide security for an amount covering more than the forecasted costs of decommissioning as a buffer.
  - *Establishment of trust fund:* Although cash deposits are an unlikely form of security in practice because JOA partners will not want to tie up cash flow, any cash deposits should be paid into a trust fund which is protected from the reach of liquidators. Should a partner become insolvent, the proceeds from the triggered security should be paid into this fund, thus protecting them.
- *Withdrawal and transfer of interests:* A partner withdrawing from the JOA and the field should be required to put in place (should it already not be in place), or maintain, security for its share of future decommissioning costs. The need to have security in place as soon as possible in the lifecycle of the joint venture is highlighted by the example of a withdrawing partner. Should a partner decide to withdraw prior to it putting security in place and it then refuse to provide security as required as a condition of its withdrawal, this could result in that partner exiting the joint venture under the default mechanism in the JOA absent the necessary security being provided. This is an undesirable position for the remaining partners. A transfer of an interest by a party to another should be conditional upon the transferee assuming the decommissioning obligations of the transferor, including in respect of decommissioning security.

Although this chapter provides an overview of the issues which decommissioning gives rise to for joint ventures from a general international stand-point, it is important to highlight that one size will not fit all in terms of approach. The provisions in the JOA must be adjusted in order that they are fully compatible with, and reflect, the decommissioning obligations set out in the host state's law, regulations and concession on a case-by-case basis. Reflecting the host state's governing regime relating to decommissioning can be complex and will require a skilled draughtsman with an understanding of the regime in question.

The question arises as to what approach should be taken where the host state's governing regime does not address decommissioning or is under-developed in this regard. In such circumstances, it will not be possible to accurately determine the regime which may apply in the future, but nevertheless it remains important for participants to ensure that their JOA partners are allocated a fair share of the decommissioning liabilities and that they have sufficient financial resources to meet such liabilities if/when they crystallise, as a minimum.

A clue as to the likely content of the future decommissioning obligations to which the joint venture may be subject might be in the international law to which the host-state is subject. The host state's obligations under UNCLOS should be considered alongside the content of any Regional Seas Programme and Action Plan to which the host state is a party as a start-point when attempting to draft decommissioning provisions. The decommissioning provisions should be drafted to take into account the obligations which are on the host state insofar as it possible. It is prudent to recognise in the provisions that should a decommissioning regime be developed by the host state then the provisions will be subject to review and amendment to reflect the requirements of the new regime.

STANDARDS AND PRACTICES IN JOAs ACROSS THE PETROLEUM INDUSTRY

Yanal Abul Failat and Eduardo G. Pereira

1. INTRODUCTION

Upstream oil and gas operations around the world almost inevitably involve a vertical relationship between:

(i) the state who controls and/or owns the petroleum and wishes to maximise commercial recovery from its resources; and
(ii) an upstream petroleum company (or a joint venture), which is seeking to explore and extract petroleum for profitable commercial production.

This usually involves the state granting the petroleum company the right to explore, exploit, appraise and produce petroleum by way of a licence, a production-sharing contract, a service contract or a combination or variation of any of these instruments (Petroleum Agreement).

A range of factors including regulatory, commercial and practical considerations defines the intricacies of each project and of most importance is the level of technical complexity and financial standing required for each Petroleum Agreement. In cases where a project involves less complex exploration, commonly in shallow depth drilling or onshore petroleum, a petroleum company may hold the Petroleum Agreement solely if it has the technology and the financial capacity to perform the obligations under the agreement on its own.[1]

Most projects, however, involve complex exploration, deep drilling and/or deep offshore production, raising the need to minimise the high cost and

[1] P. Roberts, *Petroleum Contracts: English Law and Practice*, 3rd edn, Oxford University Press, Oxford 2013, p. 38.

spread of the risks.[2] For this reason, the rights granted under a Petroleum Agreement are hardly ever exercised by a single entity but rather by a number of petroleum companies who have agreed to jointly undertake a project and allocate responsibilities and profits amongst themselves.[3]

This approach has led to the creation of the widespread concept of joint ventures (JVs) since the Petroleum Agreement itself does not deal with the sharing of rights and obligations as between the concessionaires/contractors. Whilst the central idea is to share costs, property and production (if successful) in proportion to their respective percentage interests, the synergistic nature of a JV allows participants to enjoy the financial standing and the skills of their associates.[4]

For such collaborations, it is customary to seek an unincorporated contractual association such as the JOA as opposed to incorporated associations (i.e. setting up a company in which co-ventures have shareholdings in proportion to their JV interests).[5] This means that the JV has no separate legal personality and therefore cannot be sued in its own name. This type of arrangement is attractive to co-venturers as they enjoy:

(i) a flexible contractual framework;
(ii) a preferential tax system (whereby the parties are taxed separately and each party is separately liable);
(iii) the ability to pool assets, technology, financial resources and management skills;
(iv) independence with regard to liabilities and financial contributions;
(v) the opportunity to outlay their investment in multiple ventures increasing their chances of finding petroleum; and
(vi) an inherent element of flexibility where parties can freely choose and change their co-venturers without this meaning the JV coming to an end.[6]

The JOA is a well-established form of private agreement. It is the constitution for the JV, defining the relationship between the parties to a concession and governing the entire lifecycle of the relevant upstream petroleum project, namely exploration, appraisal, development, production and decommissioning. In simple terms, the contract morphs the 'joint' nature of a Petroleum Agreement into

---

2 S. Styles, 'Joint Operating Agreements', in G. Gordon, J. Paterson and E. Usenmez (eds.), *Oil and Gas Law: Current Practice and Emerging Trends*, Dundee University Press, Dundee 2011, p. 359.
3 A.C. Inkpen and M.H. Moffet, *The Global Oil and Gas Industry: Management, Strategy and Finance*, PenWell Books, Oklahoma 2011, p. 200.
4 J.L. Nolan, *Philippines Business: the Portable Encyclopaedia for Doing Business with the Philippines*, World Trade Press, California 1996, p. 177.
5 C.M. Miles, 'AIPN 2002 Model Form Joint Operating Agreement in Oil and Gas Joint Ventures' (2003) 45 *Australian Resources and Energy Law Journal* 22(2), 153.
6 LXL LLP, *A Guide to the Energy Industry for the In-House Lawyer, focusing in 2012 on LNG*, LXL LLP, London 2012, p. 35.

several rights and obligations as between the concessionaires/contractors who are receiving this right from the State.[7] In the early stages of the project, the JOA serves the JV by allocating capital, operating expenses and risk.[8] If an upstream project is successful and production commences, the JOA's role in that phase would largely be to regulate the smooth operation of a field and to allocate the rewards.[9] At the end of the project, further expenditure and risk, including the quantification of decommissioning liabilities, would be dealt with by the JOA.[10]

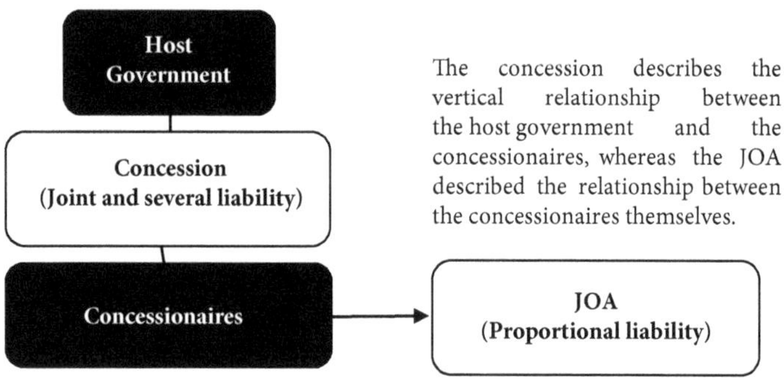

2. RATIONALE FOR USING MODEL FORM JOAs

Rarely do parties draft a JOA from scratch or use a model JOA in its published form. Rather, the parties firstly choose a model JOA that best suits their particular situation and use that the basis for negotiating and drafting the JOA. The parties then tailor and amend this agreement to reflect the arrangements of the JV and the relevant upstream project. Conine describes this situation as follows:

> 'As with oil and gas leases, there is not a "standard operating agreement." Specific provisions vary to allow for the peculiar needs of the parties to the instrument and special concerns inherent in the immediate transaction. Nevertheless, there is considerable similarity in the basic provisions of most operating agreements. This results in large part from the development of model forms of the instrument, which have received widespread acceptance in the industry. Over time, these model forms have contributed greatly to the simplification of negotiations, the standardization of technical terms and, to a more limited degree, consistency in legal interpretations.'[11]

7 Ibid.

8 LXL LLP, *A Guide to the Energy Industry for the In-House Lawyer, focusing in 2015 financial collateral and credit support*, LXL LLP, London 2015, p. 23.

9 *Ibid.*

10 *Ibid.*

11 G.B. Conine, 'Property Provisions of the Operating Agreement, Interpretation, Validity, and Enforceability' (1988) 19 *Texas Tech Law Review* 1265.

Model JOAs have been developed over many years in line with industry practice and have been subject to continuous scrutiny and revision, thus allowing JOAs to develop and reflect the needs of the ever-changing oil and gas sector. Although the substantive provisions found in one JOA may be similar to those found in another, the various model JOAs tend to differ because the different institutions that prepared them were responsible for preparing agreements to suit different legal views and investment environments. Inevitably, further differences arise from JOAs that are governed by different jurisdictions or that deal with a different type of project (i.e. conventional versus unconventional or onshore versus offshore). Martin describes this situation as follows:

> 'The North Sea environment still stands apart from the mingling of JOA concepts seen in some other jurisdictions. Companies operating in the United Kingdom have never really taken to the AIPN model JOA and have always rejected the North-American-style onshore JOAs.[12]
>
> ...
>
> Model contracts have been developed and used in a wide variety of ways in different jurisdictions. They are extremely flexible tools that allow users to draft effective petroleum contracts quickly and efficiently. They have spread throughout the global petroleum industry because of the significant benefits and immense value they provide to the entire business cycle. As a result, model contracts in the international industry will undoubtedly expand in their development and application in the future.'[13]

The parties must understand these differences as they can affect their choice of model JOA when setting up a JV. This is important where a petroleum company that has an international portfolio of assets is seeking consistency across the various JOAs that it would be party to or where a company is entering a new jurisdiction for the first time and is unfamiliar with the standard JOA or arrangement used therein.[14]

3. MODEL FORM JOAs

The following is a list of the most popular domestic and international well-established model form JOAs that are used as a basis for oil and gas JOAs.

---

12 A.T. Martin, 'Model Contracts: a Survey of the Global Petroleum Industry' (2004) 22 *J. Energy & Nat. Resources L.* 284.

13 *Ibid.*, p. 339.

14 P. Roberts and J. Derrick, 'OGUK and AIPN Joint Operating Agreements: Differences on Operator Liability' (International Law Office 2011) <http://www.internationallawoffice.com/Account/Register.aspx?ReturnUrl=http%3a%2f%2fwww.internationallawoffice.com%2fnewsletters%2fdetail.aspx%3fg%3dc3db9ed1-f9a0-47ed-9916-c1c38536e7f4> accessed 02.06.2015.

3.1. ASSOCIATION OF INTERNATIONAL PETROLEUM NEGOTIATORS (AIPN)

The AIPN JOA is one of the most popular and widely used model form JOA. For over 25 years, the AIPN JOA has set an international standard for oil and gas JVs internationally. The first AIPN JOA was published in 1990 and was revised and modified in 1995, 2002 and 2012. Moreover, in 2014, AIPN published a new model form JOA for JV exploring and producing unconventional resources. Petroleum companies operating in emerging markets have warmly welcomed the AIPN JOA, and even when not used, its provisions have become the standard against which upstream oil and gas JVs are compared. The AIPN JOA contains various optional provisions and allows the agreement to be tailored to both common law and civil law jurisdictions. AIPN further supports the international use of JOAs in different jurisdictions by continuously working towards issuing official translations of its JOA.

AIPN has also issued a number of related model form agreements, including:

(i) Accounting Procedure (2012);
(ii) Petroleum Lifting Agreement (2001); and
(iii) Unitization and Unit Operating (2006).[15]

3.2. AMERICAN ASSOCIATION OF PROFESSIONAL LANDMEN (AAPL)

The AAPL JOA can be said to be the first model form JOA and was considered state of the art at the time of publication as it incorporated many of the substantive provisions commonly found in company form operating agreements and therefore represented industry practice at the time. AAPL has over the years published three forms of JOA, namely:

- Form 610 for onshore operations, which was first published in 1956 as Form 610 for onshore operations and revised and modified in 1977, 1982, 1989 and 2013;
- Form 710 for offshore continental shelf operations, which was first published in 1998 and then revised and modified 2002 and 2007; and
- Form 810 for offshore deepwater operations, which was first published in 1996 and revised and modified in 2000.

AAPL also published an appendix to be applied for projects involving coalbed methane in 1982, which was revised and modified in 1989. The appendix

[15] The AIPN JOA and the related documents are available at <www.aipn.org>.

provides alternative provisions that address matters including sharing of roads, pads and production facilities.[16]

3.3. OIL AND GAS UK (OGUK)

The OGUK JOA, which was largely influenced by AAPL's 1956 JOA, was introduced in the UK's First Licensing Round in 1964 for offshore operations. The first step towards standardising UK JOAs however was taken in the Fifth Licensing Round in 1977 as drafted by the United Kingdom Offshore Operators Association, which was later succeeded by OGUK in 2007. The 1977 JOA eventually formed the basis for the latest UK JOA issued in the 20th Licensing Round and revised in 2009. The revision was mainly aimed at harmonising the OGUK JOA and the standard Decommissioning Security Agreement also issued by OGUK.[17] Further guidance and a minor revision were issued in 2011 and 2013 respectively. In association with the Oil Industry Finance Association, OGUK also published, as an alternative to the original Annex A to the OGUK JOA, a long form Accounting Procedure.[18]

3.4. CANADIAN ASSOCIATION OF PETROLEUM LANDMEN OPERATING PROCEDURE (CAPL)

The CAPL JOA is the industry standard for exploration and production operations undertaken in Canada. It was first published in 1971 and was then revised and modified in 1974, 1981, 1990, 2007, and most recently in 2015. CAPL's latest revision had the prime objective of offering greater functionality for horizontal wells in the context of an increasing number of 'long reach wells' on resource plays.[19]

3.5. AUSTRALIAN MINING PETROLEUM LAW ASSOCIATION (AMPLA)

In 2011, AMPLA issued its first model JOAs, namely the AMPLA Model Petroleum Joint Operating Agreement and the AMPLA Model Exploration Joint Operating Agreement even though it has been issuing joint venture agreements

---

16 The AAPL JOA and the CBM Appendix are available at <www.landman.org>.
17 Styles, *supra* n. 2, p. 360.
18 The OGUK JOA and the Accounting Procedure are available at <www.oilandgasuk.org.uk>.
19 The CAPL JOA is available at <www.landman.ca>.

for mining operations for over thirty years. Both model agreements state that they are principally drafted for onshore use (which can also be used for similar projects offshore) they are intended for use in non-complex oil and gas exploration projects in Australia, which are generally basic three party JVs. The agreements also clearly state that the AMPLA JOAs are not intended as rigid precedents to be adopted without amendment but rather a guide that includes representative provisions across all matters normally covered in JOAs. AMPLA has also issued a number of related model form agreements, including:

- Petroleum Joint Operating Agreement – Alternative and Optional Clauses;
- Cross Security Document; and
- Financier's Deed of Covenant (Priority Deed).[20]

3.6. THE ROCKY MOUNTAIN MINERAL LAW FOUNDATION (RMMLF)

The Rocky Mineral Mountain Law Foundation 'is a collaborative educational non-profit organization dedicated to the scholarly and practical study of the law and regulations relating to mining, oil and gas, water, public lands, land use'.[21] The RMMLF JOA model form was published in 1968 and focused on US onshore operations.[22] It is important to note that E&P operations in the US started in the 19thcentury and because of that companies have adopted different model form JOAs, such as those from the AAPL, AIPN, API and RMMLF. However, the most common model form JOAs for US operations are those from the AAPL, as they have had far more acceptance than the others.[23]

3.7. NORWEGIAN PETROLEUM DIRECTORATE (NPD)

JOAs were introduced in Norway in the first licensing round in 1965 and then again in 1972. Norway's concessionary system, however, was established in the third licensing round whereby the NPD JOA was introduced based on the JOAs issued in the preceding licensing rounds as well as influences from the first AAPL JOA. The NPD JOA is a mandatory agreement that parties are required to enter

20 The AMPLA JOAs are available at <www.ampla.org>.

21 The RMMLF JOA is available at <http://www.rmmlf.org/pubs/order.htm>.

22 Martin, *supra* n. 12, pp. 293-294: 'The RMMLF developed this model JOA for joint venture operations in the US Rocky Mountain area where there is no field-wide federal unit involved. It incorporates similar concepts found in other model JOAs where there is a sharing of financial risk and benefits by the parties. It was issued in 1968 and never revised. It is referred to as Form 3 in the RMMLF catalogue'.

23 E.E. Smith et al., *International Petroleum Transactions*, 2nd edn, Rocky Mountain Mineral Law Foundation, Denver 2010, p. 538.

into when holding a concession jointly. The Norwegian Ministry of Petroleum and Energy (MPE) must approve the JOA. The NPD JOA is in essence published in its 'final' form with the most recent version being the version issued for the Norwegian 22nd licensing round in 2007 accompanied by accounting procedures and special provisions. The parties cannot deviate from the terms of the contract without the permission and approval of the MPE. In fact, the MPE rarely allows amendments – this ensures a uniform JOA across Norwegian JVs with absolute terms.

3.8. GREENLAND'S BUREAU OF MINERALS AND PETROLEUM (GBMP)

In Greenland, there was no single form of JOA until the first licensing round in 2002. At this date the Ministry of Industry and Mineral Resources issued a model form JOA (accompanied by a model form of cooperation agreement and accounting procedure) for each licensing round. Model form JOAs have already been published for the upcoming 16th, 17th and 18th licensing rounds. Similarly to the NDP JOA, GBMP JOAs must be used as prescribed save for minor changes approved by the government. GBMP JOAs provide for the mandatory participation of the Nunaoil A/S, a state-owned company, which would hold a share of 8–12.5%.[24]

3.9. DANISH ENERGY AGENCY (DEA)

In Denmark, since the first licensing round in 1986, the DEA has been issuing a model form JOA for each licensing round whether it is a tendering round or an open door procedure. The three most recent licensing rounds were the 4th licensing round in 1995, the 5th in 1998, the 6th in 2006 and the 7th in 2014. The model form JOA that has to be approved by the DEA provides that on behalf of the state the Danish North Sea Fund is a mandatory concessionaire holding 20% of any concession. In conjunction with the JOA, the DEA also publishes a model form accounting procedure.[25]

4. THE SCOPE OF A JOA

The scope of a JOA must be clear and well defined and should carefully address the fundamental elements associated with the conduct and promotion of the relevant upstream project. The defined scope in the JOA must reflect and address

---

24 The GBMP JOAs and related documents are available at <www.govmin.gl>.

25 The DEA JOA and accounting procedure are available at <www.ens.dk>.

any and all activities stipulated in the concession. Therefore, there is a strong link between defining the scope of the JOA and meeting the obligations of the concession. Most JOAs deal with this by listing all the joint operations as well as by expressly excluding certain activities from that list.

The model form JOAs have taken different approaches to defining joint operations.

Model JOA	Definition
AIPN JOA	'Joint Operations means the operations and activities within the scope of this Agreement (or whose purpose at the time undertaken was within the scope of this Agreement) conducted by Operator on behalf of all Parties, including Exploration Operations, Appraisal Operations, Development Operations, Production Operations, and operations and activities for the purposes of decommissioning.
AAPL JOA	Joint Operations is not defined.'
OGUK	'Joint Operations means all operations approved, or deemed to be approved, by the Joint Operating Committee and conducted in accordance with this Agreement after the date of commencement of this Agreement as provided in clause 1 and in the case of operations under a development Programme and Budget, in respect of which all Participants are obliged to participate in carrying out such development Programme and Budget.'
AMPLA JOA	'Joint Operations means those operations and activities carried out by Operator pursuant to this Agreement, the costs of which are chargeable to all Parties.'
CAPL JOA	'Joint Operations means an Operation authorised and conducted hereunder for the Joint Account.'
NPD JOA	'Joint Operations shall mean all activities carried out under the provisions of the Joint Operating Agreement for all the Parties jointly.'
GBMP JOA	'Joint Operations means all joint operations of the Parties conducted in accordance with this Agreement.'
DEA JOA	'Joint Operations means all Joint Operations of the Parties conducted in accordance with this Agreement.'

Both the AIPN and AMPLA JOAs take an economic approach to defining joint operations, as it is emphasised that all parties undertake the costs.[26] Notably, and unlike the other definitions set out above, AIPN's approach to defining joint operations is more technical in that it refers to each of the stages of an upstream project despite the fact that such segregation of a project's lifecycle is not necessarily representative of all upstream projects. Although not forming part of OGUK's definition of joint operations, clause 3.1 similarly expands the scope of the JOA (with reference to the concession) to cover exploration and

[26] P. Roberts, *Joint Operating Agreement: a Practical Guide*, 3rd edn, Globe Law and Business, London 2015, p. 58.

production of petroleum, treatment of storage and transportation of petroleum, decommissioning and disposal of joint property. The above table illustrates a simpler approach taken by other JOAs by widely defining joint operations as operations conducted (by the operator) in accordance with the agreement.[27]

As it is important to define and make clear that certain activities form part of the joint operations, expressly excluding certain activities from the definition of joint operation serves the same purpose. This is very important for the parties as it also protects them from being dragged into activities that are not necessarily directly related to the concession. Matters commonly excluded from joint operations include activities that would be conducted outside a concession area, matters related to other concessions, downstream activities, and the joint marketing and sale of petroleum. The rationale for this exclusion is to keep the main spirit behind an incorporate joint venture as the JV parties are keen to share the risks and costs up to the production as later each member has their own decision to make concerning what to do with their share of production. But this rationale could change for a smaller participant in specific situations where they could benefit from extending the scope of the JOA to benefit from the midstream/downstream support from their co-venturers.

5. DURATION, TERM AND TERMINATION

Due to the nature and purpose of a JOA, save for surviving provisions such as confidentiality obligations, its duration is usually aligned to the term of the relevant Petroleum Agreement with the exception of any surviving provisions (commonly confidentiality and decommissioning obligations). This also means that any extensions or variations of the concession will almost invariably involve the parties varying the term of the JOA accordingly.

Like any agreement, a JOA is signed and dated by participants upon execution, but this date will not necessarily be the effective date of the agreement and the participants can negotiate an earlier (or later) date to be counted as the commencement or the effective date. In such cases, the JOA would stipulate conditions precedent that would determine the effective date of the contract – for instance the award of the concession or the approval of the state in jurisdictions such as Norway where their model form JOA is essentially a mandatory standard.

---

27 It is important to note that whilst the CAPL JOA defines joint operations in a wide manner, it expands this definition by providing an exhaustive definition of 'operation' which means any drilling, deepening, side-tracking, completion, recompletion, equipping, reworking, abandonment or other activity provided for or conducted hereunder, including the recovery of petroleum substances from wells, the construction, installation, modification, expansion or operation of any production facility and the conduct of any geological, geophysical, environmental, biophysical or engineering programme or study respecting the joint lands and any other lands within the scope of that approved programme or study.

In most model form JOAs, the effective date is deemed the date on which the parties sign and execute the agreement. The AIPN, OGUK, CAPL and AAPL do not specify any conditions precedent for the effectiveness of the JOA but rather they assume that the concession has been entered into or that the necessary licence interest has been awarded and define the effective date as the date on which the parties have signed and executed the agreement.[28] The AMPLA JOA, however, provides that save for certain obligations, the agreement comes into force on the 'Commencement Date' which is defined as the 'date on which the last of the Conditions Precedent has been satisfied or waived in accordance with [the JOA] or, if there are no Conditions Precedent, then the date of [the JOA]'.[29] Schedule 1 of the AMPLA JOA also sets out optional conditions precedent including the obtaining of all authorisations necessary by law, the execution and delivery of a cross security and deed of covenant.[30]

In all model form JOAs, it is common to see a provision stating that the JOA shall continue to exist until the earlier of (i) completing the joint operations including meeting decommissioning obligations or (ii) the parties terminating the JOA. Having said that, the parties are of course able to unanimously vote to terminate the JOA in any event. Termination provisions in JOAs however tend to be uniform across all model forms and customarily include: (i) termination by a party withdrawing their interest, (ii) forfeiture of a defaulting party's interest, and (iii) a consequential termination of the JOA because of the termination of the concession. Unless expressly stated, JOAs do not exclude any termination rights provided by the laws governing the JOA.

6. THE PARTIES TO THE JOA

6.1. PARTIES AND PARTICIPATING INTERESTS

In the recitals of any JOA, the initial parties to the agreement are identified and their negotiated percentage interests are apportioned.[31] Different model form JOAs do so in differing manners or by using different terminology, but what is consistent is the effect and role of the JOA in serving a 'proprietorial function' in the form of percentages enforced via the incorporation of an interest clause.[32] These percentages mirror the extent to which parties bear their rights and

---

28 AIPN JOA, recitals; OGUK JOA, recitals; CAPL JOA and AAPL JOA; Roberts, *supra* n. 26, p. 35.

29 AMPLA JOA, clause 1.1.

30 AMPLA JOA, Schedule 1.

31 S. Shaw, 'Joint Operating Agreements' in M.R. David (ed.), *Upstream Oil and Gas Agreements*, Sweet & Maxwell, London 1996, p. 16.

32 Styles, *supra* n. 2, p. 365.

duties.[33] Such interest clauses provide words of severance, establishing what is in English law known as a tenancy in common upon entry into the JOA. A tenant in common holds an 'undivided interest'; however, it is the distinct share of the whole which is allocated to the co-venturers.[34]

Commonly, the JOA stipulates that the co-venturers receive their share of production in kind, giving all parties direct ownership of the project and the production.[35] This is a privilege, which is considered a fundamental advantage of JOA when compared to joint venture corporations where shareholders do not have direct ownership.[36]

By virtue of the JOA, its parties own the equipment and facilities of the project as 'joint property'.[37] The model form JOAs define joint property in different ways and these are set out in the table below:

Model JOA	**Definition**
AIPN JOA	'Joint Property means, at any point in time, all wells, facilities, equipment, materials, information, funds, and property (other than Hydrocarbons) held for use in Joint Operations.'
AAPL JOA	Joint property is not defined.
OGUK, GBMP and DEA JOAs	'Joint Property means all property acquired or held for use in connection with the Joint Operations.'
AMPLA JOA	'Joint Venture Property means all rights, titles, interest, claims, benefits and all other property of whatever kind, real or personal, from time to time owned by any Participant for the purposes of the Joint Venture, and includes the Petroleum Titles, JV intellectual Property, and all items listed in the Joint Venture Asset Register, and includes petroleum before delivery to a Participant at the Delivery Point.'
CAPL JOA	'Joint Property means the Joint Lands, together with all other tangible and intangible property held for the relevant time, including funds, wells, Production Facilities and other equipment and materials.'
NPD JOA	'Joint Property shall mean equipment acquired for the Joint Operations and fixed property subordinated the Joint Operating Agreement.'

Roberts notes that whilst AIPN's definition (and similarly in the CAPL JOA) of joint property is expanded to expressly cover physical infrastructure, the

33 M. Taylor, T. Winsor and S. Tyne, *Joint Operating Agreements*, 2nd edn, Longman, London 1992, p. 23.

34 D. Chappelle, *Land Law*, 8th edn, Pearson Education, Essex 2008, p. 180.

35 K.W. Blinn, C. Duval, H.L. Leuch and A. Pertuzio, *International Petroleum Exploration and Exploitation Agreements, Legal, Economic and Policy Aspects*, Euromoney plc, London 1986, p. 194.

36 T. El-Emadi, 'Joint Venture Contracts (JVCs) among Current Negotiated Petroleum contracts: a Literature Review of JVCs Development, Concept and Elements' (2010) 1 *Georgetown Journal of International Law* 645, 663.

37 *Ibid.*

definition adopted in the OGUK, GMBP and DEA JOAs are simpler, yet wide enough to include any property used for the joint operations.[38]

In certain jurisdictions, including Denmark, Greenland and Norway, the law stipulates a mandatory right of participation for the government, via a state-owned company, which can elect to become a party to the concession and consequently the JOA. Depending on whether the state elects to participate before or after the JOA was entered into, amendments to re-allocate the parties, participating interests may be necessary. AIPN has an express provision dealing with this, which reads: 'If Government Oil and Gas Company elects to participate in the rights and obligations of Parties ... the Parties shall contribute, in proportion to their respective Participating Interests, to the interest to be acquired'.[39] The AIPN JOA also offers an alternative option clause, which stipulates that the parties enter into a separate JOA with the state with respect to the rights and obligations on the one hand, and the parties on the other.[40] Of course, in the case of a sole concessionaire, a new JOA will need to be entered into to reflect the joint participation of the private and the state-owned company. In the case of the NPD JOA, for instance, the state also has a pre-emption right when and if a party agrees to assign its participating interest at an agreed price and terms with that buyer.[41] The Norwegian State exerts further control over the field development by virtue of its right to select the participants to the licence/JOA as well as appointing the operator.[42]

In many cases where the state has a right to participate in the concession, drafters consider incorporating a carry provision, that is paying the cash calls for the percentage share to be repaid only if there is sufficient production share available for it to be repaid.[43] This is a common way for the state to participate in projects without incurring exploration and appraisal expenses in unsuccessful projects. Both the AIPN and the GBMP JOAs have exhaustive provisions that define the 'carry' and the carried interest, as well as other matters such as when and how to pay the 'carry'.[44]

6.2. THE OPERATOR

There is usually one party designated as the operator who would be responsible for conducting the day-to-day responsibilities (including negotiation and entry into various support contracts with third parties for e.g. seismic surveys, drilling,

38 Roberts, *supra* n. 26, p. 49.
39 AIPN JOA, clause 3.4.A.
40 AIPN JOA 3.4.B.
41 NPD JOA, clause 23.
42 Sections 3–4 and 3–4 of the Norwegian Petroleum Activities Act 1996.
43 LXL LLP, *supra* n. 6.
44 GBMP JOA, clause 2; AIPN JOA, clause 3.4.C.

testing, decommissioning) and the joint operations on behalf of the JV.[45] Other scenarios include the appointment of an operator nominated by the terms of the concession or by using either a contracted, incorporated or a split operator model.[46]

It is uncommon for model form JOAs to set requirements relating to the percentage interest of an operator, even though some petroleum legal regimes (e.g. Brazil) might require a minimum participating interest for this position. It is typical for the operator to be the party with the largest percentage interest.[47] This is usually considered imperative by the non-operators because it motivates the operator to invest and commit to the project more than it would have had it held a smaller percentage interest.[48] Adopting the AAPL JOA and an optional provision from the AIPN JOA, however, may influence the parties' allocation of percentage interest as it provides that an operator may be removed following an assignment that reduces its percentage interest to less than the percentage interest of a non-operating party, subject to a vote by the other parties.[49]

6.2.1. *Duties and Liabilities of the Operator*

Generally, the operator's main duties include:

(i) the preparation of programmes, budgets and Authorisations for Expenditure ('AFE');
(ii) the implementation of OpCom approved programmes; and
(iii) the provision to each of the co-venturers of reports, data and information.[50]

As the operator is the *de facto* day-to-day manager of the upstream project and in most cases the agent of the JV, the operator owes a duty of care to the non-operators. The provisions of the JOA would normally obligate the operator to perform its duties in 'a proper and workman like manner in accordance with good oilfield practice.'[51] The different model form JOAs define this standard in similar ways.

---

45 AIPN JOA, clause 4.1; AAPL JOA, clause 4.1; OGUK JOA, clause 5.1; CAPL JOA, clause 2.
46 See Roberts, *supra* n. 26, pp. 83–95.
47 LXL LLP, *supra* n. 6, p. 36.
48 N. Etteh, 'Joint Operating Agreements: which issues are likely to be the most sensitive to the parties and how can a good contract design limit the damage from such disputes?', Centre for Energy, Petroleum and Mineral Law and Policy, http://www.dundee.ac.uk/cepmlp/gateway/?news=31272 accessed 08.06.2015.
49 AAPL JOA, clause 4.4.1 and AIPN JOA, clause 4.
50 Typically, the operator's list of responsibilities is more exhaustive – see AIPN JOA, clause 4.2.B; OGUK JOA, clause 6; CAPL JOA, clause 3, amongst others.
51 B. Taverne, *Petroleum, Industry, and Governments: a Study of the Involvement of Industry and Governments in the Production, and Use of Petroleum*, Kluwer Law International, the Netherlands 2008, p. 142.

The AIPN JOA for instance provides that the operator is obliged to perform its duties 'in a diligent, safe and efficient manner in accordance with good and prudent petroleum industry practices and field conservation principles generally followed by the international petroleum industry under similar circumstances.'[52]

The AAPL JOA provides that the operator 'shall timely commence and conduct all activities or operations in a good and workmanlike manner, as would a prudent operator under the same or similar circumstances'.[53]

The OGUK JOA provides the same standard by defining good oilfield practice as:

> '[T]he application of those methods and practices customarily used in good and prudent oil and gas field practice in the UKCS with that degree of diligence and prudence reasonably and ordinarily exercised by experienced operators engaged in the UKCS in a similar activity under similar circumstances and conditions.'[54]

The GBMP and DEA JOAs take a similar position. The CAPL JOA also provides a similar standard by requiring the operator to conduct its duties 'diligently, in a good and workmanlike manner and in accordance with good oilfield practice, including prudent reservoir management and conservation principles'.[55]

It can be seen that there is no uniform definition of this standard, but what is common amongst the model JOAs is how they aim to define what a reasonable and prudent operator is by viewing each circumstance objectively and evaluating what other operators would do in the same circumstances. Therefore, the precise nature of what is reasonable and prudent or what is good oilfield practice is dependent on the circumstances, which will change as technology develops.[56]

As the operator is not remunerated for their operatorship, they are not held legally liable with respect to any damage or loss suffered by third parties or non-operators when acting on behalf of the venture.[57] The non-operators and the operator (in its capacity as a JV participant) will hold any liabilities that arise as a result of the JV and particularly the joint operations jointly.[58] The operator's liability will be limited to any loss or damage resulting from its wilful misconduct or its failure to obtain and maintain insurance even though some JOAs might provide further hurdles before this personal liability is fully met.[59]

---

52 AIPN JOA, clause 4.2.B.2.

53 AAPL JOA, clause 5.2.

54 OGUK JOA, clause 6.2.2.

55 CAPL JOA, clause 3.4.

56 Styles, *supra* n. 2, p. 377.

57 J. Easo, 'Managing the Risk of Catastrophic Events on the UK Continental Shelf', International Law Office, 2010 <www.internationallawoffice.com/Newsletters/detail.aspx?g=a0790066-73b8-41b1-a596-bb3739c4c6a0&redir=1> accessed 04.11.2013.

58 T.C. Daintith, G.D.M. Willoughby and A.D.G. Hill, *United Kingdom Oil and Gas: Loose Leaf*, Sweet and Maxwell, London 1984, para. 1-627.

59 For instance AIPN JOA, clause 4.7.

The definition of wilful misconduct raises uncertainty. For instance, this is the case in the UK where the ambit of the definition under case law is still vague; accordingly, it is standard for drafters to limit its scope by incorporating a narrow definition of the phrase, namely a 'deliberate or reckless action resulting in loss'.[60] What is certain is that if is established that an operator's conduct was regarded as wilful misconduct, it is established English law that the operator would not be indemnified.[61] This is narrower than the US approach whereby the operator's liability also extends to cover gross negligence.[62] The position in the various model form JOAs is as follows:

The AIPN JOA defines wilful misconduct and gross negligence together to mean:

> 'Any act or failure to act (whether sole, joint or concurrent) by any person or entity that was intended to cause, or was in reckless disregard of or wanton indifference to, harmful consequences such person or entity knew, or should have known, such act or failure would have on the safety or property of another person or entity.'[63]

The AAPL and CAPL JOAs provide a less elaborate position on the liabilities of the operator but clearly limits its liability incurred because of gross negligence or wilful misconduct.[64] The former does not define either terms, but like the AIPN JOA, the CAPL JOA provides a combined definition of the terms to mean:

> 'Any act, omission or failure to act (whether sole, joint or concurrent) by a person that was intended to cause, or was in reckless disregard of, or wanton indifference to, the harmful consequences to the safety or property of another person or to the environment which the person acting or failing to act knew (or should have known) would result from such act, omission, or failure to act.'[65]

The CAPL JOA also goes on to expressly exclude certain acts from the definition including acts constituting mere negligence and acts that were approved by all parties.[66]

The OGUK JOA has only a definition for wilful misconduct, which reads:

> 'an intentional, conscious or reckless disregard by Senior Managerial Personnel of good and prudent oil and gas field practice or any of the terms of this Agreement in utter disregard of avoidable and harmful consequences but shall not include any act, omission,

---

60 Styles, *supra* n. 2.
61 *Porter v Magill* [2002] 2 AC 357.
62 *Shell Rocky Mountain Production, LLC v Ultra Resources, Inc*, 415 F 3d 1158 (10th Cir 2005).
63 AIPN JOA, clause 1.1.
64 AAPL JOA, clause 5.2; CAPL JOA, clause 4.
65 CAPL JOA, clause 1.1.
66 CAPL JOA, clause 1.1.

error of judgement or mistake made in the exercise in good faith of any function, authority or discretion vested in or exercisable by such Senior Managerial Personnel and which in the exercise of such good faith is justifiable by special circumstances, including but not limited to safeguarding of life, property or the environment and other emergencies.'[67]

The default definition of wilful misconduct in the OGUK JOA limits such liability to acts or omissions committed by a senior person, which includes directors, corporate officers or defined senior managers that have overall responsibility for the management of the assets in relation to the concession/JV.[68] This is available as an option in the AIPN JOA, which also offers various alternatives when seeking to define senior personnel allowing the drafters to include field supervisory managers, senior resident managers, facility managers and any managers that directly report to a senior resident manager.[69]

It is good practice to protect the operator by capping any potential liabilities and by excluding any potential liability by the operator for consequential or environmental losses even in cases of wilful misconduct; this the default position in the OGUK JOA as this amount could be extremely hard to predict beforehand and not many operators would be comfortable taking this role without some assurances and protections.[70]

6.2.2. *Appointment of the Operator*

In many countries, the state must approve the operator's appointment based on its technical and financial capability.[71] In the UK for instance, the Oil and Gas Authority (OGA) sets out the competence requirements, which include the operator's:

(i) technical experience;
(ii) ability to supervise, manage and undertake a proposed operation;
(iii) their risk assessment and hierarchy of decision making;
(iv) plans for public engagement; and
(v) scope of relevant insurance coverage for operations and well abandonment activity.

A uniform and elementary feature of JOAs is that the operator does not receive remuneration in return for its operatorship, but merely a reimbursement of

67 OGUK JOA, clause 1.1.
68 OGUK JOA, clause 1.1.
69 AIPN JOA, clause 1.1.
70 OGUK JOA, clause 6.2.4(b).
71 The Petroleum Licensing (Production) (Seaward Areas) Regulations 2008, model clause 24(1).

costs and any profit it is entitled to pursuant to its percentage interest. Oil and gas companies that are able to do so often accept or even want to assume the role of an operator to enhance their reputation and their operatorship and asset portfolios, as well as to enjoy a level of control over the joint operations. The appointment of the operator is always indefinite and it continues until the end of the life of the project (and consequently the JOA), resignation or when and if the operator is removed by the non-operators.

6.2.3. *Resignation of the Operator*

In most model form JOAs, the operator can resign at any time having given a reasonable notice as set out in the table below:

Model JOA	Notice period
NPD JOA	6 months
OGUK JOA	270 days
AIPN JOA	120 days
AMPLA JOA	180 days
GBMP JOA	180 days
DEA JOA	180 days
AAPL JOA	90 days
CAPL JOA	45 days

6.2.4. *Removal of the Operator*

Moreover, the JOA will stipulate provisions that trigger the termination of operatorship; common examples include the removal of the operator (i) if they have become insolvent;[72] (ii) if it is served a termination notice by the OpCom;[73] (iii) upon an assignment, which reduces their participating interest;[74] or (iv) by an order of the state.[75] Provisions for the replacement of the operator and for regulating the transitional period are found in most JOAs.[76]

72 AIPN JOA, clause 4.10.A; AAPL JOA, clause 4.4.2; OGUK JOA, clause 5.3.1; CAPL JOA, clause 2.2 A; NPD JOA, clause 4.2.

73 AIPN JOA, clause 4.10; AAPL JOA, clause 4.4.2; OGUK JOA, clause 5.3.1; CAPL JOA, clause 2.2 A; NPD JOA, clause 4.2; GBMP JOA, clause 3.17.2; DEA JOA, clause 3.17.2.

74 AMPLA JOA, clause 6.2.

75 AIPN JOA, clause 4.10.A, AAPL JOA, clause 4.4.2.

76 AIPN JOA, clause 4.11.E; AAPL JOA, clause 4.7; OGUK JOA, clause 5.7; CAPL JOA, clause 2.7.

6.2.5. *Capacity of the Operator*

In most JOAs, the case would be that the operator acts both as a joint principal with the non-operators as well as an agent of the individual co-venturers (as it is an unincorporated association). This is important, as the parties must be clear in what capacity the operator is acting, particularly when facing issues of third party contract enforcement or even more importantly when determining whether the operator owes any fiduciary duties to the co-venturers as principals. Generally, it is widely accepted that the role the operator undertakes does inevitably give rise to an agent-principal relationship.

For instance, in the UK, despite the fact that there have been no cases dealing with the agency of an operator in the context of JOAs, there is a strong consensus that the common law principles of agency give rise to a fiduciary relationship.[77] In the US, it has been affirmed that the operator acts as an agent and a fiduciary relationship arises.[78] Therefore, it is prudent to acknowledge in the JOA that the nature of the operator and non-operator's relationship gives rise to an agency status to the operator. The model form JOAs address the operator's capacity in differing ways and some expressly exclude the existence of an agency relationship and a fiduciary relationship.

Model JOA	Agency acknowledged or excluded?
AIPN	Excludes agency
AAPL	Excludes agency
OGUK JOA	Express agency (with respect to third party contracts)
AMPLA JOA	Express agency
GBMP JOA	Excludes agency
CAPL JOA	Excludes agency

6.3. THE NON-OPERATORS

The non-operators will typically hold small percentage interests (somewhat like minority shareholders) and their most important role is to provide a share of the funds whenever there is a cash call and to participate in the decision-making process with respect to the JV and its operations.[79] Such decision making

77 P.D. Finn, 'Good Faith, Unconscionability and Fiduciary Duties', in International Bar Association (ed.), *Energy Law '90: Changing Energy Markets – the Legal Consequences*, Graham and Trotman, London 1990, p. 113.

78 *Meinhard v Salmon* 164 NE 545 (NY 1928).

79 LXL LLP, *supra* n. 6, p.36.

relates the authorisation for expenditures (AFE) and approval of programmes proposed by the operator. This may afford non-operators a degree of control over the operators when acting on behalf of the JV in the joint operations or other matters. The representation and the retained control of the non-operators (including the operator in its capacity as participant) is enforced in the OpCom, which is a formal committee constituted by a representative of each party and which serves as the official link between the operator and non-operators. In essence, the OpCom is a medium to supervise the operator's conduct of the JV.

6.4. OPCOM

The level of supervision and control, which the operator, is subject to, depends on the model form JOA that is opted for by the parties. In the AIPN JOA, it is provided that the operator 'shall perform Joint-Operations in accordance with the Contract, the Laws, and this Agreements, and consistent with approved AFEs), and the decisions of the Operating Committee not in conflict with this Agreement'.[80] The same approach is adopted in the OGUK JOA, which provides that '[s]ubject to this Agreement, the Operator has the right and is obliged to conduct the Joint Operations by itself, its agents or its contractors under the overall supervision and control of the Joint Operating Committee.'[81] Similarly, the AMPLA, DEA, GBMP and NPD JOAs also establish an OpCom.

Other model form JOAs do not provide an OpCom and afford the non-operators less control where their role is purely of that of an investor. For instance, the AAPL JOA affords the operator complete control over the joint operations, save for certain reservations: '[t]he Operator is an independent contractor, not subject to the control or direction of Non-Operating Parties'.[82] Similarly, under the CAPL JOA, an operator would only be obliged to consult and inform the non-operators about joint operations.[83]

As part of the OpCom, the parties are subject to a voting system in which their votes are weighted in accordance with their allocated proprietary interest percentage.[84] The JOA would stipulate the necessary percentage or rather 'pass mark' for decisions and proposals to be approved.[85] Such pass marks are commonly set at 70% in order to prevent parties with large shares from exercising veto powers and thus give significance to the votes of smaller proprietors.[86]

80 AIPN JOA, clause 4.2.B.1.
81 OGUK JOA, clause 6.1.1.
82 AAPL JOA, clause 5.1.
83 CAPL JOA, clause 3.1.
84 G. BEAN, *Fiduciary Obligations in Joint Ventures*, Clarendon Press, Oxford 1995, p. 16.
85 *Ibid.*
86 Daintith, Willoughby and Hill, *supra* n. 58, para. 1-632.

The AIPN JOA voting procedure has a number of optional clauses dealing with this, including a clause that provides that OpCom decisions be only validly made by a pass mark vote of a certain number of parties.[87] However, this also means that if the operator is the party with the largest interest (which is usually the case) then the operator can carry the vote, making the provision inadequate in controlling the operator.[88] Therefore, it is prudent to reserve certain matters for unanimous vote. The OGUK JOA deals with this by providing that certain matters (particularly matters relating to decommissioning) require a unanimous vote by the OpCom.

Unanimous voting may however result in a deadlock situation whereby the votes for and against a matter are equal. On this point, Roberts states that '[m]ost JOAs demonstrate an unwillingness to impose a meaningful deadlock resolution provision, the implication being that the parties going back to the drawing board in the OpCom until some sort of mutually acceptable position is eventually hammered out.'[89]

Therefore, it is possible to suggest that the existence of an OpCom is one of the key differences between the North American model form JOAs and the others. This is a critical difference for most non-operators as the North American JOAs position non-operators almost like investors in the relevant project, rather than as co-venturers.

7. DEVIATING FROM JOINT OPERATIONS

In practice, participants in a JV will from time to time disagree on certain decisions (geological, technical, financial or commercial) aspects of a proposed operation, which may create doubts about its viability. As a result, conflicts may arise, resulting in disputes that can affect the horizontal operation of a JOA. The resolution of such disagreements rests with non-consent and sole risk clauses. The difference between the two mechanisms is the amount of support a proposal has obtained at the OpCom.[90] On the one hand, a sole risk clause permits certain parties to undertake a project at their own risk without the support of the relevant majority.[91] On the other hand, a non-consent clause allows parties to exclude themselves from programmes even if the votes have achieved the pass mark.[92] The later are less common than exclusive operations/sole risk clauses but

87 AIPN JOA, clause 5.9.
88 Etteh, *supra* n. 48, p. 6.
89 Roberts, *supra* n. 26, p. 110.
90 Styles, *supra* n. 2, p. 390.
91 Shaw, *supra* n.31, p. 23.
92 J.G. Adlam, 'Joint Venture Operating Agreements' (1989) 2 *New Zealand Cabinet Manual* 446–450.

are both in a 'very real sense inimical to the very *raison d'ètre* of a joint venture: mutual decision-making with the aim of sharing of risk, costs and production.'[93]

Most model form JOAs set out provisions for operations that are not carried out as joint operations. This is called a sole risk project by the OGUK JOA (which in this context is generally followed by the DEA, GBMP and NPD JOAs), an exclusive operation by the AIPN JOA, or an independent operation in the CAPL JOA. The AAPL JOA provides provisions for non-consent operations but not for sole risk, while by contrast the AMPLA JOA provides a mechanism for sole risk operations but not for non-consent clauses. The concept is similar across the various model form JOAs, yet slight differences exist. A sole risk project is undertaken on the basis that only the sole risk parties are responsible for funding all costs and meeting all the liabilities with respect to the sole risk endeavour and that only the sole risk parties are eligible for any proceeds arising out of the sole risk activity.[94]

Under the OGUK JOA, the determining factor as to whether a project is a sole risk project or joint operations is the pass mark. If the pass mark is achieved upon a vote, then the operation will be carried out as a joint operation; otherwise it will be carried out as a sole risk project.[95] In cases where there is more than one proposal, the proposal that obtains the highest aggregate percentage is prioritised.

The AIPN JOA adopts a combined sole risk and non-consent provision where the party proposing the exclusive operations can proceed alone if the other parties will not support or participate in the operations. This thus contrasts with the position under the OGUK JOA where joint operations can be carried out by fewer than all the parties.[96]

The CAPL JOA also provides a similar mechanism, called an independent operation, where any party can serve a notice to the other co-venturers expressing their intention to undertake a particular project, at which point the parties may elect to participate or not in that 'independent operation'.[97]

Although not exclusively, it is common for the operator to carry out the project on behalf of the sole risk party, unless either of them decides otherwise.[98] An OpCom encompassing only the sole risk parties would also manage the project.

A common feature across most model form JOAs is that any sole risk or exclusive operations must not conflict with the joint operations or any minimum work obligations.[99] Typically operations during the minimal work programme

93 Styles, *supra* n. 2, p. 391.
94 OGUK JOA, clause 18.
95 Taylor, Winsor and Tyne, *supra* n. 33. Note that the Guidance Notes to the OGUK JOA provide a short form model non-consent clause.
96 AIPN JOA, clauses 7.1–7.2.
97 CAPL JOA, clause 10.
98 OGUK JOA, clause 15.2.9; AIPN JOA, clause 7; CAPL JOA, clause 10.
99 C. Duval et al., *International Petroleum Exploration and Exploitation Agreements: Legal, Economic and Policy Aspects*, Barrows, New York 2009, p. 295; AIPN JOA, clause 7.1(a).

cannot be conducted by fewer than all parties, although in some cases it might be allowed as more work will be done for the benefit of the host government contract.[100] A list of operations that can be carried out in this context is usually provided in the model form JOAs and typically includes seismic testing, drilling, deepening or side tracking of a well, testing and logging and development, plugging back of exploration well, recompletion of exploration and appraisal well.[101] Like the AIPN JOA, the OGUK JOA indemnifies the non-sole risk parties for any damages or costs incurred while carrying out the sole risk project, but it differs by excluding from the indemnity damage inflicted to the subsurface including any reservoir.[102] The AIPN JOA moreover does state at which stage are the parties participating in the exclusive operation are liable for such operations as plugging and abandoning and restoring the surface location of the contract area, a matter on which the OGUK is silent.[103]

Although sole risk and non-consent rights are incompatible, with the philosophy of a JOA which is based on collaboration and sharing a common interest, they allow different perspectives to co-exist in an organised and structured manner.[104] This more obvious with the non-consent clauses which would entail the consenting parties paying a share of a particular project in proportions which exceed their percentage interest in the JOA.[105] The buy-back rights tend to impose heavy penalties (e.g. percentages between 100% and 2,000%) to discourage companies from engaging in operations with fewer than all parties.[106] In any case, such provisions are rarely ever exercised and their negotiation is usually a method of applying some pressure in the negotiation of proposals at the OpCom rather than in reality.[107] Finally, these clauses may be difficult to enforce in civil law jurisdictions, as they are less likely to recognise the concept of trust.

---

100 'Sole risk provisions on the other hand, are fairly universally accepted. They recognise that a proposal (drilling, appraisal or development) may be considered worthwhile by some parties buy may not meet the "majority" passmark hurdle.' S. Shaw, 'Joint Operating Agreements', in M.R. David, *Upstream Oil and Gas Agreements*, Sweet and Maxwell, London 1996, p. 23.

101 I.e. OGUK JOA, clause 15 generally; DEA JOA, clause 7; GBMP JOA, clause 7; NPD JOA clauses 18 and 19. Please note that this is contrary to the AAPL JOA which reserves the drilling of a well to be carried out as joint operations – see AAPL JOA, clause 13. Smith et al., *supra* n. 25, p. 48. Moreover, the AIPN JOA does not allow minimum work obligations to be carried out as exclusive operation – AIPN JOA, clause 7.1(d).

102 OGUK JOA, clause 15.2.5.

103 AIPN JOA, clause 7.3.

104 C. Okafor, 'A Comparative Analysis of Sole Risk Operations in Different Joint Operating Agreement and Model Form' (2013) 17 *CAR* <http://www.dundee.ac.uk/cepmlp/gateway/files.php?file=cepmlp_car17_10_502769649.pdf> accessed 18 June 2015.

105 Ibid.

106 T. Daintith, G. Willoughby and A. Hill (eds.), *United Kingdom Oil & Gas Law*, 3rd edn, Sweet & Maxwell, London 2009, pp. 1151-11533.

107 Roberts, *supra* n. 26, p. 73.

8. FINANCING STRUCTURE

In a JOA, the more complex provisions relate to financing the JV, as it is typical of upstream projects to involve high sums of capital invested into a long-term project. The most fundamental pillar of this financing structure when looking at the JOA is the participants' role in approving budgets, AFEs, award of contracts and accordingly making pro rata cash calls to the operator within a specified period. In return, the non-operators' major right is to receive pro rata their share of any production arising from the joint operations.[108]

8.1. AWARD OF CONTRACTS

Model form JOAs usually set out mechanisms to determine the level of autonomy an operator enjoys when entering into and committing to contracts with third parties of behalf of the JV. This is a common provision, as the operator is less likely to conduct most activities by itself, as it is more efficient and flexible to engage a variety of contractors with expertise on specific assignments in accordance with their assets and portfolio.

Contracting with third parties is quite common, and it is a very welcome approach by the operators who, as a result of their arrangement with the third party, negotiate the liability arising from the performance of that particular activity under the contract. The main consideration in this respect is the manner in which the JOA deals with: (i) the non-operators' ability to enforce the contact which the operator is the only party to; (ii) the selection of the contractor; and (iii) the contractor's capacity. For each of these considerations, and depending on the unique position of the relevant JOA, the agreement might incorporate procurement provisions to secure the fulfilment of the above-mentioned considerations.

As previously mentioned, the award of contracts is often a prerogative of the operator who has the authority to enter into such contracts on behalf of parties; this is the usual position. Nevertheless, the JOA will seek to limit such authority by requiring the operator to obtain consent from OpCom to enter into agreements or at least require consent for contracts above a certain value (to avoid the Operator requesting consent for every single contract).[109]

8.2. BUDGETS, WORK PROGRAMMES AND AFEs

As the authority to execute all approved programmes and budgets, the non-operators must ensure that there is an effective method of controlling expenditure

---

[108] OGUK JOA, clause 18.

[109] AIPN JOA, clause 6.7; OGUK JOA, clauses 6.5.3–6.5.5.

and how the operator enters into contracts on the JV's behalf. The most common mechanisms are provisions that require the operator to obtain express approval from the OpCom.[110] The operator would first present a programme outlining any work which the JV wishes to undertake accompanied with a budget estimate covering both drilling, development and operating costs.[111] Styles explains that:

> 'It is generally recognised that both programme and budget are 'living documents' and may require amendment as events unfold. A budget is in the way of an estimate of costs, but does not of itself authorise the operator to demand financial contributions from the JOA members; rather this is done by the eponymous [AFE].'[112]

The operator's preparation of the work programme and budget is an obligation that is not universal in all model form JOAs.[113] Some JOAs, like CAPL and AAPL (which adopts a looser formulation of the work programme and budget established in the OGUK JOA), tend to afford the non-operators control over the operator via their power to approve AFEs.[114] In general, an AFE mechanism increases the protection of any non-operator as they have the opportunity to approve the precise cost of the intended service. Nevertheless, in some cases the existence of an AFE might be a simple process of informing the non-operators about the actual cost of the service, as no approval might be required. Many operators might argue that the intended activity was approved in the relevant work programme and budget so no further approval should be required.

8.3. DEFAULT

JOAs are entered into on the assumption that the risks and the costs will be shared amongst the co-venturers. Therefore, it can be said that failing to pay a cash call issued by the operator is a fundamental breach of JOA – particularly as the JOA will stipulate that the non-defaulting co-venturers have to make good the shortfall.[115] This perhaps explains why the most sophisticated and draconian default provisions are the ones common to the oil and gas industry.[116] Initially, the defaulting party has a remedial right to pay his default, plus interest, within a specified period that is typically set at sixty days – this is often referred to as the

110 AIPN JOA, clause 6.7.B.2; CAPL JOA.
111 OGUK JOA, clause 14.3.
112 OGUK JOA, clauses 10.2, 11.2, 12.2 and 14.1.5; Styles, *supra* n. 2, p. 390.
113 Roberts, *supra* n. 26, p. 114.
114 *Ibid.*
115 Etteh, *supra* n. 48, p. 8.
116 I. Hewitt, *Hewitt on Joint Ventures*, Sweet and Maxwell, London 2011, p. 175.

grace period.[117] If the default continues after such period, the defaulting party will face escalating consequences default, ranging from suspension of rights (which starts in the early stage of the default) to outright forfeiture of interest in order to remedy the default.[118]

8.3.1. *Suspension of Defaulter's Rights*

In a JOA, the default provisions will often provide for the suspension of a defaulter's rights. This include the loss of right to vote in the OpCom, loss of entitlement to production share and property rights, loss of right of withdrawal from the JOA and loss of access to information. Although the suspension of the defaulter's rights does not necessarily remove the non-defaulting parties' burden of having to pay the cash call, it is a threat that may prove to be effective against the defaulter.[119] The suspension would usually be triggered in the grace period where the defaulting party has an opportunity to 'cure' the default by paying the default amount and any interest within a specified period. There is some doubt as to the modus operandi of this remedy as it involves suspending some of the defaulting party's rights whilst 'insisting on the performance of other JOA provisions'.[120] Nevertheless, suspension of defaulter's rights is a remedy provided by many model form JOAs including the OGUK, AIPN and AAPL JOAs, although there are some variations.[121]

In the AMPLA JOA, there is no suspension of rights during the default period.[122]

In the RMMLF JOA, there is no clear provision of suspension of the defaulting parties' rights under a JOA and so the defaulting party reserves the right to receive information and to participate in proposals of work.[123] In fact, the RMMLF JOA does not provide a procedure for default at all but leaves it to the parties to determine and creates reciprocal liens amongst the co-venturers over the defaulting party's percentage interest, property and share of production.[124]

---

117 OGUK JOA, clause 17.6.1.

118 Y. Abul Failat and B. Jensen, 'Oil and Gas Joint Operating Agreements: Default Provisions, a Dilemma by Default' (2013) 5 *Oil, Gas and Energy Law Journal* 4 <www.ogel.org> accessed 18.06.2015.

119 H. Boigon, 'The Joint Operating Agreement in a Hostile Environment: Part 2' (1978/1988) 6(11) *Oil and Gas Law Taxation Review* 320, 330.

120 Etteh, *supra* n.48.

121 OGUK JOA, clause 17; AIPN JOA, clause 8.2; AAPL JOA, clause 7.B.

122 E. Pereira, 'Protection Against Default in Long Term Petroleum Joint Ventures' (2012) *Oxford Institute for Energy Studies* 12 <www.oxfordenergy.org/wpcms/wp-content/uploads/2012/05/WPM_47.pdf> accessed 14.06.2015.

123 *Ibid.*, p. 19.

124 RMMLF JOA, clause 4.7.

8.3.2. *Forfeiture*

Forfeiture is generally considered to be the 'ultimate price paid for failure to contribute a percentage interest share of the cost of the joint venture.'[125] It involves the transfer of the defaulting party's entire interest to the non-defaulting parties, distributed pro rata in proportion to their percentage interest.[126] In the OGUK JOA, a non-defaulting party has a right to be the assignee in respect of the defaulting party's interest in the production licence free of any encumbrances except for rent and royalty under the licence.[127] The OpCom may unanimously decide to not acquire the defaulting party's interest – this would lead to the surrender of the licence, as the non-defaulting parties would be deemed to have abandoned the joint operations.[128]

In some jurisdictions, forfeiture clauses may be deemed to be punitive clauses and therefore invalid. Under English law, forfeiture is a recognised remedy – there is some judicial authority to suggest that the English courts would generally uphold such provisions if they are proportionate to the damage actually suffered by the non-defaulting parties.[129] Nevertheless, the uncertainty with respect to enforcing a forfeiture clause is a major concern for oil and gas companies and in particular when such provisions are assessed when the operations are in the production phase.[130] At this stage of the project the defaulting party will have already invested substantially in the operations; therefore, enforcing forfeiture in such circumstances could be considered by the English court for instance to be disproportionate to the 'injury' actually suffered by the non-defaulting parties and thus rendering a forfeiture clause a penalty.[131]

The AIPN JOA, a declaration is made to the effect that each party agrees that the nature and the amount of the remedies granted to non-defaulting parties are reasonable and appropriate in the circumstances.[132] In some model form JOAs, a similar express declaration stating that each party recognises forfeiture as a remedy and that it is not a penalty but rather a fair and reasonable remedy.[133] Roberts notes that although it is good for the parties to incorporate such wording

---

125 C. Golvala, 'Upstream Joint Venture – Bidding and Operating Agreements', in G. Picton-Tubervill (ed.), *Oil and Gas: a Practical Handbook*, Globe Law and Business, London 2009, p. 49.

126 P. Roberts, 'Fault Lines in Joint Operating Agreements' (2008) 7 *International Energy Law Review* 274, 275.

127 OGUK JOA, clause 17.6.2.

128 OGUK JOA, clause 17.6.2.

129 Abul Failat and Jensen, *supra* n. 118, p. 6; *Dunlop Pneumatic Tyre Co Ltd v New Garage and Motor Co Limited* [1915] AC 79.

130 Abul Failat and Jensen, *supra* n. 118, p. 6.

131 *Ibid.*

132 AIPN JOA, clause 8.6.

133 Roberts, *supra* n. 26, p. 227.

to evidence their agreement on using forfeiture as a remedy or so, it is ultimately the courts (or arbitral tribunals) that will determine the enforceability of such clauses regardless of the presence of such statements in the JOA.[134] Finally, a forfeiture is only a useful mechanism provided the project has a positive balance (i.e. more value than costs).

In addition, the creation of liens and charges over their participating interest would work in the same manner as a forfeiture mechanism.[135] In the case of a default the non-defaulting parties could enforce that mechanism to transfer the interest from the defaulting party. This option requires local advice to verify what procedures are required to create an enforceable encumbrance over their participating interest in the relevant JOAs.

8.3.3. *Withering Provision*

Where forfeiture is not enforceable, the JOA seeks to protect the non-defaulting parties via a mandatory transfer of the interest in a process known as 'withering' as compensation for damages. This transfer should be proportional to the amount of default and previous investments. Such clauses were introduced to mitigate the perceived risk of a punitive clause with respect to the enforceability of a total forfeiture clause.[136] The only model form withering interest clause is found in the AIPN JOA, which, unlike the OGUK JOA forfeiture provision, applies to the full value of the defaulting party's interests.[137]

Although, generally speaking, adopting withering interest forfeiture clauses as opposed to an outright forfeiture clause decreases the risk of the default provision being perceived as a punitive clause, the formulae used to apply can be very complicated and have generally proved unpopular.[138] The fundamental problem remains the same, where the withering provision is enforceable only if the interest which is transferred is at least of equal value to the liability of the defaulting party.[139]

8.3.4. *Buy-Out Provisions*

Another alternative to outright forfeiture clauses are buy-out provisions. Via this mechanism the JOA allows for the non-defaulting parties to buy out the

---

134 *Ibid.*

135 See J.D. Weidman, 'Oil and Gas, Operator's Liens in Bankruptcy. The Model Form Operating Agreement Versus the Trustee in Bankruptcy's Avoiding Powers' (1984) 37 Oklahoma Law Review 141.

136 J. Waite and D. Dawnorn, 'Contractual Forfeiture of Joint Venture Interests: are such clauses enforceable' (1990) 11 *Oil and Gas Law Taxation Review* 389.

137 AIPN JOA, clause 8.4.G; Roberts, *supra* n. 26, p 232.

138 Abul Failat and Jensen, *supra* n. 118, p. 6.

139 LXL LLP, *supra* n.8, p. 24.

defaulting party's interest, which may be exercised on an internal basis amongst the co-venturers or externally by third parties. In the event of disagreement over the actual buy-out price, expert determination can be instigated. In the AIPN JOA, the buy-out provision, which is set out as an alternative to forfeiture, provides that:

> '[A]ny non-defaulting Party shall have the option, exercisable in its discretion at any time, to require that the Defaulting Party offer to seek and assign all of its Participating Interest to any non-defaulting Parties wishing to purchase such Participating Interest.'

Similar to other models,[140] the buy-out price under the AIPN JOA is calculated by determining the fair market value of the defaulting party's entire interest less:

(i) the total amount in default;
(ii) all costs, including the costs of the expert, to obtain such valuation; and
(iii) an agreed percentage of the fair market value of the defaulting party's interest ('Discount').[141]

The buy-out option provision is arguably the most 'reasonable' of all the default options as it ensures fair reimbursement to the defaulting party for its past contributions during the life of the venture, whilst applying a discount factor serves to minimise the risk that a party may use the buy-out option as a mean of forcing the other partners to buy out at a fair market value. To discourage the misuse of the buy-out option parties will often want to apply significant discount factors – usually at least 25%. However, applying a high discount factor may itself consist of a punitive element, which is similar to outright forfeiture clauses.[142] This concern is further reiterated in the AIPN JOA guidance, which also warns that the discount proposed should be carefully examined to avoid objections on grounds of unconscionability.[143]

9. DECOMMISSIONING

As a hydrocarbon field matures and as continuous production results in the depletion of the relevant deposit or as certain infrastructure is longer used, decommissioning considerations become more relevant to the parties. This has become a global concern, particularly in declining fields such as the North Sea.

140 For instance AMPLA JOA, clause 16.2.
141 AIPN JOA, clause 8.4.F.2.
142 Abul Failat and Jensen, *supra* n. 118, p. 8.
143 AIPN, 'Guidance Notes to AIPN 2012 Model Joint Operating Agreement', 2012, p. 5.

Often, the governing law sets out the framework for decommissioning and thus outlines the decommissioning provisions of a JOA with respect to collateral support and decommissioning obligations. Although regulatory regimes around the world have different ways of treating decommissioning, one common feature is the calculation of the anticipated decommissioning costs to be provided for in cash on an ongoing basis or bringing forward the 'trigger date' where decommissioning is provided for only when the value/costs reach a certain ratio. In either case, this raises potentially significant issues in an industry facing financial pressure. In jurisdictions that do not require cash/collateral to be provided on an ongoing basis, there is often a 'last man standing' statutory regime, which allows recourse to parties that have had a historic interest in a project in addition to those parties with interests at the time of decommissioning.

Thus, it is understandable that when drafting a JOA it is necessary to tailor it in a manner that adheres to the applicable law and local practice. For instance, the AAPL JOA provides straightforward decommissioning formulae which provide that the operator shall conduct decommissioning (i.e. abandonment and removal of any equipment) as required by a governmental authority, and the costs risks and net proceeds of such decommissioning will be shared by the co-venturers in accordance to their percentage interest.[144] This reflects the words of Styles who describes decommissioning costs as a 'contractual primary several pro rata liability, undergirded by a potential statutory secondary joint liability.'[145]

The parties' main concern for decommissioning liabilities will be to ensure that they only bear a cost share equivalent to their percentage interests. The increasing popularity of host governments requiring parties to contribute in advance to a decommissioning fund is making decommissioning an important issue for co-venturers and should be considered from the outset of any upstream project.[146] To protect the parties, JOAs stipulate and permit several types of security to be given as collateral support, including cash deposits, parent company guarantees and letters of credit by accredited banks.[147]

Under most model form JOAs, the operator is responsible for preparing the decommissioning plan and its performance, as well as the necessary work programmes and budgets and AFEs for the decommissioning and abandonment works, all of which must be approved and authorised by the OpCom. It is worth mentioning that the allocation of decommissioning liabilities is applied in the same manner to both joint operations and exclusive operations; the AIPN JOA for instance reads:

---

144 AAPL JOA, clause 18.4.
145 Styles, *supra* n. 2, pp. 405–409.
146 Etteh, *supra* n. 48.
147 *Ibid.*

> 'This Article 10 shall apply *mutatis mutandis* to the Decommissioning of facilities and/or equipment acquired for an Exclusive Operation and abandonment of an Exclusive Well or any well in which an Exclusive Operation has been conducted (in which event all Parties having the right to conduct further operations in such well shall be notified and have the opportunity to conduct Exclusive Operations in the well under this Article 10).'[148]

Roberts notes: 'it is not inconceivable that a particular JOA might require a bespoke collateral support package to be put in place as a condition or as a consequence of the undertaking of an exclusive operation, but this degree of good housekeeping is rarely encountered in practice.'[149]

The collateralisation of the JOA with respect to defaults in decommissioning liabilities is key to protecting the parties. The rationale is that the prescribed remedies in the default provisions are inadequate at the decommissioning stage due to the fact that there is no production to look forward to and therefore the parties may not feel the pressure to remedy the default and they may well be happy to have their interest (and consequentially their liabilities) forfeited to the non-defaulting parties.

The AIPN JOA provides more than one option to deal with this, namely:

(i) either setting up a decommissioning fund which parties contribute to on a pro rata basis in proportion to their percentage interest; or
(ii) committing to a decommissioning security agreement for the costs of ceasing operations.[150]

With respect to the latter, a decommissioning security agreement is usually negotiated during the preparation of the decommissioning development plan.[151] The OGUK JOA follows the same concept and decommissioning provisions therein have been drafted on the assumption that the parties will also enter into the UK Model 2009 Decommissioning Security Agreement (DSA) which is set out as a schedule to the JOA. The DSA provides that a trust fund shall be established to pay for decommissioning when the trigger date is reached. In this way, where a default with respect to decommissioning liabilities arises, the non-defaulting parties will be able to realise the security in respect of that party.

In any case, the DSA is a separate contract and its purpose is to supplement the decommissioning provisions in the JOA. Therefore, any amendments to the DSA or the JOA should trigger consequential amendments in the other in order to ensure consistency and that the interaction between the two agreements is satisfactory.

---

148 AIPN JOA, clause 10.3.
149 Roberts, *supra* n. 26, p. 200.
150 AIPN JOA, clause 10.
151 AIPN JOA, clause 10.3.

10. LIFTING AND DISPOSAL OF PETROLEUM

Under all JOAs, each party has a right to take ownership of and dispose of a percentage interest share of the petroleum produced from a field. The JOA determines how petroleum won from a field, whether as joint operations or exclusive operations, is allocated between the entitled parties. The JOA would also stipulate a right and an obligation to 'lift' petroleum. A failure to lift will result in consequences provided for in the JOA.[152] No party is entitled to store their petroleum in the reservoir and any such petroleum stored (or not lifted) will be deemed to form part of the reserves that are available for future lifting by all parties. The lifting arrangements will vary depending on whether it is oil or gas that is being lifted, and in either case such lifting will be regulated in more detail through a separate lifting agreement.

11. BOILERPLATE CLAUSES

11.1. ASSIGNMENT CLAUSES AND PRE-EMPTION RIGHTS

A co-venturer's interests under a JOA and the licence are in essence an asset, which may be transferred to a third party. Such transfer, however, will be governed by the JOA conferring such interest, and the JOA will regulate which transfers are permissible and which transfers require consent. Ultimately, however, governmental approval is likely to be required for any indirect or direct change in the licensee/contractors. Most model JOA forms would qualify such consent by obliging the non-transferring parties to be reasonable or by stating that 'consent not to be unreasonably withheld'. There is a general understanding of what this wording means and this was addressed under English law, where it was provided that in the absence of a more detailed provision such wording means that consent can only be refused if the assignee is not sufficiently financially or technically competent to replace the assignor.[153]

Pre-emption clauses, generally speaking, give non-selling co-venturers the option to purchase the sale assets of a proposed sale before they are sold to a third party. Such clauses are seldom uniform and each must be analysed carefully on its own merits on a case-by-case basis. However, they take three forms, each of which will be bespoke in a specific model form JOA and are best explained in the context of an acquisition relating to upstream assets and interests that would be governed by the JOA:

---

[152] Golvala, *supra* n. 125, p. 53.

[153] *Ibid.*, p. 51.

(i) *a true right of pre-emption:* the seller is obliged to offer the non-transferring parties the sale interest on the same terms and conditions agreed with a third party buyer;
(ii) *a right of first refusal*: the seller offers the JV partners the sale interests before agreeing terms with a third party buyer (the seller usually cannot then sell the interests to a third party on lesser terms than those offered to a JOA co-venturer); and
(iii) *a right to negotiate*: the JOA co-venturers can negotiate with the seller to reach an agreement to purchase the interests for a specified period of time, after which the seller can freely assign the interests to a third party buyer even at a lower price than any offered by a JV partner.

Pre-emption rights are rarely ever triggered by a proposed transfer of the assets to an affiliate of the seller, i.e. in the context of an intragroup transfer. An affiliate would be a defined term in the JOA and most JOAs have a similar approach, for instance 'a legal entity that controls or is controlled by an entity that controls a party.' The main concern of a pre-emption right is for the potential buyer, as this third party might expend a lot of time and effort in completing the deal and might not get in the end.

11.2. GOVERNING LAW

All JOAs contain a governing law clause, which stipulates the body of substantive law that governs it.[154] Such governing law dictates how the provisions of the JOA are to be interpreted, as well as both the procedures and the legal concepts that apply when a dispute arises. Although one might generally assume that the JOA would be governed by the law of the place in which the upstream project takes place, New York law, French law and English law are often the parties' choice when negotiating a JOA relating to a project that is located in an emerging market – particularly if the state-owned company is a mandatory partner to the concession (and consequentially the JOA). This is because legal regimes such as the English one have undergone years and years of legal development with respect to oil and gas upstream operations and offer JV partners the assurance that their JV agreement will be construed in accordance with its own terms and that it cannot be declared void on technical grounds because no codified structure exists.

---

154 For example AIPN JOA, clause 16; OGUK JOA, clause 25.1.

11.3. TAXES

Amongst the key advantages of the JOA (as an unincorporated contractual association) is the preferential tax system that the parties enjoy by virtue of being independent with regard to liabilities and financial contributions. This is because a JOA is an unincorporated contractual association and, in contrast with incorporated contractual associations, parties to the JOA will be liable to pay corporate income tax on any profits arising from their share of the produced petroleum. Deductions can be made against losses/expenses accumulated from the production of petroleum.[155]

11.4. FORCE MAJEURE

Force majeure is not a term of art in English law.[156] The definition in the JOA will depend on the extent of relief that the parties agree to procure through a force majeure provision. Roberts notes that often JOAs apply the definition of force majeure in accordance with the definition provided in the Petroleum Agreement (when it contains one) and emphasises that the main element of such a definition is to encompass matters that would actually be outside the control of the parties or the operator.[157] Considering that force majeure clauses do not protect parties against fiscal risks such as default, it is primarily intended to relieve the operator from any liability for a failure to perform as required in circumstances where such failure arose from a matter outside the operator's control.[158]

11.5. DISPUTE RESOLUTION

JOAs invariably contain a dispute resolution clause providing for how disputes are address and how they should be dealt with to ensure the effective operation of the JV.[159] Commonly, parties choose a final and binding arbitration procedure to resolve any disputes that may arise during the course of operations even though some might prefer local courts. This is often supplemented by pre-arbitration measures, including mediation or negotiation, that the parties must

---

155 For example AIPN JOA, clause 14; OGUK JOA, clause 22.3; AMPLA JOA, clauses 22 and 23.
156 *Hackney Borough Council v Dore* [1922] 1 KB 431.
157 Roberts, *supra* n. 26, p. 266.
158 Roberts, *supra* n. 1, p. 256.
159 For example AIPN JOA, clause 18; OGUK JOA, clause 29; AMPLA JOA, clause 19.

explore before resorting to arbitration. Moreover, JOAs often provide that certain disputes (e.g. regarding the assessment of whether a buy-out provision is proportionate) shall be resolved by expert determination. As with any other agreements, if the parties opt for arbitration, they will also choose the rules and the seat of the arbitration.

12. CONCLUSION

A JOA is fairly a complex agreement, and whilst the model form JOAs have many similarities they do collectively offer a bundle of provisions that have developed over many years of practice and could vary in content from one region to another. A model form JOA might not be used entirely in its published form but does nevertheless offer a truly comprehensive and industry-based starting point which oil and gas companies can learn from and adopt when negotiating and drafting a JOA for an upstream project. This approach is crucial to protect the parties, who are subject to the unique characteristics of a project, including the range of parties participating, the host government mineral laws, the geology, the available technology and the risks associated with the relevant concession and the local laws.

Therefore, using a standard JOA might save a lot of time and costs during the negotiation period, but it should not simply replace the negotiation and considerations of how to adapt the JOA to the particular case at hand. Although it might be possible to use any standard form for any region, this is unlikely to occur as it would take far more time and effort to make sure the relevant provisions are applicable to that jurisdiction. However, in some jurisdictions the standard forms cannot be modified without governmental approval (e.eg. in Norway) as they might be issued or approved by the relevant host government. In this case, the negotiation of the JOA is minimal or close to non-existent as the consortium should follow the local laws and regulations.

MODIFYING THE STANDARD JOA TO ACCOMMODATE UNCONVENTIONAL PETROLEUM PROJECTS

Peter Roberts

This chapter examines how a conventional JOA will need to be modified to reflect the nuances of an unconventional petroleum project. A JOA that is to be applied to the management of such a project will require modification in a number of ways. In 2014 a JOA specifically tailored to unconventional petroleum operations was issued by the AIPN.

'Unconventional' petroleum is any petroleum deposit which is developed through anything other than conventional means (that is, essentially, vertical and horizontal drilling). This includes any of shale oil and shale gas (where oil or gas is fixed within relatively fissile shale rock strata, requiring hydraulic fractionation (or fracking) for its liberation), coal bed methane (also called coal seam gas, which is methane adsorbed onto the surface of coal deposits), tight gas (gas which is trapped within rock formations of such low permeability that fracking is essential) and hydrates (gas trapped within ice-like crystalline water structures).

The focus of this chapter is principally on the structuring of a JOA for the development of onshore shale deposits, although many of the points made here will be of general application to any unconventional petroleum deposit (and particularly one where fracking is a necessity).

1. UNDERSTANDING THE OPERATIONAL PREMISE

An unconventional petroleum project will differ from its conventional project cousin in a number of ways.

A conventional petroleum development project is commonly represented by the drilling of a single exploration well (typically drilled vertically, albeit with the possibility of lateral (horizontal) deviations) that (if successful) is then appraised and is worked over to become a development lead, and then a production well. Once petroleum production is underway inherent capillary pressure within the target petroleum reservoir will lead to the free flow of petroleum from the wellbore, and petroleum flow rates from that well will ordinarily be characterised by a steady ramp-up and a smooth plateau production profile, before an eventual decline phase and the permanent cessation of production.

The wider petroleum production project within which the development well sits might be the subject of a phased programme of the tie-back of satellite development wells, in order to maximise petroleum production. Production could be shut-in for certain periods of time and later restored according to the commercial and/or operational needs of the parties.

In contrast, an unconventional petroleum development project has a number of different operational aspects to note.

1.1. PETROLEUM LIBERATION

Because of the nature of the fissile material within which the unconventional petroleum deposits are located, those deposits ordinarily have insufficient matrix permeability to allow the free migration of the captive petroleum into an incoming wellbore. The production of unconventional petroleum in commercial quantities requires significant manual manipulation in order to deliver the necessary permeability. That manipulation takes the form of the fracking of the fissile material within a target stratum, and the injection of considerable volumes of water (under high pressure) and certain chemicals and proppants in order to liberate the captive petroleum.

1.2. THE DRILLING PROGRAMME

A key component of an unconventional petroleum development project will be the drilling of significant numbers of vertical wells within relatively condensed surface areas, and also the drilling of lengthy horizontal wellbores in order to access the captive petroleum within a particular stratum. Conventional drilling is targeted to exploit reservoir high points near mature source rocks, whereas unconventional drilling needs to exploit much wider, basin-focused depocentres. Horizontal drilling maximises the ratio of borehole-to-shale surface area contact and allows greater quantities of unconventional petroleum to be exploited. The selection of drilling sites and the management of the drilling programme will be essential to the project's success.

1.3. ENVIRONMENTAL IMPACTS

An inevitable and very obvious consequence of the manner in which unconventional petroleum is liberated onshore is the recovery of significant volumes of dirty waste water (flowback) from the original water injection process, which is typically stored in artificially made surface ponds to await restorative treatment. Not all of the injected water will be so recovered however. A proportion will remain in-ground, where it has at least the capacity to contaminate latent groundwater aquifers. Unconventional petroleum operations have become controversial principally because of this perceived risk of contamination (although the probability is that poor well design and construction could have a greater role to play than any inherent problem with the unconventional petroleum deposit, which is a more controllable risk). Environmental issues are exacerbated where unconventional petroleum operations are proximate to population centres.

1.4. PETROLEUM PRODUCTION PROFILES

In comparison with a conventional petroleum project development, an unconventional petroleum project typically offers much more uncertainty as to how it will perform over time. Recovery rates are lower and depletion rates are faster than is the case for conventional petroleum deposits. Petroleum flow rates will be variable, as individual wellbores deplete and new wellbores are drilled, appraised and brought on-stream, and will present a relatively up-and-down production profile across an entire programme, compared to the relatively steady production profile that typifies a conventional project. Drilling unconventional petroleum deposits is an ongoing process throughout the lifetime of the project. Neither can petroleum production be readily shut-in (for example, during times when market prices are depressed), because of the relatively greater difficulty of restoring production from multiple low pressure wells.

1.5. PROJECT COST PROFILES

For any unconventional petroleum project more wells will need to be drilled than is the case for a conventional project. Individual wells will be less rewarding because a well will typically liberate petroleum only from its proximate fractures, compared to a conventional wellbore where the wellbore will allow migratory petroleum flow from across a reservoir. This can lead to greater proportionate levels of project expenditure.

1.6. THE OVERALL PROJECT PROFILE

The most significant difference between an unconventional and a conventional petroleum production project is the overall project profile, which is represented by a combination of factors. In an unconventional project exploration activities could be ongoing (such that exploration costs increase), and petroleum production levels could drop off (such that project revenues diminish) throughout the lifetime of the project. At times expense will outweigh income. The accounting procedure that is appended to the JOA will need to account for simultaneous revenue inflows and outflows. The overall project development plan will be in continuous evolution within a cycle of exploration, appraisal, development, production and decommissioning. The emergence of new technologies could also intervene to redirect the manner in which the project is operated. In essence, the development profile of an unconventional project is constantly changing.

1.7. CONCESSION TERMS

Under the terms of a conventional petroleum project concession there will be a relatively short initial exploration phase and then (if a commercial discovery is made) a relatively lengthy production period. For an unconventional petroleum project the concession might be modified to reflect the reality that there will frequently be an overlap between the activities of exploration and production, and the exploration and approval activity will be iterative over the lifetime of the project. Extended concession terms could be critical. What constitutes a commercial discovery will also necessarily differ by definition between the conventional and the unconventional worlds, because of the quite different profile for incurring expenditure and realising income that an unconventional petroleum project development cycle presents.

The concession will define a concession area to which it applies and in which the concession holder will possess the rights to exploit petroleum. This concession area will typically be bounded by areal coordinates, but could also define a certain stratigraphic depth. The discovery of petroleum (whether conventional or unconventional) at different stratigraphic depths within the same areal coordinates could lead to discussions regarding the feasibility of sharing of joint property and joint development opportunities (see below).

The development of unconventional petroleum deposits under a single concession could indicate the presence of such deposits at different horizontal levels. The concession is likely to be awarded in respect of particular areal and stratigraphic coordinates. In the alternative to allowing separated operations in different horizons the concession might be subdivided between different horizons (with separate JOAs to govern the horizon splits accordingly).

2. THE DEFINITION OF PETROLEUM

The very definition of petroleum, for the purposes of the JOA and the concession, will require some different thinking in the context of an unconventional petroleum project development.

In a conventional context the term petroleum will reference crude oil, natural gas or associated liquids, but in an unconventional JOA a different world becomes apparent. Petroleum could be defined by reference to the nature of the resource to which the concession relates (whether shale gas or shale oil, coal bed methane or tight gas), although the concession might not be so specific in its ambit. The form of licence that is granted in the United Kingdom for onshore exploration and production, for example, applies the same definition of petroleum as is applied to offshore projects and does not seek to differentiate the nature of the particular commodity.

Alternatively, the JOA could define petroleum not by reference to the nature of the commodity to be produced but simply by reference simply to the very manner of its exploitation. Thus, in some unconventional JOAs petroleum is defined simply as petroleum that cannot be recovered from a wellbore by conventional methods of petroleum recovery, or that cannot be recovered without interventions such as fracking.

It is likely therefore that the concession will relate generically to the exploitation of petroleum (according to its widest definition) within the defined concession area and not specifically to any particular form of unconventional petroleum. This will be of particular relevance to issues connected with sharing joint property and joint development opportunities (see below).

3. THE ROLE OF THE OPERATOR

The experience and the ability of the person appointed to act as the operator under the JOA in managing an unconventional petroleum development project will be critical.

The operator must of course be skilled in managing vertical and horizontal drilling programmes, in undertaking fracking with minimal associated impact, and in managing the project's overall environmental performance.

The quality of the drilling programme that the operator undertakes, together with the manner of the manipulation of the unconventional petroleum deposit, will be key to the production of such petroleum and the mitigation of costs in order to sustain a commercially viable project that is sufficient to deliver the required returns to the parties.

Where a horizontal drilling programme requires deep level drilling through land owned by third parties, the scope of the JOA should extend also to the operator's right (and obligation) to negotiate way leaves with third-party landowners, so as to avoid later claims for deep trespass. This will be a particular issue where unconventional petroleum exploration and production takes place within land areas of relatively dense occupancy.

In further definition of the operator's customary obligation to act prudently, because of the essential differences that exist between developing conventional and unconventional petroleum projects, a reference in the JOA to a test for good and prudent oil and gas field practice (or similar) that draws from analogous projects in the same jurisdiction will have little real meaning where that jurisdiction is witnessing the undertaking of unconventional projects work for the first time. Thus, such a test should draw instead from analogues from other, unrelated, jurisdictions (such as the United States) where there is a much greater track record of developing unconventional petroleum projects.

The issue of fiduciary duties owed by the operator to the non-operating parties in the JOA will also require some careful consideration. The operator of a particular concession could be the operator of a number of adjacent concessions and could have its own views as the best method of developing those concession areas as part of a much wider estate of interests. The operator's preference here could be at odds however with the views of the non-operating parties in respect of a particular concession who are not also the owners of that wider estate.

This issue could also be related to the possibility of a wider joint development (see below).

Given the criticality of the role of the operator to the success of the joint venture, the JOA might also seek to lock in the operator for a defined period of time and the operator's resignation rights will be curtailed.

4. DEFINING JOINT PROPERTY

In an unconventional petroleum project the key property interest of the parties will be the ownership of, or at least a right of access to, the surface area land interests from which the drilling and fracking operations will be conducted and upon which the storage of the flowback will take place. These land interests could be held severally between each of the parties (according to their respective participating interests in the project) but this fractional entitlement, with its multiple and distinct sets of interests, could be particularly difficult to effect in the context of land ownership.

It could be preferable therefore to vest the unconventional petroleum project's land interests in a joint venture company, within which each of the project participants would hold shares. Such a structure would simplify the arrangements for future transfers by the parties of their interests in the project and its joint property, and would also allow the addition of further land interests by acquisition. This is particularly the case where land interests are unregistered, which leads to greater complexity in transferring title interests.

Any way leaves that are required for deep drilling through third-party lands could also be applied for and owned by that joint venture company.

5. SCOPE

Conventional JOAs confine the scope of the joint venture to petroleum exploration and production, and the joint development of processing and transportation infrastructure is typically declared to be excluded from the JOA's scope. In an unconventional petroleum project however, because of the essential need to develop petroleum through processing and transportation infrastructure, then such an activity might specifically be included within the JOA's scope.

Where petroleum deposits (of whatever nature) exist at different stratigraphic depths with the boundary of a single set of areal coordinates then it could be attractive for joint property that exists in relation to a JOA (such as gas processing and gas gathering and gas transportation facilities at the surface) to be used collaboratively for the exploitation of other petroleum deposits within other concession areas, in order to generate further revenue for the parties to the JOA.

6. ONGOING PROJECT DEVELOPMENT

Because of the variable economic and operational profiles of an unconventional petroleum project (see above) the operator could require a significant degree of flexibility in order to respond to changing circumstances as the project unfolds. Because of the ongoing process nature of unconventional petroleum project development, multi-year work programmes and budgets are more likely to be the norm. The operator could also require the right to adjust the agreed overall project development plan (and individual work programmes), and also the associated budgets, without the need for formal approval by the non-operating parties through the OpCom (if indeed the JOA is one that applies the concept of an OpCom).

The technologies needed to explore for unconventional petroleum are relatively untried and a realistic assessment of a deposit's economic and technical viability will result only from extensive programmes of targeted exploration drilling, fracking and stimulation and then production testing. The JOA will need to reserve to the operator the corresponding latitude to explore, give up and explore again in search of a viable depocentre, and to repeat that cycle as often as may be necessary.

Thus, in an unconventional petroleum JOA the operator could have discretion to adjust the operational parameters of the project and to overspend against budget in respect of a particular period of time, beyond the levels of flexibility customarily encountered in conventional JOAs. This could make the non-operating parties nervous however, and so some limits might, nevertheless, be applied to such greater discretion.

7. EXCLUSIVE OPERATIONS

It is arguable that, because of the variable economic and productive profile of an unconventional petroleum project (see above), a non-consent right should simply not exist within the JOA. A party should be fully committed to the agreed joint operation that the agreed overall project development plan represents and should not have the right to absent itself from any part of that operation, through the exercise of a non-consent right, just because that party has taken a dim view of the overall profile of the project at a particular point in time. A similar philosophy applies to condition the right of a party to withdraw from a project (see below).

It is also arguable that a sole risk right is inappropriate in the context of an unconventional petroleum project development, because of the need for very careful management of the resource base in order to maximise the recovery of petroleum from a deposit that typically presents a very narrow range of realisable opportunity. Vertical and horizontal drilling programmes must be exercised with great care, in order to allow for the most effective exploitation of the target stratum. Allowing a party to undertake sole risk activities could be to the detriment of the wider interests of the project.

Thus, the essential elements of an exclusive operation in a conventional petroleum project, relative to the clear separation of exclusive activities and resultant petroleum production, could simply be unattainable in an unconventional project, and an unconventional petroleum JOA could simply do away with the exclusive operations provision (in whatever form it takes).

8. WITHDRAWAL

In a conventional petroleum production project the ability to simply walk away from any continued involvement that the withdrawal right represents could be applied, for example, as soon as after the minimum work obligations required by the terms of the concession have been performed and a sequence of first exploration, appraisal and well-testing fails to offer the requisite levels of encouragement for the prospects of a commercial development.

In an unconventional petroleum project however the withdrawal right might be further conditioned in its potential application. Because of the variable economic profile of an unconventional petroleum project (see above) and the need for the parties to stay the course, the JOA could declare that the right of a party to withdraw from the project is declared inapplicable for a defined period of time from the inception of the project, so as to allow the project to be fully developed between the parties according to a certain development timetable.

Alternatively, in order to ensure that the envisaged project is fully funded, the JOA could provide that the right of a party to withdraw requires the withdrawing party to commit to funding a certain share of future project development costs as a condition of that withdrawal.

9. OPTIONS FOR PETROLEUM COMMERCIALISATION

Under a conventional petroleum project JOA, the parties typically have a right and an obligation to take delivery of their respective participating interest shares of the resultant petroleum at the point of its production. In furtherance of this, the parties usually make their own individual arrangements to sell their particular interests in the produced petroleum, and also to transport that petroleum away from the point of production (through pipeline access, for example).

In an unconventional project development these premises could need to be modified however.

The obligation of a project participant to take delivery of its share of overall petroleum production could be disapplied, as part of the wider disapplication of the commitment to several sales and transportation arrangements, in favour of a single joint sales and transportation arrangement that is entered into by all of the project participants (subject to any applicable competition law constraints on joint selling or joint commercialisation). This is attributable, at least in part, to the possibility that well sites for an unconventional petroleum project could be located in a relatively remote area, far from consumption markets, and so petroleum transportation infrastructure and petroleum sales arrangements have to be entered into collectively.

10. ENVIRONMENTAL AND HSE ISSUES, AND OPERATOR LIABILITIES

Any JOA will be careful to define the regime for the management of the HSE issues that are associated with the project to which the JOA relates. The development of an onshore unconventional petroleum project has the scope for a more obvious and immediate impact on the local environment than is the case for the development of an offshore unconventional petroleum project, where out of sight means out of mind for most people. Managing the environmental impact of a large-scale onshore development project, or at least the perception of the impact, can be challenging. There could be significant social objections to the introduction of such a project from affected local communities.

Local concerns relating to the perceived adverse environmental impact associated with unconventional petroleum project developments are manifested initially in response to the threatened activity of exploring for petroleum, and yet paradoxically it is the production phase (with the attendant fracking) that has the greater potential for an adverse environmental impact – and a poor exploration result could indeed eliminate any prospects of production.

Even a relatively small environmental event could lead to very visible and very public consequences, and to significant reputational damage for the project participants. Thus, for an unconventional petroleum project the JOA might say something different about how HSE matters are to be addressed.

In an unconventional petroleum project all of the parties could be involved in the initial development, and also in the ongoing implementation, of the HSE plan. Ultimately, this could even result in the right of a non-operating party to intervene in the conduct of the project in order to arrest a perceived environmental risk. This right of intervention is not something that the operator would typically be comfortable with.

11. OPERATOR LIABILITY

A further related issue involves the operator's liability to the non-operating parties for loss or liability caused by the operator's acts or omissions in the performance of the joint operations.

Applying the customary parameters of the limitation of the operator's liability to an unconventional petroleum project, where there has been a significant environmental event that exposes all of the JOA parties to a claim made by a regulatory agency (or to claims made by affected third parties) the non-operating parties could be unable to pass that liability through to the party that was principally responsible for the offending event (that is, the operator). Thus, in an unconventional petroleum JOA the operator could be required to assume a much greater level of liability to the non-operating parties for any environmental loss or liability that has occurred as a consequence of the performance of the project.

In response to this, apart from reciting the customary operator antipathy towards any prospect of liability, the operator could argue that if it has afforded much greater rights of involvement to the non-operating parties in the development and implementation of the HSE plan (see above) then the operator should not then be made singularly responsible amongst all of the parties for any environmental loss or liability. In this respect, says the operator, the non-operating parties cannot have the best of both worlds.

Where, in an onshore unconventional petroleum project, there is deep drilling through adjacent third-party lands (see above) the operator could expose the parties to the JOA to a claim for damages for deep trespass, if the operator has not negotiated an appropriate way leave with the third-party landowner. This, the non-operating parties might argue, is an area where the operator should assume a direct, or at least a greater level of, liability for its acts and omissions.

12. UNITISATION AND JOINT DEVELOPMENT OPPORTUNITIES

The supervening mineral law or the terms of the concession could reserve a right for a state agency or for the grantor of the concession to implement a scheme of unitisation in respect of the concession area and other adjacent concession areas where there is a suggestion of contiguous petroleum deposits (assuming that the petroleum is of the same character and composition). Alternatively, the parties to the concession might come to a view themselves that some form of joint project development across a cross-concession area is a practical necessity in the interests of maximising petroleum recovery.

The process of unitisation (particularly with reference to the manner of estimation of petroleum volumes initially in place and the determination of tract participations) will necessarily be quite different for unconventional projects, and the JOA should reflect that.

The relative paucity of petroleum recovery from a single concession area could also be the inspiration for a wider collaborative joint venture, without recourse to a programme of unitisation. The JOA could also therefore recognise the possibility that there could be non-unitised joint development areas, as a means of maximising the overall recovery of petroleum from the overall resource area. The possibilities of a joint development might also be trailed within some form of area of mutual interest agreement.

A joint development programme, with shared use of joint property (see above), could be of particular relevance where petroleum deposits (of whatever nature – see above) exist at different stratigraphic depths with the boundary of a single set of areal coordinates. This is not an absolute proposition however, since the drilling of a conventional well and also a well to be used for the liberation of unconventional petroleum within the footprint of single set of areal coordinates would require separate wellbores, given the very different natures of the ensuing methods of petroleum production.

13. DECOMMISSIONING

The principle of decommissioning, reflecting that at the end of the productive life of a petroleum deposit the production wells should be permanently plugged and abandoned and that any necessary production and transportation infrastructure should be safely and effectively removed, is effectively the same between conventional and unconventional projects, but in an unconventional petroleum project there are a number of operational differences to note.

Because of the production profile of an unconventional petroleum production project (see above) it could be required that individual wells be plugged and abandoned during the lifetime of the project and whilst production is ongoing from other wells. Thus, there is not a distinct decommissioning phase such as occurs at the end of the lifetime of the deposit.

The costs of decommissioning will also therefore need to be funded during the lifetime of the project, which has an immediate cash-flow impact but which also reduces the size of the decommissioning costs at the end of the project's life. This in turn should moderate the need to provide security for unfunded decommissioning costs. Onshore decommissioning works are also obviously much easier to inspect than offshore works, which removes a certain measure of costs contingency and reduces the required levels of the associated security.

PART II

SETTING UP A JOA

Oil and gas resources will almost always be owned by the host government(s) of the country(ies) where these natural resources are located.[1] If a company has an interest in searching for and producing oil and gas, it is necessary for them to obtain permission from the relevant host government.[2] Petroleum licences, production sharing agreements (PSAs), service agreements or combinations of these all exist as established ways to grant this authorisation, and without them the contracting party has no possibility of conducting exploration and production operations.[3]

Oil and gas projects are likely to be technically challenging and capital intensive. There is a long lead-time from initial investment until revenues can be collected. Quite often petroleum activities are carried out in harsh and hostile natural environments and remote areas. As a natural consequence, this increases the challenges of finding and agreeing on adequate technical solutions, cost planning and financing, and risk management.

Although it is possible to negotiate and sign a host government contract with a single entity, this is unlikely to happen. The inherent risks in the petroleum industry encourage oil and gas companies to share risks and rewards through joint ventures. This forms the background for the JOA (i.e. unincorporated joint venture), which is basically an instrument to regulate the relationship between JV parties.

Part II of this book is divided into two subsections. The first subsection covers general clauses in the JOA, such as the scope, insurance, transfer of

---

1 Most jurisdictions provide that natural resources located in the subsoil belong to the government and it could be only explored if authorised by the respective government. However, there are exceptions to this rule such as United States (US) jurisdiction. See B.G. Taverne, *Petroluem, Industry and Governments: A Study of the Involvement of Industry and Government with the Production and use of Petroleum*, 2nd edn, Kluwer Law International, Alphen aan den Rijn 2008, p. 380.

2 'The JOA does not operate in isolation: It has to be viewed on the background of the production licence (PL), to which it is made a formal condition. And further: The PL is based on the Petroleum Act, and has to be viewed in this context.' J. Knut Kaasen, 'Scope of Joint Operating Agreements in Norway', Petroleum Law Seminar, St. Raphael, 2000, p. 8.

3 For the purposes of this research, a licence or PSA or service agreement might be referred individually but they always refer to the petroleum title signed between the private party and the host government.

interest, governing law and dispute resolution, exclusive operations, and HSE. The second subsection addresses the control of operations and expenses.

Why two subsections, rather than grouping all of these chapters into only one category? To answer this question it is necessary to understand the basic background of most JOAs.

An operator acts on behalf of each party to the consortium when directing joint operations. This typical relationship formed by the JOA allows one party to conduct and manage the operation of said consortium, but understandably causes non-operators to see this as a primary concern as they will not conduct these operations and all JOA parties will be affected by each operation and desire to control operations.

Consequently, irrespective of the level of involvement of each non-operator, from pro-active to dormant, they will be eager to oversee the joint operations to confirm whether the joint operations are being executed diligently, efficiently and in the best interests of the JV.[4]

Control of operations therefore exists to allow the non-operators to have a viable input into the performance of a joint operation and control the power of the operator. It can be the only option available for non-operators to influence and participate the conduct of the operations. This concern of control arises from the fact that the operator commonly has the final and sometimes sole say in the conduct of joint operations. The non-operator may have only very limited opportunities to participate and influence in the joint operation.[5]

Therefore, control of operations is equally a basic duty for the operator and a fundamental right for the non-operators as the operator shall conduct the operations on the behalf of all parties.

Control of operations refers not only to the pace and quality of the work performed by the operator, but also to the costs of the joint operations. This is because at the heart of the consortium is the stipulation that the parties shall share risks and costs related to the joint operations. In this context, it is clear why

---

4 This principle is clearly consolidated in the oil and gas industry. See: B. Taverne, *An Introduction to the Regulation of the Petroleum Industry: Law, Contracts and Conventions*, Graham & Trotman, London 1994, p. 136; B.G. Taverne, *Co-Operative Agreements in the Extractive Petroleum Industry*, Kluwer Law International, Hague 1996, pp. 66-68; S. Shaw, 'Joint Operating Agreements', in M.R. David, *Upstream Oil and Gas Agreements*, Sweet and Maxwell, London 1996, p. 16; S. Styles, 'Joint Operating Agreements', in J. Paterson and G. Gordon (eds.), *Oil and Gas Law: Current Practice and Emerging Trends*, Dundee University Presss, Dundee 2007, pp. 278-279; P. Roberts, *Joint Operating Agreements: A Practical Guide*, Globe Law Business, London 2010, pp. 82-86.

5 'It is not always the case that the Operator has the largest interest. The Operator of the Ninian field development in the East Shetland basin of the United Kingdom Continental Shelf, for example, has a smaller Interest than a number of the other Participants.' K.C. Mildwaters, *Joint Operating Agreements. A Consideration of Legal Aspects Relevant to Joint Operating Agreements used in Great Britain and Australia by Participants thereto to Regulate the Joint Undertaking of Exploration for Petroleum in Offshore Areas with Particular Reference to their Rights and Duties*, PhD Thesis, University of Dundee, 1990, p. 427.

this is one of the most critical issues for the JOA, as the final aspiration of any party is to maximise their 'profits'.

This control is necessary because all those involved in the consortium will have a financial input and contribute to the expenditure of a particular operation according to the Participating Interest.[6] Taking into account the numerous different factors that can affect the operations, the non-operator, as a party that will not conduct joint operations, needs to have the ability and awareness to exert control over any decision concerning the destination of capital spent in the joint operations.[7] This clearly affects all non-operators, both proactive and dormant, as even those that are solely investing will certainly seek to secure their investments by approving expenditures and subsequently controlling the overall expenditure system.[8]

The operator, however, will seek the discretion to determine the expenditure of the joint operations as early as possible, without any further delay from formal procedures and/or gaining consent from the non-operators. Thus, this can be a critical, although usual, area of tension between the operator and non-operators.[9]

It is important to remember that although the structure of the JOA is based on the operator, who has taken on this responsibility, handling the joint operations, during that time the operator is obliged to maintain the 'good standing' of the JOA, i.e. it has to obey the arrangements established in the petroleum legal regime, in addition to any other applicable regulations and procedures established in the JOA.[10] In this sense, the exercise of excessive control by non-operators might affect the good standing of the operations.

In summary, there are several procedures in place to manage the operations and expenditures in a JOA.[11] The following topics shall be analysed under this section as they serve to allow the parties to control the pace, risks and costs of the consortium: (i) the US experience on handling the expenditures of the consortium; (ii) useful mechanisms to protect payments; (iii) the different type of conduct of operations; (iv) relevant issues from the accounting procedures; (v) operator liabilities; and (vi) different ways for the non-operators to be involved in a project.

---

6 C. Thorpe, *Fundamentals of Upstream Petroleum Agreements*, C.P. Thorpe, UK 2008, p. 126.

7 Styles, *supra* n. 4, p. 288.

8 T. Daintith, G. Willoughby and A. Hill (eds.), *United Kingdom Oil & Gas Law*, 3rd edn, Sweet & Maxwell, London 2009, pp. 1143-1150.

9 Roberts, *supra* n. 4, p. 105.

10 B.G. Taverne, *Co-Operative Agreements, supra* n. 4, pp. 66-67; J. Wilkinson, *Introduction to Oil & Gas Joint Ventures: Volume I, United Kingdom Continental Shelf*, OPL, Ledbury 1997, pp. 49-40.

11 C. Gonvala, 'Upstream joint ventures – bidding and operating agreements', in G. Picton-Tubervill (ed.), *Oil and Gas: A practical handbook*, Globe Law and Business, London 2009, p. 47.

PART II.A

GENERAL CONSIDERATIONS

THE SCOPE OF THE JOA

Harry W. SULLIVAN, Jr.

1. INTRODUCTION

As we know, the JOA is a contract that is needed whenever there is more than one owner of oil and gas rights under the same granting instrument in the same block or area. Absent a JOA, the co-owners of such oil and gas rights would need to rely on the provisions of local law, if any, applicable to co-ownership to determine each co-owner's individual right to explore for or exploit oil and gas rights within the commonly owned block and the other co-owner's obligation, if any, to contribute to costs related to such activities concurrently as they are incurred. Depending on the jurisdiction, exploration and exploitation of oil and gas may be blocked except where all co-owners agree to conduct the activities. Alternatively, the local law may allow individual co-owners to act on their own to conduct exploration and exploitation activities, but at their sole cost and risk without any obligation on the other co-owners to contribute concurrently to such costs. The JOA supplements and clarifies the provisions of law addressing co-ownership, and establishes the respective rights and obligations of the co-owners to conduct exploration and exploitation of oil and gas under the granting instrument.

The JOA does not and cannot amend or modify the granting instrument. All of the rights and obligations of the co-owners under the granting instrument vis-à-vis the government/national oil company/agency counterparty continue unaffected by the addition of the JOA. The government/national oil company/

agency counterparty in its/their capacity as the counterparty to the granting instrument is not a signatory to nor bound by the provisions of the JOA, although a national oil company in a separate capacity, namely as a co-owner of oil and gas rights under the granting instrument in the same block or area, may be a signatory to and separately bound by the provisions of the JOA.

Nonetheless the scope and purpose of the JOA intersects with the granting instrument in two important respects: (1) the JOA is the contractual platform that enables the co-owner group to collectively exercise its rights and perform its obligations under the granting instrument; and (2) the JOA allocates obligations and liabilities among the co-owners in accordance with their participating interest in the ownership of the granting instrument or on another contractually agreed basis, as opposed to the joint and several liability that is customarily imposed on co-owners under granting instruments.

2. STRUCTURE TO COLLECTIVELY EXERCISE RIGHTS AND FULFIL COMMON OBLIGATIONS

When more than one owner acquires oil and gas rights under the same granting instrument in the same block or area there is a need for the owners to establish a structure to enable them to collectively exercise the rights and perform the obligations under the granting instrument. An incorporated entity can be established for this purpose, which is common in connection with oil and gas activities in Russia and some parts of Eastern Europe. The advantage of an incorporated entity is the legal structure and governance provided by applicable law. However, this legal structure and governance may also present a challenge and a disadvantage depending on the requirements of applicable law. For example, local law may provide no or minimum minority interest protections. Additional disadvantages of an incorporated entity include likely additional taxes on the separately incorporated entity and on the distributions and dividends from the incorporated entity, and difficulty in providing for marketing of oil and gas by individual co-owners instead of by the incorporated entity. For these and other reasons, the upstream oil and gas industry tends to strongly prefer an unincorporated structure to enable them to collectively perform the obligations under the granting instrument. The JOA is in reality a species of unincorporated joint venture, notwithstanding language often included in the JOA similar to the following:

> 'It is not the intention of the Parties to create, nor shall this Agreement be deemed or construed to create, a mining or other partnership, joint venture or association or (except as explicitly provided in this Agreement) a trust.'[1]

---

1 See Association of International Petroleum Negotiators (AIPN) Model Form Operating Agreement 2012, Article 14.1. See also similar language in the Association of Professional Landmen Model – AAPL Model Form 610 – 1989 Model Form Operating Agreement, Article VII. A.

Why the disclaimer of joint venture status? The main concern lies in the fact that joint ventures in most legal systems entail some level of fiduciary duty and fidelity among the co-owners of oil and gas rights who are, in reality, competitors outside of the common granting instrument and co-owned block or area. As such each co-owner typically acts in its own best interest, rather than in the best interest of the venture or of the other co-owners in the venture. The desire to negate any fiduciary duty or fidelity obligations underlies the joint venture declaimer and leads to a view that the co-owners are co-venturers, as opposed to joint venturers, within the common granting instrument covered by the JOA, but otherwise are competitors.

The AAPL Model Form 610-1989 summarises this in the following provision:

> 'In their relations with each other under this agreement, the parties shall not be considered fiduciaries or to have established a confidential relationship but rather shall be free to act on an arm's-length basis in accordance with their own respective self-interest, subject, however, to the obligation of the parties to act in good faith in their dealings with each other with respect to activities hereunder.'[2]

Structural considerations, while integral to the scope of the JOA, are generally not included in the scope or purpose clause of the JOA, but rather are detailed in the provisions of the JOA dealing with taxation and the relationship of the parties.[3]

3. PHILOSOPHY OF AIPN JOA: A GUIDE TO THE SCOPE

The co-chairs of the drafting committee for the AIPN Model Form Operating Agreement 2012 often stated that the philosophy of the AIPN JOAs[4] has always been based on four points:

- each party should do what it has promised or committed to do;
- each party should be able to do what it wants to do;
- no party should have to do what it has not promised or committed to do or does not want to do; and
- no party that does what it has promised or committed to do should be harmed if it does not want to participate in other activities.

2 Article VII. A.
3 See Article 14 of the AIPN Model Form Operating Agreement 2012.
4 AIPN has produced Model Form Operating Agreements in 1990, 1995, 2002 and 2012.

Each of these points is founded on the belief that joint operations by all of the co-owners to comply with the obligations of the granting instrument must be the paramount concern of the JOA and strongly encouraged.

The first point recognises that the granting instrument contains certain collective obligations[5] binding on all co-owners under the granting instrument. All co-owners have promised and committed in the granting instrument to perform these obligations, generally on a joint and several liability basis. Consequently it is critical that the JOA ensure that each co-owner fulfils its participating interest share of such common obligations. This is done through the encouragement of 'Joint Operations', which is defined in the AIPN Model Form Operating Agreement 2012 as meaning 'the operations and activities within the scope of this Agreement (or whose purpose at the time undertaken was within the scope of this Agreement) conducted by Operator on behalf of all Parties, including Exploration Operations, Appraisal Operations, Development Operations, Production Operations, and operations and activities for the purposes of Decommissioning'. The JOA contains a voting procedure whereby the consent of a designated percentage of ownership will compel all co-owners to comply with these common obligations.

The second point recognises that beyond the common obligations provided for in the granting instrument, the JOA should be flexible enough to enable each co-owner to perform other activities or operations that it wants to perform under the granting instrument in the common block or area, even where one or more co-owners do not want to conduct the other activities or operations. These operations are often referred to as 'sole risk' operations, undertaken by one or more co-owners at their separate cost and risk.[6] The JOA contains a voting procedure whereby a co-owner may propose operations or activities that have not been approved by the designated percentage of ownership required to approve an operation or activity.

The third point is a corollary to the second point, in that the JOA should be flexible enough to not require a co-owner to participate in activities or operations that it does not want to participate in and which are not a part of the collective obligations under the granting instrument. The second and third points are the basis for the JOA permitting sole risk operations or what the AIPN Model Form Operating Agreement 2012 refers to as 'Exclusive Operations', namely operations and activities carried out under the JOA and the granting instrument in the common block or area, the costs of which are chargeable to the account of fewer than all of the co-owners.

---

5 The AIPN Model Form Operating Agreement 2012 defines such collective obligations as the Minimum Work Obligations.

6 See Article 15 of the JOA developed by Oil and Gas UK (OGUK), a representative body for the UK offshore oil and gas industry, for use in offshore operations on the UK continental shelf.

The fourth point flows from the second and third points, in that any co-owner that decides not to participate in an exclusive operation, to be conducted by one or more of the other co-owners, will not be responsible for any of the costs, risks or liabilities associated with such exclusive operations. There are consequences to a decision not to participate in an operation or activity undertaken as an exclusive operation in the form of a limited right and premium to later participate in a successful operation or activity, but absent an election to later participate in the successful operation or activity the consequences do not include the non-participating co-owner having any responsibility for the costs, risks or liabilities of such exclusive operations.

The AIPN JOA includes in the scope clause a provision related to the first point, discussed below, but provisions regarding exclusive operations are included in later articles.[7]

4. PARTICIPATING INTERESTS, OWNERSHIP, OBLIGATIONS AND LIABILITIES

In its scope clause, the AIPN Model Form Operating Agreement 2012 includes a list of the participating interests of the co-owners in the rights, duties and obligations under the JOA. The extent of a co-owner's participating interest is not really crucial to the scope of the JOA and could be included in other JOA provisions.[8]

Two items that are crucial to the scope of the JOA are the key principles that: (1) each co-owner is entitled to its participating interest share of all rights and interests, and any hydrocarbons produced under the granting instrument from the common block or area; and (2) each co-owner is responsible for its participating interest share of all costs and liabilities incurred under the granting instrument from the common block or area. These two principles are set forth in Articles 3.3.A and 3.3.B of the AIPN Model Form Operating Agreement 2012 as follows:

> 3.3.A 'Unless otherwise provided in this Agreement, all the rights and interests in and under the Contract, all Joint Property, and any Hydrocarbons produced from the Contract Area shall, subject to the terms of the Contract, be owned by the Parties in proportion to their respective Participating Interests.'

> 3.3.B 'Unless otherwise provided in this Agreement, the obligations of the Parties under the Contract and all costs and liabilities incurred by Operator (or by

---

7 See Articles 5 and 7 of the AIPN Model Form Operating Agreement 2012.

8 For example the OGUK includes the participating interest in a separate article, namely Article 4. The AAPL Model Form 610-1989 includes the interest of the parties in a separate article, Article III. A. and Exhibit A.

> any Party on behalf of all Parties, as set out in this Agreement) in connection with Joint Operations shall be charged to the Joint Account and all credits to the Joint Account shall be shared by the Parties, in proportion to their respective Participating Interests.'

These principles lead to the obligation and commitment undertaken by all co-owners in Article 3.3.C of the AIPN Model Form Operating Agreement 2012, namely that each 'Party shall pay when due, in accordance with the Accounting Procedure, its Participating Interest share of Joint Account charges, including Cash Calls and interest, accrued under this Agreement'. This commitment by each co-owner is integral to the smooth operation of the JOA and has the effect, at least as among the co-owners, of converting the co-owners' joint and several liability in the granting instrument to proportionate individual liability.

In one recent JOA negotiation, a co-owner required that there be a cross-indemnity to backstop the commitment in Article 3.3.C of the AIPN Model Form Operating Agreement. At first blush, an indemnity seems superfluous; however, the AIPN Model Form Operating Agreement 2012 provides specific indemnities to the operator in connection with its limitation of liability,[9] to non-consenting parties in connection with exclusive operations,[10] taking over of facilities and wells and withdrawal,[11] tax,[12] and in connection with compliance with anti-bribery laws and obligations.[13] The scope of the JOA is to ensure that each co-owner bears its share of costs and liabilities for common obligations under the granting instrument. Consequently a cross-indemnity can be within the ambit of this part of the scope of the JOA.

The implementation of the two principles is found throughout the remaining provisions of the JOA.

5. GOVERNMENT PARTICIPATION

Under many granting instruments, the government or the national oil company has a right to acquire a direct participation in the rights and obligations under the granting instrument at some specified time or times during the term of the granting instrument, generally at the time a discovery is determined to be commercially exploitable. If the government or national oil company exercises its right to acquire a direct participation, there are two issues that bear on the

9 See Article 4.6.
10 See Article 7.3.
11 See Article 10.
12 See Article 14.
13 See Article 20.1.

scope of the JOA: (1) which co-owners are obligated to contribute to the direct participation to be acquired by the government or national oil company; and (2) whether the government or national oil company as a direct participant in the rights and obligations under the granting instrument will join in a novation of the existing JOA among the co-owners or enter into a separate and distinct JOA.

The AIPN Model Form Operating Agreement 2012 handles both of these issues as an optional provision in the scope clause.[14]

As to contributions for the direct participation interest to be acquired by the government or national oil company, the AIPN Model Form Operating Agreement 2012 provides that each co-owner will contribute proportionately to the interest to be acquired and all payments received for the transfer of such interest shall be shared among the existing co-owners in proportion to their participating interests. While this can be changed by contract, the optional provision is consistent with the stated principle that all co-owners are responsible for their participating interest share of all common obligations.

Having the government or national oil company as a party to the JOA is a proposition that companies can differ on; consequently the AIPN Model Form Operating Agreement 2012 provides two alternatives: (1) the government or national oil company will become a party to a novation of the existing JOA; or (2) a separate JOA will be entered into with the government or national oil company. Both alternatives recognise the need for the government or national oil company, as a co-owner under the granting instrument in the same block or area, to be a party to a JOA, albeit maybe a second or separate JOA. Having a separate JOA for the government or national oil company is not an optimum solution and can lead to misapplied terms if the two JOAs are not fully compatible. However, sometimes this may be necessary because the government or national oil company will not accept some of the terms previously agreed upon or required by the co-owners. The better practice is to have all co-owners as parties to the same JOA.

In 2012, AIPN considered including provisions regarding payment by the government or national oil company as additional alternative provisions in Article 3.4 of the Model Form Operating Agreement 2012. These provisions are typically included in the granting instrument or petroleum law creating the right to acquire a direct participation interest. It was felt that such provisions are not within the scope of the JOA, and were not included in AIPN's Model Form, although some of the same wording was included in the Guidance Notes to the 2012 JOA.

---

14 See Article 3.4.

6. COOPERATIVE ACTIVITIES AND OPERATIONS; EXCLUDED ACTIVITIES AND OPERATIONS

Each of the main model form JOAs has a laundry list of activities or operations that is intended to fall within the scope or ambit of the JOA and a list of activities excluded from the scope of the JOA. For example, the AIPN Model Form Operating Agreement 2012 provides that the scope includes: 'the joint exploration, appraisal, development, production of Hydrocarbons (including treatment, storage, and handling of produced Hydrocarbons upstream of the Delivery Point), the determination of Entitlements at the Delivery Point, and Decommissioning'. The AAPL Model Form 810 Deepwater Model Form Operating Agreement includes the following within the scope: 'the exploration, appraisal, development, operation, production, treatment, gathering, and storage of Hydrocarbons'. The OGUK JOA's scope extends to: 'the exploration for, and the appraisal, development and production of Petroleum' under the granting instrument; 'the treatment, storage and transportation of Petroleum using Joint Property'; 'the decommissioning or other disposal of Joint Property'; and 'the conditions for the carrying out of Sole Risk Projects in the License Area'.

Each of these permitted activities or operations reflect the operational lifecycle stages of the oil and gas industry. The main difference in the permitted activities and operations in these different JOAs relates to the extent to which each extends beyond the point where oil and gas is produced or extracted from the ground. The AIPN JOA draws a bright line at the Delivery Point as the farthest point downstream of production or extraction that the co-owners agree under the JOA to cooperate. Further cooperation may occur, but not under the JOA. The OGUK JOA extends the cooperation of the JOA a bit to the extent that there is Joint Property beyond the Delivery Point. Nonetheless, in all of the cited JOAs each co-owner has, under a separate provision, a right and obligation to take in kind and separately dispose of its own participating interest share of production. In none of the cited JOAs does cooperation extend to joint marketing of production. In fact, both the AIPN JOA and the OGUK JOA expressly exclude joint marketing or joint sales of hydrocarbons. This is both for anti-trust/anti-competition reasons and to negate any joint profit motive that might lead to additional taxation of the JOA similar to an incorporated entity.

The AIPN JOA specifically excludes the following from its scope: construction, operation, ownership, maintenance, repair, and removal of facilities downstream from the delivery point; transportation of the parties' entitlements downstream from the delivery point; marketing and sales of hydrocarbons, except where expressly authorised (sole risk, failure or refusal to lift creating an operation issue, and default); acquisition of rights to explore for, appraise, develop or produce hydrocarbons outside of the common block or area (other than through unitisation); and exploration, appraisal development, or production of minerals other than hydrocarbons, whether inside or outside of the common block or area. The OGUK JOA specifically excludes the following from the scope of the JOA: any joint financing arrangements; joint marketing or joint sales of petroleum; the consideration of any commercial terms in connection with the treatment, storage and transportation of petroleum under the licence using third-party infrastructure; and consideration of any commercial terms in connection with the use of joint property by third parties.

The main concern with including a specific list of excluded activities is to ensure that the technical parameters of what the co-owners are obligated, or want, to do under the granting instrument are recognised and empowered. For example, if the granting instrument requires the co-owners to transport natural gas to shore, this should be within the scope of the JOA. Similarly if the granting instrument requires the co-owners to develop a gas-fired power station to consume natural gas produced under the granting instrument, this needs to be added to the scope of the JOA. Often in the early stages of exploration, the co-owners may not fully appreciate the ultimate scope requirements of the JOA. This is especially true concerning transportation options for oil and gas, which may evolve during the preparation of a development plan.

7. CONCLUSION

The main scope issue in a JOA is to establish the respective rights and obligations of multiple co-owners of oil and gas rights under a granting instrument in a common Block or area in such a manner as to enable the co-owners to exercise their rights and fulfil their common obligations under the granting instrument. Scope should include the entire lifecycle of an oil and gas project, including exploration, appraisal, development, production and decommissioning. Joint marketing is typically excluded from the scope of the JOA for anti-trust/anti-competition and tax reasons. While the scope of the JOA can be amended by the unanimous approval of all co-owners, if they agree, it is better to anticipate the technical needs for cooperation under the JOA and establish a workable scope from the beginning of the JOA.

ADDRESSING HEALTH, SAFETY AND ENVIRONMENT MATTERS

Katie WINTERBOURNE

1. OVERVIEW

A catastrophic safety or environment incident can cripple both the reputation and financial capacity of a participant in the petroleum industry quicker and more absolutely than almost any other risk. All participants in a petroleum field, whether operators of a facility or non-operating titleholders, can suffer loss and incur liability following such an incident and must manage this risk. Managing the risk associated with a health, safety and environment (HSE) incident involves balancing the severity of the consequences of an incident with the likelihood of occurrence and the costs of implementing preventative measures. Understanding the regulatory regime in the jurisdiction of operations to assess the scope and extent of liability for an HSE incident is key to managing HSE risk. It is also important to understand the role of the relevant regulator and the regulator's powers to enforce strict regulatory compliance even before a severe HSE incident occurs.

The complexity of managing HSE risk increases with the number of parties involved in activities within a field, as operator or owner of a facility, contractors and non-operating participants. Where exploration or production activities occur under a JOA, the consequences of a severe HSE incident for each participant highlights the inherent tension between operators and non-operators and the tension between accepted principles of risk allocation under a JOA and general principles of risk allocation under which the party best able to manage or control a risk bears that risk.

Yet participants have only recently begun to give detailed consideration to HSE matters in JOAs, which is also reflected in recent model form JOAs. For example, the Association of International Petroleum Negotiators first incorporated a specific HSE provision in its 2002 Model Form International Operating Agreement to reflect industry practices. The HSE provisions have continued into the AIPN 2012 Model Form JOA (AIPN JOA).[1] The AIPN JOA, as the most commonly used model agreement internationally for offshore production, provides a good starting point for analysing the HSE provisions under a JOA.

With a focus on the AIPN JOA, this chapter considers the development of standards in and regulation of the petroleum industry to: minimise the risk of HSE incidents occurring; respond to HSE incidents that do occur; and bear responsibility for the impacts of those incidents. The chapter identifies some additional matters that participants negotiating amendments to model form JOAs should consider and discusses the tension between an operator and non-operators in the context of addressing HSE risks.

This chapter concludes that that all participants negotiating a JOA should understand the HSE regulation applicable to the petroleum field and associated operations, the powers of the regulators to enforce strict compliance with regulations, trends in HSE standards and best practice, and the implications for each participant. The participants should then develop a regime under the JOA to comply with regulation, minimise the risk of HSE incidents occurring and, in the event a HSE incident or regulatory non-compliance occurs, clarify how each participant should respond, both financially and otherwise.

---

1 Other model form JOAs also include HSE provisions, including those issued by the American Association of Professional Landmen, the Canadian Association of Petroleum Landmen, Oil and Gas UK Limited (for use on the UK Continental Shelf) and the Australian Mining and Petroleum Law Association (used primarily onshore).

2. DRIVERS BEHIND A RECENT FOCUS ON HSE IN THE JOA

Recent industry focus on HSE risk management reflects regulatory developments and changing industry practices to respond to catastrophic safety and environmental incidents that have occurred at offshore facilities causing widespread loss and damage, including loss of life. Over the last 25 years three major HSE incidents at petroleum facilities have driven and continue to drive change within the offshore petroleum industry. These are, of course, not the only major HSE incidents to have occurred either at facilities or more broadly within the petroleum industry, but have each driven significant regulatory change and industry reflection.

2.1. PIPER ALPHA INCIDENT

In 1988, a series of explosions on the Piper Alpha production platform in the North Sea claimed the lives of 165 people on the facility. The subsequent public inquiry and report by Lord Cullen (Cullen Report) made two important recommendations, which have fundamentally changed safety regulation, and, more recently, environmental regulation of the petroleum industry.[2] One of the key recommendations of the Cullen Report was the adoption of the safety case, requiring the operator of a facility to formally document how safety is to be managed within the facility. In the safety case, the operator must demonstrate that the major hazards and risks have been identified and reduced to 'as low as reasonably practicable' (ALARP), appropriate management controls have been put in place to prevent incidents occurring, and that there is adequate provision for safe evacuation and rescue in the event of an emergency. A closely associated recommendation of the Cullen Report was the shift from prescriptive to objective-based regulation.

Although prescriptive regulation remains to some extent in most jurisdictions in which the petroleum industry operates, HSE regulation has shifted towards requiring operators to demonstrate how they will achieve specified HSE objectives or outcomes. Objective-based regulation of the petroleum industry has extended beyond safety matters to address environmental risks too. Most jurisdictions will require operators to produce a safety case. Many jurisdictions will also require operators or titleholders to produce an

---

[2] The Hon. Lord Cullen, *The Public Enquiry into the Piper Alpha Disaster, Report to Parliament by the Secretary of State for Energy by Command of Her Majesty*, Volumes 1 and 2, United Kingdom, November 1990.

environment plan to demonstrate how they will manage environmental risks to the ALARP standard. Other management plans, such as a well operations management plan addressing risks associated with well integrity, may also be required.[3]

The theory behind objective-based regulation is that the operator, and more broadly the industry, is better placed to identify sources of risk and determine what processes and actions are required during operations or other activities to achieve a specified regulatory objective. With a focus on outcomes, industry can employ innovation and flexibility to continually improve standards to reduce risk. However, a key challenge is that objective-based regulation lacks certainty, which can lead to significant resourcing costs and administrative burden for industry. Further, the regulator is still expected to hold sufficient skills and experience to provide guidance to industry on what it considers is required to achieve best practice management of risk. Regulatory oversight and enforcement action is also still required to ensure that operators meet acceptable minimum standards.

2.2. DEEPWATER HORIZON INCIDENT

Regulatory standards were again scrutinised following the explosion and sinking of the Deepwater Horizon oil drilling rig, located in the Macondo field of the Gulf of Mexico, in 2010. Eleven lives were lost, and extensive ongoing damage to the environment occurred. The report of the United States National Commission on the Deepwater Horizon Oil Spill and Offshore Drilling (Deepwater Horizon Report)[4] found that the causes of the incident included systemic failures in relation to risk management, placing in doubt the safety culture of the industry, and the role of the regulator. The Deepwater Horizon Report recommended a shift in United States regulatory policy from a prescriptive model to a less prescriptive 'safety case' approach.

Besides regulatory change, the Deepwater Horizon incident also highlighted for petroleum industry participants other potentially significant consequences of a serious HSE incident, which must also be considered at the beginning of a venture, during JOA negotiations. First, the incident highlighted and continues to highlight that the costs and liability of an HSE incident can be exorbitant, far-reaching and ongoing. The operator and others involved in the incident

---

3 For example, despite the close links between well integrity and safety and environmental risks, in Australia, a well operations management plan is required as well as a safety case and an environment plan under the Offshore Petroleum and Greehouse Gas Storage Act 2006 (Cth) and associated regulations.

4 *National Commission of the Deepwater Horizon Oil Spill and Offshore Drilling's Final Report*, United States of America, January 2011.

continued to incur costs associated with clean-up, settlement compensation claims for property damage and economic loss, and various litigation and penalties under the United States Clean Water Act,[5] not to mention significant reputational damage, long after the incident occurred. The potential costs and how to make provision for such costs must be considered at the beginning of a venture.

Second, the litigation claims among the various parties involved in the Deepwater Horizon drilling and the Macondo field emphasise the importance of understanding the contractual allocation of risk and responsibility from the start. For all participants in a field, it is important to understand the extent to which non-operators will be liable under a JOA for costs that may have arisen through the gross negligence or recklessness of the operator, and, indeed, what those terms mean under the JOA and the laws governing the JOA.

2.3. MONTARA INCIDENT

Particularly in the context of Australian offshore regulatory developments, the explosion on the Montara wellhead platform in the Timor Sea in 2009, just one year before the Deepwater Horizon incident, also contributed to a renewed focus on environmental regulation. The Report of the Montara Commission of Inquiry[6] found that, generally, the regulator had sufficient powers to effectively monitor and enforce regulatory compliance at offshore petroleum operations. The safety case regime and some requirements for an environment plan to demonstrate management of environmental risks were already entrenched in the regulatory regime in Australia. The identified inadequacies related to the implementation of the regime by the regulator. As a result, a new regulator was created to regulate offshore petroleum safety and environmental matters. Despite this, an extensive overhaul of offshore environmental regulation followed and, six years after the incident occurred, the regulatory changes continue. Further, when a regulator is scrutinised in this manner, it often leads to a reticence to make decisions and grant approvals and a tendency to strictly enforce any remaining prescriptive regulation. Both regulatory change and changes in the enforcement approach of regulators leads to significant administrative burden and cost for participants, which should be acknowledged in the negotiated JOA.

---

5 Clean Water Act 33 U.S.C. §1251 et seq. (1972).

6 D. Borthwick, *Report of the Montara Commission for Inquiry*, Montara Commission of Inquiry, Commonwealth of Australia, June 2010.

2.4. IMPLICATIONS FOR JOINT OPERATING AGREEMENTS

It is still too soon for the consequences of recent changes to HSE regulation or the full ramifications of the Deepwater Horizon incident for all those bearing responsibility to be fully understood by industry, or those tasked with revising model form JOAs. Yet, in this context, parties continue to negotiate JOAs.

Model form JOAs, such as the AIPN JOA, were developed for broad application and must be adapted to meet specific circumstances of the regulatory jurisdiction, the operations and the participants. Model form JOAs cannot be expected to address the nuances of the HSE regulatory regime applicable to all operations or respond quickly to developments in specific areas of law. Particularly in an area where there are changing laws and standards, participants must specifically consider their risks, circumstances and objectives when negotiating a JOA. Participants must assess the local HSE regulatory regime applicable to the field and the laws of the relevant jurisdiction governing the JOA. Participants must also analyse trends in industry HSE standards to be able to predict regulatory developments that may occur throughout the life of the JOA.

The next section considers how the developing industry standards to reduce HSE risk are incorporated into the AIPN JOA and some additional considerations for participants negotiating a JOA.

3. MINIMISING THE RISK OF AN HSE INCIDENT OCCURRING

Following from the recommendations of the Cullen Report, the basic standard for HSE risk management in the petroleum industry is to identify major hazards and risks and put in place controls to reduce these risks to the ALARP standard. This analysis is documented in a plan, so that implementation of the controls can be monitored and the controls can be adjusted as new risks and more effective controls are identified.

Although a single incident will often have both safety and environmental impacts, the measures put in place to reduce the risk of safety or environmental consequences occurring will often be quite different. Further, the range of environmental risks and potential impacts is wider and less easily identified than the risks to the health and safety of individuals in proximity to a facility. Therefore, although the safety case and the environment risk management plan must always be consistent, they are usually separate plans, following separate risk identification processes and employing different technical expertise to establish controls to reduce those risks to the ALARP standard.

3.1. ESTABLISHING HSE PLANS

3.1.1. Requirements under the Model JOA

The AIPN JOA requires the operator to establish and implement an HSE Plan which complies with the concession or licence, laws relating to health, safety and the environment of the jurisdiction governing the concession or licence, generally accepted practices of the international petroleum industry, and decisions of the operating committee.[7] As well as to comply with relevant laws, the objectives of the HSE Plan are to achieve safe and reliable conduct of activities, to avoid significant and unintended impact on the safety and health of people, on property and on the environment. Consistent with a true objective-based obligation, the AIPN JOA does not outline how the operator should achieve the objectives of the HSE Plan.

However, the AIPN JOA also expressly directs the operator to enforce rules related to alcohol, controlled substances and weapons within the area of operations. It seems incongruous with the objective-based standard of the HSE Plan to include prescriptive rules on such matters. Presumably any HSE Plan complying with the requirements of the AIPN JOA would prescribe controls after identifying these as matters as safety hazards. Although on its face, it does no harm to prescribe specific prohibitions, it does create a risk that other HSE issues that are not similarly prescribed in the JOA are perceived to have less significance.

The AIPN JOA provides options for varying degrees of control and oversight by the operating committee in reviewing and approving the HSE Plan. The AIPN also provides for ongoing monitoring by the operating committee, which is discussed further below. At one end of the scale, the operating committee must review and approve the HSE Plan itself. The other option requires the operator to satisfy the operating committee of the effectiveness of the HSE Plan. Under this alternative, the operator must provide an HSE report and letter of assurance to the operating committee, which shows there is an HSE Plan in place that meets the objectives and requirements under the JOA. The operating committee's level of control is limited to determining the form of the letter of assurance and the HSE report. It is not clear whether the HSE Plan must be approved by the operating committee before it is submitted to a regulator, where this is required under local laws. It is also not clear what the consequences might be if the regulator requires amendments to an HSE Plan previously approved by the operating committee, or if the operating committee subsequently requires changes beyond any requirements of a regulator.

---

7 Article 6.6, AIPN JOA.

The AIPN JOA requires the operator to implement the HSE Plan. As would be expected, the operator must require its contractors, and others undertaking activities for the joint account to manage HSE risks in accordance with the HSE Plan. However, as with most other obligations of the operator under a standard JOA, it is unlikely that a non-operating participant will have any remedies available to it to enforce these requirements.

3.1.2. Additional Considerations in Negotiating a JOA

As appropriate for a model form agreement intended to apply internationally, the AIPN JOA requires the preparation of a single HSE Plan, albeit one that is annually reviewed and subject to change. To the extent that the relevant jurisdiction of operations has limited HSE requirements governing the concession or licence, the AIPN JOA ensures that the operator must, at minimum, prepare an HSE Plan to avoid significant and unintended impact on safety, health and the environment in compliance with international petroleum industry standards.

However, as identified above, the range of safety and environmental impacts and risks differ and should be addressed differently. Further, many jurisdictions will have more extensive requirements to prepare, have approved and implement approved HSE plans than those set out under the broad objectives of the AIPN JOA. Many jurisdictions will have obligations to prepare separate safety cases and environment plans, often with different requirements for exploration activities and different phases of operations. Jurisdictions may also require other related management plans to be produced, such as the well operations management plan in Australia. This creates uncertainty under the JOA and may lead to inconsistency between obligations at law and under the JOA. Although the parties can determine a process under the JOA for resolving conflicts between different obligations, ultimately the regulatory obligations will always prevail. To the extent that local laws require more onerous requirements, a better approach is to reflect, or at least acknowledge, the relevant regulatory process under the JOA in the first place.

The AIPN JOA requirement to prepare an HSE Plan is included within the article that covers work programmes and budgets. Parties negotiating a JOA should consider the likely administrative and compliance costs of meeting the HSE risk management requirements under the relevant laws and ensure that these costs will be adequately allocated under the JOA.

In circumstances where regulators must accept that adequate risk management plans are in place before activities can commence, the regulatory style of relevant regulators will have a significant bearing on timing and approval of plans.[8] The regulator's interpretation of regulatory requirements can have a

---

8 A good discussion about some of the initial difficulties faced by industry in having environment plans accepted by the newly created regulator in Australia following the

significant impact on the scope of work to produce the plans and the level of detail and number of revisions required before a plan is deemed to be acceptable.

Parties negotiating a JOA should also consider whether there are other HSE regulatory approvals that must be obtained before activities can commence. Although the AIPN JOA focuses on risk management plans, many jurisdictions will also require extensive environmental impact assessment of a proposal likely to have a significant impact on the environment before that proposal can proceed. Often these requirements can arise under environmental, rather than petroleum industry-focused, laws. A further complexity can arise in jurisdictions where different levels of government have powers to regulate environmental matters, as this may lead to an additional administrative burden or even potentially conflicting requirements.

The role of the non-operating parties in contributing to and reviewing the relevant HSE plans should also be considered. This will be relevant to the role of the operating committee in approving the HSE Plan, or other HSE risk management plans as may be described under the negotiated JOA. The general principle under a JOA is that the operator brings skill and expertise to the venture and is best placed to manage the risk management process and, where necessary, liaise with regulators to ensure that the regulatory HSE requirements are satisfied. Further, it is the operator that will be required to comply with the management plan during operations. The non-operating participants have a limited role in contributing to the preparation of management plans or liaising with regulators to obtain regulatory approvals. This may be appropriate where non-operating participants hold a minor interest in the field and, therefore, bear a comparatively small share of the costs and liability risk associated with the operations. However, these general principles should be re-assessed where the non-operating participants hold a greater proportion of the interest under the JOA and in the field, and as a consequence a higher proportion of the total costs and liability risk or where a non-operating participant holds relevant expertise, particularly in dealing with the local regulator in relation to other ventures.

3.2. REVIEW OF THE PLAN

In a similar manner to the process for approving an HSE Plan, the AIPN JOA provides options for varying degrees of control and oversight by the operating committee in reviewing and monitoring its effectiveness. Under the first option, the operating committee must, at least annually, review and approve the details

Montara incident is set out in J. Chandler and T. Daintith, 'Offshore Petroleum Regulation After Montara: The New Regulatory Style' (2015) 34 *Australian Resources and Energy Law Journal* 34.

of the HSE Plan, its implementation and its effectiveness. Alternatively, the operating committee must, once again at least annually, review and approve an HSE report and letter of assurance from the operator providing adequate evidence that: the HSE Plan fulfils the requirements of the JOA and is being properly implemented; that major HSE issues have been brought to the attention of the operating committee and are being properly managed; and that the HSE Plan is effective.

The AIPN JOA also provides options for an assessment or audit of the HSE Plan against its objectives. The first option requires the operator to undertake regular HSE assessments to review the practice and performance of the HSE systems and procedures to establish whether the HSE Plan is being properly implemented and achieving its objectives. The frequency of such assessments is not prescribed in the provision but must occur, at minimum, before any significant or new joint operation activity is undertaken. It is not clear how such assessments tie into the reporting obligations to the operating committee, who decides whether the HSE assessment has identified unsatisfactory practices and how any requisite changes are implemented. Non-operators have the right to participate in the assessment. However, they have no right to require change to practices or require further investigation. The second option requires the operator to establish an annual independent audit programme. A further optional provision permits non-operators, individually or jointly, to conduct their own audit of the HSE Plan at their own risk and cost. This is supported by the operator's duty to permit representatives of non-operators, upon reasonable advance notice, to conduct HSE audits.

Parties negotiating a JOA should consider what the consequences should be if the internal monitoring and reporting processes or the audit process indicates that either the HSE Plan or the manner in which is it is implemented could be improved. As drafted under the AIPN JOA, it is likely that non-operators would need to rely on the power of the operating committee to withhold approval to bring any pressure to bear on the operator to implement changes identified in a non-operator's or independent audit.

HSE regulations usually provide for inspections, audits and reviews of HSE risk management plans to be undertaken by a regulator. The consequences of failing to comply with the findings of a regulator following inspection can range from improvement orders and penalties, to directions to suspend operations until inadequate performance is rectified. Therefore, there are greater incentives for an operator and, indeed, non-operating participants to focus on effective implementation of and continuous improvement in risk management where there is regulatory oversight through a robust regulatory regime. In these circumstances, internal monitoring and auditing processes under the JOA should support the regulatory processes and the timing should be consistent to avoid unnecessary administrative costs.

4. RESPONDING TO AN HSE INCIDENT

4.1. RESPONSE PLANS

Although the AIPN JOA provides that the operator must implement the HSE Plan and there is some scope for the operating committee to monitor the effectiveness of the HSE Plan, there is no guidance on how the operator must respond if the HSE Plan does not achieve its objectives and an HSE incident occurs. The objects of the HSE Plan under the AIPN JOA focus on avoiding unintended HSE impacts.

In the case of an emergency, which would include any major HSE incident, the operator has a duty to take all necessary and proper measures for the protection of life, health, the environment and property and report to non-operators about the event and any measures the operator has taken or plans to take in response.[9] However, there is no requirement to prepare contingency or response plans under the AIPN JOA. Arguably these are an integral part of any best practice HSE Plan and an HSE incident response plan is required under most HSE regulation. The Cullen Report recommendations indicated that a component of a safety case included demonstrating that there was adequate provision for safe evacuation and rescue in the event of an emergency. In a similar manner, an environment risk management plan should demonstrate adequate provision to rapidly contain any discharge that could lead to an environmental impact. However, the requirement to prepare such response plans should be explicitly required under the JOA to give non-operators, who will likely bear liability as titleholders under the relevant jurisdiction's regulatory regime, comfort that the operator can adequately manage a serious HSE incident.

A well-documented incident response plan can also minimise the risk that the parties will incur unnecessary financial and resourcing costs in responding to an incident. In a similar manner as the HSE Plan should be regularly reviewed for its effectiveness, the incident response plan should be regularly reviewed and approved in accordance with industry best practice.

4.2. FINANCIAL PROVISION FOR RESPONSE TO AN INCIDENT

Under the AIPN JOA, the operator must effect and maintain certain insurances in respect of the joint operations.[10] The AIPN JOA is not prescriptive about the various insurances that the operator is required to procure and often parties to a JOA will outline insurance requirements in more detail, especially the

9 Article 4.2.B.14, AIPN JOA.
10 Article 4.7, AIPN JOA.

essential insurances. Essential insurances should include liability cover for the impacts of safety and environmental incidents. However, the extent of liability for environmental incidents and the associated level and scope of cover requires particular focus. Following a safety incident, the injured parties are relatively easily identified and liability risks are confined. By contrast, the third parties affected by an environmental incident who may seek to recover their loss from participants can be difficult to identify, depending on the sensitivity of the local environment, the area and permanence of impacts, and the extent of use of other affected resources. Particularly in the aftermath of the Deepwater Horizon incident, the parties to a JOA should carefully assess the scope of their environmental risks and determine whether all liability and costs are insurable and at what cost. JOA parties also need to assess how they will respond to any gaps they identify.

In some cases, the relevant regulatory regime may prescribe the essential insurance or other financial assurance that the operator is required to procure. In the United Kingdom, operators that are members of the Offshore Pollution Liability Agreement[11] (OPOL) accept strict liability for oil spills in the North Sea up to a capped amount. If any operator defaults on the payment of clean-up costs, the OPOL scheme will respond up to the capped amount. Operators must show evidence of financial responsibility for this amount either through insurance or other means. Membership of the OPOL scheme is voluntary. However, a condition of licences[12] either requires membership or requires an operator to otherwise have the same coverage. Although membership of the OPOL scheme does not prevent additional claims beyond the capped strict liability amount, JOAs will often limit financial assurance requirements to the OPOL limits.

In Australia, titleholders must maintain sufficient financial assurance to meet the costs, expenses and liabilities associated with carrying out petroleum activities.[13] This is likely to include the costs associated with responding to an incident, cleaning up and ongoing monitoring and may extend to costs of compensating third parties for loss or damage. The regulator cannot accept an environment plan until it is satisfied that the titleholders have sufficient financial assurance in place and, at other times, can require titleholders to provide evidence of their financial assurance. Titleholders can use a combination of forms of financial assurance and, although the duty is imposed on all titleholders, it can be satisfied by one or a combination of titleholders.

Although it may be possible to satisfy financial assurance obligations through insurance, titleholders will need to confirm that adequate coverage is obtained to meet the financial assurance duty. In many cases, there may be gaps that will

---

11 American Society of International Law, 'Offshore Pollution Liability Agreement 1974' (1974) 13 *International Legal Materials* 1403.

12 Granted under the Petroleum Act 1998 (UK).

13 Section 571, Offshore Petroleum and Greenhouse Gas Storage Act 2006 (Cth).

need to be filled through other forms of financial assurance. To ensure that all titleholders continue to meet their obligations, parties negotiating a JOA within Australian waters should consider addressing these obligations in the JOA. The parties should consider: outlining the process through which the operator should estimate the total costs, expenses and liabilities associated with carrying out the relevant petroleum activities; confirming which parties are responsible for procuring financial assurances and for what amount; and determining to what information each party needs access to be able to sign any declaration of financial assurance provided to the regulator.

Generally, as the full extent of costs and liability for the Deepwater Horizon incident become apparent, it is no longer sufficient for parties negotiating a JOA to rely on broad duties of the operator to obtain and maintain insurances. Participants should evaluate the potential risks of operations and ensure that they can meet the financial consequences of a severe HSE incident, acknowledging that liability is rarely capped for such an incident occurring at an offshore petroleum facility.

4.3. UNDERTAKING INTERNAL INVESTIGATIONS

The process to undertake internal investigations following an HSE incident is also invariably overlooked in the JOA. By contrast, an operator would generally require its contractors to co-operate in any investigation conducted by the operator. Parties to a JOA should consider whether non-operating participants should have a right to relevant information obtained during post-incident investigations to enable them to defend prosecutions against both the company, and where relevant, its officers and managers. This, of course, needs to be balanced against the right of the operator to conduct its own investigations without the risk that it could be compelled to provide non-operating participants with information that they could later use in claims against the operator.

The principles that would need to be considered in determining an appropriate process under the JOA for conducting internal investigations is, first, whether legal professional privilege (attorney–client privilege) will apply to the investigation documents and report and, then, whether that privilege is waived by providing the documents to non-operating participants. Although different tests will apply, in common law jurisdictions legal professional privilege will generally apply to documents created for the dominant purpose of seeking legal advice or in anticipation of litigation. This can include investigation documents. Although privilege would generally be lost by providing those documents to a third party, it may be maintained if the third party has a common interest in the receipt of the privileged documents, and the parties do not have conflicting interests.

5. RESPONSIBILITY FOR AN HSE INCIDENT

The operator is expected to bring skill and expertise to a venture, increasing the likelihood of maximising the benefits to all participants of resource production. However, the operator's key expectation is that it will not bear any liability to the non-operators or to any third party, beyond the operator's participation interest, as a result of it acting as operator. The general principle is that an operator should not make a profit or suffer a loss through acting as operator. However, non-operators are frequently concerned about the extent of liability they may incur through the JOA and, directly, under local laws applicable to the operations arising out of an operator's actions over which the non-operators had no control. The tension is greater where the non-operating participants have similar capacity, expertise and experience to conduct operations as the operator and where the participating interests of all participants are closely aligned.

5.1. ALLOCATION OF LIABILITY UNDER THE JOA

Under the JOA, the operator will undertake to comply with all applicable laws, including the requirements of the concession or conditions of the title, and to conduct all activities in a diligent, safe and efficient manner in accordance with good oilfield practices. The AIPN JOA states that the operator shall conduct joint operations in a 'diligent, safe and efficient manner in accordance with good and prudent petroleum industry practices generally followed by the international petroleum industry under similar circumstances'.[14] However, non-operating participants have limited recourse under the JOA if the operator fails to comply with its duties.

Often these duties are further defined in a JOA to confirm the standards of performance expected of the operator and the measures open to non-operating participants to require compliance on an ongoing basis. Such measures are generally limited to review, audit and approval powers of the operating committee. For certainty, any standards of performance prescribed under the JOA should be consistent with the standards required of the operator under the relevant local laws. The JOA should also consider whether the applicable local laws require different standards for different HSE matters and ensure that the operator is required to meet the highest of those standards.

Following the Deepwater Horizon incident, industry participants continue to debate the standards of performance to be expected of the operator and, in particular, the circumstances in which the operator might retain responsibility under the JOA for its acts or omissions contributing to an HSE incident.

---

[14] Article 4.2.B.2, AIPN JOA.

However, the general principle that titleholders should share liability according to their participating interests has not shifted under the AIPN JOA.

The AIPN JOA releases the operator from liability to non-operating participants resulting from the performance or failure to perform the duties and function of the operator and the participants indemnify the operator against any claims arising out of or incidental to the joint operations even though caused by the negligence, strict liability or other fault of the operator.[15] The AIPN JOA provides optional provisions to prescribe that the operator will remain liable for its gross negligence or wilful misconduct, which is defined in terms of a reckless disregard or wanton indifference to harmful consequences. However, many major operators are refusing to accept even this risk of liability during JOA negotiations, particularly in the wake of the Deepwater Horizon incident. Frequently, minor participants need to balance the advantage of an experienced operator against the risk of liability under the JOA arising out of HSE incidents regardless of cause. Even if the JOA does impose liability on the operator for a loss or liability caused by its gross negligence or wilful misconduct, the JOA may impose a cap on that liability, which is generally a cap on a per claim or annual basis with an aggregate cap over the term of the JOA.

Given the customary lack of responsibility under the JOA for an operator's breach and the limited remedies available to non-operators, the JOA could do more to prescribe the required standards of the operator's performance and to give a measure of control over the operator to the non-operating parties, which could be applied so as to limit the scope for a breach of contract by the operator. However, it is likely that the capacity to negotiate such changes to the standard position will only rest with those non-operators that have sufficient capacity and experience to meaningfully contribute to risk management and where the participating interests and, therefore, financial contributions are comparable.

5.2. SOURCES OF LIABILITY UNDER LOCAL LAWS

Significant increases in liability and uncertainty about allocation of responsibility for HSE incidents highlight the importance for all participants and contractors to understand where that liability may fall within the jurisdiction in which they operate, and whether that liability is or can be shifted by the JOA.

Identifying the sources of liability for HSE incidents under local law can be complex. Despite wide recognition of the value of a single international regime to deal with responsibility for pollution from offshore facilities, a lack of international political consensus requires continued reliance on regional conventions and state legislation to regulate pollution from the offshore

[15] Article 4.6, AIPN JOA.

petroleum industry.[16] Similarly, there is no uniform health and safety regime to consistently guide those operating in the offshore petroleum industry. Further, in many jurisdictions operating as a federation of states or provinces, there are layers of regulation commensurate with levels of government. Particularly in the context of environmental laws, regulatory offences and civil liability regimes can arise under petroleum industry-specific legislation and general legislation for the protection of the environment.

Further, although civil liability to third parties and costs of clean-up can be allocated under the JOA according to participants' interests, some sources of loss or liability cannot be shifted. Penalties imposed following the prosecution of offences will lie with the party or individual found guilty of the offence and, in these circumstances, indemnities are often unenforceable. The costs associated with reputational damage are also unrecoverable. The concern for the operator is that it will generally be the primary party prosecuted for an offence under HSE laws. However, it is also the party best able to manage HSE risks. The concern for non-operators is that, as a titleholder, often they too can be charged with an offence. However, unlike the operator, they may have little opportunity under the JOA to control risks. Further, a feature of many environmental laws is that directors, officers and managers of a party charged with an offence can often be charged with the same offence, and in some cases can be deemed to have committed the same offence. In some circumstances, a defence may be available to the non-operating party or its management personnel if they can establish that they had no control over the commission of the offence.

6. CONCLUSIONS

Given the significant costs, liabilities and reputational damage associated with a severe HSE incident, parties negotiating a JOA should closely evaluate the regulatory requirements under local laws, local circumstances and industry best practice to manage HSE risks at the outset. Participants should consider the enforcement approach of regulators and how this might affect the administrative burden of regulatory compliance. Both operators and non-operators should consider the processes and management structures to best demonstrate that risks are reduced to the ALARP standard, the venture is committed to ongoing review and improvement of management plans and response plans, and financial resources are in place. These processes should then be documented in the JOA.

---

16 S. Bosma, 'The Regulation of Marine Pollution Arising from Offshore Oil and Gas Facilities – An Evaluation of the Adequacy of Current Regulatory Regimes and the Responsibility of States to Implement a New Liability Regime' (2012) 26 *Australia and New Zealand Maritime Law Journal* 89.

In the context of recent HSE incidents within the petroleum industry and developing regulation and standards, it is no longer sufficient to rely on the bare approach provided in model form JOAs.

The inherent tension between the operator and non-operating participants under the accepted principles of risk allocation under a JOA is also highlighted in the context of HSE incidents. Non-operators should consider whether it is to their benefit to negotiate greater control and oversight of the operator in relation to HSE matters in the JOA. Those pursuing such options should only do so if they are confident of their capacity to meaningfully reduce risks. Otherwise, they could increase both their administrative burden and exposure to penalties if a serious HSE event occurs.

INSURANCE: WHAT SHOULD BE INSURED, WHO SHOULD BE LIABLE FOR IT AND TO WHAT EXTENT?

Birgitte JENSEN

1. INTRODUCTION

The JOA is the private agreement which 'splits' the joint and several liability imposed by the terms of the licence (as awarded by the relevant state) and regulates the relationship, obligations and rights between the joint venture (JV).[1] A JOA will cover many aspects of the partners' investment and is generally designed to last the lifetime of the investment through exploration to production and (in some examples) cessation of production. It addresses the

[1] B. Jensen and Y. Abul Failat, 'Oil and Gas Joint Operating Agreements – Default Provisions, A Dilemma by Default' (2014) 5 *OGEL* 1 <www.ogel.org>.

parties' rights, obligations and liabilities, how the JV is to be run and funded, the default mechanisms for failing to comply with various obligations, provisions for decision making, and specifies the duties and limitations of liabilities for the party which is responsible for the day-to-day running of the co-venture and petroleum operations namely, the operator. The operator is the party who usually enjoys the highest participating interest in the JV and often boasts a higher financial and technical standing compared to the non-operator parties. The high-risk, high-cost (but ultimately high-reward) environment in which oil and gas companies operate is the main reason why JVs are established and it allows these companies to share the high expenditures and uncertainties across a portfolio of investments around the world in order to maximise profits. JVs can take the form of a corporation, limited liability or company, although in the oil and gas industry JVs are usually unincorporated, which means that the JV does not have a distinct legal personality and therefore cannot be taxed, sued or sue in its own name.[2]

The risks associated with oil and gas activities are vast and potentially catastrophic. Commonly cited risks include technical, geological, environmental and political risks, each set against the backdrop of the specific region in which operations are conducted and the world economy whose hunger for petroleum ultimately dictates whether the risk/reward offset was worth its price. As explained above, the JV structure permits oil and gas companies to share and thereby mitigate the risks. The skill and performance of the operator in conducting petroleum operations will play a significant role in the level of operational risk exposure. The strength and diversification of the relevant oil and gas company's investment portfolio, the capital balance sheets, management and hedging strategy may go some way to withstand some of the inherent financial, fiscal and economic risks for which no insurance 'can save the day'. However, in the post-Mocando oil spill era it is questionable to what extent the usual contractual allocation of liability rules between the operator and the non-operator parties as well as the operator and third party contractors and the insurance policies for catastrophic disasters will be able to withstand such events. As explored further below, it is an industry standard principle that the operator in the context of a JV structure, is obliged to procure and maintain insurance for certain policies required by law (or as agreed by the parties). Slight differences do however exist in the model JOAs[3], for example with respect to the extent the non-operators indemnify the operator against his duties to procure and maintain the insurance policies required in petroleum operations and

---

2 *Ibid.*

3 Model JOAs meaning the industry standard joint operating contracts issued by various national and international associations involved in standardising and enhancing petroleum agreements. Examples include Association of International Petroleum Negotiators (AIPN), Oil and Gas UK (UKOG), and the American Association of Professional Landmen (AAPL).

pursuant to the JOA. The JOA is the key agreement which sets out what happens in the event of loss; it is therefore important that the JOA deals adequately with risk allocation, the parties' liabilities and responsibilities for obtaining and maintaining insurance policies that are obligatory as opposed to non-obligatory, and the circumstances in which a JV party can opt in or out of certain insurance policies. Unless otherwise stated, this chapter generally focuses on the position in relation to the UK legal regime and practices.

2. THE MEANING OF INSURANCE

It is interesting to consider that there is no defined term for a contract of insurance under English or EU law. Despite the lack of an exhaustive definition of a contract of insurance, the EU courts have given some helpful guidance. In particular the case of *Card Protection Plan v Customs and Excise Commissioners*[4] gives a succinct description:

> '[T]he essentials of an insurance transaction are, as generally understood, that the insurer undertakes, in return for prior payment of a premium, to provide the insured, in the event of materialisation of the risk covered, with the service agreed when the contract was concluded. It is not essential that the service the insurer has undertaken to provide in the event of loss consists in the payment of a sum of money, as that service may also take the form of the provision of assistance in cash or in kind'.

In the UK, a well-known and often-cited case setting out the most common characteristics of a contract of insurance is *Prudential v Commissioners of Inland Revenue*. The case sets out certain features that would be typical of a contract of insurance, namely:

- 'The event should be one which involves some amount of uncertainty. This relates to whether or not the event will actually occur or not as well as uncertainty in respect of the time at which it may/will happen;[5]
- A contract of insurance must be a contract which for some consideration, usually but not necessarily in periodic payments called premiums, you secure ... some benefit, usually but not necessarily the payment of some money, upon the happening of some event;[6]
- The uncertain event must be adverse to the interest of the assured.'[7]

---

4 (Case C-349/96) [1999] 2 AC 601.

5 *Prudential v Commissioners of Inland Revenue* [1904] 2 KB 658 para. 663.

6 *Ibid.*

7 *Ibid.*

A contract of insurance has also been defined as an 'agreement to confer upon the insured a contractual right which, prima facie, comes into existence immediately when loss is suffered by the happening of an event insured against, to be put by the insurer into the same position in which the insured would have been had the event not occurred, but in no better position'.[8]

The features of a contract of insurance are therefore similar to an indemnity, in that the obligation to insure is a primary obligation and not an accessory obligation.[9]

3. LIABILITY AND INSURANCE

3.1. GENERAL DUTY TO PROCURE INSURANCE

In common with most model JOA forms, the UK Oil and Gas Model JOA states that the operator is obliged to acquire and maintain all appropriate insurances in compliance with the requirements of the licence and any other applicable legislation, or of 'any contract entered into by the operator in furtherance of Joint Operations',[10] except in respect of any insurance which the operator must take out in its own name.[11] The cost of insurance is charged between the co-venturers in proportion to their respective percentage interests unless a co-venturer chooses not to participate in the insurance.[12]

The only required insurances, under the UK regime, are those for employee protection[13] (which will be carried in the operator's own name) and, as explored below in detail, an operator must be a member of Offshore Pollution Liability Association (OPOL),[14] which is a requirement under the licence as granted by the UK Secretary of State.[15]

The operator will also take out, on behalf of the entire JV, any other insurance which the Joint Operating Committee thinks appropriate.[16] The most common form of optional insurance taken out by a JV is Construction All Risk (CAR)

8 *Callaghan v Dominion Insurance Co* [1997] 2 Lloyd's Rep 541.

9 P. Roberts, *Petroleum Contracts English Law and Practice*, Oxford University Press, Oxford 2013, p. 344.

10 UKOG Model JOA, clause 8.1.

11 S. Styles, *Oil and Gas Law – Current Practice and Emerging Trends*, 2nd edn, Dundee University Press, Dundee 2011, p. 381.

12 UKOG Model JOA, clause 8.1.1.

13 Under the Employers' Liability (Compulsory Insurance) Act 1969 employers must provide insurance for all employees working in the UK, and this legislation has been extended offshore.

14 The most recent version, 1 January 2010, of OPOL is available: Under OPOL, member operating companies agree to accept strict liability for pollution damage and the cost of remedial measures.

15 UKOG Model JOA, clause 8.2.

16 UKOG Model JOA, clause 8.1.1.

insurance to cover the construction of the installation and any other joint developments.[17]

Except to the extent that an operator must by law or contract obtain insurance for the benefit of the JV, it is common for all model JOAs to provide and allow for the non-operating parties to procure their own insurance. In electing not to participate in the insurance obtained by the operator, the parties who opt out must notify the operator and the other parties of this and agree not to interfere with the operator's negotiations to obtain insurance for the benefit of the parties who have opted in. Each of the non-participating parties have to ensure that, in proportion to their participating interest share of any liability which may arise in connection with joint operations, they obtain and maintain equivalent insurance to that of the operator. The policies taken out by the non-participating parties should also include waivers of subrogation in favour of the other parties. Subrogation is a remedy that allows rights enjoyed by one person to be transferred to another without formal assignment.[18] In the context of insurance, upon an insurer making payments to the insured person the insurer can ordinarily benefit from all the rights and remedies of the insured party against the party who caused the underlying loss, the insurer is thus allowed to sue upon the rights and remedies (in the name of the insured person) and is thereby subrogated to the rights of the insured.[19] Therefore, in order to make sure that the other partners stand to benefit instead of the insurer, there has to be a waiver of rights of subrogation in favour of the other contractual parties – this would have to be procured from and negotiated with the insurers as part of the overall process of insuring that party's interest in the JV project.[20]

In practice, the most common reason for a party to procure its own insurance is that it already benefits from insurance as part of larger group policy. International oil and gas companies may have large insurance teams who are responsible for insuring all group/subsidiary companies taking into account the specific region and applicable legislation within which these entities are present. Most joint venture parties therefore insure under their own (group) policies. Indeed if insurance cover were to be arranged for each individual interest held, it would be very difficult for the insurers to consider such company's total exposure. Some of the larger oil and gas companies do not insure with the market, meaning that they 'self-insure'. Self-insurance, in brief terms, is a risk management method whereby a calculated amount is set aside using actuaries to compensate for a potential future loss.

---

17 Styles, *supra* n. 11, p. 382.

18 P. Roberts, *supra* n. 9, p. 159.

19 *Ibid.*

20 *Ibid.*

3.2. LIABILITY AND DUTY OF THE OPERATOR TO INSURE

As explained above, the operator acts as a manager for the JV and has overall control over conducting exploration and production operations. Under the auspices of the Joint Operating Committee, the duty of the operator extends to 'conduct[ing] the Joint Operations by itself, its agents or its contractors'.[21] Therefore the operator would be responsible *inter alia* for preparing work programmes and budgets, granting authorisations for expenditure, implementing/carrying out approved programmes, dealing with and contracting with contractors who undertake work for the benefit of the JV, and providing the JV parties with certain information and data.

Significantly, the operator, in light of it being responsible for the joint operations (even if it does not conduct any of the joint operations itself)[22] for no remuneration, and thereby assuming additional risk and exposure to third party and JV partner claims, is indemnified and held harmless by the other JV parties. The only exception to this principle is in the case of the operator's wilful misconduct or also, as is the case under the general UK regime, if the operator fails 'to obtain or maintain insurance which it is required to obtain and maintain ... except where the Operator has used all reasonable endeavours to obtain or maintain any such insurance but has been unable to do so and has promptly notified the Participants participating or proposing to participate therein'.[23] It is interesting to note that only the UK regime (and the standard JOA used in Denmark and Greenland) specifically state that the operator can be found liable and held responsible by the other JV partners if it fails to obtain and maintain insurance. The UK Model therefore, on the face of it, affords the non-operating parties an added level of protection or recourse against the operator which would not require them to have to prove wilful misconduct, which is notoriously difficult. The obligation in respect of the operator and insurance is set out in Clause 8.8.1 of the Model JOA which states:

> 'The Operator shall obtain and maintain, in respect of the Joint Operations[24] and the Joint Property, all insurance required under the Licence or any other applicable law or as may be required by any contract entered into by the Operator in furtherance of Joint Operations and such other insurance as the Joint Operating Committee may from time to time determine'.

21 UKOG Model JOA, clause 5.

22 Styles, *supra* n. 11, p. 376.

23 UKOG Model JOA, clause 6.2.4. The position is the same in the Greenland Model JOA, clause 3.3.3.

24 This means all operations which are conducted by the operator on behalf of all of the participants in accordance with this agreement after the date of commencement of this agreement – UKOG Model JOA.

The first limb of the obligation set out above is for the operator to acquire and maintain insurance under the licence or any other applicable law for joint operations and property. The 'Licence' is a reference to a UK Petroleum Production Licence,[25] which would include the 'Model Clauses'.[26] The Model Clauses, the Licence and the Petroleum Act do not identify any mandatory or specific insurance policies which the operator must obtain as such. Rather, the Model Clauses, together with regulations made under the authority of the UK Parliament and general common law, impose certain obligations on operators (and licensees generally) which are underpinned by schemes supported by the oil and gas industry.[27] In particular, Model Clause 23(9) provides: '[t]he Licensee shall comply with any reasonable instructions from time to time given by the Minister with a view to ensuring that funds are available to discharge any liability for damage attributable to the release or escape of Petroleum in the course of activities connected with the exercise of rights granted by this licence'.

The operator is thus compelled to demonstrate its competencies and financial standing to the Secretary of State for Energy and Climate Change (Secretary). Under the Model Clauses this would also include prior approval from the Secretary to become an operator, which would mean satisfying various criteria including that it has the relevant insurance coverage for operations and well abandonment and that it is a member of OPOL (discussed below). The Secretary has also, in the wake of the Macondo incident, scrutinised the demonstration of financial capabilities of licensees before consent may be granted for exploration and appraisal wells on the UK Continental Shelf. The operator must inform the Secretary of the cost of well control and the cost of financial remediation and compensation and demonstrate financial responsibility to meet such costs by means of reliance on credit/financial strength, parent company guarantees and insurance.

In relation to the meaning of 'or any other applicable law' this would include the governing law of the JOA as well as the relevant governing law of any other contract which the operator entered into in furtherance of joint operations. Applicable law would mean statutory law and under English law the law of negligence. An example of legislation which would fall under applicable law (and which is not necessarily specific to the oil and gas community) relates to an employer's legal obligation to obtain insurance for its employees.[28] Therefore, to the extent that the operator's employees carries out functions for the benefit of joint operations and the operator failed to adequately insure its employees and this directly resulted in the non-operating parties incurring loss as a result,

25 Pursuant to the Petroleum Act 1998.
26 The Petroleum Licensing (Production) (Seaward Areas) Regulations 2008.
27 N. Scott, 'Offshore Industry Compensation Regime', presentation paper, OPOL <www.interspill.org_previous-events:2012_14_March_pdfs_OffshoreForum Panel>.
28 Employers' Liability (Compulsory Insurance) Act 1969.

the non-operating parties would theoretically, have a direct recourse against the operator.

The second limb of Clause 8.8.1 of the Model JOA relates to '... or as may be required by any contract entered into by the Operator in furtherance of Joint Operations and such other insurance as the Joint Operating Committee may from time to time determine'. This imposes a direct contractual right on the operator to obtain and maintain any insurance which may be required in any contract he enters into when carrying out joint operations or any insurance which the Joint Operating Committee has determined as necessary. Therefore, unless the operator can show that he used all reasonable endeavours to obtain or maintain any such insurance but had been unable to do so and informed the non-operating parties accordingly, failure to comply with this obligation would give the non-operating partners recourse to claim against the operator.

That it prima facie falls to the operator to maintain and obtain insurance for joint operations is a logical allocation of liability bearing in mind the role that he performs and the general oil and gas legislation (in particular relating to environment and pollution) which imposes a fault based and strict liability regime which looks straight to the operator to: (i) take steps to prevent damage or further damage and notify the authority in the event of any damage covered by the relevant regulations; (ii) provide information and undertake preventive and remedial measures as required by the relevant authority; (iii) submit proposal for remediation as required; and (iv) pay costs claimed by the relevant authority in relation to environmental damage.

The reason the operator is liable to the non-operating parties for reasonably obtaining insurance is simply due to the significant losses the non-operating parties would incur if the operator did not properly insure and an event occurred for which the operator should be culpable.[29] However, the type of occurrences which would lead to an operator to be held accountable supposes that the operator may in fact be liable for failures other than not obtaining or maintaining insurance[30] – although to prove such culpability the non-operating parties would have to demonstrate that the operator's misconduct was wilful. As is common with most model JOAs, the operator is held harmless from any consequential loss that the non-operating may suffer as a result of the operator's performance/misperformance.[31] The meaning of consequential loss is usually defined in the relevant JOA as it can otherwise be a difficult to establish whether a loss is direct or consequential depending on the circumstances and the applicable law.

---

29 P. Roberts, *supra* n. 9, p. 350.

30 *Ibid.*

31 UKOG Model JOA, clause 6.2.4 (b).

4. OPOL

As set out above the Model Clauses require licensees to demonstrate that funds are available to meet liability for escape or discharge of petroleum. The Secretary therefore requires all operators active in offshore exploration and production in the UK Continental Shelf to be a party to the Offshore Pollution Liability Agreement dated 4 September 1974 ('OPOL Agreement'). Under the OPOL scheme, operating companies agree to accept strict liability for pollution damage and the cost of remedial measures, with only certain exceptions, up to a maximum of US$250,000,000 per incident. OPOL has currently 133 members and also allows applications from operators of offshore facilities outside of the UK Continental Shelf (including those located in Denmark, Germany, France, the Republic of Ireland, the Netherlands, Norway and Greenland).

The underlying purpose of OPOL is to: (i) provide means for the expeditious settlement of claims arising out of an escape or discharge of oil; (ii) to encourage immediate remedial action by the parties; (iii) to ensure financial responsibility of the parties to meet their obligations; (iv) to provide a mechanism for ensuring that claims are met up to the maximum liability under OPOL; and (v) to avoid complicated jurisdictional problems.[32] OPOL decided that it could only be operators who should be parties to the agreement since they are more directly involved and in a better position than non-operators to assume the obligations imposed by OPOL; for example, facilities such as pipeline systems can serve a number of different participants, but only have a single operator whose responsibility is usually defined by an operating agreement.[33] Furthermore, in the case of a JV arrangement, it is the operator who assumes the obligations under OPOL for all other participants.

The OPOL Agreement sets out three key elements, namely it: (i) provides for reimbursement/compensation; (ii) creates a financial responsibility regime; and (iii) provides guarantees against default by a member. Under the financial responsibility regime, OPOL requires that its members give evidence of financial responsibility which must be provided for an amount of not less than US$250 million for any one incident and US$500 million in the annual aggregate – evidence of this responsibility can be in the form of (i) certificates of insurance from an insurer or broker; (ii) surety bond issues by a company acceptable to the board of OPOL; (iii) a guarantee issued by an accepted guarantor; or (iv) qualification of a member as a self-insurer, provided it demonstrates financial responsibility. If a member fails to make a payment to a claimant for any sums due under the agreement, the other members of OPOL agree that they will contribute pro rata to such payment according to the number of facilities

---

32 Offshore Pollution Liability Association Ltd <http://www.opol.org.uk/about.htm> (February 2015).

33 *Ibid.*

operated by them at the time of the relevant incident. The claims that will arise under OPOL would either be reimbursement of public authorities for remedial measures and/or compensation to third parties for pollution damage.

Clause 8.2 of the UK Model JOA ensures that the operator of the JV is bound by OPOL and that OPOL applies to the JV offshore facilities. It is also made clear that if an operator has to pay in relation to remedial measures and pollution damage[34] or for any other reason pursuant to the OPOL Agreement, such payments are for the joint account.

It is important to appreciate that OPOL is not a fund and the operator may be held liable for losses which exceed the maximum recovery limit or for losses which go beyond the scope of the OPOL scheme.[35] Further it should be remembered that the operator can also be held liable for pollution, oil spills and a range of offences by virtue of the law of negligence as well as statute (such as the Environmental Damage (Prevention and Remediation) Regulations 2009).

5. WHAT TYPE OF INSURANCE SHOULD BE IN PLACE?

As stated above, the OPOL regime insures up to a pre-determined amount of US$250 million per incident. This limit was the subject of consideration of a joint study between Oil and Gas UK and OPOL which modelled well blowout scenarios for four representative locations around the UK for a release duration of thirty days based on the use of a 'capping device'.[36] The conclusion of the report was that the OPOL limit of US$250 million per incident is adequate for the vast majority of UK well operations. Nonetheless, most oil and gas companies will also carry insurance for their own and other liabilities beyond the OPOL limit, usually covering loss or damage to property and Operators' Extra Expenses (OEE), discussed further below.

The past decade or so has witnessed a huge shift towards oil and gas companies venturing into more extreme deepwater drilling environments, which has resulted in the costs and risks of offshore drilling increasing. The Macondo incident in the deep waters of the Gulf of Mexico exposed the difficulties and complexities associated with a major oil spill in deepwater and managing the risks in such environments, as well as the profound challenges of dealing with environmental damage and pollution. In the post-Mancondo era, many oil and gas companies have had to re-evaluate their pollution cover as well as their risk exposure more generally, recognising that pollution liability will be accompanied

---

34 Offshore Pollution Liability Agreement, clause IV <http://www.opol.org.uk/downloads/OPOL-Agreement-From-1april2015.pdf>.

35 P. Cameron, 'Liability for Catastrophic Risk in the Oil and Gas Industry' (2012) *IELR* 211.

36 See 'Oil Spill Cost Study – OPOL Financial Limits' >http://www.oilandgasuk.co.uk/knowledgecentre/Key_issues.cfm?.

with a need for additional cover for items such as well control, physical damage, business interruption and removal of wreckage.

5.1. THE OEE POLICY

Prior to the Macondo incident, insurers did not really pay much attention to the scope of cover and pricing capacity for pollution arising from offshore wells – this risk is covered in the OEE policy,[37] which specifically includes controlling a well, re-drilling, third party legal liability and further pollution liability cover. The part of the cover which had previously received the most attention (from an insurer's perspective) was well control cost, together with the cost of making a well safe (re-drilling), as these were the parts of the cover in relation to which many claims were paid out and particularly as witnessed during the hurricane events in the Gulf of Mexico in 2004/2005 and 2008.[38] However, this focus has changed somewhat after the Macondo incident.

The standard template policy form for the OEE, as developed by the London Insurance Market and covering well control and associated risk for offshore (and onshore) drilling, is the Energy Exploration and Development 8/86 policy form (EED 8/86). The OEE policy as reflected in the EED 8/86 wording is a composite policy which is designed to 'stand alone', meaning that it is not designed to be included in an oil and gas company's package placement (although it is very likely to be included).[39] The core of the EED 8/86 policy is the section on control of well, to which various endorsements have been added over time.[40]

5.1.1. *Control of Well*

The control of well coverage is triggered by a well becoming 'out of control' as defined in the policy. The definition is therefore key and relates to a flow of well fluids originating from the well bore above the surface of the ground or water that cannot be controlled by certain defined actions as specifically set out in the policy, which will include the activation of blowout prevention equipment or ridding of excess pressure in the well.[41] There are also similarly detailed definitions as to when a well is brought under control and when the insurer's liability for well control ceases.[42]

---

37 A. Rees and D. Sharp, 'Energy – Drilling in Extreme Environments: Challenges and Implications for the energy insurance industry', Lloyd's, 2011, p. 29.

38 *Ibid.*, p. 27.

39 *Ibid.*, p. 31.

40 C.L. Stuart, 'Downhole, Offshore and Blowouts – A Primer on Oil and Gas Coverage: The Offsore Energy Package Policy', University of Texas School of Law, Houston, Texas, 2013, p. 3.

41 A. Rees and D. Sharp, *supra* n. 37, p. 31.

42 *Ibid.*

5.1.2. *Re-drilling*

Once a well is under control it may need to be re-drilled/restored. This is when the second limb of the policy kicks in whereby (so long as the conditions as defined in the policy are satisfied) the insurer will pay for the costs incurred in re-drilling to a level at which control was lost. However, the insurers' liability is capped using a formula based on the policy indemnity and the percentage of the original expense of drilling the well.[43] However, in return for an increased premium, insurers often do not apply this limitation. There are also certain limits relating to the methodology of the re-drilling and time limits for the commencement of the restoration or re-drill.

5.1.3. *Pollution*

The third section of the OEE cover is coverage for pollution resulting from blowouts, but not pollution from other facilities or reasons (although it is possible to include cover for pollution from the production facility so long as the original cause is the blowout).[44] The pollution cover is for accidental and sudden incidents, the three main subparts relating to: (i) legal liability for damages in relation to third party property damage and injury; (ii) costs for clean-up or attempted clean-up (which does not require legal liability); and (iii) legal defence costs. To satisfy the obligations under OPOL, oil and gas companies can purchase an endorsement to the OEE policy which will satisfy the obligations of OPOL[45] (i.e. the means of demonstrating financial responsibility by means of insurance). In order to be sure that they comply with OPOL, oil and gas companies obtain agreement from their insurers that OPOL criteria have priority in allocation of the limit and often purchase a dedicated limit for the pollution risk.[46]

5.1.4. *Other Endorsements/Policies under OEE*

In addition to the three main types of cover described above, most oil and gas companies also purchase additional coverage as part of their OEE policy for a range of risk factors. Examples include:

- care custody and control;[47]
- underground control of well;[48]

---

43 *Ibid.*

44 *Ibid.*

45 *Ibid.*

46 *Ibid.*

47 This relates to property owned by another party (e.g. leased equipment) but which is legally under the insured's control or possession.

48 As the 'Control of Well' coverage relates only to a blowout which emerges at the surface of the ground or water bottom, this optional extension of cover relates to underground blowouts.

- resultant plugging and abandonment endorsement;
- evacuation expenses;
- deliberate well firing;
- farm-out well endorsement;
- contingent joint venture liability;[49]
- making wells safe;
- priority of payments;
- turnkey endorsement;
- loss of production income; and
- development drilling wells endorsement.

5.2. CORPORATE LIABILITY

A majority of oil and gas companies will (in addition to OEE) also have corporate liability policy or perhaps a string of policies to protect their entire scope of activities. The most common standard London insurance market policy is JL 2003/06 or LSW 244. Coverage under this policy includes: (i) bodily injury; (ii) personal injury; (iii) property damage; and (iv) advertising injury[50] – directly or indirectly caused by or arising out of seepage, pollution or contamination however caused, whenever or wherever happening. There are however strict exclusions to the policy, including pollution from the well, which in effect means the policies include full pollution exclusions. There are 'buy back' options to cover property damage and injury to third parties from seepage and pollution so long as the event happened during the policy term and was discovered and reported within a specific time limit. However, there is no specific cover for clean-up costs, meaning that the insured would have to show that the clean-up action was conducted to avoid property damage. This may be further frustrated by an exclusion disallowing cover where liability arises due to statutory obligations on the operator for pollution clean-up.[51] To overcome these restrictions would require specific endorsements to supersede the provisions, although it is unlikely that many insureds would have such an endorsement.[52]

Pollution cover under the OEE policy is therefore the more comprehensive cover for pollution risk as opposed to liability policies on the basis that the OEE regime offers cover for compensation to third parties for property damage and injury as well as clean-up costs (regardless of this being on a first or third party basis).[53]

49 This relates to the risk of a JV partner not paying for its share of a loss.

50 This relates to injury caused to a third party as a result of defamation, trademark infringement resulting from another business' advertising.

51 A. Rees and D. Sharp, *supra* n. 37.

52 *Ibid.*

53 *Ibid.*

5.3. OTHER TYPES OF INSURANCE

Other endorsements and complementary policies which may be bundled together with the OEE policy and which each offer separate coverage include: (i) physical damage (which may include removal of debris, property damage, oil in line, property in transit); (ii) business interruption (elements of which can include loss of production income, loss of hire, contingent business interruption, delay of start up); (iv) windstorm; (v) political risk; (vi) war and related risks; (vii) construction policy (as further discussed below); (viii) crude oil storage; and (ix) first-of-kind technology.

5.4. CONSTRUCTION ALL RISK POLICY

The construction phase of any project, and in particular offshore projects, carries considerable risk and costs to the parties responsible for commissioning the project as well as contractors and subcontractors. Standard Construction All Risks (CAR) policies have developed in the offshore insurance market to address the specific risks associated with construction, the most well-known being the 2001 Offshore Construction Project Insurance Wording (WELCAR 2001).[54] Under this policy there is *inter alia* cover for all risks of physical loss/damage to the project works, including materials which are to become part of completed project; cover is also given for damage caused by defective parts but not for the defective part itself. The policy is intended to provide cover for all parties involved in the construction of the project and therefore includes 'other asssureds' and not just the named insureds. It is also commonplace for the insurers to agree to waive rights of subrogation against the insureds and other assureds which effectively means that there is diminished risk of the insurers bringing claims against the parties involved in the project. There are specific exclusions in WELCAR, including damage to vessels or floating materials used as part of the process unless such items are to become permanent part of the completed structure, the cost of repairing faulty welds and cost of repairing wear and tear.

6. CONTRACTOR'S LIABILITY VERSUS OPERATOR'S LIABILITY

On the basis that the operator assumes the upfront risks for oil and gas operations, the insurance policies/products available for such risks cater to and are aimed

---

[54] On 30 September 2011, the Joint Rig Committee at Lloyd's revised and released new WELCAR wording.

at operators. However, after the Macondo incident in 2010, the traditional allocation of contractual risk between the operator and the contractor is being challenged and the insurance industry is reacting accordingly.

A 'knock for knock' indemnity in the context of the oil and gas industry provides for one party X to indemnify the other party Y against claims relating to the death or personal injury to party X's employees, loss or damage to party X's property and pollution deriving from party X's property. Party Y gives reciprocal indemnities in favour of party X. The usual 'knock for knock' indemnities stand regardless of any party's negligence or breach. These arrangements are commonly found in the standard contracts entered into between the operator and the contractors the operator uses to carry out joint operations. In terms of insurance obligations, the operator and the contractor are each only required to insure against the death of, or injury to, its own employees and pollution emanating from its own property. Following the Macondo incident, which laid bare the unprecedented level of costs for which an operator could be held liable, operators are increasingly seeking to contest the 'knock for knock' regime and the extent to which contractors should be able escape without picking up any costs for pollution or third party liability following a catastrophic incident.

> 'Traditionally, operators have carried risks via insurance or self-insurance, on the understanding that such risks are counter-balanced by the considerable rewards of E&P success; these occur across the portfolio of the operators' licences, each with decades of revenue-earning ability, and which the contractor cannot share in. In this way, the risk-reward relationship has structured the liability relationship and related insurance.'[55]

It is a widely accepted principle in the oil and gas industry that the risks are allocated to the party best in control of and able to sustain the risk;[56] therefore, until 2012 when litigation arose from the Macondo disaster, it was completely unchallenged that operators, as opposed to the contractors who make up the supply chain, should bear any pollution/environmental damage risk. The idea that a party other than the operator (who controls the decision-making process and all information relating to a well or operations, stands to reap huge rewards, and is generally held responsible vis-à-vis the various regulators) should take ultimate responsibility disrupts the traditional allocation of responsibility.

However, following the Macondo incident and the 2012 oil spill in Brazil involving Chevron and Transocean, regulators have pursued contractors in addition to the operator, imposing substantial fines that cannot be indemnified (by the operator) on policy grounds.[57] Operators are increasingly seeking to hold contractors liable for an allocation of subsurface pollution including well

55 P. Cameron, *supra* n. 35, p. 207.
56 *Ibid.*, p. 209.
57 *Ibid.*, p. 210.

control, clean-up and third party liability in circumstances where contractors are (grossly) negligent. However, to the extent that licensees remain responsible to the relevant licensing authority for activities associated with the licence, including absolute responsibility for pollution and well control, the risk is that the burden and cost of insurance will remain with the oil and gas companies as opposed to the relevant contractors. To delegate such responsibility to the supply chain would effectively mean that the operator would have to monitor the financial responsibility and capability of each of its contractors, which would be a near-impossible task. Further, placing responsibility down the chain would in any event most likely pass the cost of insurance back to the oil and gas companies, as they are the only ones capable of absorbing the risks and costs, of seeking protection globally from the insurance market as a whole and achieving economies of scale.[58] Not surprisingly, therefore, despite the increasing number of insurance products available to contractors to supposedly cover their increased risk profile, the insurance market is generally nervous of increasing contractor liability and simply does not offer cover for events such as blowouts, well control, etc., which are the responsibilities of the operator. This is why the OEE policy was developed in relation to the operator and not the contractor.

58 A. Rees and D. Sharp, *supra* n. 37, p. 29.

TRANSFER OF INTEREST AND CHANGE OF CONTROL IN JOAs

Michael POLKINGHORNE*

* The author wishes to thank James Hart (Associate at White & Case LLP) for reviewing and providing comments on the chapter, particularly with regard to the English law on penalties.

1. INTRODUCTION

A joint operating agreement (JOA) is a contract that regulates the relationship between parties who share the benefit of a right to explore and produce mineral resources which exist below the surface of land,[1] which is often granted by way of a (state) licence.[2] Each party to the JOA has an interest in 'the rights, interests, obligations, and liabilities'[3] derived from the JO`A and the underlying contract[4] (Participating Interest).[5]

---

1 K. O'Gorman and M. Stadnyk, *Arbitration and Joint Operating Agreements: An Overview*, International Energy and Minerals Arbitration, Paper 10, Rocky Mt. Min. L. Fdn. 2013, pp. 10–11: 'the JOA provides the contractual process for regulating the relationship between the parties involved.'

2 A. Jennings, *Oil and Gas Exploration Contracts*, Sweet & Maxwell, London 2002, para. 2-01: 'The oil company or group will have been granted a lease or licence (depending on the local law) … in order to secure the necessary rights to recover petroleum (normally defined as both oil and gas).'

3 See the definition of Participating Interest in Article 1.1 2012 JOA: 'Participating Interest means each Party's undivided share (expressed as a percentage to ___ (_) decimal places) of the total shares of all Parties in the rights, interests, obligations, and liabilities of the Parties derived from the Contract and this Agreement.' In other words, a Participating Interest is the percentage interest in the JOA operations owned by each of the JOA parties individually as a percentage of the total interests of all the JOA parties. See also the definition of Contract in Article 1.1 2012 JOA: 'the instrument identified in the recitals to this Agreement, including any extensions, renewals and/or amendments.' See also the definition of Agreement in Article 1.1 2012 JOA: 'this agreement, together with the Exhibits attached to this agreement, and any extension, renewal, or amendment agreed to in writing by the Parties.'

4 Reference to 'underlying contract' is to the licence or concession. For definition of licence or concession see note 14 below.

5 O'Gorman and Stadnyk, *supra* n. 1, pp. 10–11: 'The JOA governs the terms on which a mineral right, such as a hydrocarbons license, is shared and exercised in practice by its co-tenants. Many JOAs allocate participating interest shares in such assets between its parties.

The Model International Joint Operating Agreement published by the Association of International Petroleum Negotiators[6] (AIPN JOA) is widely used in the oil and gas industry[7] and will be the bedrock of this chapter as it explores the treatment of transfer and change in control provisions in the 2012 version of the AIPN JOA, (2012 JOA) and how they have evolved from earlier versions of the AIPN JOA. Indeed, the new version has increased in complexity in relation to this issue.[8]

A JOA governs what is anticipated to be a long-term relationship between the parties for the conduct of oil and gas exploration and production. It is accordingly possible that during the JOA's lifetime, one or multiple parties to the agreement will want to transfer their Participating Interest in the underlying project[9] to a third party. There could be a variety of commercial reasons for a party's desire to move on, such as wanting to diversify its portfolio, looking to farm out all or part of an interest in order to be carried, a decision to move out of a given geographical area, or – as we have seen recently with BP – a need for cash to fund other liabilities. Moreover, the current oil price environment has seen a wave of exits by international oil companies, with fields no longer being commercially viable. Finally, because of the duration of oil and gas exploration projects, other 'transformational events'[10] such as a change in operator[11] or the insolvency of one of the JOA parties could also lead to a transfer. The parties to the JOA need to ensure that their agreement provides for such situations.[12]

These participating interest shares affect the extent of the parties' stakes in costs, liabilities, and anticipated oil and gas production.'

6 'The Association of International Petroleum Negotiators (AIPN) is a non-profit organization founded in 1981 to enhance the professionalism of cross-border energy negotiators throughout the world.' <https://www.aipn.org/about_AIPN.aspx>.

7 R. Major, 'A Practical Look at Pre-emption Provisions in Upstream Oil and Gas Contracts' [May 2005] IELTR Issue 5, p. 121: 'The [JOA] form used by the Association of International Petroleum Negotiators ("AIPN") is, in particular used extensively.'

8 O'Gorman and Stadnyk, *supra* n. 1, pp. 10–18: 'The AIPN Model International JOA has grown increasingly complex to reflect the nature of modern international joint operations. It provides a panoply of options and alternative clauses from which contract drafters may select.'

9 See the definition of Participating Interest, *supra* n. 3.

10 M. Hammerson, *Upstream Oil and Gas: Cases, Materials and Commentary*, Globe Law and Business, London 2011, p. 178.

11 An operator in the context of a JOA is a JOA party who carries out the JOA operations (typically oil and gas exploration and production) on behalf of all the JOA parties. The remaining JOA parties who are not the operator, i.e. the non-operators, will reimburse the operator for the cost of carrying out the joint operations by way of cash-calls. The operator will often have a substantial interest in the joint operations and be technically competent.

12 C. Purdie, *The Joint Operating Agreement – Notes from the Field – An English Law Perspective on the Oil & Gas Market*: 'During the lifetime of the JOA, a party may wish to transfer its interests in the licence, the JOA and the wider project to a third party in order to realise some of the value of the asset. The JOA should make provision for such an occurrence.' <http://www.andrewskurth.com/pressroom-publications-1044.html>. See also P. Roberts, *Joint Operating*

This chapter will begin by outlining the concepts of assignment and novation under English and French law (as good examples of how common and civil law systems deal with this issue). It will then explore the concept of transfer of interest under a JOA and explain the notion of an indirect change in the context of a change in control (the situation where the ultimate shareholder sells not the interest itself but the subsidiary or special purpose vehicle holding that interest). In this respect, attention will be paid to the types of preferential rights[13] that can be incorporated into a JOA, the arguments for and against doing so, and the differing judicial treatment of those rights in common law and civil law jurisdictions. This chapter will also deal with the eventuality of a transfer occurring in the context of a JOA party defaulting in respect of its obligations, as well as the various mechanics for withdrawal by a JOA party or consent to the substitution of a third party. Finally, certain common practical implications of transfer and change in control provisions will be considered.

2. TRANSFER OF INTEREST

2.1. DEFINITION

The definition of transfer in the 2012 JOA is expressed to include a transfer by means of a sale, assignment or novation of rights or obligations under the JOA and the contract underlying it.[14] Notably, the definition of transfer in the

---

Agreements: A Practical Guide, Globe Law and Business, London 2012, p. 129: 'During the lifetime of a JOA, a party might wish to realise the value of that asset. The principal method of achieving this is for that party to transfer its interests in the JOA (and in the concession and the wider petroleum project) to another person. That other person may be an existing other party to the JOA, an affiliate of the transferor or an entirely unrelated third party. The JOA should be alive to this possibility, which is an inevitable aspect of the evolution of the relationships which the JOA represents … subject to the principle that a transfer of interests should not be detrimental to the interests of the non-transferring parties.'

13 Reference in this article to 'preferential rights' is to both pre-emption rights and rights of first refusal. The difference between these two types of preferential rights is the timing. Rights of pre-emption give the other JOA parties the right to be given the opportunity to buy the Participating Interest *after* the proposed transferor has found a prospective buyer and there have been negotiations between the buyer and the proposed transferor. In contrast, rights of first refusal are triggered much earlier; they are triggered before negotiations with a prospective buyer have even commenced. Pre-emption rights will be discussed in section 4 below.

14 See the definition of 'transfer' in Article 1.1 2012 JOA: 'Transfer means any sale, assignment, novation, Encumbrance or other disposition by a Party of any rights or obligations derived from the Contract or this Agreement (including its Participating Interest), other than its Entitlement and its rights to any credits, refunds or payments under this Agreement, and excluding any direct or indirect Change in Control of a Party.' See the definitions of 'agreement' and 'contract' in Article 1.1 2012 JOA, *supra* n. 3. The underlying contract will often be a

2012 JOA excludes changes in control of a JOA party, and 'change in control' is defined separately (and will thus be dealt with separately in this article; see section 3 below).

The 1995 AIPN JOA was narrow in scope in relation to transfers. The transfer provisions only applied if one of the parties transferred their Participating Interest and not any other rights. The definition of 'transfer' under the 2002 AIPN JOA and the 2012 JOA however is much broader, including transfers of (rights and) obligations derived from the JOA and the underlying contract.[15] The AIPN JOA developments thus acknowledge the interrelated nature of the many contracts that form part of an oil and gas exploration project.[16] The transfers provided for by the JOA will commonly occur by way of assignment or novation, which have different legal implications depending on the jurisdiction in which they arise, as set out below.

2.2. BACK TO BASICS: WHAT ARE ASSIGNMENT AND NOVATION?

2.2.1. Assignment

Assignment is a legal device which allows one party (the assignor) to transfer its rights under a contract to another party (the assignee). When the assignment takes place in the JOA framework, its consequences will depend on the applicable law governing the contract.

Under English law, only the benefit (the rights) under a contract and not the burden (the obligations) can be assigned.[17] The rights under a JOA can be

---

licence or concession. A licence a governmental grant providing authority to specific parties for the undertaking of oil and gas exploration. A concession is: 'The duration for which the private sector will operate the service/asset for. At end of the concession the asset is handed back to the government authority in a pre-agreed condition.' <http://www.people.hbs.edu/besty/projfinportal/glossary.htm>.

15 P. Weems and M. Bolton, 'Highlights of Key Revisions – 2002 AIPN Model Form International Operating Agreement' [June 2003] IELTR, Issue 6, p. 178: 'The Revision Committee sought to deal with this potential loophole by incorporating the transfer definition into the Model Form, and extending restrictions on transferability to include rights or obligations conferred under the contract or the operating agreement itself.'

16 Some JOAs go further and require that linked project agreements be transferred together. See Roberts, *supra* n. 12, p. 135: 'The JOA might also require that any transfer by a party of its interests in the JOA be accompanied by a corresponding transfer of that party's interests in any other relevant project documents, so that chain of title within the overall petroleum project is kept intact. Principally, this requirement will apply to the concession, but it will also apply, for example, to any unitisation and unit operating agreement ... and to any other project agreements.'

17 *Linden Gardens Trust Ltd v Lenesta Sludge Disposals Ltd* [1993] UKHL 4: 'The burden of a contract can never be assigned without the consent of the other party to the contract in which event such consent will give rise to a novation.'

transferred without the need for the consent of the other JOA parties.[18] The assignor must, however, give notice of the assignment to the other JOA parties (and will, of course, retain its obligations).[19]

Under French law a *cession de créance* (transfer of a right, claim or receivable) is similarly distinguished from a *cession de dette* (transfer of an obligation), although it is possible for both a *cession de créance* and a *cession de dette* to be transferred simultaneously through a *contrat de cession*.[20] Here again the assignor can transfer his rights to a third party if the former notifies the other assignee of this – there is no requirement for consent. By contrast, a *cession de dette* is possible only if the beneficiary of the obligation gives its consent.[21]

2.2.2. *Novation*

Novation is a method of transfer of rights and obligations by which – as a matter of legal theory – an existing contract is replaced by a new one, with the consent of the existing and new contractual parties.[22]

Under English law, novation occurs when 'two contracting parties agree that a third party, who also agrees, shall stand in relation of either of them to the other.'[23] This mechanism allows a third party to become responsible for the burden of a contract, so that the transferor can break away from its rights and obligations under that contract.[24] One has to be careful, however, when drafting clauses involving transfers as nomenclature is not always identical in different common law jurisdictions. The writer has, for example, seen contracts in South Africa which speak not of assignment, but of 'cession', and 'delegation' for novation; when using these terms it is best to add what exactly is being transferred (rights and/or obligations).[25]

---

18 Roberts, *supra* n. 12, p. 130: 'A party (the transferor) [can] freely transfer the benefit of its rights only in the JOA to another person (the transferee) by bilateral assignment of those rights without the need for the consent of any of the non-transferring parties, subject only to notice of the assignment of those rights being given to the non-transferring parties to be effective as a legal assignment.'

19 Section 136 Law of Property Act 1925.

20 A *cession de créance* is governed by Articles 1689–1695 of the French Civil Code. This has certain practical advantages over a novation, e.g. no extinction of a pre-existing legal relationship.

21 Cour de cassation, civ. 1, 30 April 2009, Bull. Civ. I, No. 82.

22 Roberts, *supra* n. 12, p. 130: 'Under a novation, the transferor will be replaced completely in favour of the transferee and effectively a new agreement will be created with the consent of all relevant parties.'

23 *Chitty on Contracts*, 31st edn, para. 19-086.

24 A. Bénabent, *Droit des obligations*, 14th edn, Montchrestien-Lextenso éd, Paris 2014, p. 526.

25 In India, the somewhat loose usage of the term 'assignment' (by drafters) can be seen in one of the major cases on the subject. In *Khardah Company Ltd v Raymon and Co. India (Pvt.) Ltd*, AIR 1962 SC 1810, T.L. Venkataramiah J. who spoke for the Bench has observed thus (at p. 1817 of AIR): 'The law on the subject is well settled and might be stated in simple

The position under French law is more or less the same. Novation is defined by the French Civil Code as the extinction of a legal relationship, followed by the creation of a new one to replace it.[26] This substitution allows a third party to replace one of the contracting parties. Novation under French law also requires the express consent of the original contractual parties and the third party.

The key difference between assignment and novation as those terms are employed in the AIPN JOA is that in the case of an assignment, the transferor will remain liable to the other JOA parties for the obligations under the JOA,[27] subject to the governing law of the contract in question.

2.3. TYPES OF TRANSFER

The main types of transfer under the 2012 JOA are transfers to third parties, assignments of operatorship, and transfers to affiliates.

2.3.1. Transfer to a Third Party

Transfers to a third party – a non-JOA party – are dealt with by Article 12.2 of the 2012 JOA. The most important provisions are the optional provisions on preferential rights,[28] which give the other non-transferring JOA parties the right to purchase the Participating Interest of the proposed transferor, over and above a prospective or existing buyer. Preferential rights will be discussed further at section 4 below.

2.3.2. Assignment of Operatorship

A new optional provision, contained in Article 4.12 of the 2012 JOA, concerns the assignment of operatorship to an affiliate.[29] An operator under a JOA usually

terms. An assignment of a contract might result by transfer either of the rights or of the obligations thereunder. But there is a well-recognised distinction between these two classes of assignments. As a rule obligations under a contract cannot be assigned except with the consent of the promise, and when such consent is given, it is really a novation resulting in substitution of liabilities. On the other hand rights under a contract are assignable unless the contract is personal in its nature or the rights are incapable of assignment either under the law or under an agreement between the parties.'

26 Novation is governed by Articles 1271–1281 of the French Civil Code.

27 Roberts, *supra* n. 12, p. 130: 'The critical difference between an assignment (of rights) and a novation (of rights and obligations) is that under the assignment, the transferor remains liable to any non-transferring party to perform its continuing obligations under the JOA.'

28 See *supra* n. 13 and section 4.1 for explanation of preferential rights.

29 Ashurst Energy briefing, *AIPN releases new 2012 version of its model Joint Operating Agreement:* 'The 2012 JOA [AIPN] includes an optional provision to allow the operator to assign operatorship to any of its affiliates provided that certain conditions are met.' <https://www.ashurst.com/doc.aspx?id_Content=7443>.

conducts oil and gas exploration and production activities on behalf of all the JOA parties, and is reimbursed by the other JOA parties for the cost of those activities in proportion to the Participating Interest of each. The operator will usually have a large stake in the project and is often chosen as a result of the size of its Participating Interest and/or its technical expertise.

The new provision on assignment of operatorship provides for the assignment of all (but not part) of the rights and obligations of the operator to an affiliate, subject to a number of conditions, including that the affiliate has sufficient technical competence and financial capacity to fulfil the duties of an operator.[30] As an alternative, the operator (or another affiliate of the operator with technical competence and financial resources) may provide a guarantee to the effect that it will remain responsible for the performance of the affiliate operator's duties.[31] In addition, there is a provision requiring the affiliate to enter into a written instrument accepting all of the operator's rights and obligations.[32] In practice, the transfer of operatorship to an affiliate will mean that the original operator will remain a party to the JOA, but the function of operator will be performed by the affiliate company. This provision may be helpful for companies that would like to take advantage of the tax benefits resulting from a different company taking on the role of operator and there could also be group re-organisation reasons for wanting to transfer operatorship to another member of the relevant entity's corporate group.[33] There is also a provision 'for re-assignment of the operatorship in cases where an affiliate ceases to be the affiliate of the assigning operator'[34] contained in Article 4.12.C of the 2012 JOA.

Another optional provision relating to assignment of operatorship was added to the 2002 AIPN JOA (see p. 211) and retained in the 2012 JOA.[35] It provides that when the operator transfers all of its Participating Interest to an affiliate, the affiliate will be automatically deemed to be the operator. Some commentary maintains that there is 'no obvious logic for this as there is no guarantee that the affiliate-transferee will have the necessary technical competence to act as the operator.'[36] However, this may be ameliorated, to an extent, by the fact that assignment is conditional on the original operator remaining liable for the affiliate's performance of its obligations under the JOA.[37] In addition, it is likely

30 See Article 4.12.A 2012 JOA.
31 See Article 4.12.A 2012 JOA.
32 See Article 4.12.B 2012 JOA.
33 Ashurst Energy briefing, *supra* n. 29: 'This option may be useful for oil and gas companies that prefer for the operatorship function to be performed by a separate company due to group structuring or tax reasons.'
34 Roberts, *supra* n. 12, p. 132.
35 See Article 12.2(B) 2002 JOA and Article 12.2.B 2012 JOA.
36 Roberts, *supra* n. 12, p. 132.
37 See Article 12.2.B 2012 JOA.

that the government that granted the licence or concession will have a right of veto on the appointment of a new operator.

2.3.3. *Transfer to an Affiliate*

This type of transfer concerns a JOA party transferring its Participating Interest to an affiliate company. Transfers to an affiliate do not typically trigger preferential rights.[38] Article 12.2.F of the 2012 JOA provides that transfers will be subject to preferential rights in the event of a transfer *unless* the transfer is to an affiliate, defined as 'a legal entity that at any tier Controls, is Controlled by, or is Controlled by an entity that Controls, a Party.'[39] As this transfer to an affiliate may be a part of a JOA party's group re-organisation, it may make commercial sense that such internal transfer does not trigger the other JOA parties' right to acquire the Participating Interest of the transferring party.[40] That being said, the 2012 JOA contains a safeguard which provides that the original JOA party remains liable for the affiliate's performance of its obligations.[41]

3. CHANGE IN CONTROL

3.1. DEFINITION

A change in control in the context of a JOA occurs when the entity controlling the majority interest in a JOA party changes. Change in control is defined in the 2012 JOA as a direct or indirect change of the majority interest in a JOA party, by way of a variety of means including a share sale. The change in control must be one in which the market value of the Participating Interest represents an agreed percentage of the market value of the assets of both (i) the JOA party subject to a change in control and (ii) its affiliates.[42] The thinking behind this is said to

---

38 Major, *supra* n. 7, p. 123: 'Generally assignments to affiliates will be excluded from pre-emption right provisions.'

39 Article 1.1 2012 JOA. See also the definition of Control in the 2012 JOA: 'the ownership directly or indirectly of more than fifty (50) percent [or] fifty (50) percent or more of the voting rights in a legal entity.'

40 Major, *supra* n. 7, p. 123: 'Co-Venturers should not be able to acquire interests simply due to another Co-Venturer's group reorganisation.'

41 See Article 12.2.D.3 2012 JOA: '[a transferee has no rights in the Contract or Agreement unless and until] in the case of a Transfer to an Affiliate, each Party has consented in writing to such Transfer, which consent shall be denied only if the transferee fails to establish to the reasonable satisfaction of each Party its ability to comply with the provisions of Article 20.1, and the transferring Party agrees in an instrument reasonably satisfactory to the other Parties to remain liable for its Affiliate's performance of its obligations' (emphasis added).

42 See the definition of 'change in control' in Article 1.1 2012 JOA: 'Change in Control means a direct or indirect change in Control of a Party (whether through merger, spin-off, sale of

cover situations where a change in control is only a small part of a much larger transaction (think Exxon Mobil), and to ensure that the provision will 'bite' only in those cases where the underlying transfer/change in control is the aim, or an important part of the aim, of the overall exercise (see below).

3.2. HISTORY OF CHANGE IN CONTROL PROVISIONS IN THE AIPN JOA

The change in control provisions in Article 12 of the 2012 JOA have evolved substantially from previous versions, the earliest of which contained no definition at all.[43] Change in control was originally intended to fall within the provisions on transfer – the 1995 JOA defined transfer as '[a]ny transfer of all or a portion of Participating Interest whether directly *or indirectly* by assignment, merger, consolidation, or sale of stock, or other conveyance, other than with or to an Affiliate.'[44] This 'sweeping language'[45] was intended to stop JOA parties from circumventing preferential rights by, for example, selling stock in a JOA party or its parent company.'[46] This, however, had unintended results, as it was unclear whether changes in control in a parent company, particularly where the Participating Interest of its subsidiary 'played a relatively insignificant role in the transaction', triggered pre-emption rights.

A number of disputes arose where changes in control at parent level led to arbitration proceedings, as it was unclear whether pre-emptive rights within the JOA had been triggered (since it was the subsidiary and not the parent who was the express party to the JOA).[47] As a result, the 2012 JOA now defines change in control separately from the provisions on transfer.

---

shares or other equity interests, or otherwise) through a single transaction or series of related transactions, from one or more transferors to one or more transferees, in which the market value of the Party's Participating Interest represents more than [___] percent of the aggregate market value of the assets of the Party and its Affiliates that are subject to the change in Control. For this definition, market value will be determined based upon the cash a willing buyer would pay a willing seller in an arm's length transaction.' Corresponding definition can be found in Article 12.1 2002 JOA.

43 Weems and Bolton, *supra* n. 15, p. 180: 'Historically, a change in control was undefined.'

44 Article 12.1(G) 1995 JOA. Our emphasis.

45 Weems and Bolton, *supra* n. 15, p. 180.

46 *Ibid.*, p. 180: 'Although the original intention behind the broad effect of the 1990 [and 1995] Version was to prevent a party from easily circumventing the pre-emption by selling the stock of the party or one of its parent companies, the Revision Committee noted that the sweeping language has led to unintended results.'

47 'The email Survey of AIPN members undertaken before drafting began on the Model Form revealed that Art. 12 in the 1995 Version was a key source of JOA disputes … the Revision Committee was aware of recent disputes in which a change of control (by merger of publicly traded corporations) at the parent company level resulted in an arbitration over whether preemptive rights were triggered with respect to the parent company's subsidiary which owned

3.3. GENERAL CONSIDERATIONS

The operative provisions on change in control are contained in Article 12.3 of the 2012 JOA. The parties can, in a similar fashion to the JOA provisions on transfer, provide for preferential rights to be triggered on a change of control. Note, for example, that when an affiliate takes control, this does not trigger preferential rights provisions.[48]

This new change in control provision uses 'both vote and value thresholds for determining whether a change in control occurs'.[49] As for the value aspect, a relevant change occurs when there is a takeover of the requisite JOA party (or its parent) and the market value of that party's Participating Interest constitutes a specified percentage of the market value of the overall assets of that party, and its affiliate.[50]

The financial position of the new entity is addressed by the optional provision contained in Article 12.3.B of the 2012 JOA, which requires that the party subject to the change in control provide information to the other parties indicating that it will still have the financial ability to uphold its payment obligations under the JOA and underlying contract. If this information is not provided, the other JOA parties can then require the party subject to the change in control to provide replacement security.[51]

---

a participating interest in a venture operating under the 1990 Version [of the AIPN JOA].' Note that the definition of transfer under the 1990 and 1995 versions are virtually identical.

48 See Article 12.3.C 2012 JOA: 'Any Change in Control of a Party, other than one that results in ongoing Control by an Affiliate shall be subject to the following [pre-emptive rights] procedure' (emphasis added).

49 Weems and Bolton, *supra* n. 15, p. 180.

50 A. Dann and G. Byrneon, *AIPN launches new joint operating agreement*, BLP Expert Legal Insights, 31.03.2012: 'A 'Change in Control' now only applies if the value of the relevant participating interests exceeds a percentage (to be nominated) of the assignor's group value, implying that the clause is intended to target only pre-emption avoidance, not financial capability. This proposed new standard wording may not be acceptable to many users of the document.' <http://www.blplaw.com/expert-legal-insights/articles/aipn-launches-new-joint-operating-agreement/>.

51 Weems and Bolton, *supra* n. 15, p. 180: 'The change in control provisions also include an option requiring satisfactory evidence of continued financial capability after a change in control. In the event that such evidence is not provided, the parties can require security for its participating interest share of 'any obligations or liabilities which the parties may reasonably be expected to incur' under the contract and the JOA.' See also Article 12.3.B JOA 2012: 'A Party subject to a Change in Control shall provide evidence reasonably satisfactory to the other Parties that after the Change in Control such Party shall continue to have the financial capability to satisfy its payment obligations under the Contract and this Agreement. If the Party that is subject to the Change in Control fail to provide such evidence, any other Party, by notice to such Party, may require such Party to provide Security satisfactory to the other Parties concerning its Participating Interest share of any obligations or liabilities that the Parties may reasonably be expected to incur under the Contract and this Agreement during the then-current Exploration or Exploitation Period or phase of the Contract.'

4. PREFERENTIAL RIGHTS TO PURCHASE

4.1. WHAT ARE THEY?

In contrast to an option, a preferential right may be exercised only once a trigger event has occurred, i.e. on the occurrence of a transfer or change in control. Preferential rights to purchase[52] give the holder of the right (Preferential Rights Holder) an opportunity to purchase the Participating Interest of a JOA party who wishes to transfer their interest or that is subject to a change in control, before the proposed transfer or change in control occurs.[53]

The general procedure in relation to preferential rights is that the JOA party that wishes either to transfer its Participating Interest, or is subject to a change in control, must notify the Preferential Rights Holders of their right to purchase the Participating Interest. The Preferential Rights Holders are notified of the terms and conditions under which they can exercise their preferential rights and are given a period of time within which to accept the offer.[54]

Another feature of preferential rights to purchase in the context of JOAs is that even if a JOA party decides not to exercise its right of pre-emption on a particular occasion, the right is not extinguished.[55] It survives as long as the Preferential Rights Holder is a party to the JOA and the JOA term is still running.[56]

If a third party purchases a Participating Interest that gives preferential rights to the other JOA parties, the preferential rights can generally be exercised against this third party by the other JOA parties even though the third party was not an original party to the JOA.[57] Indeed, the third party may itself inherit the

---

52 In this article reference to 'preferential rights' is to rights of pre-emption and rights of first refusal. See *supra* n. 13 for further explanation.

53 The timing of the notification by party proposing to transfer their interest in the JOA or that is subject to a change in control to the parties with the benefit of a preferential right will depend on the type of preferential right provided for in the JOA, i.e. pre-emption right or right of first refusal (see below section 4.2).

54 P.S. Murphy, *Perspectives in Preferential Rights to Purchase in Oil and Gas Agreements*, p. A-16: 'Once a preferential right holder has been notified of the terms and conditions under which it must exercise its rights, the holder then has an offer from the owner which is open for acceptance.' <www.aipn.org/documents/confDocs/PrefrightspaperfinalHunt.doc>.

55 E.B. Poitevent, II and C.L. Hewitt, *Preferential Rights, Rights of First Refusal and Options: The Whys and Wherefores*, American Association of Petroleum Landmen, New Orleans, Louisiana, June 2000, p. 4: 'The fact that the preferential right may not be exercised therefore has no extinguishing effect on the right.' <http://www.kslaw.com/library/pdf/PreferentialRights.pdf>.

56 *Ibid.*, p. 3: 'The holder of a preferential right, however, also holds on to his right for the duration of the operating agreement.'

57 *Ibid.*, p. 3: 'if the holder of a preferential right allows a sale to a third party to proceed, the holder may nevertheless exercise the preferential right when the third party himself decides to sell the interest'. See also Article 20.4 of the 2012 JOA: 'Subject to the limitations on Transfer contained in Article 12, this Agreement shall inure to the benefit of and be binding upon the successors and assignees of the Parties.'

benefit of the preferential rights of its predecessor.[58] If the JOA parties thus want to limit pre-emption rights to the original parties, they should expressly provide for this in the JOA.[59]

4.2. TYPES OF PREFERENTIAL RIGHTS

Preferential rights come in various forms, and each affects the specific procedure to be followed in relation to the right.[60] The 2012 JOA gives various options in this regard. The principal difference lies, logically, in the timing of the notification to the Preferential Rights Holder(s).[61]

4.2.1. Pre-emption Right

Pre-emption rights give JOA parties the opportunity to purchase a Participating Interest of the JOA party that is proposing to transfer the same, or is subject to a change in control, once the final terms of the transfer or change have been fully negotiated.

In the case of a transfer, the pre-emption rights provision in the 2012 JOA provides that '[o]nce the final terms and conditions of transfer have been fully negotiated',[62] the party wishing to transfer its Participating Interest must notify the Preferential Rights Holders of the 'final terms and conditions relevant to the acquisition',[63] after which the Preferential Rights Holders will have thirty days to deliver a counter-notification, where they may accept the terms and conditions 'without reservations or conditions'.[64] If more than one Preferential Rights

---

58 *Ibid.*, p. 4: 'A purchaser of a mineral interest, moreover, may become the holder of a preferential right or option held by his or her predecessor-in-interest.'

59 *Ibid.*, p. 4: 'If a party granting a preferential right or option desires to limit that right to the grantee, rather than the grantee and his or her transferees, then special attention should be paid during the process of drafting the JOA. In that case, special effort should be made to specify that the option or right of first refusal is personal in nature to the grantee and/or limited in time.' See also Roberts, *supra* n. 12, p. 138: 'pre-emption rights might be limited to application to only the first generation of parties to the JOA and could be expressed not to apply in respect of any subsequent transferees that later wish to transfer their interests.'

60 Poitevent and Hewitt, *supra* n. 55, p. 4: 'The procedure for exercising an option or preferential right varies according to the type of right at issue and the wording of the clause granting the right or option.'

61 The timing has often been a cause of disputes. See Weems and Bolton, *supra* n. 15, p. 178: 'The [2002 JOA] Revision Committee also took note of disputes that pertain to the timing of the exercise of the right of first negotiation (i.e. prior to the commencement of any third-party negotiations regarding a potential disposition versus at any time prior to the actual closing of the transfer of the transferor's participating interest).'

62 Article 12.2.F.1 (Optional Alternative #1 – Preferential Rights) 2012 JOA.

63 *Ibid.*

64 *Ibid.*

Holder counter-notifies the proposed transferor, then each party will acquire a portion of the Participating Interest 'equal to the ratio of its own Participating Interest to the total Participating Interests of all the counter-notifying Parties.'[65]

Similarly, in the context of a change in control under the 2012 JOA, only once the final terms of a change in control have been negotiated must the party subject to the change notify the Preferential Rights Holders, by disclosing the terms and conditions of the acquisition of the Participating Interest and by attributing a cash value to that interest (which can of course be a delicate and critical exercise where the sale is part of a larger overall transaction).[66] The Preferential Rights Holders would then have the right to acquire this Participating Interest on these terms, again by delivering a counter-notification.[67] Similarly, if more than one Preferential Rights Holder is interested in purchasing the Participating Interest, they may do so in proportion to their respective interests.[68] The right to purchase the Participating Interest is, however, extinguished if the change of control does not go ahead.[69]

4.2.2. *Right of first refusal*

A right of first refusal is similar to a pre-emption right in that it allows a Preferential Rights Holder to purchase the Participating Interest of a JOA party, over and above a third party. A right of first refusal, however, is triggered much earlier in the negotiation process.

In the context of a transfer in the 2012 JOA, rights of first refusal are triggered before the negotiations with third parties have even commenced.[70] Therefore, these rights arise before there is any written agreement with the third party[71] and prohibit the proposed transferor from entering into a non-binding written

---

65 Article 12.2.F.2 (Optional Alternative #1 – Preferential Rights) 2012 JOA.

66 Article 12.3.C.1 (Optional Alternative #1 – Preemptive Rights) 2012 JOA: 'Once the final terms and conditions of a Change in Control have been fully negotiated, the Acquired Party shall disclose all such final terms and conditions as are relevant to the acquisition of such Party's Participating Interest and the determination of the Cash Value of that Participating Interest in a notice to the other Parties.'

67 *Ibid.*

68 Article 12.3.C.2 (Optional Alternative #1 – Preemptive Rights) 2012 JOA.

69 Article 12.3.C.3 (Optional Alternative #1 – Preemptive Rights): 'No Party may acquire the Acquired Party's Participating Interest under this Article 12.3.C unless and until completion of the Change in Control. If for any reason the Change in Control agreement terminates without completion, the other Parties' rights to acquire the Participating Interest subject to the proposed Change in Control shall also terminate.'

70 Hammerson, *supra* n. 10, p. 202: 'Rights of first refusal are triggered prior to any third-party sale process having commenced.'

71 Article 12.2.F.1 (Optional Alternative #2 – Right of First Refusal) 2012 JOA provides for rights of first refusal to be triggered 'before the transferor enters into a written agreement providing for such a Transfer.'

agreement with that third party.[72] Rights of first refusal in the 2012 JOA require the proposed transferor to invite the Preferential Rights Holders to make an offer for the Participating Interest (by way of counter-notification).[73] The Preferential Rights Holder and the proposed transferor are then obliged to negotiate for a period of sixty days in good faith.[74] Once this sixty-day period has elapsed, and in the event that they do not find the offer of the Preferential Rights Holder acceptable, the transferor can transfer the Participating Interest to a third party.[75]

There is an important optional provision stating that the proposed transferor can accept the offer of the third party only if it is on more favourable terms than those of the Preferential Rights Holders proposing to acquire the interest.[76] In the event that more than one Preferential Rights Holder is interested in making an offer to buy the Participating Interest, the interested JOA parties should meet and make a joint offer[77] which, if successful, enables them to purchase the Participating Interest *pro rata* to their Participating Interests.[78]

The provisions on rights of first negotiation in the 2012 JOA (in the context of a change in control) follow the same procedure as outlined above. The only difference is that the trigger event arises when the affiliates of a JOA party, rather than the JOA party itself, seek to enter into a transaction that will result in a change in control of that JOA party.[79]

4.3. ARGUMENTS IN FAVOUR OF PREFERENTIAL RIGHTS

There are a variety of reasons why preferential rights may be considered desirable. One of the most obvious is that they allow the JOA parties to have some control over the identity of their fellow JOA parties,[80] enabling the exclusion of third parties that either do not have the financial means by which to comply with the

72 Weems and Bolton, *supra* n. 15, p. 20: 'the right of first negotiation prohibits a transferor from even entering into a non-binding heads of agreement or memorandum of understanding'. See also Article 12.2.F.1 2012 JOA (Optional Alternative #2 – Right of First Refusal) 'whether or not such agreement is binding.'

73 Article 12.2.F.1 (Optional Alternative #2 – Right of First Refusal) 2012 JOA: 'If a Party wishes to transfer any part or all of its Participating Interest, before the transferor enters into a written agreement providing for such a Transfer (whether or not such agreement is binding) the transferor shall send the other Parties notice of its intention and invite them to submit offers for the Participating Interest subject to the Transfer.'

74 *Ibid.*

75 *Ibid.*

76 Article 12.2.F.1 (Optional Alternative #2 – Right of First Refusal) 2012 JOA.

77 Article 12.2.F.3 (Optional Alternative #2 – Right of First Refusal) 2012 JOA.

78 Article 12.2.F.2 (Optional Alternative #2 – Right of First Refusal) 2012 JOA.

79 Article 12.3.C.1 (Optional Alternative #2 – Right of First Negotiation) 2012 JOA.

80 Poitevent and Hewitt, *supra* n. 55, p. 2: 'a preferential right allows its holder to control whom his business partners will be in future lease operations.'

obligations of the JOA,[81] or do not have the expertise required to be beneficial to the joint operations.[82] The third party may also have a business philosophy which is not compatible with that of the other JOA parties,[83] thereby posing the risk of disruption to the decision-making process.[84] In some cases the incumbents may want the ability to prevent a third party from becoming a JOA party for political reasons.[85] Put in the most general terms, JOA parties may hence want preferential rights in the JOA in order to 'help to preserve the culture and cohesion of the original joint venture'.[86]

From a commercial perspective, it may be cost effective to give JOA parties the right to buy a further stake in an asset in which they already hold an interest, as it allows them to profit from the due diligence already conducted on the asset, and to consolidate their interest in that asset.[87]

4.4. ARGUMENTS AGAINST PREFERENTIAL RIGHTS

There are similarly many arguments against preferential rights. For example, preferential provisions can fetter the ability of a JOA party to dispose of its proprietary interest, thus affecting the marketability of that interest[88] to potential purchasers.[89] In particular, if the JOA gives a right of pre-emption (rather than a right of first refusal) to the other JOA parties, the third party could suffer substantial wastage of time, money and resources. Consider where that party spends a great deal on negotiations and due diligence to the point that it has agreed a set of final terms.[90] These final terms would, of course, have to be

---

81 Poitevent and Hewitt, *supra* n. 55, p. 2.

82 Murphy, *supra* n. 54, p. A-3: '[a company may] want the ability to exclude certain parties that are not compatible with [their] company or that are financially or technically weak.'

83 Poitevent and Hewitt, *supra* n. 55, p. 2: 'A preferential right, moreover, will allow its holder to exclude a third party from the JOA that has an operational or engineering philosophy that differs from that of the current owners.'

84 Major, *supra* n. 7, p. 118: 'concern about introducing further Co-Venturers into a project thus creating potentially more complicated decision-making procedures.'

85 Major, *supra* n. 7, p. 118: '[there are] more complex reasons for not wanting to be in a venture with a particular Potential Buyer such as political reasons'.

86 Roberts, *supra* n. 12, p. 138.

87 Murphy, *supra* n. 54, p. A-3: '[preferential rights allow JOA parties to] buy properties in which [they] already own an interest, consolidating [their] holdings, and thereby reducing [their] costs.'

88 Murphy, *supra* n. 54, p. A-3: '[preferential rights] diminish the value and marketability of a property.'

89 P. Dighton, 'Pre-emptive rights jettisoned in the North Sea' (2003) 22 *Australian Resources & Energy L.J.* 146, 150: '[preferential rights] are an unreasonable fetter on alienation which is likely to make the interest worth less and more difficult to market.'

90 Poitevent and Hewitt, *supra* n. 55, p. 2: 'a potential buyer will be reluctant to enter into extended negotiations to purchase the interest on beneficial terms when those terms may be

conditional on the Preferential Rights Holders not taking up their rights.[91] If they decide to exercise those rights, then the potential purchaser will have done it all for nought.[92] The costly and time-consuming nature of the preferential rights procedure itself acts as a deterrent to potential purchasers.[93]

Another issue is that because potential buyers may be deterred by the presence of preferential rights provisions,[94] the resultant decrease in the number of potential buyers will reduce competitive tension. As a result, the price offered for the Participating Interest may be lower than it otherwise would be.[95] From the seller's point of view, preferential rights are uncommercial because they limit its flexibility to dispose of the Participating Interest and adjust its portfolio of investments.[96]

As explained above, there is considerable debate over the inclusion of provisions for preferential rights in JOAs. Whilst some companies view them as incentivising in oil and gas exploration and production (as they allow JOA parties to control with whom they will engage in these activities), others see preferential rights as limiting commercial flexibility.[97]

4.5. APPROACH TO PREFERENTIAL RIGHTS

4.5.1. *Common Law*

The treatment of pre-emption provisions in common law jurisdictions has been inconsistent. This has created a degree of uncertainty surrounding the

used to co-opt the deal for another party to the JOA. The potential for lost time and needless expense almost certainly impacts the market value of interests subject to these [preferential] rights.'

91 If the terms are not conditional then the transferring party – and in the circumstances that the third party was aware of the existence of the preferential right, the third party – may be liable to the Preferential Rights Holders for breach of contract.

92 Murphy, *supra* n. 54, p. A-3: 'Some potential purchasers will decline to review the technical and financial data on the property because of opportunity costs, administrative costs, etc.'

93 Roberts, *supra* n. 12, p. 138: 'The application of pre-emption rights is often accused of stultifying the free transferability of petroleum project interests, through the implication of extra costs of contracting associated with their exercise [and] the imposition of delays in the sale process.' See also Major, *supra* n. 7, p. 120: 'a pre-emption right will almost certainly cause delays and a certain amount of completion uncertainty.'

94 Roberts, *supra* n. 12, p. 138: 'transferees are potentially deterred from bidding because of uncertainty about whether the non-transferring parties will exercise their pre-emption rights.'

95 Murphy, *supra* n. 54, p. A-4: 'Assuming there are fewer bidders due to the [preferential rights], the bids that are tendered may be lower because of perceived lower competition.'

96 *Ibid.*, p. A-4: '[preferential rights] limit the flexibility on the sellers to adjust their portfolios.'

97 *Ibid.*, p. A-3: 'Some companies view preferential rights to purchase ("PRTP") as an important part of their joint venture with others in the exploration for and production of hydrocarbons. They view PRPT as a way of controlling with whom they will participate in joint venture

treatment of such clauses that is unappealing to commercial parties.[98] Indeed, '[c]ases involving pre-emption rights are essentially exercises in interpretation, which means the decision is usually specific to the particular drafting and circumstances, making it difficult to extract generic principles.'[99]

4.5.1.1. England

A well-cited English law authority on the willingness of the English courts to facilitate the exercise of pre-emption rights in the context of JOAs is *Texas Eastern Corporation (Delaware) and Ors v Enterprise Oil Plc & Ors*.[100] Against a complex background of changes of ownership of the underlying interest, the JOA contained a provision giving the other operators sixty days from the receipt of a notice from the operator wishing to sell its interest 'the prior and preferred option, in the ratio of the respective Percentages of Interest of those electing to purchase, to purchase the interest covered by said offer'.[101]

In the High Court, Evans J had found that the pre-emption provision was invalid as, based on the wording of the JOA, it was not workable in practice,[102] as the percentage of each party's interest was too difficult to quantify as a result of changes of ownership of the interests under the original licence.[103] Evans J held that it was not the duty of the court to remedy the agreement between the parties by implying the required terms to enable it to work.[104]

The Court of Appeal, however, took a different approach, overturning the decision of the Commercial Court, and reading the provision in light of the commercial intentions of the parties, thereby interpreting the pre-emption clause widely so as to make it workable. This was accomplished by finding

activities. Others view PRPT as an undesirable clause that should be avoided because it diminishes the value of their property and limits their flexibility in managing their portfolio.'

98 Dighton, *supra* n. 89, p. 146: 'Frustration with the uncertainty surrounding these clauses, and the disputes that have arisen, has led to recent intervention by the UK government in respect of North Sea petroleum licences.'

99 *Ibid.*, p. 148.

100 Unreported, Court of Appeal (England), 21 July 1989.

101 See *Texas Eastern Corporation (Delaware) and Ors v Enterprise Oil Plc & Ors*, Unreported, Court of Appeal (England), 21 July 1989, p. 3.

102 See *Texas Eastern Corporation (Delaware) and Ors v Enterprise Oil Plc & Ors*, Unreported, Court of Appeal (England), 21 July 1989, p. 1.

103 Dighton, *supra* n. 89, p. 149: 'the complications were that the different participants owned different parts of the [licence area] plus [TENSI] owned interests in other fields ... when the other participants exercised their rights, entitling them to purchase according to their existing 'Percentages of Interest', it was almost impossible to stipulate who was entitled to what.' See also Hammerson, *supra* n. 10, p. 202: 'the ownership of different sub-areas diverged from the licence area as a whole [which] made the implementation of pre-emption rights difficult to operate.'

104 Dighton, *supra* n. 89, p. 149: 'Evans J held that the Court could not imply terms to make a pre-emption clause work.'

that the percentage interests of each other party should be determined by an expert and that if the result was not acceptable, allowing the parties to return to court.[105] The Court of Appeal, therefore, found that the pre-emptive rights were valid,[106] demonstrating a willingness to make pre-emption provisions work. This decision, however, is not free from controversy; according to one writer 'the decision is generally criticised as redrafting the clause for the parties.'[107]

4.5.1.2. Australia

In *Beaconsfield Gold NL & Ors v Allstate Prospecting Pty Ltd & Ors*,[108] a dispute arose out of a joint venture. Although this is not strictly a JOA scenario, a JOA is in essence an unincorporated joint venture;[109] therefore the case may give some indication as to how preferential rights would be interpreted in a JOA).

While the decision, strictly speaking, principally concerns how to interpret a change in control provision, it demonstrates, in the writer's view, the courts' general inclination towards the protection of the commercial bargain behind these types of provisions.

---

105 *Ibid.*, p. 149: 'On appeal the Court of Appeal, in overturning this decision, exercised a remarkable degree of judicial creativity by formulating an approach where the differing interests were to be valued by an expert and if that did not deliver an acceptable result the parties could come back to the Court!'.

106 The reasoning of Dillon L J in *Texas Eastern v Enterprise Oil* was as follows: 'the position is as if there were a contract for sale at a reasonable price, which involves assessing value, and it was said that the parties have not agreed whether the appropriate method of valuing is so many years' purchase of expected rent or so much per square foot of floor area and, therefore, it is necessary to have expert evidence as to what is the appropriate method. The court would say it is to be the reasonable method in the circumstances of effecting the valuation which will produce the reasonable price.' See *Texas Eastern Corporation (Delaware) and Ors v Enterprise Oil Plc & Ors*, Unreported, Court of Appeal (England), 21 July 1989, p. 10.

107 S. Damson Garba, 'Pre-emption Right in the Commercial Viability of JOA Interest: Is the UK approach a Model for other Jurisdictions?', p. 8 <http://www.dundee.ac.uk/cepmlp/gateway/files.php?file=cepmlp_car14_23_708009940.pdf>.

108 [2006] VSC 320 (8 September 2006).

109 Hammerson, *supra* n. 10, p. 176: 'The form of unincorporated petroleum joint venture is commonly known by the contract that establishes it – the joint operating agreement.' See also O'Gorman and Stadnyk, *supra* n. 1, pp. 10–16: 'The JOA is essentially an unincorporated joint venture.' See also B. Jensen and Y. Abul Failat, 'Oil and Gas Joint Operating Agreements - Default Provisions, a Dilemma by Default' (2013) 11(5) *Oil, Gas & Energy Law Intelligence* 3: 'JVs can take the form of a corporation, limited liability company or partnership although in the oil and gas industry JVs are usually unincorporated which means that they do not have a distinct legal personality and therefore cannot be taxed, sued or sue in their own name.' See also F. Solimene, 'Production-sharing Contracts, Joint Ventures and Service Contracts: Analysis and Drafting Consideration' (2014) 32(5) IELR 176: 'JVAs are agreements where 'venturing firms combine subsets of their assets for a specific business purpose and for a limited period of time (usually from ten to fifteen years or less)'. The most important kind of JVA used in the oil and gas industry is a joint operating agreement.'

The pre-emption clause in the joint venture agreement in this case came into effect if and when the joint venture partner[110] became 'at any time a subsidiary of another corporation'.[111] The meaning of 'subsidiary of another corporation' was fundamental to the case. The judge stated that the meaning should be determined objectively, by a reasonable person in the position of the parties to the contract, construing the words in a commercially sensible manner.[112]

Ultimately, the judge in the case held that pre-emption rights would be triggered even if the change in control did not occur in the immediate holding company of the JOA party, but occurred in a parent company further up the corporate tree. The court considered that the pre-emption provisions in the JVA had 'an obvious anti-avoidance purpose'.[113] The judge also expressed the view that the objectives of pre-emption rights generally 'may be defeated if pre-emptive rights provisions are interpreted narrowly'.[114] The judge, therefore, held that '[w]here there are two interpretations of a pre-emptive rights clause in a joint venture agreement which are reasonably open, that which accords with the objective purpose of the provision should be preferred.'[115]

4.5.2. Civil Law

The Guidance Notes to the 2012 JOA state the following regarding pre-emption rights: 'In certain Civil Law jurisdictions, pre-emption rights may result from statutory law. For instance, in some Civil Law jurisdictions, the co-owners of property and the co-holders of contractual rights may pre-empt by law transfers of any of such properties and/or contractual rights to third parties. If the Parties wish not to have pre-emption rights at all, it is advisable to include a clear exclusion provision in the Operating Agreement.'[116] The writer has seen provisions of this type involved in various Russian projects, for example.

From a more contractual perspective, under French law, preferential rights, also known as *droits préférentiels*, *droit de priorité/faveur* or *droit de preemption*, may result from a *pacte de préférence* (preferential agreement) or from a *clause de cession préférentielle* (preferential rights clause) or *clause de rachat prioritaire* (preferential buy-out clause) included in the agreement.[117] In the absence of

---

110 The joint venture partner in these circumstances may be compared to a JOA party.

111 *Beaconsfield Gold NL and Ors v Allstate Prospecting Property Ltd* [2006] VSC 320 (8 September 2006), para. 8.

112 *Ibid.*, para. 9.

113 *Ibid.*, para. 32.

114 *Ibid.*, para. 34.

115 *Ibid.*, para. 34.

116 AIPN 2012 Guidance Notes, p. 6.

117 B. Mallet-Bricout, 'Le droit de préemption du cocontractant – pas de pitié pour le bénéficiaire!', *La Semaine Juridique Notariale et Immobilière* n° 40, 7 octobre 2011, 1266, LexisNexis.

specific legal texts on preferential rights agreements or clauses,[118] the regime governing preferential rights clauses falls under the general French legal principles on contracts.[119]

5. TRANSFERS IN THE CONTEXT OF A DEFAULT

The transfers discussed up to this point have involved exercises where the proposed transferor has wanted, and been willing, to transfer its Participating Interest. In contrast, a transferor may be forced to transfer its interest against its will, as a result of its default of particular obligations under the JOA.

The provisions on default are contained in Article 8 of the 2012 JOA, under which a default arises where a JOA party fails to pay charges under the joint account (including cash calls) or provide or maintain security when required to do so under the JOA or underlying contract.[120] There is also an option to provide that a failure to perform indemnity obligations will also constitute a default.[121]

The default provisions in Article 8 have undergone a series of substantial changes over the years, resulting in their increased complexity. The revisions to Article 8 of the 2002 JOA have, for example, focused on the remedies available against a defaulting party and the clarification of issues including the rights lost as a result of default.[122] The biggest change to the 2002 JOA, however, was the addition of an optional forfeiture provision requiring the defaulting party to withdraw from the agreement and licence,[123] and the optional buy-out

118 Some preferential rights clauses are governed by specific legal dispositions under French law, such as for shareholders, in real estate, etc.

119 The general governing principles of contractual freedom and party autonomy remain, as provided by Article 1134 of the French Civil Code: 'Agreements lawfully entered into take the place of the law for those who have made them. They may be revoked only by mutual consent, or for causes authorized by law. They must be performed in good faith.' The validity of an agreement, such as the assignment of a company's participating interest to another entity, is governed by Article 1108 of the French Civil Code, which establishes four conditions for the validity of a contract: 'Four requisites are essential for the validity of an agreement: The consent of the party who binds himself; His capacity to contract; A definite object which forms the subject-matter of the undertaking; A lawful cause in the obligation.' (English translations provided by Legifrance.)

120 See Article 8.1.A 2012 JOA: 'Any Party that fails to pay when due its share of Joint Account charges (including Cash Calls and interest), or provide when due and maintain any Security required of such Party under the Contract or this Agreement … shall be in default under this Agreement.'

121 Article 8.1.A 2012 JOA.

122 Weems and Bolton, *supra* n. 15, p. 12: 'In general, revisions to the default provisions centred on addressing possible enforceability of remedies as well as clarification of certain default rights (such as rights lost during a default and the effects of a default caused by a failure to post financial security).'

123 Article 8.4(D) (Alternative 1) 2002 JOA.

provision, providing for the non-defaulting parties to buy out the defaulting party's Participating Interest.[124]

The 2012 JOA built on the Articles of the 2002 JOA,[125] particularly with the addition of a withering clause, which gives the option to require a defaulting party to sell and assign a portion of its Participating Interest using a formula which takes into account, *inter alia*, the amount already contributed by the defaulting party and the amount in default.[126] In addition, the 2012 JOA added a provision allowing for a defaulting party to transfer its Participating Interest so long as it cures its default prior to the transfer or on the closing of the transfer.[127] The result of the amendments over the years is that the 2012 JOA now provides for three different options to be taken by JOA parties in response to a default, some details of which are provided below.

Under the 2012 JOA, the process commences with the operator giving notice of default, which it is obliged to do promptly upon learning of the default. The default period begins five days after the default notice is given.[128] As soon as the default period commences, the defaulting party loses various rights under the JOA, including certain rights in relation to transfers.[129]

5.1. FORFEITURE

Traditionally, the remedy of forfeiture in the context of default remedies in JOAs has been a source of what can best be termed anxiety, particularly regarding whether the remedy will be considered a penalty and therefore unenforceable.[130] Indeed, although the forfeiture remedy may be considered to be a fair way to ensure that the JOA parties uphold their payment obligations under the JOA,

---

124 Article 8.4(D) (Alternative 2) 2002 JOA.

125 Gilbert & Tobin, *The New 2012 AIPN Model International Joint Operating Agreement*, March 2012: 'The 2012 JOA contains updated provisions dealing with protracted and more complex types of default.'

126 Article 8.4.G 2012 JOA.

127 Article 8.3.C 2012 JOA.

128 See the definition of Default Period in Article 1.1 2012 JOA: 'the period beginning on the fifth (5th) Business Day after the date that the Default Notice is received under Article 8.1.A and ending when the Defaulting Party has remedied its default in full by paying the Total Amount in Default.'

129 See Article 8.2.A.5 2012 JOA: 'the Defaulting Party has no right, during the Default Period, to: ... Consent to or reject any Transfer or otherwise exercise any other rights with respect to Transfers under this Article 8 or under Article 12.'

130 Peter Roberts, *Fault Lines in Joint Operating Agreement: Forfeiture* [2008] IELR 275: 'Historically, the principal nervousness around the operation of the forfeiture remedy by the non-defaulting parties has revolved around whether the remedy might be determined to be penal in nature and so unenforceable.'

it is 'a powerful tool which must be exercised with great care and responsibility and which is fraught with uncertainty about its legal validity.'[131] Forfeiture is considered to be the 'ultimate price paid for failure to contribute a percentage interest share of the cost of the joint venture.'[132]

5.1.1. England

The English law on penalties was the subject of a recent and comprehensive restatement by the Supreme Court in the case of *Cavendish Square Holding BV v Makdessi*.[133] For present purposes, three important principles emerge from the decision (two relating to the scope of the rule against penalties, and one on the substance of the test to be applied in determining whether a given provision constitutes a penalty).

First, the court accepted that a clause which imposes a forced transfer for no consideration or for consideration which does not reflect the value of the asset transferred could amount to a penalty.[134] The court also considered that it was possible for a clause to be both a penalty clause and a forfeiture clause.[135] A measure of confusion had existed in English law as to the relationship between the equitable doctrine of relief against forfeiture and the rule against penalties. Although the Supreme Court did not come to a definitive view, the approach they preferred was summed up by Lord Clarke in the following terms: 'the court should ask first whether, as a matter of construction, the clause is a penalty and, if it answers that question in the negative, it should ask (where relevant) whether relief against forfeiture should be granted in equity having regard to the position of each of the parties after the breach'.[136]

Accordingly, it appears that forfeiture clauses in JOAs are, at least in principle, capable of amounting to penalty clauses.[137]

Second, the Supreme Court reiterated the position that the rule against penalties applied to terms which are so-called 'secondary obligations'. These are, in simple terms, contractual remedies which arise upon the breach of a primary

---

131 *Ibid.*, p. 275: 'The customary tone of the various commentaries on the efficacy of the default provision under the JOA is to suggest that the forfeiture remedy, whilst providing a fair measure of protection to all the parties to the JOA to ensure that they each pay their way according to their defined shares (without which the risks associated with the JOA might simply not be undertaken), is a powerful tool which must be exercised with great care and responsibility and which is fraught with uncertainty about its legal validity.'

132 C. Golvala, 'Upstream Joint Ventures – Bidding and Operating Agreements', in G. Picton-Turbervill (ed.), *Oil and Gas: a Practical Handbook*, Globe Law and Business, London 2009, p. 49.

133 *Cavendish Square Holding BV v Makdessi; ParkingEye Ltd v Beavis* [2015] UKSC 67.

134 *Ibid.*, para. 183.

135 *Ibid.*, paras. 18, 160, 227, 291 and 292.

136 *Ibid.*, para. 291.

137 Roberts, *supra* n. 130, p. 275: 'Although the forfeiture will be of the defaulting party's property interests, rather than the obligation of the defaulting party to make payment of a sum of money as is the case with a conventional penalty obligation, the principles which will arise for consideration will be much the same.'

contractual obligation (such as an obligation to pay a certain amount of money upon failure to comply with a primary obligation to deliver goods).[138]

Third, the court recast the test for determining whether a particular provision constitutes a penalty. The recast test asks, first, whether (at the time of contracting) there was a 'legitimate interest' to be protected. Then, if the non-defaulting party can be said to have had a legitimate interest in contractual performance of the primary obligation by the defaulting party, the court must ask whether the means of protection were 'out of all proportion' or 'exorbitant or unconscionable' when regard is had to the interest in question.[139]

As to whether the forfeiture remedy will be considered a penalty under this recast test, it seems that a powerful case can be made in relation to the first limb of the test. That is to say, there are a number of arguments weighing in favour of concluding that a non-defaulting partner did have a legitimate interest in the performance of the various primary obligations contained in JOAs. For example, the terms requiring prompt payment of cash calls allow the project to progress and enable the parties to meet their commitments under work programmes and the licence or concession itself. In so doing, the negative consequences of failing to meet these commitments are avoided. On that basis, the non-defaulting partner does appear to have a legitimate interest in ensuring, for example, that the defaulting party promptly pays cash calls.

However, as to the second limb of the test – the question of whether the application of the forfeiture clause will be considered 'out of all proportion' or 'exorbitant or unconscionable' to the legitimate interest – this is likely to turn on the particular facts of the case. For example, if JOA parties were to pursue forfeiture in a situation where the amount owed by the defaulting party was much less that the value of its Participating Interest, then this could be a factor weighing in favour of finding that the clause amounts to a penalty. On the other hand, the fact that the forfeiture clause is theoretically applicable to all parties may weigh in favour of finding it is not a penalty. What seems clear is that enforcing forfeiture provisions as a result of a payment default in certain circumstances 'could be considered by the English courts to be disproportionate to the injury actually suffered by the [non-defaulting parties] and thus rendering the forfeiture clause a penalty'.[140]

5.1.2. *France*

By contrast, French law upholds liquidated damages clauses (termed *clauses pénales*) which specify a reasonable amount of damages for breach of contract[141] whilst, pursuant to the French Civil Code, providing judicial discretion to adjust

138 *Cavendish Square Holding BV v Makdessi; ParkingEye Ltd v Beavis* [2015] UKSC 67, para. 14.

139 *Ibid.*, paras. 32, 152, 255 and 293.

140 Jensen and Abul Failat, *supra* n. 109, p. 5.

141 Article 1152 of the French Civil Code provides as follows: 'Where an agreement provides that he who fails to perform it will pay a certain sum as damages, the other party may not be awarded a greater or lesser sum.'

the agreed amount of damages 'where it is obviously excessive or ridiculously low'. This gives scope for arbitral tribunals applying French law as the substantive law in the proceedings to modify a *clause pénale*.

The risk that forfeiture provisions may be unenforceable under English and French law means that JOA parties need to exercise caution when choosing and exercising default provisions. There is often, as a result of these concerns, a temptation for JOA parties to instead provide for withering or buy-out provisions as a remedy against default, but even these remedies are not without their own issues.[142]

Assuming that the JOA parties do decide to exercise the forfeiture remedy, the 2012 JOA requires a defaulting party to completely withdraw from the agreement and assign its Participating Interest to the non-defaulting parties.[143] The assignment to the non-defaulting parties should be in proportion to the Participating Interests of those other parties, excluding any non-defaulting party which declines such assignment.[144]

There is also a new optional provision in the 2012 JOA for expedited forfeiture for subsequent default.[145] This provision provides that in those circumstances where a second default occurs in the same twelve-month period, the defaulting party has only fifteen, and not thirty, days until the forfeiture remedy can be exercised by the non-defaulting parties.[146] This addresses the inconvenience to JOA parties who are subjected to repeated late payments. As well as inconvenience, late payments can result in the non-defaulting parties having to arrange an interim funding facility to remedy the late paying party's behaviour.[147]

---

142 Jensen and Abul Failat, *supra* n. 109, p. 1: 'Therefore whilst it may be tempting for JV partners to choose the alternative default provisions to forfeiture (namely, withering options and buy-out provisions) on the pretext that this will bring JV partners on safer ground, these provisions themselves may in fact hide some risks more commonly associated with outright forfeiture clauses.'

143 Article 8.4.D.1 2012 JOA: 'any non-defaulting Party shall have the option, exercisable in its discretion at any time, to require that the Defaulting Party offer to completely withdraw from this Agreement and assign all of its Participating Interest, as described in Article 8.4.E.'

144 Article 8.4.E 2012 JOA.

145 Article 8.4.D – Optional Provision 2012 JOA.

146 Article 8.4.D 2012 JOA: 'If a Defaulting Party fails to fully remedy all its defaults by the thirtieth (30th) Day of the Default Period, or by the fifteenth (15th) Day of the corresponding Default Period of any subsequent default occurring within twelve (12) Months of the preceding default.'

147 Roberts, *supra* n. 130, p. 274 'a party [may commit] persistent but eventually remedied defaults, which will also inconvenience the non-defaulting parties.' See also Roberts, *supra* n. 12, p. 187: 'The principal definition of a "default" implies the total failure of a party to pay its share of a cash call or an invoice request by a due date, but it might also be that a party's behaviour is characterised by repeatedly making late payments. These late payments will eventually be remedied each time by the defaulting party, but this pattern will inconvenience the non-defaulting parties, which will effectively be required to act as a form of interim funding facility in order to make good the defaulting party's late payments.'

5.2. BUY-OUT

The buy-out provision introduced by 2012 JOA 'is arguably the most 'reasonable' of all default options as it ensures fair reimbursement to the [Defaulting Party] for its past contributions during the life of the venture.'[148] It is less harsh in nature than the forfeiture provision because although the defaulting party is still forced to transfer its Participating Interest, the defaulting party receives consideration for this transfer from the non-defaulting parties who are willing to buy out the interest.[149]

There is the option under the 2012 JOA to allow that either each non-defaulting party, or a majority in interest of the non-defaulting parties, buy out the defaulting party.[150] The procedure involves the non-defaulting parties exercising their buy-out option and giving the defaulting party a notice specifying the value offered for the acquisition of the defaulting party's Participating Interest.[151] If the defaulting party does not accept the value in this notice, then the determination of the relevant value will be referred to an independent expert.[152]

When drafting the JOA, the parties may choose to include a percentage discount which is to be applied to the consideration paid by the non-defaulting parties for the defaulting party's Participating Interest in any buy-out.[153] The percentage to be applied is negotiated by the parties when drafting the JOA. The application of this percentage may also lead to problems in practice. On the one hand, the discount factor is helpful because it 'serves to minimise the risk that a [defaulting] party may use the buy-out option as a mean of forcing the other [JOA parties] to buy-out at fair market value'[154] when its involvement in the JOA has become less profitable. Indeed, for the purpose of deterring JOA parties from misusing the buy-out provisions 'parties will often want to apply significant discount factors – of say at least 25%'.[155] However, there is the risk

---

148 Jensen and Abul Failat, *supra* n. 109, p. 6.

149 Article 8.4.D.2 2012 JOA: 'any non-defaulting Party shall have the option, exercisable in its discretion at any time, to require that the Defaulting Party offer to sell and assign all of its Participating Interest to any non-defaulting Parties wishing to purchase such Participating Interest, as described in Article 8.4.F.'

150 Article 8.4.F.1 (Alternative #1 and Alternative #2) 2012 JOA.

151 Article 8.4.F.2 2012 JOA: 'Each Acquiring Party shall specify in its Buy-Out Notice a value for the Defaulting Party's entire Participating Interest.'

152 Article 8.4.F.2 2012 JOA: 'the Defaulting Party shall (i) notify the Acquiring Parties that it accepts, with respect to each Acquiring Party, such Acquiring Party's proportionate share of the value specified by such Acquiring Party in its Buy-Out Notice (in which case this value is, with respect to such Acquiring Party, the "Buy-Out Price"); or (ii) refer the Dispute to an independent expert pursuant to Article 18.3 for determination of the value of its entire Participating Interest.'

153 Article 8.4.F.2(c) 2012 JOA.

154 Jensen and Abul Failat, *supra* n. 109, p. 6.

155 *Ibid.*

that this discount factor may be considered to be punitive to the point of being a penalty.[156] This concern is highlighted in the 2012 JOA Guidance Notes which state that the percentage of the discount should be 'carefully examined in order to avoid any objection on grounds of unconscionability.'[157]

5.3. WITHERING PROVISIONS

Withering provisions provide that in the event of a default, the non-defaulting parties have the option to decrease the Participating Interest of a defaulting party.[158] Pursuant to such provisions, the amount by which the defaulting party's Participating Interest is decreased (Withering Interest) is determined and assigned to the non-defaulting parties.[159] The Withering Interest is calculated using a formula specified in the JOA.[160] In the 2012 JOA the factors taken into account in this formula include the costs paid by the defaulting party in the development plan before the default[161] and the defaulting party's share of the estimated total costs.[162]

Again, there is choice in the 2012 JOA to provide that either (i) each non-defaulting party, or (ii) a majority in interest of the non-defaulting parties, may exercise their withering option on a default.[163] If each non-defaulting party is given the right to exercise its withering option and more than one non-defaulting party exercises the same option, the Withering Interest will be assigned to each of the parties *pro rata*.[164]

---

156 Roberts, *supra* n. 130, p. 276: 'This is something of a paradox since it partly reintroduces the principle of penalisation of the defaulting party into a mechanism which was initially intended to ameliorate the punitive nature of the forfeiture provision.'

157 AIPN 2012 Guidance Notes, p. 5.

158 Article 8.4.D.3 2012 JOA: 'any non-defaulting Party shall have the option, exercisable in its discretion with respect to a default occurring at any time under an approved Development Plan, to require that the Defaulting Party offer to assign a part of the Defaulting Party's Participating Interest in the corresponding Exploitation Area to any non-defaulting Parties wishing to accept assignment of such part, as described in Article 8.4.G.'

159 Article 8.4.G.1 2012 JOA.

160 Article 8.4.G.2 2012 JOA.

161 Article 8.4.G.2 2012 JOA: 'aggregate costs paid by the Defaulting Party regarding the applicable Development Plan before the date of the Cash Call giving rise to the default.'

162 Article 8.4.G.2 2012 JOA: 'Defaulting Party's Participating Interest share of the Estimated Total Costs.'

163 Article 8.4.G.1 2012 JOA.

164 Article 8.4.G.1 2012 JOA: 'Any non-defaulting Party that fails to exercise its Withering Option during such thirty (30) Day period shall be deemed to have elected not to become an Acquiring Party and its Withering Option regarding the Defaulting Party shall terminate. Each Acquiring Party shall be deemed to have proposed to acquire a proportion of the Withering Interest of the Defaulting Party equal to the ratio of such Acquiring Party's Participating Interest to the total Participating Interests of all Acquiring Parties and pay such proportion of the Withering Price, unless they otherwise agree.'

Withering provisions are less harsh than forfeiture clauses. However, the formula used to calculate the withering interest can be quite complicated and has therefore 'generally proved unpopular'.[165] There is also the risk that withering clauses provide temptation for JOA parties to downsize their liabilities, should they feel that the project is not profitable. Indeed, the provisions may 'operate as an escape for a party that wishes to reduce their liabilities, particularly in relation to less productive assets'[166] by deliberately defaulting.

6. WITHDRAWAL PROVISIONS

Whereas the default remedies described in section 5 above are vehicle by which a JOA party can be 'expelled against its will',[167] withdrawal is a method by which a JOA party can resign from the JOA of its own free will.

The withdrawal provisions are contained in Article 13 of the 2012 JOA. Under this article, a JOA party has the right to withdraw from a JOA by notice to the other parties[168] and the withdrawal may be partial or complete.[169] As a result of the withdrawal, the withdrawing party must assign its Participating Interest to the non-withdrawing parties free of cost.[170] There is also a provision stating that that if the host government does not approve of the withdrawal, the withdrawing party can have its interest held in trust.[171]

Some commentary maintains that including a right to withdraw in a JOA should be given careful consideration. This is because withdrawal provisions effectively allow a JOA party to abandon its rights and obligations.[172] As a result, it may be preferable to provide that withdrawal can occur only in certain circumstances. For example, a JOA parties may want to specify periods where withdrawal is prohibited. Indeed, '[i]t may be prudent to provide for withdrawal during the exploration phase only, and only after the minimum work obligations

165 Jensen and Abul Failat, *supra* n. 109, p. 6.

166 SNR Denton, *Briefing: Key Differences Between the 2012 AIPN Joint Operating Agreement and the 2012 Joint Operating Agreement*, October 2012 <http://www.dentons.com/en/insights/articles/2012/october/3/key-differences-between-the-2002-and-2012-aipn-joint-operating-agreements>.

167 Roberts, *supra* n. 130, p. 277.

168 Article 13.1.A 2012 JOA.

169 Article 13.2 2012 JOA.

170 Article 13.6 2012 JOA.

171 Article 13.7 2012 JOA.

172 Purdie, *supra* n. 12: 'The inclusion in the JOA of the right of a party to withdraw from the JOA should be considered carefully. Withdrawal provisions allow the withdrawing party to surrender its interests in the JOA and the licence to the other parties, in effect abandoning its rights and obligations.'

have been satisfied within such phase.'[173] Furthermore, '[c]aution must also be exercised in respect of withdrawal near the end of the licence's life.'[174]

JOA parties should try to achieve a balance which is commercially acceptable to all of the parties, focusing on 'ensuring the delivery of their joint venture intentions and providing for withdrawal where the project risk and uncertainty make such a concept acceptable.'[175]

7. CONSENT PROVISIONS

Consent provisions provide a second level of protection for JOA parties against newcomers.[176] Indeed, it is common for preferential rights to be accompanied by these provisions.[177] Generally, they will provide that consent should be obtained from the other JOA parties and/or the host government in the event of a prospective transfer.

Usually, this freedom of consent (or refusal) of the other JOA parties will not be without its limits.[178] The right to refuse consent will frequently be limited to situations where it is commercially reasonable to do so,[179] and such scenarios will usually be explicitly delineated (as they are in the 2012 JOA). For example, in Article 12.2.D.2, a transfer can be completed if consent is obtained from all the co-venturers, but this consent can be denied only in certain circumstances. The 2012 JOA gives two alternatives. The first is that consent can be denied if the proposed transferor cannot establish its financial capacity and technical ability. The other provides for this but adds an option for consent to be refused – in the case of transfer to an affiliate – if the transferor does not agree to remain liable for the performance of the affiliate's obligations.[180] Even if the 2012 JOA

---

173 *Ibid.*: 'Consideration should be given to the inclusion of prohibited periods, particularly in respect of the period up until the satisfaction of the minimum work obligations under the licence. It may be prudent to provide for withdrawal during the exploration phase only, and only after the minimum work obligations have been satisfied within such phase.'

174 *Ibid.*

175 *Ibid.*

176 Hammerson, *supra* n. 10, p. 201.

177 Major, *supra* n. 7, p. 118: 'Pre-emption/first refusal rights are generally accompanied by separate consent provisions whereby consent to a potential transfer must be obtained from the Other Co-Venturers and/or the NOC and/or the host government.'

178 *Ibid.*, p. 118: 'However, it is unusual that consent provisions will give total discretion to the other parties to a project to veto a Potential Buyer. A right to refuse consent is generally limited to circumstances where the Other Co-Venturers have genuine concerns about the financial and/or technical capabilities of the Potential Buyer.'

179 *Ibid.*, p. 118: 'A right to refuse consent is generally limited to circumstances where the Other Co-Venturers have genuine concerns about the financial and/or technical capabilities of the Potential Buyer.'

180 Article 12.2.D.1 2012 JOA.

is not used, it is usual for consent provisions in JOAs to provide that consent to transfers should not be unreasonably withheld.[181]

Various provisions relating to transfers and changes in control in the 2012 JOA feature the need to obtain governmental consent or approval,[182] but the 2012 JOA does not address whether any limitations exist in respect of such consent. ICC Case 14108 of 2008[183] provides some indication of how arbitral tribunals might be expected to deal with the procedural and financial issues surrounding government consent in general. In that case, a requirement of the renewal and extension agreement entered into between the claimant company and the respondent ministry in respect of a production sharing agreement (PSA) was that a partial amendment agreement (PAA) with the re-negotiated terms of the PSA extension be approved by the respondent's Parliament, which would bind the parties 'upon exhaustion of the constitutional procedures in the [Respondent's] State'. Upon the Parliament's refusal to ratify the renewal and the PAA, and substitution of a state-owned company for the claimant following the expiry of the PSA, the claimant sought compensation for the volume of oil to which it would have been entitled during the PSA extension. The Tribunal, finding that the PSA had not been extended as the necessary constitutional procedures had not been exhausted, dismissed the claim for damages for breach of contract, but awarded compensation on the grounds of estoppel for the claimant's exploration costs incurred through its reliance on the behaviour of the respondent's government.

It does not seem shocking that a tribunal respect a government's right to withhold consent, but as seen above the matter need not end there. As regards changes in control which are subject to governmental approval, ICC Case 14108 should be borne in mind in relation to the timing and costs issues of obtaining, or failing to obtain, government approval.

Another issue, very common but perhaps beyond the scope of this chapter, is what happens in the interim between contracting for a transfer and government approval of the same. Does the original transferor remain in place? Does a trust in favour of the assignee exist (a notion which is largely foreign in those civil law jurisdictions where the notion of trust and/or beneficial interest are not generally recognised) or does the assignee come in 'unofficially', as it were, pending the requisite approvals (as often a transferring party may wish to get out due to concerns about funding ongoing operations)? These issues are not always clear.

---

181 Hammerson, *supra* n. 10, p. 201: 'there is a considerable body of case law (mainly from landlord and tenant disputes) which provide examples of where refusal of consent will be considered reasonable.'

182 E.g. Article 13.7 2012 JOA (withdrawal), Article 12.2.F.1 – Alternative #1 2012 JOA (pre-emption rights on transfer) and Article 12.2.F.1 – Alternative #2 2012 JOA (right of first refusal on transfer).

183 See *ICC International Court of Arbitration Bulletin* (Vol. 25/No. 2-2014), pp. 23–24 and 67–71.

8. PROBLEMS IN PRACTICE

8.1. SELLING 'UPSTAIRS' AND 'DOWNSTAIRS'

The circumvention of preferential rights has long been an issue in relation to JOAs, and the awareness of such circumvention led to major amendments to change in control provisions in the 2002 JOA.[184] Hence, much (albeit not all) of what follows concerns agreements which do *not* take advantage of the AIPN's most recent recommendation(s).

Absent well-drafted change of control provisions, there remains a debate as to whether clauses speaking purely of transfers, even indirect ones, catch a change up the ownership chain. On the one hand, a literal, or some would say logical, construction would say there is no transfer by the JOA party and the matter should end there. On the other hand, the writer has seen it argued (under Indian law in the case in question) that one should not be able to do indirectly that which is prohibited directly. Of course, the problem can then become how far a court or tribunal should go in fashioning the bargain (in terms of valuation of any interest etc.) where, for example, a change in control involves more than one asset.

On the other hand, it is arguable whether a change at the parent level of a very large company, which has Participating Interests in hundreds of projects, should trigger the requirement to obtain partners' consent in all of these projects. Is it a question of drafting, or the intention behind the drafting; and are the transferors' motives in structuring the transaction as a change in control a relevant consideration?

In contrast to 'selling upstairs', a JOA party may in circumstances be able to avoid triggering preferential rights by selling 'downstairs', i.e., in an example given by US writers over a decade ago, consider where the parent company transfers the interest to a subsidiary (which falls outside of the preferential rights clause of the AIPN JOA due to carve outs for transfers to affiliates)[185] and then sells off the subsidiary (assuming changes in control are not caught).[186] In these circumstances, the JOA parties may also feel that they have been cheated of the opportunity to buy the Participating Interest in accordance with preferential rights in the JOA.[187] As a solution to this, commentators have suggested that in

184 See section 3.2 above.

185 See section 3.2 above.

186 Poitevent and Hewitt, *supra* n. 55, p. 9: 'Changes in the ownership of corporations that hold mineral interests have been the subject of innumerable preferential rights disputes. Usually, the corporation is itself sold or the corporation transfers the interest to a subsidiary, which is then sold. Holders of preferential rights often feel cheated under these circumstances, since the ownership of the interest, while not conveyed to any party, has effectively changed hands to a third party.'

187 *Ibid.*

these circumstances, there could be a provision for the subsidiary to re-convey the Participating Interest to the original owner.[188]

8.2. PACKAGE SALES

A package sale, in the context of transfers and preferential rights, occurs where the Participating Interest subject to the preferential right is sold in conjunction with a number of other assets.[189] Two main issues arise in practice as a result of package sales in the context of JOAs. Firstly, using carve-outs for package sales as a way to avoid triggering preferential rights, and secondly, the difficulty of allocating a price for the Participating Interest where only a global price for the package as a whole has been agreed. How will the other parties know if, in the case of an operation involving numerous interests, the value of the relevant interest under their JOA has met or not the JOA's percentage criteria triggering a right? The answer is far from simple and the problem arises frequently in practice, as discussed below.

8.2.1. Avoidance of Preferential Rights

If an interest is sold under a more extensive arrangement where there is an agreed overall value and agreed terms for the entire package, arguably it is difficult to ascribe a separate value to the specific interest subject to the preferential rights.[190]

As a result, some JOAs will exempt package sales from preferential rights.[191] The 2012 JOA, however, does not provide for this carve-out. Rather it provides that in the event of a package sale, and where pre-emption rights are provided for, a cash value must be ascribed and included in the notice from the proposed transferor to the other JOA parties.[192]

---

188 Major, *supra* n. 7, p. 118: 'The definition of "affiliates" should be considered carefully. In addition, care should also be taken to ensure that such a clause cannot be used to avoid pre-emption/consent rights by transferring the interest to an affiliate as permitted under the agreement and then disposing of the affiliate. The drafting therefore needs to provide, for example, that if the affiliate transferee ceases to be an affiliate of the transferor within two years, the interest must be transferred back to the transferor.' This is why certain JOAs (including the AIPN) have provisions that damages for breach are not necessarily an adequate remedy and that specific performance of a transfer obligation to the other JOA parties is considered an important, even essential remedy (discussed further below).

189 *Ibid.*, p. 122: 'A "package" deal is where the asset covered by a pre-emption right is to be sold with a number of other assets.'

190 *Ibid.*: 'The argument is that, where the deal is a package deal, there is no way of ascertaining the terms and price applicable to the specific interest which is the subject of the pre-emption right and therefore the pre-emption right cannot apply.'

191 Dighton, *supra* n. 89, p. 151: 'there may be a carve-out [from preferential rights] for package deals.'

192 Article 12.2.F.3 2012 JOA: 'If a Transfer that is not a Cash Transfer or involves other properties included in a wider transaction (package deal), the transferor shall include in its notification

A carve-out of package sales from preferential rights may of course tempt a transferor 'to dress the transaction up as a package when in reality it is not'.[193] This could be achieved by including another minor interest as part of the package.[194] The JOA parties may perceive this as unfair and should give careful consideration to drafting mechanisms to remedy this.

For example, if the JOA parties decide to depart from the 2012 JOA and include a carve-out provision for package sales, it may be sensible to 'restrict the carve-out to "*bona fide*" package deals'.[195] This wording is 'commonly used'[196] in JOAs in such circumstances and could serve the purpose of deterring the avoidance of pre-emption rights. However, the inclusion of this wording may also give rise to issues in itself because '[t]he difficulty is that packages at each end of the spectrum might be easier to classify than those in the middle.'[197] For example, in circumstances where a sizeable percentage of their asset(s) to be sold as part of the package sale is included (e.g. 50%) it is easier to conclude that the sale is a bona fide package deal, than if 1%, for example, of the asset(s) were included (even if this transaction were actually bona fide).[198] Indeed, it is hard to determine the point or specific percentage at which a sale becomes bona fide, and, accordingly, any stipulation in the contract to that effect could be considered arbitrary.[199]

Of the same accord, and as mentioned above, the drafting parties may also consider whether the carve-out should only apply 'if the additional asset(s) represents a certain minimum percentage value of the entire deal'.[200] And again as mentioned above, this percentage may be considered to be an arbitrary figure, and lead to its issues of valuation, certain of which will be dealt with below.

---

to the other Parties a statement of the Cash Value of the Participating Interest subject to the proposed Transfer, and each other Party shall have a right to acquire such Participating Interest on the same final terms and conditions as were negotiated with the proposed transferee except that the acquiring Party shall pay the Cash Value in immediately available funds at the closing of the Transfer instead of the consideration payable in the third party offer, and the terms and conditions of the applicable instruments shall be modified as necessary to reflect the acquisition of a Participating Interest for cash.'

193 Dighton, *supra* n. 89, p. 151.

194 *Ibid.*, p. 151: 'Alternatively there may be a carve-out for package deals, but an unscrupulous transferor may attempt to circumvent by adding minor interests in other assets to dress the transaction up as a package when in reality it is not.'

195 *Ibid.*

196 *Ibid.*

197 *Ibid.*

198 *Ibid.*, pp. 151–152: 'a package where a substantial percentage of another asset e.g. 50%, is also included might well be regarded as bona fide, just as the addition of a 1% interest in the same asset might fail an objective test (even if it is bona fide). Does this mean then that, applying the "straw that broke the camel's back" principle, that somewhere between these limits is a magic point which might be identified as the point at which a specific percentage interest in the asset becomes bona fide? Clearly this is illogical.'

199 *Ibid.*

200 *Ibid.*, p. 152.

8.2.2. *Ascertaining and Allocating Price*

If an attempt is made to ascribe a set value to the specific interest subject to pre-emption rights, the transferor may be tempted to 'allocate an inflated portion of the package price to that interest which is subject to pre-emption rights, in order to discourage exercise of the pre-emption rights.'[201] Of course, some contracts for package sales may include a provision to the effect that the asset be allocated a price which is of market value, or a fair and reasonable value.[202] However, even this approach is not without its risks as the assets being sold together as a package may itself have an effect on the value. For example, the value of assets individually may well not be worth as much as if they are sold together, 'particularly if they use shared facilities or carry complementary tax allowances, losses and/or gains'.[203] As a result, determining a market value or a fair value for the individual interest is not always as easy as it may at first seem.[204]

The 2012 JOA addresses this issue by providing that the Participating Interest subject to the pre-emptive rights, which is being included in the package sale, should be allocated a cash value and that this should be included in the notice given to the Preferential Rights Holders.[205] 'Cash Value' has two possible definitions in the 2012 JOA for the drafters to choose from.[206] One definition is that the cash value ascribed is the total monetary value that could be 'reasonably allocated' to the Participating Interest, taking into consideration tax savings, cash or other assets. In so doing, the 2012 JOA recognises that the cash value of a specific asset may be affected by other factors. The alternative is for cash value to be defined as the market value of the Participating Interest that a 'willing buyer would pay a willing seller in an arm's length transaction'.[207] The 2012 JOA does not provide for an expert procedure in respect of the determination of cash value with respect to package sales, unlike its positon with respect to non-cash transfers, but perhaps it should, and the writer has certainly seen this in other agreements.[208]

---

201 Major, *supra* n. 7, p. 122.

202 *Ibid.*, p. 122: 'Sometimes contracts expressly provide that the price allocated to the asset in question must be "market price" or a "fair and reasonable price."'

203 *Ibid.*

204 *Ibid.*: 'However, a collection of assets may well have a different value when sold together to the value they have if sold individually, particularly if they use shared facilities or carry complementary tax allowances, losses and/or gains and it is therefore not always easy to arrive at a price which is fair for all parties involved.'

205 Article 12.2.F.3 2012 JOA.

206 See the definition of 'cash value' in Article 1.1 2012 JOA.

207 See the definition of 'cash value' in Article 1.1 2012 JOA.

208 Major, *supra* n. 7, p. 122: 'Some kind of expert determination procedure should be included in any case as there is clearly scope for debate.'

8.3. NON-CASH TRANSFERS

Non-cash transfers (i.e. share swaps) can be particularly problematic in the context of preferential rights in JOAs. Transfers are evidently more straightforward if the consideration for the transfer is for cash or is easily convertible into cash.[209]

The impracticalities of non-cash transfers are reflected in the 2012 JOA by giving the JOA parties the option to carve out non-cash transfers from pre-emption rights provisions. This option was introduced in the 2002 JOA and maintained in the 2012 JOA.[210]

However, tinkering with these types of transactions may 'den[y] a participant the ability to negotiate a package deal or swaps, involving different assets, or shares, with or without a cash adjustment',[211] which may be considered to be unacceptable to some JOA parties, as '[m]any companies require the unfettered ability to be able to negotiate these types of deals.'[212] The difficulty which arises out of a transaction for non-cash consideration, however, is that the JOA party wishing to exercise its pre-emption rights will never be able to match the offer of the third party exactly, because they obviously do not own the assets that the third party is offering.[213]

As a result, the 2012 JOA provides a procedure whereby the JOA parties pay a cash equivalent value[214] of the asset that the third party is offering in exchange for the transferor's Participating Interest. In the 2012 JOA this is contained in Article 12.2.F.3.[215] The procedure begins with the proposed transferor stating the cash value of the Participating Interest in its notice to pre-emption rights holders.

It is clearly possible that the other JOA parties will not agree with the cash value allocated to the Participating Interest by the proposed transferor. The 2012 JOA provides for this situation in Article 12.2.F.4. The value attributed to the Participating Interest by the proposed transferor is deemed to be correct unless a notice is given to the proposed transferor by one or more of the JOA parties, stating that they disagree with the valuation.[216] The notice should provide

209 Dighton, *supra* n. 89, p. 151: 'Pre-emptive rights are less complicated where there is cash consideration in a proposed sale. Thus many agreements provide that the consideration must be in cash or assets readily convertible to cash.'

210 This option for pre-emption rights to apply *only* to cash transfers was introduced by Article 12.2(G) 2002 JOA and retained in Article 12.2.G 2012 JOA.

211 Dighton, *supra* n. 89, p. 151.

212 *Ibid.*

213 *Ibid.*: 'The obvious difficulty with translating such a deal for pre-emption purposes is that a co-venturer wanting to pre-empt is unable to match the offer exactly because it does not own those specific assets which form part of the consideration.'

214 See section 8.2 above for the definition of 'cash value' in Article 1.1 2012 JOA.

215 Article 12.2.F.3 2012 JOA.

216 Article 12.2.F.4 2012 JOA.

reasons for this if possible. The JOA parties, under this same clause, will then have a period during which to negotiate an agreed attributable cash value. In the event that the parties cannot agree, determination of an appropriate cash value will be left to an expert under Article 18.3. However, this 'last resort' of expert determination also has its issues as '[q]uite apart from the delay caused by this valuation process, most corporations would shy away from losing control of the deal by placing an important commercial factor, namely price, in the hands of a third party.'[217]

8.4. PRE-ACTION DISCOVERY

Establishing the cash value in a package sale or the cash equivalent value in a non-cash transfer will become especially problematic if arbitral proceedings are commenced, as it will form not only part of the quantum for damages, but also the grounds for applications for interim relief. For example, the party objecting to the transfer may seek document production or even pre-action discovery in order to ascertain whether an accurate cash value has been attributed to the relevant asset(s). However, the parties to the proposed transfer are unlikely to agree to production of documents for the purposes of such valuation, on the basis that those documents are protected by the proposed transaction's confidentiality.

Further, obtaining pre-action discovery or document production in arbitration is highly problematic and rarely obtainable. In *EDO Corporation v Ultra Electronics Limited*,[218] it was held that the English court did not have power to grant pre-action disclosure in respect of a supply sub-contract which provided for any dispute arising out of that contract to be referred to ICC arbitration. The claimant had applied for pre-action disclosure on the basis that it believed the defendant had misused confidential information in relation to a contract between the defendant and Australian Navy in breach of a restriction in the sub-contract. The court, in reinforcing the aim of the English Arbitration Act 1996 to minimise court intervention in arbitration,[219] dismissed the application, finding that although the 1998 ICC Rules recognised the power of the court to grant interim measures prior to the constitution of the arbitral tribunal,[220] such power was not relevant as neither party had formulated a substantive claim

217 Dighton, *supra* n. 89, p. 151.

218 [2009] EWHC 682.

219 See s. 1(c), which provides that 'the court should not intervene except as provided by this Part'.

220 See Article 23(2), which provides that '[t]he application of a party to a judicial authority for such measures or for the implementation of any such measures ordered by an Arbitral Tribunal shall not be deemed to be an infringement or a waiver of the arbitration agreement and shall not affect the relevant powers reserved to the Arbitral Tribunal.'

or commenced arbitral proceedings. Furthermore, the 1998 ICC Rules did not confer powers on the High Court beyond those granted by Parliament,[221] which are supportive rather than supervisory in nature.

From an English law perspective at least, it is thus unlikely that the objecting party would be able to obtain interim relief from the courts to ascertain the cash value from documents produced under pre-action discovery.

The likelihood of pre-arbitration discovery in civil law jurisdictions is similarly problematic as document production is extremely limited, even once a case has commenced.

8.5. SPECIFIC PERFORMANCE

Even if the objecting party succeeds in arbitration, it may not want – as a Preferential Rights Holder – to be awarded damages; for example, as an owner of a Participating Interest, damages are often not an adequate remedy. The 2012 JOA addresses this by specifically providing for specific performance as a remedy – this was introduced in the 2002 version.[222] Specific performance is defined as 'a remedy available ... to compel a person to actually perform the contractual obligation.'[223] Therefore the remedy of specific performance would require the proposed transferor to perform its contractual obligation to follow the preferential rights procedure, if the JOA contains such provisions. This remedy may also be potentially helpful if the transfer has already taken place before a Preferential Rights Holder claims that it has the right to buy the Participating Interest. However, ordering specific performance of the contract in these circumstances could prove troublesome, as it would involve the re-transfer of the interest from an (innocent) third party, who is not a party to the original contract.

Nonetheless, the enforceability of such provision providing for specific performance must be considered in the context of the applicable law of the JOA. Indeed, the Guidance Notes to the 2012 JOA recognise that different remedies may be preferred in different jurisdictions.[224]

---

221 Section 44 sets out the court powers exercisable in support of arbitral proceedings, but does not include pre-action disclosure.

222 See Article 12.1.B 2012 JOA (Alternative #1). Specific performance as a remedy was introduced by the 2002 JOA.

223 *Chitty on Contracts*, 31st edn, para. 27-004.

224 2012 JOA Guidance Notes, p. 5: 'Under Civil Law jurisdictions a judge would normally consider a damages award in the event of default, whereas under Common Law the equitable "specific performance" remedy could also be available.'

8.5.1. *Common Law – England*

Under English law, specific performance is a discretionary remedy and, therefore, 'not available as of right.'[225] There are 'stringent constraints'[226] on whether specific performance can be awarded.[227] The resistance of the English courts to the award of specific performance is demonstrated in the case of *Co-operative Insurance Society Ltd v Argyll Stores (Holdings) Ltd.*[228] That said, where the parties have explicitly agreed to specific performance as a remedy (per the 2012 JOA wording) there is a greater chance that such remedy will be imposed under English law on the basis of freedom of contract.[229] Clauses expressly providing for specific performance, however, have not been subject to much discussion in the English courts so the correct approach under English law is uncertain. There are, for example, a number of cases which show 'the likely reticence of the English courts towards clauses that would oust their discretion'.[230] For example, in *Quadrant Visual Communications Ltd v Hutchison Telephone (UK) Ltd* Stocker LJ held '[o]nce the court is asked for the equitable remedy of specific performance, its discretion cannot be fettered. Once the assistance of the court is involved by one of the parties in a discretionary matter, that party is bound by the general discretion of the court to grant or refuse the remedy sought.'[231] Therefore, the position under English law appears to be that even if specific performance is provided for, the award of such a remedy will still be at the discretion of the court.

It is also worth noting the fact that most of these disputes are dealt with by way of arbitration, where tribunals are notoriously reticent in giving orders for specific performance.

---

225 S. Rowan, 'For recognition of remedial terms agreed inter partes' [2010] *Law Quarterly Review* 449.

226 *Ibid.*

227 The requirements include the inadequacy of damages, the requirement of constant supervision, severe hardship. See *Chitty on Contracts*, 31st edn, Chapter 27.

228 [1998] AC 1 (HL).

229 Rowan, *supra* n. 226, p. 450: 'An intermediate solution capable both of reconciliation with *Co-operative v Argyll* and of assimilation into English law would be for specific relief to be granted at the behest of the contracting parties. The wishes of the parties would be expressed in a clause providing that specific performance and/or injunctive relief should be available at the election of the injured party on the occurrence of a breach. Not only would the enforcement of such clauses give effect to the common intention of the parties and uphold the fundamental principle of freedom to contract, but it would also allow specific remedies to be claimed where they would otherwise be unavailable or where it is uncertain that they would be awarded.'

230 *Ibid.*, p. 451.

231 [1993] BCLC 442 CA.

8.5.2. *Civil Law – France*

Under Article 1184(2) of the French Civil Code a non-breaching party has the option to either compel a breaching party to fulfil the agreement – so long as it is capable of being fulfilled – or to request termination of the agreement and damages. This provision appears to grant a non-breaching party the right to seek specific performance for the breach of any contractual obligation.

While this principle is seemingly contradicted by the broad wording of Article 1142 of the French Civil Code (which provides that any obligation to do something or refrain from doing something should be resolved by way of damages, if the breaching party does not fulfil its performance obligations), the French *Cour de cassation* has reduced the ambit of Article 1142 to cases of non-performance of a personal obligation to do something or refrain from doing something.[232] Examples of this include obligations involving personal creativity.[233]

Therefore, French courts have generally confirmed the right of a non-breaching party to choose specific performance as a remedy for breach regardless of the seriousness of the contractual breach.[234] In addition, the French courts generally only apply the limitation set out in Article 1142 where the obligations at stake are of a personal nature.

That being said, it is the writer's experience that French courts (and by necessary implication, arbitral tribunals applying French law) are nonetheless extremely parsimonious in granting such relief.

9. CONCLUSION

A JOA provides a structure by which to regulate the relationship between the JOA parties, ensuring a level of certainty of the rights and obligations of the JOA parties. The 2012 JOA has been bolstered in order to try and provide for an even greater degree of certainty and flexibility in relation to transfers and changes in control. However, these complex provisions may give rise to problems in practice which practitioners should be aware of when drafting a JOA. It remains to be seen if and how these provisions will undergo further changes in the next version of the AIPN JOA.

---

232 See Cass. Civ., 20 jan. 1953.

233 E.g. Cass. civ., 20 jan. 1953; Cass. soc., 20 apr. 1956.

234 See Cass. civ. 3e, 22 mai 2013.

GOVERNING LAW AND DISPUTE RESOLUTION CLAUSES IN JOAs

Tuuli TIMONEN and Anaïs HARLÉ*

CONTENTS

---

* The authors would like to thank Sahana Jayakumar for her support in the drafting of this chapter. The views expressed in this chapter are strictly those of the authors and should not be attributed in any way to White & Case LLP.

1. INTRODUCTION

A JOA is a contractual framework that regulates the relationship between participants to major oil and gas projects.[1] These projects bring together

---

[1] K. O'Gorman and M. Stadnyk, 'Arbitration and Joint Operating Agreements' (2013) *IEMA (International Energy and Minerals Arbitration)* Paper 10, pp. 1–2.

several actors, who each play different roles in the exploration, development and production of the projects. A JOA permits the allocation of risks and costs between the participants and determines the way the production and profit will be shared.

JOAs are most often international in nature, as oil and gas projects usually necessitate cooperation between state entities and foreign private parties. Indeed, states will usually entrust the task of developing and administering the concession to a public entity established for this purpose. This public entity will then enter into a joint venture with a private, usually foreign, entity, which will operate the concession and conduct the day-to-day business of the joint venture.

In addition to the operator, who is in charge of the day-to-day management, a JOA usually involves private parties who will essentially have a supervisory and investing role, namely the non-operator(s).[2] These non-operators – who may be of several different nationalities – will participate in the operation of the JOA and impact, or be impacted by, the operator's performance under the JOA, as the operator enters into an intricate set of agreements, such as sub-contracts with local or foreign suppliers. Furthermore, at least part of the funding of oil and gas projects typically comes from private actors who may or may not be parties to the JOA. All these private parties (operators or non-operators) share operational and financial responsibilities in accordance with their respective participative interest in the project.[3]

JOAs thus organise long-term cooperation between parties whose interests may diverge in several respects at different stages of the project. A well-drafted and thought-through agreement is crucial to establish a clear, transparent relationship that will permit the parties to conduct joint operations on a lasting and stable basis. Careful drafting is also important to avoid disputes in the future. As, however, disputes cannot always be avoided in such long and complex projects with significant monetary (and other) interests at stake, the

---

2 See 2012 Association of International Petroleum Negotiators Model International Joint Operating Agreement (the AIPN Model JOA). The Association of International Petroleum Negotiators (AIPN) has produced a Model Contract which is commonly used for JOAs in oil and gas exploration projects. It provides that the operator 'shall have exclusive charge of Joint Operations, and shall conduct all Joint Operations'. (2012 AIPN Model International Joint Operating Agreement, Article 4.2.A.). The operator is the focal point of the operations and handles the different phases of the project on the field for the non-operators. The success of the project and the return on the investment of the non-operators are between the operator's hands. JOAs attempt to address the scope and limits of the operator's duties vis-à-vis the other parties to the JOA. (A.B. Derman, M. Hallake, A. Golding, W.M. Katz Jr and P.A. Vermillion, 'Choice of Law Provisions when Drafting Arbitration Provisions for International Oil and Gas Agreements' (2006) 3(2) *TDM* 3.) An operating committee composed of all the parties, operator and non-operator, may be established in order to authorise and supervise the joint operations but it is not always the case. Non-operating parties may indeed decide to have a purely passive role.

3 O'Gorman and Stadnyk, *supra* n. 1, pp. 1–2.

parties must foresee mechanisms that permit prompt and effective resolution of their possible disputes.

Two clauses are of particular importance in this regard, although the parties at times underestimate the importance of these clauses because they do not directly touch upon the core functions of the JOA. First, governing law clauses[4] provide the framework in which the parties' JOA operates. These clauses will be discussed in section 2 of this chapter. Second, dispute resolution clauses become fundamental if a party needs to enforce its rights under a JOA through dispute resolution mechanisms. Because of the complexity of the operation itself on the one hand and the contractual relationships that typically surround oil and gas projects on the other, it is important to choose a mechanism that is not only efficient in terms of time and cost but that can also accommodate the multiparty element of the operation. Dispute resolution clauses in JOAs are discussed in section 3 of this chapter.

2. GOVERNING LAW CLAUSES IN JOAs

With a governing law clause, the parties subject their agreement to a law of their choice, which law may or may not otherwise relate to the performance of the agreement. Depending on the scope of the clause, this law will govern a variety of matters under the JOA. In the absence of a choice in their JOA – and if the parties cannot later agree on the governing law – it will be for a third party decision maker to determine which law will regulate an array of matters under the agreement, should a dispute arise. In order to avoid the uncertainty that relates to a third party's decision and, most importantly, to displace an otherwise applicable law that may not be the best adapted to the contract, the parties to a JOA quasi-systematically insert a clause into their contract in which they choose the law that will govern their contractual relationship.

This section will address the importance of choosing the governing law (section 2.1), the role of the governing law in the context of a JOA (section 2.2),

4 Several laws may have a bearing on issues that can arise out of, or relate to, a JOA in case of a dispute, such as: (i) the law, or legal rules, that the parties have chosen as the law governing the substance of the dispute; (ii) mandatory rules that apply regardless of the parties' choice, as well as rules of public policy; (iv) other applicable rules and non-binding guidelines and recommendations; (iv) the law governing the arbitration agreement (or other dispute resolution clause); (v) the law governing the dispute resolution procedure; (vi) the law of the recognition and enforcement of the award or court decision (some or all of these laws may, of course, coincide, but researching the laws that govern the issues listed here requires different considerations with respect to each issue). See N. Blackaby, C. Partasides, A. Redfern and M. Hunter, *Redfern and Hunter on International Arbitration*, 5th edn, Oxford University Press, Oxford 2009, Section 3.07. By 'governing law', this chapter refers to the law that applies to determine the parties' rights and obligations under the JOA – in other words, the substance of the dispute. The term 'governing law' is mostly used to refer to the law that the parties have themselves chosen in the JOA.

the potential limits to the parties' choice of law (section 2.3) and will give indications on how to draft an efficient choice of law clause (section 2.4).

2.1. CHOOSING THE GOVERNING LAW

2.1.1. Freedom of Choice and the Importance of Making a Choice

As a principle, parties to a JOA can choose the law that will govern their relationship. Indeed, it is widely recognised under most national laws and in international conventions that parties to an international agreement are free to select the law applicable to their contract.

For instance, in England and Canada, courts have held that if the parties expressly state their choice of law in the contract, this choice will be upheld, subject to certain limitations (e.g. legality and public policy).[5] A similar approach is adopted in the United States, where the parties' choice is upheld, as long as the choice has a reasonable basis, is in accordance with public policy and has a 'substantial relationship to the parties or the transaction'.[6] In Russia, Article 1210 of the Civil Code provides that the parties may select the law applicable to their contract.[7]

In the European Union, the Rome I Regulation on the Law Applicable to Contractual Obligations ('Rome I Regulation') firmly establishes the principle of party autonomy.[8] Article 3 of this Regulation, entitled 'freedom of choice', provides that 'a contract shall be governed by the law chosen by the parties'.[9]

Choosing the appropriate law is of particular importance in the context of JOAs, as the parties often come from different legal backgrounds, and the operations are complex and require a sophisticated legal regime to regulate the contractual relationship, should the need arise. The parties may also wish to subject their contract to a 'neutral' law to avoid having to rely on the host state's

---

5 T.B. Heersche, 'International Resources Law and Projects, Chapter 9: Selection of Governing Law', 103B Rocky Mountain Mineral Law Special Institute 9 (April 2009), p. 7.

6 Restatement (Second) of Conflict of Laws, Section 187, 'Law of the State Chosen by the Parties'.

7 Civil Code of the Russian Federation, W.E. Butler (translation and ed.), Wildy, Simmonds & Hill Publishing 2010, p. 390, Article 1210(1): 'The parties of a contract may when concluding a contract or subsequently choose by agreement between them the law which shall be subject to application to their rights and duties under this contract. The law chosen by the parties shall apply to the arising and termination of the right of ownership and other rights to things to moveable property without prejudice to the rights of third persons.'

8 Regulation (EC) No 593/2008 of the European Parliament and of the Council of 17 June 2008 on the law applicable to contractual obligations. In order to make an effective choice, the parties should clearly indicate that they choose to subject the contract's interpretation to a certain law. The Rome I Regulation provides that the choice must be 'express' or 'clearly demonstrated by the terms of the contract or the circumstances of the case'.

9 Article 3 of Rome I Regulation.

legal system. Where the parties fail to choose the governing law, an arbitral tribunal or a court will have to first select the applicable law before turning its attention to the substance of the dispute itself. This can be an expensive and lengthy process, causing greater uncertainty than if the parties had simply addressed the choice of law question in the first place.[10] It can also lead to an outcome that neither party wishes for and that may not be in the best interest of the project.

In the absence of a choice by the parties, a tribunal or a court is likely to apply the law of the place of operation, which will ordinarily be the law of the host state.[11] This is because the decision maker will typically search for the law that has the 'closest connection' to the agreement,[12] which in all likelihood is the law of the place where the operation takes place. This solution may seem unfavourable to foreign parties or unduly advantageous to the state party: private companies involved in JOAs may feel uncomfortable with the application of the law of the state where they operate, particularly as that law may evolve following internal political changes or fluctuations in the oil and gas market with a detrimental impact on private parties' position under the contract. In addition, this law may not be the best suited to govern a complex contractual operation, as it may not address all the questions that arise from the parties' relationship.

Thus, it is important that the parties exercise the freedom of selecting the law of their contract and make a choice. As will be seen below, the legal system that the parties opt for can potentially change the course of their contractual relationship and shape their respective rights and obligations under the JOA.

2.1.2. Making the Right Choice

Even developed, modern legal regimes have different approaches to certain questions that may become determinant in scoping the parties' respective obligations. These differences are particularly apparent when comparing common law and civil law systems, which vary in their approaches to several questions. Conscious of these differences, the Guidance Notes to the AIPN 2012 Model JOA state that the Model JOA, although 'written for use in a wide variety of types of jurisdictions', contains concepts and mechanisms that are 'taken from the common law and may need to be adapted for use in jurisdictions other than those based on a common law tradition.'[13] The Guidance Notes therefore give

---

10 Blackaby, Partasides, Redfern and Hunter, *supra* n. 4, Sections 3.203-3.205.

11 C. Otero García-Castrillón, 'Reflections on the law applicable to international oil contracts' (2013) 6(2) *J. World Energy Law Bus.* 11.

12 See e.g. Article 4(4) of the Rome I Regulation. See also, *Goode on Commercial Law*, 4th edn. (Penguin Books 2010), p. 1230.

13 Guidance Notes to AIPN 2012 Model Joint Operating Agreement, Guidance Note on Civil Law, p. 2.

information on issues that may require particular attention should the parties wish to adopt the 'laws of a Civil Law jurisdictions ... as governing law.'[14]

Like the AIPN Model JOA, many complex, international contracts are based on common law model contracts. Thus, opting for French law, for example, in a contract that adopts a contract model based on a common law system may make interpretation of certain clauses difficult and possibly result in their invalidity.

Before choosing a law, the parties should therefore assess which issues are most likely to necessitate recourse to the governing law and how the contemplated governing law treats those situations. Although these issues are not always easy to predict, the parties would still be well advised to study how certain key items are treated in the law that they are contemplating. This exercise entails looking into not only the written provisions of the chosen law, but also the jurisprudence and legal doctrine, as they will guide the interpretation and application of the governing law. In the heat of the contract negotiations, this evaluation is often overlooked. This chapter will therefore seek to provide guidance to the parties when making that choice.

2.2. ROLE OF THE GOVERNING LAW

The governing law plays its biggest role where the terms of a JOA are unclear or where the agreement fails to allocate the risk for a particular issue.[15] It is therefore worth exploring issues that may arise under a JOA that typically call for the application of the governing law to see how the choice of law can impact their resolution.

2.2.1. Contract Interpretation

Where the parties disagree on the interpretation of a certain contract term, it will be for the court or tribunal to determine what each party's obligation encompasses. The governing law will provide the interpretation rules that the decision maker will follow.

2.2.1.1. Interpreting Ambiguous Contract Terms

In most civil and common law jurisdictions, interpreting ambiguous contract terms involves researching what the parties' intention could reasonably have been when they concluded the agreement. However, the particular factors that the court or tribunal will take into account in determining the parties' intention,

---

14 Guidance Notes to AIPN 2012 Model Joint Operating Agreement, Guidance Note on Civil Law, p. 2.

15 M. Polkinghorne and C. Kirkman, 'Paris Energy Series No. 4: Choice of Law in Oil & Gas Agreements: What difference does it make?', White & Case (June 2010), p. 3.

and the breadth of that inquiry, vary according to the applicable law. For instance, the willingness to look beyond the four corners of the contract differs from one jurisdiction to another and the importance of pre-contract negotiations is not the same under every law. It has been said that civil law jurisdictions are more concerned with the 'justice in the individual case' and therefore look more into the relationship between the parties by taking into account the 'true state of mind of one of the parties', than common law lawyers.[16] Common law, for its part, is said to be more concerned with 'commercial convenience and the security of transactions' and therefore pays more attention to the 'appearance of consent'.[17]

Under US law, section 214 of the Restatement (Second) of Contracts provides that:

> 'Agreements and negotiations prior to or contemporaneous with the adoption of a writing are admissible in evidence to establish ... the meaning of the writing ...'[18]

The range of factors that fall within such 'agreements and negotiations' is very broad. The court or tribunal may consider, among other factors, the parties' purposes at the moment of the formation of the contract, past dealings, market conditions, conduct prior to the conclusion of the contract and the parties' knowledge of their situation.[19]

By contrast, the approach taken under English law is much more restrictive. The starting point for interpreting an unclear contractual term is that the court or tribunal may look into the factual background against which the terms were agreed in order to determine the parties' intentions from the context.[20] However, case law has explicitly made clear that this exercise does not extend to considering parties' actions or statements made during negotiation.[21]

To take the example of a civil law system, French law follows a similar approach to that under US law, arguably going even further.[22] Article 1156 of the

---

16 B. Nicholas, *The French Law of Contract*, 2nd edn, Clarendon Press, Oxford 1992, p. 48. See also Polkinghorne and Kirkman, *supra* n. 15, pp. 1–2.

17 B. Nicholas, *supra* n. 16, p. 48. See also Polkinghorne and Kirkman, *supra* n. 15, pp. 1–2.

18 2 ALI Contracts 2nd §214.

19 M.N. Kniffin, *Corbin on Contracts*, Vol. 5, Interpretation of Contracts, Lexis Law Publishing, 1998, §24.10, pp. 83–86.

20 *Reardon Smith Line Ltd v Yngvar Hansen-Tangen* [1976] 1 WLR 989, 995–996. See also *Investors Compensation Scheme Ltd v West Bromwich Building Society* [1998] 1 WLR 896.

21 *Chartbrook Ltd v Persimmon Homes Ltd* [2009] UKHL 38. Lord Hoffmann asserted that 'the admission of pre-contractual negotiations would create greater uncertainty of outcome in disputes over interpretation and add to the cost of advice, litigation or arbitration. Everyone engaged in the exercise would have to read the correspondence and statements would have to be taken from those who took part in oral negotiations. Not only would this be time-consuming and expensive but the scope for disagreement over whether the material affected the construction of the agreement (as in the *Yoshimoto* case) would be considerably increased.'

22 At the time of drafting of this chapter (Autumn 2015), a reform of the French contract law was under preparation. The new French contract law, if adopted, will apply to contracts concluded

Code Civil provides that '[o]ne must in agreements seek the common intention of the contracting parties, rather than stop at the literal meaning of the words.'[23] In other words, French law considers that the true intention of the parties is more important than the plain text of the agreement.[24] Applying Article 1156, French courts' jurisprudence specifies that, when seeking the common intention of the parties, the court or tribunal may look into the parties' behaviour following the conclusion of the contract.[25] They may also examine the parties' actions before the conclusion of the contract, their correspondence and any previous agreements concluded between them.[26]

2.2.1.2. Inferring Implicit Terms into the Contract

Under US law, a term may be implied into the contract in certain circumstances, where the parties have not allocated a risk under the contract. Section 204 of the Restatement (Second) of Contracts provides that:

> 'When the parties to a bargain sufficiently defined to be a contract have not agreed with respect to a term which is essential to a determination of their rights and duties, a term which is reasonable in the circumstances is supplied by the court.'[27]

Under English law, the tribunal must first be satisfied that the following test is met before a particular term can be implied into the contract: (1) 'it must be reasonable and equitable'; (2) it must be 'necessary to give business efficacy to the contract so that no term will be implied if the contract is effective without it'; (3) it must be 'so obvious that "it goes without saying"'; (4) it must be 'capable of clear expression'; and (5) it must 'not contradict any express term of the contract'.[28]

Article 1135 of the French Civil Code provides that judges may fill gaps in a contract by referring to 'equity, usage or law'.[29] The reference to equity permits

---

after its entry into force (which is planned for Autumn 2016) and the rules described in this chapter will continue to apply to contracts concluded before its entry into force.

23 Article 1156 of the French Civil Code. (Translation provided by <www.legifrance.gouv.fr>, available at <http://www.legifrance.gouv.fr/Traductions/en-English/Legifrance-translations>). In French: '*On doit dans les conventions rechercher quelle a été la commune intention des parties contractantes, plutôt que de s'arrêter au sens littéral des termes.*'

24 F. Terré, P. Simler and Y. Lequette, *Les obligations*, 11th edn, Dalloz, Paris 2013, n°450, p. 500.

25 *Cour de Cassation*, Third Civil Chamber, 5 Feb. 1971, *D.* 1971.281. In French: '*il appartenait aux juges du fond de rechercher l'intention des parties contractantes dans les termes employés par elles comme dans tout comportement ultérieur de nature à la manifester*'. See also A. Bénabent, *Droit des obligations*, 14th edn, LGDJ, Paris 2014, n°273, p. 216.

26 Bénabent, *ibid.*, n°273, p. 216.

27 2 ALI Contracts 2nd §204.

28 See *Attorney General of Belize v Belize Telecom Ltd* [2009] UKPC 10, para. 26, referring to *BP Refinery (Westernport) Pty Ltd v Shire of Hastings* (1977) 180 CLR 266, 282–283.

29 Article 1135 of the French Civil Code: 'Agreements bind not only as to what is therein expressed, but also as to all the consequences that equity, usage, or law impose upon the obligation

judges to infer new obligations on the parties, even if the parties did not foresee such obligations when concluding the contract.[30]

Thus, the applicable law will determine the emphasis that a court or tribunal will place on the parties' behaviour surrounding the contract when determining the intention of the parties. This law will also determine how readily the tribunals will infer implied contract terms from the parties' behaviour. It is therefore worthwhile for the parties to be aware of these differences to be able to anticipate how a court or tribunal will determine the meaning of any ambiguous clauses.

2.2.2. Operator's Liability vis-à-vis Non-Operators

Disputes between the parties to JOAs often arise in relation to the standard of care owed by the operator to the non-operators.[31] The 2012 AIPN Model JOA provides that the operator shall conduct the joint operations in 'a diligent, safe, and efficient manner in accordance with good and prudent petroleum industry practices and field conservation principles generally followed by the international petroleum industry under similar circumstances'.[32] Nevertheless, JOAs often seek to limit the operator's liability vis-à-vis non-operators, 'reflecting the principle that the former ought neither gain a profit nor suffer a loss as a result of being the operator.'[33] Such restrictions may be subject to gross or wilful negligence exceptions.[34]

The validity of such exculpatory clauses will depend on the applicable law, which may set limits to these clauses. For instance, the applicable law can lay down conditions as to the standard of care that the operator must exercise. The failure to exercise such standard of care can well lead to the operator's liability towards the non-operator, despite the exculpatory clause. For example, New York courts regard with disfavour contracts in which a party is trying to avoid all consequences arising from its own negligence.[35] They therefore require that the contract 'specifically state in clear, unequivocal, and unmistakable language that

according to its nature.' (Translation provided by <www.legifrance.gouv.fr>, available at <http://www.legifrance.gouv.fr/Traductions/en-English/Legifrance-translations>). In French: '*Les conventions obligent non seulement à ce qui y est exprimé, mais encore à toutes les suites que l'équité, l'usage ou la loi donnent à l'obligation d'après sa nature.*'

30 P. Malaurie, L. Aynès and P. Stoffel-Muck, *Les obligations*, 6th edn, LGDJ, Paris 2013, n°774, p. 384.

31 O'Gorman and Stadnyk, *supra* n. 1, p. 13.

32 AIPN Model JOA, Article 4.2.B.2.

33 O'Gorman and Stadnyk, *supra* n. 1, p. 14.

34 See e.g. AIPN Model JOA, Optional Article 4.6.D: 'Despite Article 4.6.A or 4.6.B, if any Senior Supervisory Personnel of Operator or its Affiliates engage in Gross Negligence / Willful Misconduct that proximately causes the Parties to incur damage, loss, cost, or liability for claims, demands or causes of action referred to in Article 4.6.A or 4.6.B, then, in addition to its Participating Interest share: Operator shall bear all such damages, losses, costs, and liabilities.'

35 Derman, Hallake, Golding, Katz and Vermillion, *supra* n. 2, p. 13.

one party is absolving another from future liability for negligence.'[36] In addition, under French law, exculpatory clauses must not negate the essential obligation in the contract.[37] Therefore, if an exculpatory clause reduces drastically the compensation that a party who breaches an 'essential contractual obligation' would otherwise need to pay to the damaged party, the clause can be nullified for negating the very purpose of the contract. In addition, exculpatory clauses are not valid in case of gross or wilful negligence.[38]

The applicable law will also determine the scope of the operator's potential liability, such as whether indirect damages fall on the operator.

2.2.3. Impact of Changes in the Contractual Framework over Time

The parties entering into a JOA typically have in sight a long-term project in which their relationship is meant to evolve over time and the circumstances in which the parties operate are likely to change. As explained by certain authors:

> 'The long-term nature of the contracts at issue makes them vulnerable to disruption from unforeseen events or events which the parties – for whatever reason – did not and perhaps could not deal with in the contract with sufficient time and in sufficient detail. The longer-term an agreement and the more exposed to geological, commercial and political risk, the more it becomes vulnerable to external events. Such events can make the operation of the contract partially impracticable or, from a commercial and financial perspective, no longer viable for one party.'[39]

Thus, the parties need to plan in advance how they will deal with sudden and unexpected changes in the set-up of their operations. JOAs therefore almost always contain *force majeure* clauses that allow for the suspension or termination of the operations in case of a *force majeure* event, and limit the liability of a party in case of such event. If the clause does not clearly define what types of events constitute *force majeure*, or if the clause is incomplete or unclear, the law applicable to the contract will come into play as the clause will need to be interpreted in light of the surrounding circumstances.

---

36 *Ibid.*, p. 13, referring to *Carr v Champagne Trucking, Inc.*, Case No. 52572, 2004 WL 396484, at *3 (N.Y. Sup. Ct. 2204).

37 *Cour de Cassation*, Commercial Chamber, 29 June 2010, *Faurecia*, n°09-11.841, in French: "*est réputée non écrite la clause limitative de réparation qui contredit la portée de l'obligation essentielle souscrite par le débiteur*".

38 *Cour de Cassation*, Commercial Chamber, 15 June 1959, n°57-12.362. In French: "*seuls, le dol ou la faute lourde de la partie qui invoque, pour se soustraire à son obligation, une clause d'irresponsabilité insérée au contrat et acceptée par l'autre partie, peuvent faire échec à l'application de ladite clause*".

39 A. Kolo and T.W. Wälde, 'Renegotiation and Contract Adaptation in the International Investment Projects: Applicable Legal Principles & Industry Practices' (2004) 1(1) *TDM* 1.

If the JOA does not contain a *force majeure* clause or a renegotiation clause in case of changes of circumstances, then a party seeking to invoke the change of circumstances will need to rely on the remedies available under the governing law. Although virtually all legislations recognise the principle of *pacta sunt servanda*, many of them are willing to depart from this principle in case of an unforeseeable change in the circumstances beyond the parties' control.[40] But the threshold that different national laws require in order to depart from the principle differs. Civil law systems typically contain provisions for situations of *force majeure* and hardship, whereas in common law jurisdictions relief is available in the case of frustration, impossibility or commercial impracticability. Thus, the law that the parties have chosen to govern their relationship will have a bearing when interpreting whether or not the *force majeure* (or hardship) exception applies.

2.2.3.1. Civil Law: Force Majeure

Under French law, an event will traditionally amount to *force majeure* if it is unforeseeable, irresistible and external to the control of the parties.[41] A clear distinction is drawn between events that make performance impossible and those that simply make it more difficult or onerous, with only the former qualifying as *force majeure*.[42] When the contract performance has become impossible, the parties have different mechanisms at their disposal to deal with the changed circumstances depending on the nature of the impossibility: if the impossibility to perform is only temporary, the contract can be suspended,[43] whereas in case of a complete impossibility, the contract can be terminated.[44]

Certain Northern African jurisdictions, whose civil codes are heavily influenced by the French Code, also incorporate *force majeure* provisions.[45]

Some civil law jurisdictions also recognise the doctrine of 'hardship' as a limitation or exclusion of liability. Hardship differs from *force majeure* in that it concerns situations in which performance of the contract has become more difficult but not impossible. As a result, the remedy for hardship is not

---

40 Polkinghorne and Kirkman, *supra* n. 15, pp. 5, 3.

41 A. Bénabent, *supra* n. 25, p. 332.

42 *Cour de Cassation*, Civil Chamber, 5 Dec. 1927: DH 1928.84; *Cour de Cassation*, First Civil Chamber, 8 Dec. 1998, Bull. Civ. I, n°346.

43 *Cour de Cassation*, First Civil Chamber, 24 February 1981, Bull. civ., I, n°65, D. 1982.479, note D. Martin.

44 If a party cannot perform at all, the contract will be terminated and voided with retroactive effect (*Cour de Cassation*, Commercial Chamber, 28 April 1982, Bull. civ. IV, n°145). If performance of the contract is only impossible for the future, it will be terminated with no retroactive effect (*Cour de Cassation*, Chambre Mixte, 23 Nov. 1990, D. 1991.121, note Larroumet).

45 See e.g. Article 127 of the Algerian Civil Code; Articles 282 and 283 of the Tunisian Code of Obligations and Contracts; Articles 268 and 269 of the Moroccan Code of Obligations and Contract; and Article 165 of the Egyptian Civil Code.

termination or suspension, but the possibility of altering the terms of the contract.[46] To qualify for hardship, the events in question must be unforeseeable and beyond the control of the party invoking it.[47]

The Egyptian Civil Code, for example, expressly provides for hardship:

> 'The contract makes the law of the parties. It can be revoked or altered only by mutual consent of the parties or for reasons provided for by law. When, however, as a result of exceptional and unpredictable events of a general character, the performance of the contractual obligation, without becoming impossible, becomes excessively onerous in such way as to threaten the debtor with exorbitant loss, the judge may according to the circumstances, and after taking into consideration the interests of both parties, reduce to reasonable limits, the obligation that has become excessive. Any agreement to the contrary is void.'[48]

Similar provisions can be found in the Algerian Civil Code and in the laws of UAE, Qatar and Kuwait.[49] On the contrary, under French law, a well-established principle dictates that the judge has no power to modify the terms of the contract if there is a fundamental change in circumstances that does not amount to *force majeure*.[50] Therefore, if the JOA is governed by French law, the parties should include a renegotiation clause into their contract if they want to be able to renegotiate the JOA in case of fundamental changes in circumstances that do not make performance of the contract impossible.

Even when the chosen law allows a decision maker to adjust the contractual obligations in case of hardship, the national laws' hardship provisions may not be sufficient to protect the performing party in case of changed circumstances, even if that party considers the change 'drastic'. By way of example, the following did not constitute hardship according to certain courts and tribunals:

- dramatic changes in market prices for products;
- unfavorable general economic circumstances in a country;
- currency fluctuations, even severe;
- failure of a central bank to grant authorization to pay in foreign currency when foreign exchange control regulations were in place at the time of contracting; and
- armed hostilities between countries with a history of antagonism.[51]

---

46 Fucci, *supra* n. 46, p. 11.

47 See UNIDROIT Principles, Article 6.2.2.

48 Article 147 of the Egyptian Civil Code.

49 See Article 107 of the Algerian Civil Code; Article 249 of the UAE Civil Code; Article 171 of the Qatar Civil Code; and Article 198 of the Kuwait Civil Code.

50 *Cour de Cassation*, Civil Chamber, 8 March 1876, *Canal de Craponne*, D. 1876.I.193. This well-established principle was modified by the reform of French contract law. See, Article 1195, paragraph two, as revised by the ordinance of 11 February 2016, No. 2016-131 (see <https://www.legifrance.gouv.fr/affichTexte.do?cidTexte=JORFTEXT000032004939&categorieLien=id>).

51 Fucci, *supra* n. 46, p. 18.

It is therefore recommended to include a hardship clause in the parties' agreement, specifying what type of events shall necessarily lead to a renegotiation of the agreement. In the context of a JOA, such circumstances could, for instance, be a substantial increase in the price of raw materials.

2.2.3.2. Common Law: Commercial Impracticability and Frustration

Common law systems usually do not contain express rules on hardship and *force majeure*. Therefore, if parties who have opted for US or English law in their contract and wish for *force majeure* or hardship exceptions to apply, they should include an explicit clause to that effect.[52]

That being said, common law jurisdictions also have mechanisms to cope with similar circumstances that civil law jurisdictions address under the headings of *force majeure* and 'hardship'. US law, for instance, allows the parties to rely on the concepts of impossibility, commercial impracticability and frustration in certain circumstances.

Impossibility is a defence that may be invoked when one party's non-performance results from a change in circumstances that has made the performance impossible. In such circumstances, the party whose performance has become impossible may avoid performance altogether. Commercial impracticability operates where subsequent events make the circumstances so different from the parties' assumptions at the time of contracting that it would be unfair to hold the parties liable for non-performance.[53] Such events permit the parties to refrain from performing the contract, but they do not allow for adjustment of the contract.[54]

Close to impracticability is the doctrine of frustration of purpose:

> 'Where, after a contract is made, a party's principal purpose is substantially frustrated without his fault by the occurrence of an event the non-occurrence of which was a basic assumption on which the contract was made, his remaining duties to render performance are discharged, unless the language or the circumstances indicate the contrary.'[55]

Under English law, the courts recognise the concept of frustration where:

> 'there supervenes an event (without default of either party and for which the contract makes no sufficient provision) which so significantly changes the nature (not merely the expense or onerousness) of the outstanding contractual rights and/or obligations

52 Polkinghorne and Kirkman, *supra* n. 15, p. 6. See also, *Goode on Commercial Law*, *supra* n. 12, p. 150.
53 2 ALI Contracts 2nd §261.
54 Fucci, *supra* n. 46, para. I. B.
55 2 ALI Contracts 2nd §265.

> from what the parties could reasonably have contemplated at the time of its execution that it would be unjust to hold them to the literal sense of its stipulations in the new circumstances: in such case the law declares both parties to be discharged from further performance.'[56]

The effect of frustration is to bring the contract to an end, independently of the will of the parties.[57] There is no duty to renegotiate the contract terms, even if performance has become really burdensome.[58] Frustration is defined very narrowly by English courts, so that a finding of frustration involves a standard much more difficult to meet than hardship.[59]

Thus, the parties' choice of law can impact the consequences that a change in the circumstances surrounding their contractual operation will have on their respective obligations.

2.2.4. *Liquidated Damages or Penalty Clauses*

The governing law may have a role to play even in situations in which the contract contains no gaps or uncertainties. It is very common to find liquidated damages provisions in JOAs, as the parties wish to avoid lengthy disputes on the calculation of damages. Here again, the validity and interpretation of the clause will depend on the applicable law.

Under English law, a clause will either be upheld as a liquidated damages provision, which is valid and allows the damaged party to recover the stipulated sums in the event of a breach, or it will be classified as a penalty, which is void and the stipulated sum is irrecoverable.[60] Traditionally, the qualification of the clause as a liquidated damages clause or as a penalty depends on whether the court or tribunal considers the sum to be 'a genuine pre-estimate of [the party's] probable or possible interest in the due performance of the contract.'[61] This does not, however, mean that the clause will be qualified as a penalty only because it does not correspond to the exact amount of the damages suffered. A disparity can exist between the two amounts, as long as it is not excessive and the parties are

---

56 *National Carriers Ltd v Panalpina (Northern) Ltd* [1981] AC 675 at 700, restating the test in *Davis Contractors Ltd v Fareham UDC* [1956] AC 696.

57 *Goode on Commercial Law*, *supra* n. 12, p. 150.

58 *Ibid.*, p. 150.

59 Z.A. Al Qurashi, 'Renegotiation of International Petroleum Agreements' (2005) 22(4) *Journal of International Arbitration* 270–71. See also *Goode on Commercial Law*, *supra* n. 12, p. 151, holding that, at common law: 'The general principle is that the parties are free to qualify or to limit the obligations which they assume to one another but, once an obligation has been assumed, the law will only exceptionally discharge the parties from the obligations which they have expressly assumed.'

60 J. Chitty and H.G. Beale, *Chitty on Contracts,* 31st edn, Sweet & Maxwell, London 2008, para. 26-171.

61 *Dunlop Pneumatic Tyre Co. Ltd v New Garage and Motor Co. Ltd* [1915] AC 79 at 96.

allowed a 'generous margin' in this regard.[62] Generally speaking, the courts look at whether there is 'any commercial justification for a discrepancy between the sum in the clause and the amount the innocent party would have received if damages had been assessed at common law'.[63] When a clause is considered a penalty, it will not be enforced beyond the sum amounting to a party's actual loss.[64]

Another example of clauses that may be considered as unauthorised penalty clauses under English law are forfeiture clauses, in which the parties provide that if one party defaults from its obligations under the JOA (for instance, if it fails to answer positively to a cash call for a non-operator), it must transfer its participating interest in the project to the non-defaulting party or parties in part or in full. If the participating interest of the defaulting party ends up being sold at a discounted value, the forfeiture clause may be considered an unenforceable penalty clause.[65] The same reasoning is likely to apply if the clause provides that forfeiture should take place for no compensation at all.

US law takes a similar approach to liquidated damages clauses:

> 'Damages for breach by either party may be liquidated in the agreement but only at an amount that is reasonable in the light of the anticipated or actual loss caused by the breach and the difficulties of proof of loss. A term fixing unreasonably large liquidated damages is unenforceable on grounds of public policy as a penalty.'[66]

Where US and English law consider that an unreasonably large liquidated damages clause is, in principle, unenforceable and must be set aside,[67] civil law systems generally give a court or tribunal the power to modify the amount of

---

62 *Murray v Leisureplay plc* [2005] EWCA Civ 963, para. 43; see also, para. 46: 'The real question is whether the sums for which the parties have provided the paid on breach differ substantially from the sums that would be recoverable at common law and whether there is shown to be no justification for that.'

63 M. Castaneda Wilcox, 'Spotlight on the rule against penalties', *Practical Law Dispute Resolution Blog*, 21 May 2015 <http://disputeresolutionblog.practicallaw.com/spotlight-on-the-rule-against-penalties/?sourceassetid=1248169917294&source=updateemail>.

64 *Jobson v Johnson* [1989] 1 W.L.R. 1026, 1040: 'it will not be enforced ... beyond the sum which represents [his] actual loss'.

65 See e.g. *El Makdessi v Cavendish Square Holdings BV and another* [2013] EWCA Civ 1539. But see on the decision's application to JOAs, e.g. P. Ashley, J. Aldersey-Williams and D. Rutherford, 'Oil and gas: forfeiture in JOAs – new case law', *Lexology*, 28 April 2014 <http://www.lexology.com/library/detail.aspx?g=5a02f7ff-c199-4866-a0b4-4fa5aacdae03> and P. Roberts, 'Forfeiture Clauses in JOAs – New Law, Old Problems', June 2014 <http://www.andrewskurth.com/pressroom-publications-1099.html>.

66 2 ALI Contracts 2nd §356.

67 For the UK, see *Kemble v Farren* [1829] 6 Bing 141; *Dunlop Pneumatic Tyre Co. v New Garage and Motor Co. Ltd* [1915] AC 79, 86-87; *Jobson v Johnson* [1989] 1 WLR 1026; *Scandinavian Trading Tanker Co. AB v Flota Petrolera Ecuatoriana (The Scraptrade)* [1983] 2 AC 694; *Alfred McAlpine Capital Projects Ltd v Tilebox Ltd* [2005] Build. L. 271 (TCC). For the US, see Section 356 of the Restatement (Second) of Contracts, which provides that: 'Damages for breach by either party may be liquidated in the agreement but only at an amount that is reasonable in the

liquidated damages, if they find that the amount is manifestly excessive in the circumstances.[68] For example, Article 1152 of the French Civil Code provides that:

> '[T]he judge may, even of his own motion, moderate or increase the agreed penalty, where it is obviously excessive or derisory. Any stipulation to the contrary shall be deemed unwritten.'[69]

The idea of being able to adjust the amount of the parties' liquidated damages clause, in contrast to the all-or-nothing approach in common law countries, is also present in the UNIDROIT Principles of International Commercial Contracts:

> '[N]otwithstanding any agreement to the contrary the specified sum may be reduced to a reasonable amount where it is grossly excessive in relation to the harm resulting from the non-performance and to the other circumstances.'[70]

German, Swiss and Swedish laws also operate in a similar manner in relation to liquidated damages.[71]

The above were but examples of issues that the parties' chosen law will typically impact. Other issues that will also be governed by that law of the contract are (or at least may be) the very validity of the JOA, i.e. whether it is legal and enforceable in the first place. Further, the following rights and obligations have also been identified as issues that will be impacted by the governing law:

- third party beneficiary rights;
- recognition of trust concepts;

...

- possible exclusions;
- presence of fiduciary duties;
- limitation periods; and
- ability for a party to sue in both contract and tort.[72]

---

light of the anticipated or actual loss caused by the breach and the difficulties of proof of loss. A term fixing unreasonably large liquidated damages is unenforceable on grounds of public policy as a penalty.' See also Section 2–718 of the Uniform Commercial Code.

68 Polkinghorne and Kirkman, *supra* n. 15, p. 7.

69 Article 1152 of the French Civil Code. In French: '*Lorsque la convention porte que celui qui manquera de l'exécuter payera une certaine somme à titre de dommages-intérêts, il ne peut être alloué à l'autre partie une somme plus forte, ni moindre. Néanmoins, le juge peut, même d'office, modérer ou augmenter la peine qui avait été convenue, si elle est manifestement excessive ou dérisoire. Toute stipulation contraire sera réputée non écrite.*'

70 Article 7.4.13 of the UNIDROIT Principles.

71 See Section 343 of the German BGB; Article 163 of the Swiss Code of Obligations; and Chapter 1, section 36 of the Swedish Contracts Act.

72 T.B. Heersche, *supra* n. 5, pp. 2–3.

2.3. LIMITS TO THE PARTIES' CHOICE OF LAW

2.3.1. *Limited Importance of the Governing Law*

Despite advocating the importance of making a choice of law in order to avoid unpleasant surprises, the authors recognise that, in the end, the final choice may not have as big a role to play in the parties' relationship as one might think. First, the choice will usually only materialise in the event of a dispute. As long as the operation runs smoothly, or the parties are able to settle their disputes amicably, recourse to the governing law may not be needed at all.

Second, and as discussed above, the main role of the parties' choice of law is to fill in any gaps in the interpretation of the contract. Therefore, if the terms of the agreement are clear, the governing law of the contract will usually not come into play at all, since a tribunal or court will simply apply those terms as they stand.[73] This reluctance to interfere with a clearly framed contract is apparent in both civil and common law jurisdictions.[74] As JOAs are typically thoroughly negotiated and are concluded between sophisticated parties, the decision makers are more likely to try to infer the common intent of the parties from the surrounding facts and wording of the contract than to find other gap fillers from the governing law. In fact, the governing law's greatest role may well be to provide for the rules that will allow the tribunal or court to determine the parties' intent.

Finally, even in the event of a dispute, the scope of the governing law has some inherent limits, as will be explained below.

2.3.2. *Inevitable Application of Mandatory Rules*

The parties' choice of law will not be given effect where the parties are bound by mandatory rules. Mandatory rules are those provisions of the otherwise applicable law from which the parties cannot deviate. In other words, mandatory rules apply regardless of the parties' choice.

In the European Union, Article 9 of the Rome I Regulation on the law applicable to contractual obligations defines overriding mandatory provisions as 'provisions the respect for which is regarded as crucial by a country for

---

73 Polkinghorne and Kirkman, *supra* n. 15, p. 3.

74 Under English law, it is established as a general rule that: 'where the words of any written instrument are free from ambiguity in themselves, and where external circumstances do not create any doubt or difficulty as to the proper application of those words to claimants under the instrument, or the subject-matter to which the instrument relates, such instrument is always to be construed according to the strict, plain, common meaning of the words themselves.' (Tindal CJ in *Shore v Wilson* (1842) 9 Cl. & Fin. 355, 565.) Similarly under French law, where the terms of a contract are clear and precise, judges are not permitted to distort their meaning or modify them in any way (Article 1134 of the French Code Civil, as interpreted by *Civ. 15 avr. 1872 (Veuve Foucauld et Coulombe c/ Pringault)*. The original commentary reads: '*Il n'est pas permis aux juges, lorsque les termes d'une convention sont clairs et précis, de dénaturer les obligations qui en résultent et de modifier les stipulations qu'elle renferme*'.

safeguarding its public interests, such as its political, social or economic organisation, to such an extent that they are applicable to any situation falling within their scope, irrespective of the law otherwise applicable to the contract under this Regulation'.[75] These rules thus restrict party autonomy in the sense that they cannot be derogated from by contract.

Such mandatory laws may have particular relevance in the hydrocarbon field: as natural resources are often vital for the sustainability of a country's economy, they bring into play sensitive interests such as environment protection, important economic stakes and even state sovereignty.[76] These sectors are therefore heavily regulated by the host states.[77] As a consequence, local laws may well become predominant in the performance of the agreement notwithstanding the parties' choice of another law.

For instance, the host state's tax laws will apply regardless of the governing law. Similarly, the parties cannot set aside the application of criminal statutes that may become relevant in case of a major ecological catastrophe. Criminal statutes concerning the good conduct of business may also be relevant in the hydrocarbon sectors. For instance, US quoted companies are bound by the Foreign Corrupt Practices Act and cannot exclude the statute's application to their contract simply by choosing a different governing law. In fact, this law is often qualified as a 'long arm statute', as its application reaches companies that are non-resident defendants, provided that they have minimum contacts with the forum.[78] Similarly, contracting parties will not be able to exclude provisions relating to antitrust or competition law[79] or employment law. Finally, environmental laws may contain mandatory provisions that the parties must respect, regardless of the governing law clause.

2.3.3. Governing Law's 'Short Arms'

As stated above, the operation regulated by a JOA involves an intricate set of sub-agreements that are necessary to implement the project. And issues may arise out of those sub-agreements that impact the JOA's performance. For instance, a dispute may arise with a subcontractor and have an operational and/or financial impact on the parties to the JOA (e.g. if a subcontractor delays in its performance, which in turn delays the operator's performance under the JOA). Such dispute will be subject to the law governing the subcontract, and not the JOA, despite the dispute's relevance to the parties' performance under the JOA.

---

75 Article 9 of the Rome I Regulation.

76 Otero García-Castrillón, *supra* n. 11, p. 18.

77 *Ibid.*

78 *Black's Law Dictionary*, 10th edn, B.A. Garner, ed., 2014, p. 1085, defining a 'long-arm statute' as '[a] statute providing for jurisdiction over a nonresident defendant who has had contacts with the territory where the statute is in effect.'

79 Blackaby, Partasides, Redfern and Hunter, *supra* n. 4, Section 3.129.

Therefore, even if the parties make an express choice of law, they must keep in mind that that choice is confined to their contract and that, as a consequence, more than one law may impact the performance of their obligations, either directly or indirectly.[80]

2.3.4. A Choice Made in Good Faith

Most legal systems impose certain general limits to party autonomy, among which the requirement that the choice be made in good faith. English courts have, for example, stated that parties are granted wide autonomy in selecting the law of the contract, 'provided the intention expressed is bona fide and legal, and provided there is no reason for avoiding the choice on the ground of public policy'.[81] This limitation has been interpreted as requiring that (i) the choice is not illegal under the law of the forum; (ii) the choice is not intended to circumvent a mandatory rule of law that would otherwise be applicable in the absence of a choice; or (iii) the choice is not contrary to the public policy of the forum.[82] Under French law, the bona fide requirement is embodied in the concept of *fraude à la loi*, which consists in manipulating a connecting factor to evade an otherwise unfavourable law of the forum.[83] The courts will not enforce such choice.

These limitations rarely apply to JOAs as it is customary that the parties to complex, international contracts choose a law other than the one that would 'otherwise' apply to their relationship. Inferring a choice made in bad faith in this context would require exceptional circumstances.

2.4. DRAFTING AN EFFICIENT CHOICE OF LAW CLAUSE

2.4.1. Ensuring Application of the Most Adapted Rules

In selecting the governing law, the parties should opt for a system of rules that will provide clarity and certainty in case of a dispute. For this reason, parties to a JOA will often select a national legal system to govern their agreement,[84] although, in theory, they are free to select 'anational rules' (such as the UNIDROIT Principles).

---

80 In certain circumstances the parties' choice may, however, extend to third parties, such as in case of a transfer of a claim under the JOA to a third party. See e.g. Article 14.2 of Rome I Regulation ('The law governing the assigned or subrogated claim shall determine its assignability, the relationship between the assignee and the debtor, the conditions under which the assignment or subrogation can be invoked against the debtor and whether the debtor's obligations have been discharged.')

81 *Vita Food Products Inc. v Unus Shipping Co.* [1939] AC 277, at 290.

82 P. Nugh, *Autonomy in International Contracts*, Oxford University Press, Oxford 1999, p. 67.

83 *Cour of Cassation*, Civil Chamber, 18 March 1878, *Princesse de Beauffremont v Prince de Bauffremont.*

84 Blackaby, Partasides, Redfern and Hunter, *supra* n. 4, Section 3.108.

The parties may wish to choose a law that seems 'neutral' in view of the nationality of the parties involved. However, supposed neutrality does not necessarily entail efficiency in the resolution of a dispute and should therefore not automatically be the guiding consideration in the selection of the governing law. Some bodies of law are more developed than others with respect to complex contracts in general, or hydrocarbon contracts more particularly and, as a consequence, they offer more predictability in their application.[85] Therefore, although those laws may not always be 'neutral' from the perspective of the parties' respective nationality, they may be better adapted to the JOA than the more 'neutral' laws. When selecting the governing law, the parties should, for instance, pay attention to how developed the contemplated law's jurisprudence is on complex international contracts and how stable the selected law's legal environment is, instead of the law's perceived 'neutrality' vis-à-vis the parties.

The parties may, however, want to avoid the host state's law for the reasons explained above.[86] If the parties cannot bypass the application of the host state's law, foreign parties may wish to insert a 'stabilisation clause' into the agreement. By this clause, the parties 'freeze' the applicable legislation by agreeing that the applicable law will be that in force at the contract effective date, and that any subsequent changes to the host state's law will not apply, unless otherwise agreed by the parties. If the host state is party to the JOA, the contracting state may undertake not 'to annul or change the terms of the contract by legislative or administrative action', unless the counterparty approves the change in the legal regime.[87] Such clauses are intended to mitigate the negative effects that a change in the legal regime of the host state (unilaterally decided by that state) may have on the contract and on the contracting party.

In the alternative – or in addition to a stabilisation clause – the choice of law clause can contain a reference to international law principles to mitigate possible negative sides of the host state's law, as international law will generally protect fundamental rights that a local law may seek to limit.[88] The second alternative choice of law clause in the AIPN Model JOA contains a clause referring to international law:

> '18.1 Applicable Law
>
> The laws of __________, to the extent consistent with international law, shall govern this Agreement for all purposes. To the extent the laws of __________ are not consistent with international law, then international law shall prevail.'[89]

---

85 For instance the historical importance of the oil industry in Texas explains the abundant case law in respect to oil and gas contracts.

86 See above section 2.1.1.

87 Blackaby, Partasides, Redfern and Hunter, *supra* n. 4, Section 3.117.

88 Polkinghorne and Kirkman, *supra* n. 15, p. 11.

89 AIPN Model JOA, Article 18.1, 'Applicable Law'.

The JOA may also refer to anational or transnational rules of law, such as the UNIDROIT Principles,[90] in addition to containing a traditional choice of law clause. In the context of oil contracts, the parties can, for instance, refer to *lex petrolea* (i.e. oil sector-specific international rules).[91] The AIPN Model JOA provides for example that the operator shall conduct the joint operations 'in a diligent, safe, and efficient manner in accordance with good and prudent petroleum industry practices and field conservation principles generally followed by the international petroleum industry under similar circumstances'.[92]

2.4.2. *Ensuring the Broadest Application of the Governing Law*

Governing law clauses should be drafted in a broad and comprehensive manner to ensure that the same law governs the entire relationship between the parties. While it is in theory possible to submit different parts of an agreement to different national laws,[93] such setting is likely to make interpretation of the contract more difficult and can generate conflicts between different parts of the contract.[94]

It is thus advisable to provide that one law covers all issues arising out of the JOA in the broadest manner. The two alternative choice of law clauses in the AIPN Model JOA ensure this by stating that the chosen law will govern the JOA 'for all purposes'.[95]

If the governing law clause is included in the dispute resolution clause, it is important that it provides that 'any and all disputes *under and in connection with*' the JOA are submitted to the same law (or similar wording to the same effect). The small addition of 'in connection with' may become conclusive in the case of a dispute as it will, for instance, permit the inclusion of tortious claims related to the performance of the operations under the JOA within the scope of the governing law and clarify that disputes related to the validity of the JOA itself are governed by the law applicable to the agreement. The absence of such wording does not automatically mean that the governing law will not govern

---

90 UNIDROIT Principles. See also e.g. Rome I Regulation, Recital 13 that provides that: 'This Regulation does not preclude parties from incorporating by reference into their contract a non-State body of law or an international convention.'

91 Otero García-Castrillón, *supra* n. 11, pp. 12–18.

92 AIPN Model JOA, Article 4.2.B.2.

93 See e.g. Rome I Regulation, article 3(1).

94 The specific case of arbitration agreements will be discussed below in the context of dispute resolution clauses. In summary, an arbitration agreement can be, and often is, governed by a different law to the rest of the agreement because of the arbitration agreement's autonomy. This is particularly the case if the parties select a seat of arbitration that is not the same as the jurisdiction the law of which otherwise governs the JOA. On the law applicable to arbitration agreement see e.g. G.B. Born, *International Commercial Arbitration*, 2nd edn, Kluwer Law International, The Hague 2014, p. 472 *et seq.*

95 AIPN Model JOA, Article 18.1.

those questions, but the parties can avoid unnecessary uncertainty and the possible need to litigate the scope of the governing law clause by clarifying in their clause that issues 'in connection' with the JOA fall within the orbit of the chosen law in the broadest manner.

2.4.3. Ensuring the Direct Application of the Governing Law

When the parties have the freedom to choose the law that governs their contract, they should specify that that law operates in a 'direct' manner – in other words that the governing law's choice of law rules are excluded. In practice, this exclusion means that even if the governing law provides that a certain question would otherwise be answered by applying another country's law (such as the law of the place of performance), the *renvoi* will not operate and the tribunal or court will apply the substantive provisions of the law chosen by the parties. The purpose of this exclusion is at least twofold. First, it allows the parties to avoid facing complex conflict of laws questions in a contractual setting that in and of itself is already challenging, which questions are prone to lengthen and complicate possible legal proceedings. Second, it provides legal certainty to the parties' contractual relationship. Indeed, the mechanism of *renvoi* can lead to unexpected results with the tribunal or court possibly applying a law that the parties specifically wanted to exclude.

For example, a simple and well-drafted clause would read:

> 'This Agreement is governed by, and all disputes arising under or in connection with this Agreement shall be resolved in accordance with, the laws of ______ (to the exclusion of its conflict of laws rules).'[96]

Similarly, the AIPN Model JOA's first alternative for a governing law clause provides for the exclusion of choice of law rules by stating that the '*substantive* laws of ________________, *exclusive of any conflicts of laws principles* that could require the application of any other law, shall govern this Agreement for all purposes.'[97]

3. DISPUTE RESOLUTION CLAUSES IN JOAs

A JOA is designed to have a long existence because of the nature of oil and gas exploration projects, which typically expand over several years. Thus, a variety of disputes can arise during the lifespan of a JOA, particularly in view of the

---

96 P.D. Friedland, *Arbitration Clauses for International Contracts*, 2nd edn, Juris Publishing, New York 2007, p. 184.

97 AIPN Model JOA, Article 18.1 (emphasis added).

complexity of the projects that JOAs govern. Many disagreements can be settled smoothly and the parties reach an agreement without the help of a third party. But some disputes lead to a deadlock between the parties, which may even paralyse the project if the disagreement cannot be solved. In such circumstances, it is important that the JOA foresees a dispute resolution mechanism that can deal with any issues quickly and efficiently.

In order to do that, the JOA's dispute resolution mechanism must take into account the particularities of a JOA, such as the international nature of oil and gas exploration projects, as well as the multiparty and multicontract elements of a JOA. The parties may also wish to ensure that the exploration is not brought to a halt by every dispute or disagreement between the various parties that have a role to play. Thus, as noted by one author:

> 'A balance must be struck in the JOA between providing an accessible forum for the prompt and effective resolution of disputes between the parties (whether between the parties inter se or between the operator and the non-operating parties) and making it too easy for the parties to elevate every disagreement to the level of a formal dispute, which might be done in order to frustrate the commercial purpose of the JOA.'[98]

Despite its importance, the parties to a JOA often fail to pay sufficient attention to their agreement's dispute resolution provision during the contract negotiations, as their focus is on the performance of the project – not on its failure or the possible difficulties that may arise. Therefore, the dispute resolution provision is often among the last items that the parties address during their negotiations, albeit one of the 'major risks in deal' that the parties should not ignore.[99]

The following will first address the parties' needs that a JOA's dispute resolution mechanism should meet (section 3.1), before describing different mechanisms of dispute resolution to which the parties can have recourse (section 3.2). It will then discuss the scope of a JOA's dispute resolution clause, in view of the multicontract and multiparty element of the operations that JOAs typically govern (section 3.3), and provide indications as to how to draft an efficient dispute resolution clause (section 3.4).

3.1. A MULTI-TIERED DISPUTE RESOLUTION CLAUSE TO FIT THE PARTIES' NEEDS

As in every long, complex project, the parties' needs in case of a dispute arising out of a JOA may be multiple and varied. The parties will, however, typically

---

98 P. Roberts, *Joint Operating Agreements: A Practical Guide*, 2nd edn, Globe Business Publishing, London 2012, p. 207.

99 J.P. Bowman and A.T. Martin, 'Negotiating and Drafting Dispute Resolution Provisions for International Petroleum Contracts' (2007) 4 *OGEL*, slide 3.

need (i) an efficient and quick process that will not paralyse the project for any longer than necessary; (ii) a process that will, to the extent possible, preserve the parties' relationship; (iii) a process that will preserve the parties' procedural rights; and (iv) a process that will lead to an enforceable decision. The JOA's dispute resolution clause should reflect these needs. In addition, the dispute resolution mechanism should be tailored to the disputes that are most likely to arise under the JOA.

With these requirements in mind, and particularly in view of a JOA's cooperative nature, the dispute resolution clauses should provide for the obligation, or at least the possibility, of resorting to non-contentious forms of dispute resolution before elevating the dispute to litigation or arbitration. Indeed, many JOAs contain a 'multi-tiered dispute resolution clause', i.e. 'one that requires certain steps to be taken – usually negotiation or mediation or one and then the other – before an arbitration or litigation may be commenced'.[100] Such clauses are strongly recommended in the context of long, complex contracts, where the parties' relationship will usually not end with the dispute, as these clauses 'require the parties fully to explore the possibility of amicable settlement prior to the launch of often lengthy, expensive, and disruptive arbitral proceedings'.[101] These multi-tiered dispute resolution clauses typically provide for negotiation as a first recourse in case of a disagreement. Failing an agreement in the course of the negotiations, multi-tiered dispute resolution clauses may then provide for other non-contentious mechanisms, such as expert determination or mediation, before allowing the parties to bring the dispute to a decision maker, which will typically be an arbitral tribunal.

A multi-tiered dispute resolution clause is also advantageous where the parties cannot circumvent the host state's courts' jurisdiction. In such cases, it may be particularly advantageous for the foreign investor to have alternative means of dispute resolution available to it in addition to litigation in national courts.

Thus, the following description of dispute resolution mechanisms under JOAs is based on multi-tiered dispute resolution clauses.

---

100 J.M. Townsend, 'Promoting Peace Before Conflict: Integrating Alternative Methods of Dispute Resolution into the Arbitration Process', in Albert Jan van den Berg (ed.), *Arbitration Advocacy in Changing Times, ICCA Congress Series*, 2010 Rio Volume 15, Kluwer Law International, 2011, p. 35.

101 Blackaby, Partasides, Redfern and Hunter, *supra* n. 4, Section 2.84. See also M. Pryles, 'Multi-Tiered Dispute Resolution Clauses' (2001) 18(2) *Journal of International Arbitration* 159–176, indicating: 'Perhaps another reason for the employment of multi-tiered clauses lies in the great diversity of possible disputes in complex contracts, particularly construction contracts of some duration. It is an obvious fact that a dispute resolution clause inserted into a contract is designed to deal with future disputes. These future disputes can be multifarious in nature. They can involve very different issues and bear very different monetary values. In consequence a multi-tiered dispute resolution procedure is likely to contain, in one tier or another, a procedure appropriate for a particular dispute. For these reasons, and others, it seems that multi-tiered dispute resolution clauses are increasing in popularity and use.'

3.2. DIFFERENT TYPES OF DISPUTE RESOLUTION MECHANISMS AT THE PARTIES' DISPOSAL

Many different forms of dispute resolution mechanisms exist, among which the parties can choose to select those that would be the most appropriate in case of a dispute arising out of their particular contract. As noted, most contracts combine several of these methods, in order to allow the parties to attempt an amicable settlement before referring the dispute to a third party decision maker. Non-contentious forms of dispute resolution will be addressed first (section 3.2.1), before considering contentious forms of dispute resolution (section 3.2.2).

3.2.1. Non-Contentious Forms of Dispute Resolution

3.2.1.1. Negotiations

The JOA may provide that, as a first step, the parties must try to negotiate to reach an amicable agreement over their dispute. A dispute resolution clause will usually provide that negotiations must be started after reception of a written notice of the dispute. The notice will kick off the time period reserved for the negotiations and put the other side on notice that the claiming party has formally initiated the contractual dispute resolution process.

To ensure the efficiency and thus the usefulness of the negotiations, the dispute resolution clause should provide that the negotiations must be conducted between senior executives of the parties involved, who have the power to negotiate on behalf of the parties and enter into a settlement.[102] The interest of 'executive negotiations'[103] is also to elevate the dispute to a level of management not involved in the day-to-day operations of the project, with no personal considerations.[104] Senior executives are also likely to have a 'wider corporate perspective',[105] which means they are more likely to think about the commercial relationship in the long run than those involved in the day-to-day performance of the project.

The parties can also spell out in their dispute resolution provision that any settlement negotiations are undertaken 'without prejudice' to their respective positions in possible adjudication proceedings. This can provide an additional incentive to the parties to make settlement offers and to find an amicable outcome to their dispute, as the parties do not need to fear that their settlement offers will be interpreted as admissions in the future. However, such specific

---

102 See e.g. Optional Provision in AIPN Model JOA, Article 18.2.B.

103 H.R. Dundas, 'Dispute Resolution in the Oil & Gas Industry: an Oilman's Perspective' (2004) 4 *TDM* 7.

104 Townsend, *supra* n. 100, p. 36.

105 Dundas, *supra* n. 103, p. 7.

stipulation is not, in principle, necessary: many jurisdictions consider that, as a rule, a settlement offer made in the course of negotiations does not prejudice the offeror's position, should the dispute persist. In other words, an adjudicator will not infer any weakness in one party's position from that party's settlement offer.

If undertaken successfully, negotiations can lead to a prompt and cost-effective resolution of a dispute. And even if the negotiations do not end with a settlement, they may enable the parties to better frame the issues at dispute and narrow the scope of the matters that will be brought forward.

3.2.1.2. Mediation

Some dispute resolution clauses provide that the parties must – or may – have recourse to a mediator before turning to a final decision maker. Mediation is a process by which the parties are encouraged to reach an agreement on their own terms with the help of a neutral third party. The mediator does not impose any decisions on the parties. Instead, the mediator aims at facilitating the settlement of the dispute through different techniques, such as individual meetings with each side.[106] After the parties have worked through the issues separately with the mediator, the eventual aim is to bring them together at the end of the process to discuss settlement terms. If an agreement is reached, the parties may go on to sign a settlement agreement that has binding force, if they so indicate.[107] This settlement will remain confidential and the parties may, in principle, not use it in subsequent adjudication proceedings as proof against the other side.[108]

Mediation can be a lower-cost option than arbitration or litigation: the process can sometimes take place in a single day and parties are spared the time and monetary costs of document production associated with litigation or arbitration. In addition, contrary to national court's judges, mediators do not necessarily have to be legally trained – instead, they come from a range of industrial and commercial backgrounds.[109] Having a mediator with industry expertise can be a significant advantage if the parties wish to reach a commercial or technical solution rather than focusing on the legal points of their dispute.

Having reached a settlement on their own terms, albeit with the help of a mediator, the parties are often better placed to maintain their commercial relationship than those that have followed a contentious adjudication process. Reaching a consensus can be key in the context of a JOA, as the parties often

---

106 H. Brown and A. Marriot, *ADR Principles and Practice*, Sweet & Maxwell, London 1993, p. 110, points 4 and 5.

107 *Ibid.*, p. 145.

108 The parties may, however, wish to insert a confidentiality clause into their agreement to ensure that all settlement negotiations and any settlement agreement must be kept confidential and cannot be used in subsequent proceedings, although such provision is not necessary in most jurisdictions.

109 Brown and Marriot, *supra* n. 106, p. 119, point 8.

have to continue the project despite disagreement on certain aspects of their common undertaking.

However, mediation is not always the best option for parties under a JOA. If the dispute is multiparty in nature (i.e. involving several participants), it can be complicated to organise a mediation process, let alone reach a settlement, to which all parties concerned agree.[110] It is also hard to make mediation work if the parties involved are not fully committed to reaching an agreement or if the situation has already escalated to a point where one or both parties want to walk away from the project.

Another disadvantage of mediation, which may well become determinative in case of an uncooperative party, is that the settlement agreements are not directly enforceable in courts. Indeed, a settlement agreement may only be enforced as a binding contract. Therefore, a party wishing to enforce its terms would have to 'take action on it in the appropriate courts of the country having jurisdiction'[111] if the other side refuses to abide by the settlement agreement's terms.

3.2.1.3. Expert Determination/Early Neutral Evaluation

Expert determination has been credited with being 'an informal, speedy and effective way of resolving disputes, particularly disputes which are of a specific technical character or specialized kinds'.[112] This confidential process[113] involves the parties selecting a neutral third party expert to provide a determination of a particular area of the dispute. The parties can agree that the decision of the expert is binding between them, but they may also decide to keep the decision non-binding. In the latter case, the process is often referred to as 'early neutral evaluation'.

3.2.1.4. Expert Determination

Since expert determination is a consensual process, the parties are able to decide the scope of the issues in dispute that the expert is to consider and the powers

---

110 For a different view, see Brown and Marriot, *supra* n. 106, p. 150, stating that: 'There is, however, another view, namely that ADR is particularly appropriate for multi-party disputes because such disputes are complex and expensive to litigate, and impossible to arbitrate without the consent of all parties, and because the processes of ADR can work just as effectively with numerous parties as with two parties.'

111 *Ibid.*, p. 379, specifying that: 'As with the enforcement of all contracts, the remedy may be damages or, where appropriate, specific performance or an injunction.'

112 *Heart Research Institute Ltd v Psiron Ltd* [2002] NWSC 646 at [16], quoted in J. Bailey, *Construction Law*, Vol. III, Informa Law, Abingdon 2011, para. 23.21.

113 See Brown and Marriot, *supra* n. 106, p. 356: 'The neutral's duty of confidentiality may arise from the agreement to enter into the process, from the code of practice regulating it, and/or from representations made when the ADR service was offered to the parties.'

that the expert will be able to exercise.[114] The process of hearing evidence from the parties and making a decision is carried out on a short time-scale. In general, the parties produce a limited amount of evidence to the expert (usually because the expert is only deciding on a specific, narrowly defined issue) and the decision can be rendered as soon as 14 days later.[115]

On the surface, expert determination may appear indistinguishable from arbitration with a single arbitrator. However, the system can, and should, be demarcated from conventional arbitration since its function and approach are different.[116] For example, the time-scale of an expert determination is intended to be much shorter than that of arbitration.[117] In addition, arbitrators are generally bound by duties of legal nature, such as the duty to afford the parties due process and to listen to all sides of the argument, whereas an expert is only bound by what the parties have agreed upon.[118] An expert is not normally required to give reasons for his/her decision or to adhere to principles of due process (unless the parties have specified that he/she is to do so).[119] Finally, as briefly mentioned above, there are no formal rules regarding evidence and no provision for cross-examination of witnesses.[120] In this sense, the process of expert determination is much less formalistic than arbitration and litigation, thereby adding to its reputation for serving as a quick and informal way to receive a decision on a particular topic or issue. In order to seal this separation from arbitration, it is often common for parties to include a clause expressly stating that their expert is to act as an expert and not as an arbitrator.[121]

The decision of an expert is to be respected by the parties, as failure to do so would constitute a breach of the contract that provided for recourse to expert

---

114 Bailey, *supra* n. 112, para. 23.22.

115 American Arbitration Association, 'Early Neutral Evaluation: Getting An Expert's Assessment' <https://www.adr.org/aaa/faces/services/disputeavoidanceservices/earlyneutral evaluation;jsessionid=9CYYVpZZk1lD1rcGWjNVjJpfhn1LTTHz1zy457QzZkN3qG HcLkxH!-784978660?_afrLoop=161508029331995&_afrWindowMode=0&_afrWindowId=null#%40%3F_afrWindowId%3Dnull%26_afrLoop%3D161508029331995%26_afrWindow Mode%3D0%26_adf.ctrl-state%3D14u2rw8wn1_4>.

116 Arbitration will be discussed in more detail below.

117 Also, the determination and the expert him/herself is not bound by statutory provisions and duties in the same way as an arbitrator in arbitration proceedings whereas arbitration agreements between parties are supported by legislative provisions of the seat of the arbitration and so any 'gaps' will be filled in by the courts. Bailey, *supra* n. 112, para. 23.23. In addition, expert determinations covered by an 'expert determination agreement' are purely contractual and any disagreement about an expert's scope or duties would be decided by the court in the usual way, whereas the arbitrators are typically the judges of their own competence.

118 Bailey, *supra* n. 112, para. 23.23.

119 *Ibid.*, para. 23.28.

120 American Arbitration Association, 'Early Neutral Evaluation: Getting An Expert's Assessment', *supra* n. 115.

121 Bailey, *supra* n. 112, para. 23.27.

determination.[122] Consequently, parties have to go to court if they want to enforce this decision, as they would do to enforce a contract.

Expert determination is at its most effective when a technical issue needs to be resolved. In the context of a JOA, the most common topics for expert determination include, for instance, the value of a party's interests where there is a transfer of interests, whether a particular circumstance can constitute *force majeure* under a contract, or the attribution of cash values to non-cash consideration where a pre-emption right so applies.[123]

3.2.1.5. Early Neutral Evaluation

If the parties decide that the expert's decision will not be binding on them, i.e. they opt for the 'early neutral evaluation', the purpose of the expert's intervention is somewhat different from expert determination. Indeed, in the case of early neutral evaluation, the expert's determination will serve more as a 'guide as to how the dispute might be resolved if elevated to arbitration or litigation' instead of an authoritative decision.[124] In certain cases, the expert may evaluate the issues in dispute as a whole, setting out the best and worst case alternatives that confront the parties to the dispute.[125] Such non-binding decision can avoid the escalation of the dispute and may provide the parties with more focus in their settlement discussions.

3.2.2. Contentious Forms of Dispute Resolution

3.2.2.1. Litigation

In certain circumstances, the parties have no other alternative than to submit their disputes to national courts if, for instance, the host state's legislation forbids the state entities from concluding international arbitration agreements. But the parties to a JOA may also choose to submit their disputes to a national court without being obliged to do so, in which case they can usually select which country's courts they wish to have recourse to. A clause by which the parties submit their dispute to a certain court is at times referred to as the 'choice of forum' clause.

---

122 Brown and Marriot, *supra* n. 106, p. 376, indicating that '[e]nforcement is accomplished by way of an action on the contract: the determination does not have authority or effect of an arbitration award.'

123 Roberts, *supra* n. 98, p. 209.

124 Bailey, *supra* n. 112, para. 23.30. See also American Arbitration Association, 'Early Neutral Evaluation: Getting an Expert's Opinion', *supra* n. 115.

125 American Arbitration Association, 'Early Neutral Evaluation: Getting an Expert's Opinion', *supra* n. 115.

The reasons for opting for a choice of forum clause may vary, but typically the parties wish to extract the dispute from the jurisdiction of the otherwise competent court (such as the court of the host state), all the while preserving the certainty that national litigation proceedings offer – or at least are said to offer. Indeed, litigating provides a degree of certainty in the sense that the procedural rules of most jurisdictions contain detailed, well-established and clear provisions, eliminating the need for the JOA's dispute resolution clause to address such procedural issues.[126] Where there is a choice of forum clause, the procedure for bringing the case before the courts will depend on the procedural rules of the jurisdiction that the parties choose in their clause.[127] Furthermore, national courts have significant powers in relation to, for example, joining third parties, providing interim remedies and striking out unmeritorious claims,[128] and their decision will be enforceable within their own jurisdiction.[129]

However, the parties forfeit a significant amount of flexibility if they opt for litigation in national courts, as they are bound to follow the procedural rules that are in place in their chosen jurisdiction. This can result in litigation in overburdened national courts that stretches out over many months, or even years, with long appeal proceedings. Such protracted litigation can have a disastrous impact on large projects that must move forward despite the parties' dispute. Indeed, solely opting for litigation to solve all disputes under a JOA may be overly burdensome. For example, where the dispute is relatively minor or involves issues of a technical nature, expert evaluation or arbitration may be a more appropriate route to take.[130] Using litigation to resolve such issues may slow down the progress of the project in the meantime which, as noted above, could lead to an undesirable commercial outcome.

Further, the parties have no control over the choice of the decision makers, which can be detrimental in view of the technical and complex issues that may arise from the operations governed by the JOA. In addition, disputes brought before national courts are public, which may have a significant adverse impact

---

126 Roberts, *supra* n. 98, p. 211.

127 Parties to international contracts should specify in their choice of forum clause which courts have jurisdiction over the dispute and whether this jurisdiction is exclusive. If the parties have not specified which courts of their chosen jurisdiction are competent to hear their dispute, the law of the chosen jurisdiction will determine where the dispute will be heard.

128 Most arbitral institutions' rules give similar powers to arbitrators, but the arbitrators' powers have certain limitations that national courts' do not. For instance, arbitrators will typically have to seek the apparent or implied consent of the parties before joining a third party to the proceedings, whereas national courts are usually not bound by the parties' agreement in this regard in the same manner. And although arbitrators often have the power to issue interim measures under the arbitration rules, enforceability of such measures is not straightforward in some countries.

129 On the enforceability of arbitral awards, see below.

130 Roberts, *supra* n. 98, p. 211. In these instances, the author states that litigation could be 'something of a sledgehammer to crack a nut'.

on the parties' commercial interests. Finally, contrary to international arbitration awards, which are subject to the recognition and enforcement mechanism of the New York Convention (discussed below), there is no international convention that would allow for national court decisions to be systematically enforced around the globe. This adds a layer of uncertainty to the finalisation of the parties' dispute, in case the losing party does not comply with the court decision.

3.2.2.2. Arbitration

Arbitration has been found to be the 'preferred dispute resolution mechanism for transnational disputes', which is particularly true in the energy sector.[131]

Arbitration is a private method of settling disputes between parties to a contract by a neutral third party. Arbitration requires an agreement by the parties, but once the parties have agreed on arbitration, they are bound by the arbitration agreement and can, in principle, no longer have recourse to national courts to resolve the disputes falling within the ambit of their arbitration agreement. In addition, the arbitrators' decision is final and binding on the parties, which distinguishes arbitration from mediation.

Arbitration presents many advantages in the context of JOAs. The advantages of arbitration that are traditionally put forward by the advocates of this dispute resolution method are indeed particularly well-fitted to the international nature of JOAs and the types of disputes that typically arise. Arbitration is praised for the procedural flexibility it offers to parties who can tailor the procedure to their needs.[132] In addition, arbitration offers the advantage of confidentiality compared to litigation in open court[133] (provided that the parties agree to keep the proceedings and the outcome confidential). Confidentiality is particularly important for parties to JOAs, as resolving the dispute will most likely require the production of sensitive information pertaining to natural resources, among others.

Another important advantage of arbitration that has relevance in the context of JOAs is that it offers a neutral forum to parties that come from different countries.[134] This may be particularly significant to the operator, or other private party to the dispute, who may wish to avoid the (perceived) advantage that the state party will have before its national courts. As such, this (perceived) advantage could be avoided with a choice of forum clause that opts for the courts of a country other than the host state. But national courts' willingness to adjudicate matters involving a state party (or a state entity) varies, and different

131 *International Arbitration Survey: Corporate Choices in International Arbitration*, Queen Mary, University of London, 2013, pp. 21 and 6.

132 Blackaby, Partasides, Redfern and Hunter, *supra* n. 4, Section 1.73.

133 *Ibid.*, Section 1.95.

134 *Ibid.*, Sections 1.90-1.91.

jurisdictions have different approaches to state sovereignty. Such considerations have less importance in arbitration since the state has accepted in advance to submit to arbitration.

Furthermore, arbitration usually offers the parties the possibility to choose their decision makers, either from a list of arbitrators or freely from the legal or technical industry. This possibility offers the advantage of using arbitrators who have specific legal, linguistic or technical knowledge, which in view of the complexity of the operations that JOAs govern may be decisive in order to arrive at the right solution. In addition, the arbitrators' experience can significantly speed up the dispute resolution process, as they should not need to spend as much time on familiarising themselves with the matters as an inexperienced adjudicator would.

As the parties to a JOA are often of different nationalities and their assets can be dispersed all over the world, the arbitral award may need to be enforced in a variety of places. A major advantage of arbitration compared to national litigation is the existence of international conventions that provide for facilitated mechanisms of enforcement. The New York Convention, which has been signed by 154 countries, provides for the recognition and enforcement of foreign arbitral awards in all its signatory countries.[135] Signatory states of the New York Convention have undertaken to recognise and enforce arbitral awards rendered in other signatory countries, with only very limited grounds for denying their recognition or enforcement. Conversely, recognition and enforcement of a foreign court's judgment is mostly conditioned upon the existence of a bilateral treaty between the country of the courts that rendered the decision and the country where enforcement is sought.[136] In the absence of such agreement, enforcement may prove difficult.

Another specificity of arbitration is that the arbitration agreement is subject to a 'principle of separability', according to which the arbitration agreement is independent from the rest of the contract. The corollary of this principle is that the arbitration agreement's fate does not necessarily follow that of the JOA as a whole: for example, if the JOA is annulled, the arbitration agreement can continue to exist and disputes relating to the JOA's annulment may still

---

135 The United Nations Convention on the Recognition and Enforcement of Foreign Arbitral Awards, done at New York, 10 June 1958, United Nations Treaty Series (1959), Vol. 330, 3, No. 4739 (New York Convention).

136 There are certain limited regional exceptions, such as the 2007 Lugano Convention, which provides for the facilitated recognition and enforcement of judgments rendered in one of the signatory countries (Convention on jurisdiction and the enforcement of judgments in civil and commercial matters signed in Lugano on 30 October 2007, Title III, Recognition and Enforcement). Within the European Union, the Brussels I Regulation permits the same (EU Regulation No. 1215/2012 of the European Parliament and of the Council of 12 December 2012 on jurisdiction and the recognition and enforcement of judgments in civil and commercial matters, Chapter III, Recognition and Enforcement).

be decided in arbitration. The other corollary of this principle is that the law governing the arbitration agreement can be different from the law that governs the rest of the JOA. This may be a significant advantage if the JOA's governing law would, for instance, invalidate the arbitration agreement for one reason or another. The parties can explicitly choose the law that governs their arbitration agreement.[137] Where no choice is made by the parties, the agreement's validity will often be determined according to the 'law of the country where the award was made' (that is the law of the seat of arbitration),[138] although the solution is not always straightforward. As different jurisdictions have adopted different solutions in this regard, the parties should consider specifying that the law of the seat applies to their arbitration agreement, if they wish for this law to be applicable.[139]

3.3. SCOPE OF A JOA's DISPUTE RESOLUTION CLAUSE

The performance of a JOA typically necessitates several contractual relationships and implicates in one way or another third parties to the JOA. These third parties and ancillary contractual relations may impact, and be impacted by, the performance of the JOA. Therefore, the resolution of a dispute arising out of the JOA may require the participation of the parties who have not signed the JOA in the dispute resolution process.

In the case of national litigation, the solution to such third party intervention is usually quite straightforward: the court need not look into the parties' agreement to determine whether it has jurisdiction over the parties before it. Instead, the court will only consider whether its jurisdiction reaches those parties under its own procedural rules (although this may involve interpreting the scope of a choice of forum clause to some extent, as well as examining international agreements and considerations of comity). It is therefore usually possible to bring third parties to a JOA into court proceedings, if a sufficient nexus exists between the national court and either the third party in question or the operation that the third party is involved in.

The same is not true for arbitration. In principle, international arbitration agreements have a limited effect, in the sense that 'only the parties to an international arbitration agreement are either bound or benefitted by that

137 New York Convention, Article V.1(a).

138 New York Convention, Article V.1(a). In general on the law governing arbitration agreements see e.g. Born, *supra* n. 94, p. 472 *et seq.* And see V. Neelakantan and A. Goyal, 'Which Law Governs the Agreement to Arbitrate', *Global Arbitration Review*, 21 April 2015.

139 To this effect, see Neelakantan and Goyal, *supra* n. 138 (analysing the English courts' jurisprudence relating to the law governing arbitration agreements and noting that several court decisions have led to the application of the law governing the substantive contract).

agreement'.[140] Therefore, only the parties that are signatories to the arbitration agreement contained in the JOA will be parties to the arbitration proceedings, to the exclusion of sub-contractors or parent companies of the parties involved. However, there are various exceptions to this principle that can be relevant in the context of a JOA.

One illustration of a situation in which an international arbitration agreement can reach non-signatory parties is the exception of the so-called 'group of companies' doctrine. This doctrine has been defined in the following terms:

> '[W]here a company is part of a corporate group, is subject to the control of (or controls) a corporate affiliate that has executed a contract and is involved in the negotiation or performance of that contract, then that company may in some circumstances invoke or be subjected to an arbitration clause contained in that contract, notwithstanding the fact that it has not executed the contract itself.'[141]

The group of companies doctrine may become relevant in the context of a JOA, particularly if the foreign operator is only a shell of its parent company, which shell was established to shield the parent company from any liability. That being said, arbitral tribunals do not eagerly lift the corporate veil and accept jurisdiction over a non-signatory parent company absent exceptional circumstances.

An arbitration agreement can also be extended to third parties under different theories of private law, such as assignment, agency or succession.[142] It is also possible to invoke the existence of guarantor relations[143] as a closely connected contractual relationship requiring the extension of the arbitration clause. Third party beneficiaries may also invoke an arbitration agreement that a contract containing a stipulation to their benefit contains, if it is possible to infer the parties' intention to extend their arbitration agreement to such third parties.[144] The arbitration agreement may in some circumstances provide that it will benefit a party that is not a signatory to the contract or to the arbitration agreement. Clear language is therefore key, as the parties can expand or limit their arbitration clause with a careful choice of wording.

Finally, related disputes can be consolidated in a single arbitration proceeding in certain cases. Some institutional rules of arbitration provide for this possibility. For example, the ICC Rules of Arbitration provide that it is

---

140 Born, *supra* n. 94, p. 1407.

141 *Ibid.*, p. 1445.

142 Blackaby, Partasides, Redfern and Hunter, *supra* n. 4, Sections 2.47-2.51. See also, e.g., *Bridas Sapic v Government of Turkmenistan*, 345 F.3d 347 (5th Cir. 2003): 'federal courts have held that so long as there is some written agreement to arbitrate, a third party may be bound to arbitration. Ordinary principles of contract and agency law may be called upon to bind a nonsignatory to an agreement whose terms have not clearly done so.'

143 Born, *supra* n. 94, p. 551.

144 G*Ibid.*, p. 585.

possible to consolidate two or more arbitrations if the parties have all agreed to consolidation[145] or 'all of the claims in the arbitrations are made under the same arbitration agreement'.[146] Consolidation under the ICC Rules of Arbitration is also possible if the claims in the arbitrations are made under 'more than one arbitration agreement' but the arbitrations are 'between the same parties, the disputes in the arbitrations arise in connection with the same legal relationship, and the [ICC] Court finds the arbitration agreements to be compatible.'[147] This can become relevant in the case of disputes under a JOA, as there 'may be issues which are in dispute between certain of the parties to the concession which could impact on and trigger disputes under the JOA, or vice versa.'[148]

3.4. DRAFTING AN EFFICIENT DISPUTE RESOLUTION CLAUSE

Dispute resolution clauses are usually negotiated when the parties have everything but a dispute in sight. These clauses are typically reserved for the end of the negotiations, when all other issues are settled.[149] The temptation – and risk – for the parties to insert boilerplate clauses or clauses imported from other contracts that are not specifically tailored for the specificities of their JOA is, therefore, considerable. The downside of using dispute resolution clauses that are not adapted to the needs of the specific operation leads to a considerable amount of time and money spent on disputing over whether a decision maker, typically the arbitrators, have jurisdiction over a certain dispute between the parties. Of course, difficulties relating to the arbitrators' jurisdiction may arise from the very complexity of the dispute at hand, for instance, if issues arise out of several inter-related agreements. But unfortunately, often the difficulties result from poorly drafted dispute resolution clauses.

At the moment of drafting their dispute resolution clause, the parties do not yet know what their respective positions in a possible dispute will be: who will be the claimant, who the respondent and what interests they will have at stake. Nor do they know the subject matter of the disputes that may arise in the future[150] – indeed, a dispute may arise out of matters that they never thought could bring about disagreements.

---

145 Article 10(a) of the 2012 ICC Rules of Arbitration.
146 Article 10(b) of the 2012 ICC Rules of Arbitration.
147 Article 10(c) of the 2012 ICC Rules of Arbitration.
148 Roberts, *supra* n. 98, p. 213.
149 Bowman and Martin, *supra* n. 99, slide 2.
150 *Ibid.*, slide 3, advising that the JOA's dispute resolution clause should aim at simplicity and clarity, which will avoid spending time and money over the interpretation of the dispute resolution clause.

In view of these uncertainties, different elements should be taken into account when drafting a multi-tiered dispute resolution clause.

3.4.1. *Clear Indications as to the Negotiating Period*

If the dispute resolution clause obligates the parties to negotiate in good faith before initiating adjudication proceedings, the clause should be clear as to the requirements and effects of the negotiations. In fact, a surprising number of disputes arise out of improperly conducted or improperly initiated negotiations. A party willing to delay arbitration may argue that the other party has not fulfilled the negotiation requirement. Although a tribunal will rarely decline jurisdiction on this basis, and instead will only ask the parties to negotiate for the stipulated period of time, this is time and money wasted that could be avoided with properly drafted clauses (and compliance with those clauses). Firstly, the clause should specify how the negotiations are kicked off in order to determine when the negotiating period ends. For example, the clause can require that a notice must be sent to the other party, informing that the notifying party wishes to start negotiations.[151] The clause can also define the method of dispatch of the notice, the address to which the notice must be sent and how quickly the notice should be issued after the initiating event. Secondly, the clause should clearly indicate by whom the negotiations are to be conducted and for how long.[152] It should also indicate who can replace the designated person if he/she is not available at the time of the dispute (e.g. 'senior manager or other designated person with the same authority').

3.4.2. *Expert Determination and Mediation*

In order for an expert determination or mediation to be efficient, the clause should indicate how the expert or the mediator is to be selected and what qualifications he or she should have.[153] In addition, as for negotiations, the parties should specify a time frame within which the expert determination or mediation should be undertaken. It is generally advisable that the parties opt for a relatively short time period,[154] as it is useless for the parties to pursue a prolonged dispute resolution process if there is no prospect of success. In any event, the parties can always agree to extend their negotiations, mediation or expert determination period, if they feel that they are close to reaching a settlement.

---

151 Pryles, *supra* n. 101, p. 160.

152 *Ibid.*, p. 160, underlying the 'danger of using subjective criteria for determining when one tier of the dispute resolution procedure is ended and the next may be utilized'.

153 Reference to an institution may be a good option as the mediation rules of institutions often provide for a method of appointment. See e.g. Article 5 of the ICC Mediation Rules in force as of 1 January 2014.

154 Friedland, *supra* n. 96, p. 123.

In the specific context of expert determination, the parties should specify the type of decision that the expert is to render and notably whether this decision will be binding on them or not.[155]

3.4.3. *Scope and Content of the Arbitration Clause*

3.4.3.1. Scope

Firstly, the multi-contract element of an oil or gas project brings an additional challenge to the drafting of dispute resolution clauses. To the extent possible, the different agreements that ensure the performance of the oil and gas project should contain identical arbitration clauses. This will facilitate consolidating inter-related disputes before the same tribunal and thus make the dispute resolution faster and cheaper. If it proves impossible to adopt identical clauses, the parties to the inter-related agreements should try to make their arbitration agreements compatible (i.e. same arbitration institute, same applicable law, same seat, same number of arbitrators and same language) or at least harmonise them to the extent possible.

In addition, as in the case of governing law clauses, the wording of the arbitration agreement is important to clarify its scope and avoid fragmenting a dispute before different fora. A clear and efficient formulation would, for example, be that 'any and all disputes arising out of or in connection with the JOA will be submitted to arbitration'. If the parties do not extend their arbitration clause to disputes that arise 'in connection with' their agreement, the arbitration clause may be interpreted as only covering contractual claims to the exclusion of tortious claims.[156]

3.4.3.2. Governing Law

Many agreements contain, on the one hand, a governing law clause and, on the other, a dispute resolution clause, which provides that disputes arising out of the agreement will be governed by the same law as the one selected in the governing law clause. The parties should, however, consider including only one choice of law provision in their JOA in order to avoid any inadvertent inconsistency between the different clauses. If, in addition to including a separate governing law clause into the JOA, the parties nevertheless wish to specifically indicate the law that will apply to their dispute, they should note that that law applies to

155 See above the difference between expert determination and Early Neutral Evaluation, at section 3.2.1.3.

156 See G.B. Born, *International Arbitration and Forum Selection Agreements: Drafting and Enforcing*, 4th edn, Kluwer Law International, The Hague 2013, pp. 39–40.

'disputes' arising out of the agreement – and not to 'arbitration',[157] if they have selected arbitration as their adjudication method. Indeed, the procedural law of the arbitration will 'almost always' be the law of the seat of arbitration.[158] And it is in most cases in the parties' interest that the law of the seat governs those proceedings, as that law will also apply in possible annulment proceedings before the courts of the seat of arbitration. Thus, the arbitration proceedings should comply first and foremost with the law of the seat of arbitration to ensure that the future award will be recognised in those courts.

The above does not mean that the parties would not be well advised to specify which law governs their *arbitration agreement* (as opposed to the arbitration proceedings), if the JOA contains an arbitration agreement. The law governing the agreement to arbitrate is significant for several reasons: (i) it governs the validity of the arbitration agreement; (ii) it is 'crucial to the question of whether a particular dispute can be referred to arbitration or is arbitrable'; and (iii) it is relevant to deciding several other 'ancillary issues in an arbitration such as the ability to join third parties'.[159] If the parties have not chosen the law that governs the arbitration agreement specifically, the courts and arbitral tribunals will have to determine which law applies to the validity of the agreement. According to the New York Convention, the validity of the arbitration agreement is first and foremost decided according to the law 'to which the parties have subjected it' and, failing such choice, according to the law 'of the country where the award was made'[160] (i.e. the seat of arbitration). National courts have, however, different approaches to determine the law that governs the validity of the arbitration agreement failing the parties' explicit choice to that effect. Some courts apply the law of the seat of arbitration to this question,[161] others the law of the contract (i.e. the law that governs the subject matter of the dispute),[162] and some subject the question of the arbitration agreement's validity to 'general principles of international law' that allow the national courts to consider the arbitration agreement's validity based on 'the common intention of the parties' alone, without any 'reference to a national law'.[163]

To avoid any uncertainty, the parties should consider specifying explicitly the law that they wish to apply to their arbitration agreement and, at least, be

157 Bowman and Martin, *supra* n. 99, slide 4.

158 Born, *supra* n. 94, p. 1598 ('Although the procedural law of the arbitration is almost always the arbitration legislation of the arbitral seat, there are rare exceptions where the parties attempt to agree upon a foreign procedural law.').

159 Neelakantan and Goyal, *supra* n. 138.

160 New York Convention, Article V.1(a).

161 This is the case for instance in China. See Neelakantan and Goyal, *supra* n. 138.

162 This is the case of, for instance, India and, in certain circumstances, England and Wales. See Neelakantan and Goyal, *supra* n. 138.

163 This is the case of France, see *Cour de Cassation*, First Civil Chamber, 20 Dec. 1993, *Municipalité de Khoms El Magreb v Société* Dalico, 1994 Rev. Arb. 116. See also Born, *supra* n. 94, p. 481.

'alive to the issue of the law governing the agreement to arbitrate'.[164] Indeed, certain arbitral institutes have responded to the issue by revising either their default model arbitration clauses or their arbitration rules to specify the law governing the arbitration clause.[165]

3.4.3.3. Institutional and ad hoc Arbitration

An important choice to make is the selection between an ad hoc or institutional arbitration. The former 'is conducted without an administering authority and, generally, without the aid of institutional procedural rules', while the latter 'is conducted pursuant to procedural rules promulgated by a particular arbitral institution, which generally also "administers" the arbitration'.[166] Ad hoc arbitration supposedly offers more flexibility to the parties, as the parties are not guided by the institutional arbitration rules. But ad hoc arbitration may also prove more difficult to conduct in practice, if one of the parties is unwilling to participate in the arbitral proceedings.[167] State parties may, however, prefer ad hoc arbitration as it is not supervised by an institution located in a foreign country, although such localisation does not have any impact on the seat of arbitration or the place where the proceedings will take place. Institutional arbitration for its part is usually preferred by arbitration practitioners as it notably leads to 'enhanced predictability and regularity'.[168] Institutional arbitration has the advantage of providing a set of arbitration rules that guide the proceedings and the relevant institution can help the parties in a variety of circumstances, such as if the parties have difficulties in selecting an arbitrator, one party fails to participate in the proceedings, *etc.*

---

164 Neelakantan and Goyal, *supra* n. 138 (the authors note that '*as* a general rule, drafters may consider adopting the law of the country where the seat of arbitration is situated, as the law governing the arbitration agreement', as '[t]his ensures that any subsequent challenge to an award or proceedings for resisting enforcement do not throw up a surprise on this particular issue.' The authors then analyse different considerations that the parties should take into account if they wish to adopt a 'different system of law to govern the arbitration agreement.')

165 See e.g. Article 16.4 LCIA Arbitration Rules (2014) ('The law applicable to the Arbitration Agreement and the arbitration shall be the law applicable at the seat of the arbitration, unless and to the extent that the parties have agreed in writing on the application of other laws or rules of law and such agreement is not prohibited by the law applicable at the arbitral seat.'), HKIAC Model Clause (providing as an optional provision to the model clause the following: 'The law of this arbitration clause shall be … (*Hong Kong*)' (emphasis in original), and noting that '[t]his provision should be included particularly where the law of the substantive contract and the law of the seat are different. The law of the arbitration clause potentially governs matters including the formation, existence, scope, validity, legality, interpretation, termination, effects and enforceability of the arbitration clause and identities of the parties to the arbitration clause. It does not replace the law governing the substantive contract.').

166 Born, *supra* n. 156, pp. 44–45.

167 *Ibid.*, p. 65.

168 *Ibid.*, p. 65.

In general, parties to a JOA should incorporate a set of 'modern arbitration rules, instead of drafting arbitration procedures of their own or rely on [the] arbitration law at [the] place of arbitration',[169] which would risk bringing complications in proceedings that are already complex. In other words, it is generally advisable that the parties opt for institutional arbitration instead of ad hoc arbitration.

When choosing between different arbitral institutions, the parties should pay attention to the existence of a mechanism for handling multiparty disputes.[170] Indeed, as already mentioned, disputes arising out of JOAs may involve more than two parties, which can lead to complications in the arbitration proceedings unless the arbitral rules have adequate provisions to deal with such circumstances.

Finally, when selecting the institution that will administer the arbitration proceedings, the parties should indicate clearly that they intend to apply the rules of that institute to their proceedings. The parties should also avoid incorporating more than one set of rules.[171] If the parties wish to have an option between different sets of rules, they should clearly provide that the claiming party has to choose one of the several options – and not give authority to several institutions at the same time, as some courts may consider such provisions as conflicting and invalid.[172]

3.4.3.4. Seat of Arbitration, Choice and Number of Arbitrators, Confidentiality of the Proceedings

The choice of the seat of arbitration can have a great impact on the outcome of the arbitration proceedings. Although the tendency is to select a seat that is not the country of origin of any of the parties to the JOA, an even more important factor that the parties should consider when selecting the seat is the arbitration law of the country. This is because the courts of the seat of arbitration will be the courts where an unsatisfied party can seek annulment of the award after the arbitration proceedings[173] and those courts will apply their local law. Even if some countries recognise and enforce awards annulled at the seat,[174] most are reluctant to do so. Thus, annulment by local courts severely undermines the

---

169 Bowman and Martin, *supra* n. 99, slide 9.

170 See e.g. Articles 7–10 of the 2012 ICC Rules of Arbitration.

171 Bowman and Martin, *supra* n. 99, slides 10–11.

172 For example, the clause should not use such language: 'the dispute shall be referred to arbitration according to the ICC Rules of Arbitration and the LCIA Rules of Arbitration'. It should rather indicate: 'at the choice of the claiming party, either according to the ICC Rules of Arbitration or the LCIA Arbitration Rules…'.

173 Born, *supra* n. 156, p. 68.

174 See e.g. in France, *Cour de Cassation*, First Civil Chamber, *Hilmarton*, 23 March 1994, *Rev. Arb.* 1994.327, note Jarosson; *Cour de Cassation*, First Civil Chamber, *Putrabali*, 29 June 2007, 24 *Arb. Int'l* 295 (2008).

efficacy of an arbitral award and, therefore, the parties should not select their seat lightly.

The parties should, in general, choose a seat that has a well-established reputation as an 'arbitration-friendly' jurisdiction. This means that the seat should have a well-established arbitration law and jurisprudence, which provide for a liberal recognition and enforcement of arbitral awards. The law of the seat will also become relevant if the parties need the assistance of a 'support judge' in the course of their proceedings: the parties may need to have recourse to a national judge to assist them in the arbitration proceedings if, for instance, they need an antisuit injunction against their counterparty or other type of provisional measures to protect their rights pending the arbitration proceedings. Typical seats that fulfil these conditions are, for instance, Paris, Geneva, London, New York and Singapore, to name only a few.[175] The parties will also often want to avoid selecting the country of origin of their counterparty as the seat of arbitration, even if that country would be an 'arbitration-friendly' seat. The private parties will also often want to avoid the countries where the operations take place for fear that the national courts will not be completely impartial in case of annulment proceedings. This fear may well become warranted if the arbitrators misapply the local laws or if the arbitrators order a state or state entity to pay a consequent amount of damages to the private party.

The physical location of the arbitration hearings should not be confused with the seat of arbitration. The seat's only function is to provide for the applicable arbitration law and – as the case may be – the judicial support system. Thus, although the proceedings typically take place at the seat, this is not obligatory and the location of the arbitration proceedings may be somewhere completely different without that impacting the parties' selection of the seat. In fact, the entire proceedings can even take place remotely, although that is rare and often impracticable.

In addition to selecting their seat of arbitration and the physical location of the hearings, the parties are also free to determine the number of arbitrators that will adjudicate their disputes. While opting for a single arbitrator may be a cheaper option, most parties decide to have a three-arbitrator panel,[176] as it allows each side to select its own arbitrator. Usually the disputes arising out of JOAs are of such complexity and the amounts at stake sufficiently high that a three-member panel is advisable. The parties can, however, decide that only disputes exceeding a certain amount will be submitted to a three-member panel, whereas smaller disputes will be decided by a sole arbitrator.

---

175 *2010 International Arbitration Survey: Choices in International Arbitration*, Queen Mary, University of London, 2010, p. 19.

176 Born, *supra* n. 156, p. 79. See also Blackaby, Partasides, Redfern and Hunter, *supra* n. 4, Section 2.70.

The parties should also define the method of choosing their arbitrator(s). In the case of a three-member panel, each party typically chooses one arbitrator and the party-appointed arbitrators select the president. Where the parties opt for institutional arbitration, they should in particular indicate in their dispute resolution clause that they will appoint the arbitrators themselves and not leave the choice to the institution. Indeed, it is most often in the interest of the parties to have the power of choosing their own decision maker, as that will allow them to assess their particular needs in a specific dispute. In any event, the institution will retain the power of selecting the arbitrator(s) if a party fails to appoint its arbitrator in due course. If the parties decide to opt for a sole arbitrator, the dispute resolution clause will typically state that the parties will select the arbitrator together. The clause may, and should, also stipulate that if the parties fail to reach an agreement over the arbitrator within a certain period of time, the arbitration institute that they have selected will appoint an arbitrator on their behalf.

Additional aspects that the parties should consider in their arbitration clause are the language of the proceedings and, importantly, the confidentiality of the proceedings. Contrary to general belief, neither the institutional rules nor the law of the seat usually provide that the arbitration proceedings are by default confidential.[177] On the contrary, it is for the parties to provide that their proceedings should be kept confidential, if they so wish.

3.4.3.5. Right to Appeal and Enforcement of the Award

The parties can specify in the arbitration agreement that any award will be final and binding, which will often be interpreted as a waiver of any possible right to appeal the award.[178] If the parties have selected institutional arbitration rules in their arbitration clause, those rules typically contain a similar provision imposing on the parties the obligation to abide by the arbitration award.[179] Such undertaking will, however, not prevent the parties from challenging the validity of the award through annulment proceedings before the court of the place of arbitration.

The parties should also already consider the enforceability of their award when negotiating the dispute resolution clause. As it is likely that at least one

[177] Bowman and Martin, *supra* n. 99, slide 21. See, *a contrario*, Article 30 of the 2014 LCIA Arbitration Rules.

[178] For arbitrations conducted in England, the parties may want to expressly exclude the possibility of appeal under section 69 of the 1996 English Arbitration Act.

[179] The rules of most arbitral institutions so provide. See e.g. Article 34(6) of the 2012 ICC Rules of Arbitration: 'Every award shall be binding on the parties. By submitting the dispute to arbitration under the Rules, the parties undertake to carry out any award without delay and shall be deemed to have waived their right to any form of recourse insofar as such waiver can validly be made.'

party will be a state or a state entity, issues relating to state immunity may arise in the context of enforcement if that party does not comply voluntarily with the future award. While the fact that a state or state entity enters into an arbitration agreement is widely recognised as a waiver of the immunity from jurisdiction,[180] it is rarely the case for immunity from enforcement.[181] Therefore, the parties often insert waivers of sovereign immunity in their agreement. For example, the AIPN Model JOA includes a provision that reads: '[a]ny Party that now or later has a right to claim sovereign immunity for itself or any of its assets hereby waives any such immunity to the fullest extent permitted by the laws of any applicable jurisdiction.'[182]

3.4.3.6. Using Model Clauses?

Arbitration institutions offer model clauses that the parties can insert into their contracts.[183] While these clauses ensure the arbitral tribunal's power to adjudicate under the relevant rules, they are rarely adapted to the complexity of a JOA, as they do not take into account the need for a multi-tiered dispute resolution mechanism. These clauses can serve as a basis for a more elaborate arbitration clause that may be tailored to the specific needs of the parties.

The AIPN Model JOA provides for a model multi-tiered clause that is specifically adapted to the context of a JOA.[184] It contains a basic model clause that refers disputes to arbitration and then provides different optional provisions for the parties to incorporate into their agreement:

> '18.2 Dispute Resolution
>
> 18.2.A Notification. A Party who desires to submit a Dispute for resolution shall commence the Dispute resolution process by providing the other parties to the Dispute written notice of the Dispute ("Notice of Dispute"). The Notice of Dispute

---

180 G.R. Delaume, 'Judicial Decisions Related to Sovereign Immunity and Transnational Arbitration' (1987) 2 *ICSID Rev.* 403.

181 See, however, the position of French courts as regards subscription to institutional rules of arbitration: *Cour de Cassation*, First Civil Chamber, 6 July 2000, *Creighton Ltd v Ministères des Finances de l'Etat du Qatar, Clunet* 2004.1054, note Pingel.

182 AIPN Model JOA, Article 18.4, 'Waiver of Sovereign Immunity'.

183 See e.g. Standard ICC Arbitration Clause: 'All disputes arising out of or in connection with the present contract shall be finally settled under the Rules of Arbitration of the International Chamber of Commerce by one or more arbitrators appointed in accordance with the said Rules.' See also, LCIA Recommended Clause for future disputes: 'Any dispute arising out of or in connection with this contract, including any question regarding its existence, validity or termination, shall be referred to and finally resolved by arbitration under the LCIA Rules, which Rules are deemed to be incorporated by reference into this clause. The number of arbitrators shall be [one/three]. The seat, or legal place, of arbitration shall be [City and/or Country]. The language to be used in the arbitral proceedings shall be [ ]. The governing law of the contract shall be the substantive law of [ ].'

184 AIPN Model JOA, Article 18.2, 'Dispute Resolution'.

shall identify the parties to the Dispute and contain a brief statement of the nature of the Dispute and the relief requested. The submission of a Notice of Dispute shall toll any applicable statutes of limitation related to the Dispute, pending the conclusion or abandonment of Dispute resolution proceedings under this Article 18.

18.2.B Negotiations. The parties to the Dispute shall seek to resolve any Dispute by negotiation between Senior Executives. A 'Senior Executive' means any individual who has authority to negotiate the settlement of the Dispute for a Party. Within thirty (30) Days after the date of the receipt by each party to the Dispute of the Notice of Dispute (which notice shall request negotiations among Senior Executives), the Senior Executives representing the parties to the Dispute shall meet at a mutually acceptable time and place to exchange relevant information in an attempt to resolve the Dispute. If a Senior Executive intends to be accompanied at the meeting by an attorney, each other party's Senior Executive shall be given written notice of such intention at least three (3) Days in advance and may also be accompanied at the meeting by an attorney. Despite the above, any Party may initiate arbitration proceedings under Article 18.2.D or mediation proceedings under Article 18.2.C concerning such Dispute within thirty (30) Days after the date of receipt of the Notice of Dispute.

18.2.C Mediation. [Subject to the requirements of negotiation between Senior Executives under Article 18.2.B], [t]he parties to the Dispute shall seek to resolve the Dispute by mediation. Within thirty (30) Days after the date of the receipt by each party to the Dispute of the Notice of Dispute thirty (30) Days after the date of the first negotiation meeting among Senior Executives under Article 18.2.B in effect, as modified herein] by sending all other parties to the Dispute a written request that the Dispute be mediated. The Parties receiving such written request will promptly respond to the requesting Party so that all parties to the Dispute may jointly select a neutral mediator and schedule the mediation session. The mediator shall meet with the parties to the Dispute to mediate the Dispute within thirty (30) Days after the date of receipt of the written request for mediation. Despite the above, any Party may initiate arbitration proceedings under Article [18.2.D] concerning such Dispute within thirty (30) Days after the date of receipt of the Notice of Dispute within sixty (60) Days after the date of receipt of the Notice of Dispute.

18.2.D Arbitration. Any Dispute [not finally resolved by alternative Dispute resolution procedures set forth in Articles 18.2.B and 18.2.C] shall be resolved through final and binding arbitration, it being the intention of the Parties that this is a broad form arbitration agreement designed to encompass all possible Disputes, including Disputes about the arbitrability of a Dispute.'[185]

Sub-clause 18.2.D of the AIPN Model JOA also includes provisions giving details about the arbitration, such as the applicable institutional rules, the number of arbitrators, the method of appointment of the arbitrators, the place of arbitration or the language of arbitration.

---

185 AIPN Model JOA, Article 18.2, 'Dispute Resolution'.

Another example of a multi-tiered arbitration clause, adapted from the ICC Model Clause, is:

> 'In the event of any dispute arising out of or in connection with the present contract, the parties agree to submit the matter to settlement proceedings under the [ICC's ADR] Rules. If the dispute has not been settled pursuant to said Rules within [45] days following the filing of a [request for mediation] or within such other period as the parties may agree in writing, such dispute shall be finally settled under the [designated arbitral institution] by [one or more arbitrators] appointed in accordance with the said Rules of Arbitration.'[186] The seat of arbitration will be [X] and the arbitration proceedings will be conducted in [X] language.

As discussed in section 2.3.2.4, if the parties decide to opt for a model clause, they should consider specifying the law that governs their arbitration clause.

4. CONCLUSION

The most carefully drafted contract can leave room for interpretation and disputes. This is when governing law and dispute resolution clauses will come into play: if things go wrong, the law that the parties have chosen will determine (subject to the limitations discussed above) their respective rights and obligations. And those rights and obligations will be determined according to the JOA's dispute resolution mechanism. Therefore, the parties should not only opt for a choice of law provision in their JOA but also carefully consider which law is the best adapted for their contractual relationship. Similarly, the parties should pay attention to how, and by whom, they wish their disputes to be resolved.

As these clauses are not the ones that the parties usually spend the most time on in the course of the contract negotiations, they are too often overlooked. Although consulting dispute resolution lawyers at the contract negotiation stage is not common, these specialists are often the best placed to advise which law and what dispute resolution mechanism are the best adapted for the parties' JOA. Therefore, the parties should consider consulting a counsel with experience in international disputes already when drafting the JOA. In the alternative, the parties should use thoroughly thought-through standard governing law clauses, such as those in the AIPN JOA Model. The situation is somewhat different with respect to dispute resolution clauses: although recourse to standard dispute resolution clauses may be a good basis to start from, the parties should keep in mind that JOAs are complex operations that often require more tailor-made dispute resolution mechanisms.

---

186 Friedland, *supra* n. 96, Appendix Twenty-Nine, p. 259.

THE CHALLENGES OF IMPLEMENTING AN EXCLUSIVE OPERATION

Eduardo G. Pereira

1. INTRODUCTION

At the heart of the JOA lies the concept of operations being undertaken jointly by the parties thereto. However, a risk to the ongoing alignment of the JOA parties' respective interests lies in the variable nature of the characteristics of the parties forming the joint venture. Taylor and Tyne identify that 'the companies making up a licence group will often differ dramatically in size, financial resources, technical capability and in other important respects'.[1] The degree of

---

1 M.P.G. Taylor and Sally M. Tyne, *Taylor and Winsor on Joint Operating Agreements*, 2nd edn, Longman, London 1992, p. 47.

such characteristics possessed by each of the JOA parties will rarely remain static and it should be expected from the outset of the JOA that the characteristics will evolve as the joint venture progresses. The JOA parties are unlikely to maintain a unified perspective on what constitutes the best way forward for the joint venture. Styles clearly describes this reality in the following terms:

> 'In an ideal world there would be unanimous agreement among the members on all significant decisions. In practice, there will from time to time be disagreements among the members and normally these disputes will be resolved within the Opcom by means of decisions taken which secure a pass mark.'[2]

Bearing in mind that in this challenging industry we very rarely find ourselves operating in an ideal world, and that disagreements are a common occurrence in practice, it is crucial to foresee the requirement for flexibility in the JOA.[3] This perspective is noted by Shaw, who mentions that although 'a JOA is intended to be comprehensive, it cannot cover all issues and should, therefore, be a flexible, interactive framework that allows for evolution.'[4]

The concept of the exclusive operation deals with circumstances in which a proposed joint operation does not secure the necessary pass mark or does not have the support of all the parties at the Joint Operating Committee (Opcom), in that it provides a way forward for the proposed operation without the participation of all the parties to the JOA. In effect, exclusive operations clauses are an example of the practical implementation of the flexibility to which Shaw refers and they tend to be amongst the most complex clauses in a JOA.

However, the implementation and enforceability of these clauses could represent significant challenges in practical cases as quite often they were not meant to used but were rather intended as a threat to the JOA parties to remain united in joint operations.[5] This chapter analyses the key issues that an exclusive operation might encounter if implemented by a JOA party.

2. EXCLUSIVE OPERATIONS CLAUSES

Exclusive operations clauses typically exist in two forms – (i) sole risk and (ii) non-consent – and JOAs may contain neither, only one, or occasionally both.

---

2 S. Styles, 'Joint Operating Agreements', in J. Paterson and G. Gordon (eds.), *Oil and Gas Law: Current Practice and Emerging Trends*, Dundee University Press, Dundee 2007, p. 288.

3 See also *Const v Harris* (1824) Turn. & R 496; 37 ER 1191; *Blisset v Daniel* (1853) 10 Hare 493; 68 ER 1022.

4 S. Shaw, 'Joint Operating Agreements', in M.R. David, *Upstream Oil and Gas Agreements*, Sweet and Maxwell, London 1996, p. 14.

5 'On the relatively rare occasions on which sole risk have been used in the UKCS, the result has usually been to create discord among the co-venturers.' T. Daintith, G. Willoughby and A. Hill (eds.), *United Kingdom Oil & Gas Law*, 3rd edn, Sweet & Maxwell, London 2009 p. 1152.

A sole risk clause pertains to sole risk operations – operations which may be conducted when a proposal has been made to the Opcom but fails to achieve the voting pass mark required.[6] In this case, any party voting in support of a proposal which has failed to obtain such pass mark can elect to undertake the work at its sole risk and cost (to the extent the other parties are not supportive of the proposal).[7] Should more than one party support the failed proposal, then it may be that more than one party will engage in the sole risk operation.

In a non-consent clause the situation is somewhat inverted. A proposal has been made to the Opcom and has achieved the voting pass mark,[8] but such proposal did not have the support of all parties to the JOA. A non-consent clause provides for a dissenting party (or dissenting parties as the case may be) to elect not to be a participant in the approved joint operation; thus the proposed joint operation will be undertaken by the remaining parties that have chosen not to exercise such right.

The difference in purpose of the sole risk clause and the non-consent clause is highlighted by considering the outcome of the Opcom's vote. The former applies where a proposal does not reach the pass mark required by the Opcom but a party (or parties as the case may be) still decides to carry out the proposed work. The latter applies where a proposal does reach the pass mark required by the Opcom but a dissenting party (or parties as the case may be) votes against the proposal to no effect and decides not to participate in such proposal.[9] In effect, sole risk and non-consent clauses allow different interests to co-exist in the same enterprise, thus preserving, at least in theory, the cohesiveness of the joint venture.

As alluded to above, exclusive operations clauses feature variably in JOAs and they are not accepted without exception. An analysis of the suite of model form JOAs identifies that some JOAs contain only sole risk clauses,[10] some JOAs contain only non-consent clauses,[11] and some JOAs contain both (in some cases in stand-alone form[12] and in other cases in a hybrid form).[13] Sole risk clauses are more commonly present than non-consent clauses in practice outside North America.[14]

---

6 See also A. Jennings, *Oil and Gas Exploration Contracts*, 2nd edn, Sweet & Maxwell, London 2008, p. 25; T. Daintith, 'Right to explore for and exploit petroleum: the licence', in T. Daintith, G. Willoughby and A. Hill (eds.), *United Kingdom Oil & Gas Law*, 3rd edn, Sweet & Maxwell, London 2009, pp. 1151-1152.

7 The non-sole risk or non-consent party could refer to one or more parties.

8 See also: Jennings, *supra* n. 5, pp. 92-93.

9 See also: Taylor and Tyne, *supra* n. 1, p. 48; Shaw, *supra* n. 4, p. 23; Styles, *supra* n. 2, pp. 288-289.

10 See, for example, the OGUK JOA and AMPLA JOA.

11 See, for example, the AAPL JOA.

12 See, for example, the OGUK JOA guidance notes which provide a non-consent clause for insertion into the OGUK JOA should this be desired by the parties.

13 See, for example, the AIPN JOA and the CAPL JOA.

14 See also Shaw, *supra* n. 4, pp. 23-24; Daintith, *supra* n. 6, pp. 1151-1153.

The rationale for the inclusion/non-inclusion of each clause is as follows. Non-consent clauses are typically utilised in a joint venture where the operator has significant power and the non-operators have little control over activities. This situation is prevalent in US joint operations and thus a non-consent right, but not a sole-risk right, is a feature of the AAPL JOA. Conversely, in joint operations where it is convention that non-operators have a greater opportunity to represent their respective interests and potentially shape decisions in the Opcom, then this clause is of less importance.[15] This position is reflected in the UK and Australian models and thus the OGUK and AMPLA JOAs do not ordinarily feature non-consent rights, but instead feature a sole-risk right.

In practice, the application of exclusive operations can be problematic for the JOA parties. There exist a number of practical challenges to implementing an exclusive operation which act as a disincentive to the JOA parties to apply such rights. The remainder of this chapter provides a summary of some of the significant practical issues which may arise.[16]

3. POOR DRAFTING

The mechanics of exclusive operations provisions in JOAs can be complex, and accordingly the provisions are not always correctly drafted. The practical issues associated with the implementation of an exclusive operation in practice are not always sufficiently dealt with in the model form JOAs. The insufficiency of the drafting in the JOA can act as a disincentive to the implementation of an exclusive operation from the outset.[17]

The majority of the exclusive provisions are fairly standard in JOAs (e.g. notice, liabilities, buy-back, etc.). But the requirement for the creation of a new JV for the establishment of a sole risk operation is fairly unique.[18] This is probably the most significant difference from the AMPLA JOA model as it clearly deals with the fact that a *mutatis mutandis* clause is not adequate to deal with the complexities of this provision (i.e. most JOAs establish a provision

---

15 See also: P. Mandler, 'New Oil & Gas UK standard joint operating agreement (JOA)' (2008) 4 *IELR* 111, 112.

16 This is a non-exhaustive summary. To cover all possible issues in detail would be voluminous to the extent that entire text books have been dedicated to this issue. See E.G. Pereira, *Joint Operating Agreements: Mitigating Operational and Contractual Risks in Exclusive Operations*, Globe Law and Business, London 2013 for further detailed analysis.

17 For detailed discussion on the issues which should be addressed in properly drafting an exclusive operations clause, see P. Roberts, *Joint Operating Agreements*, 3rd edn, Globe Law and Business, London 2015.

18 AMPLA JOA §13.1 (d).

saying that all of the other JOA provisions shall apply *mutatis mutandis* to the exclusive operation):

> '(e) If a Sole Risk Election Notice is given, the Sole Risk Participants are deemed to have associated in a new unincorporated joint venture (*Sole Risk Joint Venture*) in respect in the Sole Risk Operation in the Sole Risk Area as Participants pro rata in the proportion that their Percentage Shares (at the date of the Sole Risk Election Notice) bear to each other, or in such other proportions which they agree (*Sole Risk Participating Interest*).
>
> (f) The Sole Risk Participants must promptly and in good faith negotiate and execute a new joint venture agreement in relation to the Sole Risk Operation in the Sole Risk Area (*Sole Risk JOA*) but unless and until they agree, the provisions of this agreement apply with necessary modification to the Sole Risk Joint Venture.
>
> (g) Upon execution of the Sole Risk JOA, the Sole Risk Area is excised from this agreement and the non-Sole Risk Participants must do all things necessary to transfer the Petroleum Title (or part thereof) over the Sole Risk Area to the Sole Risk Participants, or to facilitate the grant of a new Petroleum Title over the Sole Risk Area to the Sole Risk Participants.
>
> (h) Upon formation of a Sole Risk Joint Venture:
>
> (i) the Petroleum Title for the Sole Risk Area must be held by the holders thereof on trust for and at the expense of the Sole Risk Participants as beneficial owners; and
>
> (ii) until a new Petroleum Title is granted over the Sole Risk Area, and all Authorisations to conduct the Sole Risk Operation are obtained, the Participants and the Operator of the existing Joint Venture must act in respect of the Sole Risk Area as directed by, and at the sole cost and risk of, the Sole Risk Participants, with the Sole Risk Area being treated, as between the parties, as the legal and beneficial property of the Sole Risk Participants.'[19]

Therefore, it is possible to suggest that the AMPLA JOA model is the only agreement which clearly provides a solution to the complexities of an exclusive operation. But the creation of a sub-consortium does not solve all the questions and doubts about this matter.

4. INTERACTION WITH JOINT OPERATIONS

The JOA normally prohibits the implementation of exclusive operations which conflict with approved joint operations.[20] It may also set out an order for the

---

19 AMPLA JOA §13.3.

20 C. Duval et al., *International Petroleum and Exploration Agreements: Legal, Economic & Policy Aspects*, 2nd edn, Barrows, New York 2009, p. 295.

implementation of operations such that joint operations are carried out with priority over exclusive operations.[21] Whilst this approach is not necessarily problematic where joint operations are distinguishable from exclusive operations, there is potential for disagreement to arise where the operations are less distinguishable and/or inextricably linked.[22]

Where an exclusive operation has a relationship with a joint operation, debate may arise in relation to the degree to which it conflicts with the joint operation and the order in which its execution should take place.[23] This may result in the exclusive operation being carried out in a manner which is inefficient.

A further issue which may arise with linked exclusive and joint operations is associated with a petroleum discovery.[24] In the event a discovery is made, the question of what constitutes a fair allocation of petroleum between the joint operation and the exclusive operation will need to be answered. This can be a difficult exercise and given the likely significant monetary values at stake, it could lead to disagreement between the JOA parties.

5. FRAGMENTATION OF THE JOINT VENTURE AND GOVERNANCE OF EXCLUSIVE OPERATIONS

Taverne notes the potential for the use of exclusive operations to have a fragmenting impact on the joint venture: '[f]requent use of the non-consent

---

21 P. Roberts, *Joint Operating Agreements: A Practical Guide*, Globe Law and Business, London 2010, p. 69.

22 'In particular, there is usually a provision that sole risk operations should not interfere with joint operations (i.e. operations in which all the co-operators are participating); the definition of what constitutes "interference" is generally contentious and not easily resolved.' Daintith, Willoughby and Hill (eds.), *supra* n. 5, p. 1152.

23 'Another issue to consider is the extent to which the participants in an exclusive operation can use any of the facilities, materials or other property which is used in the performance of the joint operations.' Roberts, *supra* n. 21, pp. 75-76.

24 'One other noteworthy point is the contrast between the APEA Form (which allows a party to non-consent only in respect of the drilling of an exploratory well) and the BNOC proforma which does not allow non-consent for exploration and appraisal operations, but does allow a party to non-consent a development. This difference is not, I would submit, principally caused by the differing legal or taxation regimes, but rather by the different philosophies of those responsible for drafting the respective clauses. The BNOC draftsman was seeking to encourage exploration and appraisal, but did not wish to drag unwilling parties into development. The APEA draftsman was more concerned with the disruptive effects of a party non-consenting, and so was prepared to allow non-consent only in the early stages of exploration in a particular area. This again serves to illustrate that the dominant factor in the negotiation and drafting of these clauses will be the underlying philosophy of the parties involved and their priorities (as they then exist) in relation to exploration and development of the permit area.' K.R. Saville, 'Comment on Sole Risk in Mining and Petroleum Venturers', AMPLA Yearbook 1986.

and sole risk work options may lead to fragmentation of the joint venture ... The impact of those options may be restricted by limiting the number of distinct operations in respect of which any participant is allowed to exercise the options.'[25]

The most critical concern is the full implementation of an exclusive operation, as ultimately it will lead to the segregation of the joint operations and the potential creation of a sub-area within the same licensed area. As a result, the costs and risks may not be allocated as a unit for the entire licensed area as different areas may have different parties with different working interests. Consideration must be given to how best to address in the JOA the consequential practical issues that arise. The JOA must address how exclusive operations are regulated, with particular attention given to the allocation of risks, liabilities, costs and 'profits' related to the exclusive operation (particularly in the case of non-participating parties). The ultimate solution might be the creation of a new JOA for the sub-area pertaining to the exclusive operation and it should be attached as part of the main JOA to avoid any conflict at a later stage. Unfortunately, this is not the approach taken by the majority of the JOA models as they prefer the vague *mutatis mutandis* formulation for the relationship between the exclusive operation and the JOA.[26] As previously mentioned, the only JOA model form which recognises this issue is the AMPLA JOA, which sets out that sole risk participants are deemed to have formed a new unincorporated joint venture and that the sole risk participants must promptly and in good faith negotiate and execute a new joint venture agreement in relation to the sole risk operation and area.[27]

6. NON-CONSENT BURDEN

The exercise of a non-consent right may present the JOA parties with a significant challenge to overcome.[28] As a result of one or more parties electing not to participate in the proposed joint operation, the costs of the ensuing joint operation will be for the account of the parties that approved the proposal.[29] This will result in each of such parties funding a greater share of the costs of the operation compared to what they would be liable for in the event that all parties were in support of the operation.[30] This issue is exacerbated where the

25 B.G. Taverne, *Co-Operative Agreements in the Extractive Petroleum Industry*, Kluwer Law International, London 1996, p. 69.

26 AIPN JOA, Article 7; OGUK JOA, Article 15; Norwegian JOA, Article 18.

27 AMPLA JOA, Article 13.

28 See: J. Wilkinson, *Introduction to Oil and Gas Joint Ventures*, OPL, Ledbury 1997, pp. 42-43; Styles, *supra* n. 2, pp. 288-289.

29 Taylor and Tyne; Styles, *supra* n. 1, pp. 48-49.

30 See: H. Dundas, 'Joint Operating Agreements: An Introduction', 1994 Summer Programme: UK Oil and Gas Law, CPMLP 09/09, 1994, p. 10; B. Manning, 'Some Practical Aspects of

non-consent right has been exercised in respect of a high-cost operation and a participating party does not have sufficient funding to cover its increased share of costs arising as a result of that non-participation, which in turn will frustrate the ability to conduct the proposed operation. This issue could be particularly problematic in an unconventional or offshore project in a frontier environment as the costs are likely to be higher than usual and the practical implications of using a non-consent provision could represent a challenge to the project itself.[31]

7. OPERATOR REFUSAL

Another complexity involving an exclusive operation refers to the operatorship and host government approval.[32] The operator under the JOA is commonly the only entity authorised by the host government to conduct the joint operations in respect of the underlying concession.[33] As a natural consequence, the operator would be the only entity authorised to conduct any exclusive operations. The situation can however become complicated where the operator is a non-participating party or where the operator has the right to decline to perform exclusive operations.[34]

The JOA may provide that the parties participating in an exclusive operation should elect an operator for the purposes of carrying out that exclusive operation

Resources Joint Ventures', in W.D. Duncan, *Joint Ventures Law in Australia*, 2nd edn, The Federation Press, Sydney 2005, pp. 323-324.

31 'As mirror images of each other, these provisions can be complex and, because they run contrary to the basic premise of the joint operating agreement, the consequences of non-consent or sole risk need to be set out in detail.' C. Golvala, 'Upstream joint ventures – bidding and operating agreements', in G. Picton-Tubervill (ed.), *Oil and Gas: A practical handbook*. Globe Law and Business, London 2009, p. 48.

32 'However, if the licence operator is not participating in the sole risk project, in the case of a sole risk drilling, it may decline to carry out the drilling, and, in the case of sole risk development, the approval of all parties to the JOA is normally required before the operator is permitted to carry out the development. These conditions are designed primarily to protect the operator and the rest of the group from the danger of the operator being placed in a situation in which an obligation to carry out the sole risk operations might prejudice its ability to continue with joint operations which have been approved by the full operating committee.' Taylor and Tyne, *supra* n. 1, p. 58.

33 'The operatorship of the sole risk project is a matter for the sole riskers. If the operator approved under the licence is a member of the sole risk group then it is natural for him to be the operator for the sole risk project. If this is not so, however, it is up to the sole riskers to find an operator. That may be the licence operator carrying out the work as a contractor, or it may be one of the sole riskers, or they may get a non-group member to operator for them. The JOA usually provides that the operator may refuse to carry out a sole risk project.' V. Gayrner, 'Sole Risk and Non-Consent Under U.K. Joint Operating Agreements', 1994 Summer Programme: UK Oil and Gas Law, CPMLP 09/09, 1994, p. 5.

34 'There are contractual complications in the event that Operator is not a sole risk party, and in such circumstance UK JOAs generally provide for: Operator to opt out of acting as such; and/ or The sole risk parties to request Operator to stand aside.' Dundas, *supra* n. 30, p. 10.

from the participating parties.[35] Where the operator under the JOA is a non-participating party,[36] it is likely that the election of the new operator for the exclusive operation will require the approval of the host government.[37] Should such approval not be granted, the parties may be forced to look for a contractor-operator or in the worst case terminate the exclusive operation.[38]

Similarly, an operator may have the right under the JOA to decline to perform exclusive operations.[39] Should it exercise this right, the JOA will typically provide for a new operator to be appointed from the participating parties in respect of the joint operation.[40] This situation could represent a real challenge if the non-operators do not have the necessary technical and financial competence to conduct the operations in such area (for example, deepwater offshore). The issues associated with the approval of a new operator set out in the previous paragraph may be encountered.

8. BUY-BACK RIGHTS

A party which has undertaken a sole risk operation may desire, or may require, the participation of one or more of its JOA partners in the exclusive operation at a later date, particularly so where work is required which it cannot itself fund.[41] Following the election of a non-consent right or a sole risk operation, it is common for JOAs to provide for the non-participating parties to reinstate to varying degrees the basic philosophy of the JOA of sharing costs and risks.[42] At defined later stages, a non-participating party may have the right to join an exclusive operation subject to it paying a share of the costs incurred by the participating parties and a premium. The option to reinstate such sharing of costs and risks may however not be straightforward.

The costs of buy-back can involve a significant premium which is typically several hundred percent, designed to act as a disincentive to parties electing not

35 K.C. Mildwaters, *Joint Operating Agreements, A Consideration of Legal Aspects Relevant to Joint Operating Agreements used in Great Britain and Australia by Participants thereto to Regulate the Joint Undertaking of Exploration for Petroleum in Offshore Areas with Particular Reference to their Rights and Duties*, PhD Thesis, University of Dundee, 1990, p. 212.

36 '... may wish to reserve its right to decline to act as the operator in respect of an exclusive operation in which it is not a participant, on the basis that to do so might prejudice its ability to give its full attention to the performance of its duties in respect of any approved joint operations (or in respect of any other exclusive operations for which it is or will be acting as the operator).' Roberts, *supra* n. 21, p. 74.

37 Duval et al., *supra* n. 20, pp. 295-297.

38 *Ibid.*

39 Taylor and Tyne, *supra* n. 1, pp. 62-63.

40 *Ibid.*

41 E.E. Smith et al., *International Petroleum Transactions*, 3rd edn, RMMLF, Westminster 2010, p. 607.

42 Daintith, *supra* n. 6, p.1153.

to participate in the exclusive operation from the outset.[43] However, the size of this premium may also act as a disincentive to non-participating parties joining an exclusive operation at a later date.[44] The unwillingness of parties to pay a high premium may in turn frustrate the ability of the participating party to further develop the joint operation.

9. INTERACTION WITH CARRY ARRANGEMENTS

As consideration for the acquisition of a participating interest in a concession and associated JOA pursuant to a farm-in/farm-out agreement, the farming-in party (the 'farminee') will provide consideration in one or more forms.[45] It is not uncommon for the farminee to agree to provide a financial carry to the benefit of the farmor in respect of the cost of works which may be or are to be carried out. Such carry arrangements may apply in respect of exploration works and/or development works.

In the drafting of such carry arrangements, the parties should be precise in specifying the extent to which such carry arrangements apply (i) to joint operations, and/or (ii) to exclusive operations.[46] Should the farmor intend the carry to be available for exclusive operations to which it is a participant, this should be made clear in the drafting of the consideration provisions.

The potential for the implementation of an exclusive operation by the farmor to which carry arrangements apply is unlikely to be met with positivity by the farminee. Consequently, the farmor may be able to benefit from this position during the negotiation of proposals in the Opcom. In the knowledge that the farminee is unlikely to wish its funds to be used in an operation to which it may not benefit, the farmor may have the upper hand in the Opcom in having proposals voted through as joint operations.

A prudent farminee may specify in the farm-in/farm-out agreement that the farmor is unable to conduct an exclusive operation during such times as the carry applies. This could be implemented to such an extent that the farmor is required to vote in the Opcom in accordance with the farminee during the carry

---

43 'If at a later date a non-consenting party wishes to rejoin that part of the venture, it will normally have to buy its way back in by picking up its share of the cost, commonly together with some sort of time-based additional charge.' Golvala, *supra* n. 31, p. 49.

44 See C. Thorpe, *Fundamentals of Upstream Petroleum Agreements*, C.P. Thorpe, UK 2008, pp. 134-135; Shaw, *supra* n. 4, pp. 22-23; Dundas, *supra* n. 30, p. 10; Duval et al., *supra* n. 20, pp. 295-297; Daintith, *supra* n. 6, pp. 1151-1153; Roberts, *supra* n. 21, p. 72.

45 J.H. Waite, 'Sole Risk in Mining and Petroleum Ventures: The Australian Position', AMPLA Yearbook 1986; W.G. Holt, 'Problems Relating to Arctic Farmout and Joint Operating Agreements' (1972) 10 *Alta. L. Rev.* 450; P.R. Weems and M. Bolton, 'Highlights of Key Revisions – 2002 AIPN Model Form International Operating Agreement' (2003) 1 OGEL 5.

46 Smith et al., *supra* n. 41, p. 608.

period. The position taken by the farminee may be such that to the extent it is funding the operation, the farmor should have little or no control over its spend. Such a proposal will ultimately frustrate the ability of the farmor to implement an exclusive operation.

10. GOVERNMENT INVOLVEMENT[47]

Oil and gas resources are typically owned by the host government and as a natural consequence any company or investor intending to carry out exploration or production activities will require the consent of, and authorisation by, the relevant host government.[48] Thus, any change in the operatorship, licensed area or participating interest of the JOA parties (i.e. the key issues for any exclusive operation) should be approved by the relevant host government.[49] These issues are typically dealt with in the host government contract and the government will typically desire to control who is conducting the relevant activities and which parties constitute the consortium in any project and in the relevant concession area.[50] The host government may have its own opinions and aspirations as to which party should be responsible for operations and any deviation from its initial agreement and initial understanding of how operations will be conducted within the concession area may become problematic.

11. NATIONAL OIL COMPANY INVOLVEMENT

A national oil company (NOC) is an entity owned or controlled by a host government. This entity might not have the same perspective as an international oil company (IOC), because its ultimate shareholder is not a private entity but instead a government, which is sensitive to economic and political considerations.[51] Some JOAs might provide further protections to the NOC in order to safeguard the interests of the IOCs in the joint venture. For example,

---

47 This topic is dealt with in 'The Relationship between a JOA and a Host Government Instrument' in this volume.

48 See B.G. Taverne, *Petroluem, Industry and Governments: A Study of the Involvement of Industry and Government with the Production and Use of Petroleum*, 2nd edn, Kluwer Law International, Alphen aan den Rijn 2008, p. 380.

49 Norwegian JOA §19.5: 'If the Operator does not participate in the development, the participating Parties shall select an operator. Such selection is subject to approval by the Ministry.'

50 E.g. AIPN JOA, §7.12 and Greenlandic JOA, §7.2.8.

51 E.G. Pereira and A. Ovcharova, *Joint Operating Agreements: A Comparison between IOC and NOC Perspectives*, Globe Law and Business, London 2015.

in Morocco the consortium agreement provided by the local NOC clearly states that sole risk project rights only apply to the IOCs but not to the NOC.[52] Another example is the JOA model from Greenland, where the local NOC has a carried interest throughout the exploration phase.[53] However, it is not always the case that an NOC's rights are different from the IOCs' rights. For example, in Norway, Statoil does not have any carry provision or different rights from the IOCs. Consideration should be given to the issue of whether an NOC should have non-consent rights and rights to conduct exclusive operations in the JOA. Such rights may be prejudicial to the interests of the IOCs should there be a difference of opinions between them and the host government as to what constitutes the best way forward for the joint venture.

12. EXCLUSIVE OPERATIONS IN FRONTIER ENVIRONMENTS

The viability of exclusive operations in new plays (i.e. unconventional operations in shale and tight reservoirs)[54] and extreme frontier environments (e.g. the Arctic, ultra-deepwater, etc.) will require careful consideration as the implementation of an exclusive operation in such circumstances might arguably not be viable in the way in which such rights exist in respect of more traditional basins.

One solution in such circumstances would be the exclusion of exclusive operations. This would result in no party having the right to elect not to participate in joint operations and no party being able to conduct sole risk operations. This approach however ignores the need for parties to be able to validly opt out of joint operations and thus may result in premature termination of the joint venture. It also fails to recognise that technological improvements may lessen the challenges of conducting an exclusive operation in such circumstances over time. The AIPN guidance notes for unconventional resources maintain the possibility of conducting an exclusive operation. As a JOA could be in place for several decades, it is important that it provides for some flexibility to accommodate evolving circumstances.

If the parties decide to remove the option for an exclusive operation, then issues in relation to deadlock will arise and will need to be dealt with in an innovative way in the JOA. An exclusive operation often serves as a deadlock mechanism if the parties cannot reach the pass mark to approve a particular activity. Thus, if the JOA was designed to work with an exclusive operation but

52 ONHYM JV, Article 12.

53 Greenlandic JOA, clause 2.4.

54 See P. Roberts, 'Modifying the Standard JOA to Accommodate Unconventional Petroleum Projects' in this volume.

the parties decide to remove the exclusive operation, then further thoughts are required as to what would be the consequences for the JOA as a whole.

A more flexible approach to the issue of exclusive operations in such circumstances may be to restrict the scope of exclusive operations. Consideration could be given to the circumstances in which it might be acceptable for the parties to be able to exercise a non-consent right and a sole risk right. These could be clearly specified in the JOA and could be subject to review as and when circumstances change.

13. DEFAULT

A critical provision in any JOA is the default provision.[55] Securing payments is at the heart of any joint venture as sharing costs and risks are the key premises for forming a joint venture. Most JOAs typically impose restrictions and sanctions on the party in default with their payments and eventually insurance obligations. The initial restrictions tend to include the inability to vote in any meeting and obtain any information from the consortium. As a consequence, a party in default cannot propose an exclusive operation until they remedy their default.[56] Although they are not allowed to vote they should be considered a participant in the joint operations and non-participants in a decision which could be carried as a exclusive operation.[57]

14. UNIT OPERATING AGREEMENT

A highly complex issue in the oil and gas industry is the possibility that a reservoir could extend beyond the contractual border of a host government contract.[58] In order to avoid competitive drilling, different concessionaires or contractors should combine their efforts and develop this overlapping reservoir through a unitisation and unit operation agreement process. This agreement could be simplified as a wider JOA between different licence groups. This group can conduct unit and non-unit operations in a similar way as the joint and exclusive operations for a conventional JOA. The complexity in this agreement consists in the relationship and coordination of different JOAs between the licence groups.

---

55 Waite, *supra* n. 45; Taylor and Tyne, *supra* n. 1, pp. 55-56.

56 AIPN JOA, clause 8.2.

57 *Ibid.*

58 See E.G. Pereira and G. Carloni, 'Unitisation and Unit Operating Agreements' in this volume.

15. CIVIL LAW

Another complex area is the enforceability of JOAs in civil law countries.[59] Some concepts and principles from common law might not be applicable in civil law jurisdictions. Exclusive operation is a good example of where civil law jurisdictions might impose a variety of legal challenges to be implemented. Therefore, further thoughts and considerations should take place in the relevant civil law countries to confirm the enforceability of the exclusive operation.

16. CONCLUDING COMMENT

Sole risk and non-consent clauses represent essential elements for the survival of a JOA, as they address with flexible terms the issue of disagreements in the joint venture. This flexibility is needed to provide for the ongoing cohesion of the joint venture. However, the implementation of an exclusive operation in reality represents a complex and likely problematic process for those parties participating and those parties not participating in the exclusive operation. For these reasons the sole risk and non-consent clauses are commonly used as nothing more than tools with which to influence decisions taken in the Opcom and to remind the parties that it is better and cheaper to stay together as unit. The implementation of an exclusive operation is a rare occurrence.

---

[59] See E.G. Pereira and Y. Abul Failat, 'Key Issues Relating to JOAs in Civil Law Countries' in this volume.

PART II.B

CONTROL OF OPERATIONS AND EXPENDITURES

AUTHORISING WORK AND CONTRACTS

How is the North American System Unique?

David H. SWEENEY*

1. INTRODUCTION

An authorisation for expenditure (AFE) is 'a form which is widely used in the oil and gas industry when wells are drilled by multiple parties' that describes

* The author would like to thank his colleagues George B.H. Bibikos and Matthew Galbraith for their time and effort reviewing this article.

the proposed operation and estimates associated costs.[1] AFEs play a role in most joint operating agreements; however, their importance varies significantly depending on a number of factors, including the relative bargaining strength of the parties, applicable law, and the requirements of the underlying granting instrument(s). Similarly, a work programme and budget addresses the proposed operations to be conducted by co-owners of hydrocarbon rights during a period of time and the estimated costs of those operations. In North America, AFEs generally play a more important role in determining the proposal and approval of, and budget for, operations. Outside of North America, AFEs typically work in tandem with work programmes and budgets to determine the identity, pace and cost of operations.

This distinction is indicative of (among other things) the philosophy that underlies the relationship of the parties to a joint operating agreement inside, and outside, of North America. The property ownership aspect of the North American exploration and production business, which is largely absent elsewhere, has generally resulted in joint operating agreements in which the parties surrender autonomy only to the minimum extent practicable. Outside of North America, there is generally a greater need for the co-owners of hydrocarbon rights to act in concert, and thus a more methodical approach to operations and contract awards. These general approaches are undoubtedly different (although, as noted below, the same basic result can be achieved using forms common to either approach), but the distinction between North American and non-North American joint operating agreements in this respect is more nuanced than is commonly supposed. A careful examination of a number of forms[2] that are representative of their respective contexts, as well as actual agreements based on these forms, shows that the 'success' of a system of operational proposals, budgeting and contracting should be judged as much on the ability of the system to thrive in its environment as on the ultimate results. In this light, the North American system has generally succeeded.

---

1 H.R. Williams and C.J. Meyers, *Manual of Oil and Gas Terms*, 12th edn, Matthew Bender & Company, Newark, NJ 2003, p. 30 (citing *M&T, Inc. v Fuel Res.* Dev. Co., 518 F. Supp. 285 (D. Colo. 1981)).

2 This chapter examines the following commonly encountered form joint operating agreements as representative of their respective types: Rocky Mineral Law Foundation Forms 1 and 2 (RMMLF Form 1 and RMMLF Form 2, respectively), the 1989 version of the American Association of Professional Landmen Form 610 (AAPL 610), the 2014 version of the American Association Professional Landmen's Form 810 offshore operating agreement for US deepwater operations (AAPL 810), the American Association Professional Landmen's Form 710 offshore operating agreement for US shelf operations (AAPL 710), American Petroleum Institute Form 5UO2 (API 5UO2), the Canadian Association of Petroleum Landmen 2007 form Operating Procedure (CAPL 2007), the 2002 and 2012 versions of the Association of International Petroleum Negotiators' model form (AIPN (2002) and AIPN (2012), respectively), Oil & Gas UK's 2009 industry form operating agreement (OGUK), and AMPLA Ltd's model form joint operating agreement (AMPLA).

2. THE 'NORTH AMERICAN' SYSTEM[3]

North American joint operating agreements, by and large, can be thought of as 'AFE-centric'. AFEs are the primary manner – and sometimes the only manner – in which operations are proposed and approved. In North American joint operating agreements, work programmes and budgets are generally either for informational purposes only or are entirely absent. Further, in most onshore agreements that are based on a version of the commonly encountered AAPL 610 form that, in its many incarnations, probably encompasses the majority of North American operating agreements by number, there is neither provision for, nor a contractually mandated periodic meeting of, a committee to discuss operational plans. Agreements that govern projects in certain areas, such as the Gulf of Mexico or Canada, or with certain characteristics, such as federal exploratory units or coalbed methane or unconventional reserves, utilise work programme and budget procedures to some degree; however, these are exceptions to the rule, and, even in these types of agreements, the AFE procedure frequently remains the primary manner in which operations are proposed. Thus, although there are significant differences among the many forms of agreement commonly used in North America, the operational proposal procedures in each type of agreement generally share many characteristics.

2.1. METHOD OF PROPOSING OPERATIONS IN NORTH AMERICAN AGREEMENTS

Under most North American joint operating agreements, any party that has not relinquished its interest in a zone may generally propose an operation in that zone, regardless of whether the operation was pre-planned or discussed with the other parties.[4] A party (whether the operator or a non-operator) initiates this

---

3 Sections 2 and 3 of this article consist of a high-level summary a complex topic. A number of sources contain more detailed descriptions of AFE processes and procedures commonly encountered in both North American and non-North American joint operating agreements. See, e.g., J.R. Reeves, 'Drilling and Other Development Operations Under the Model Form Operating Agreement', Institute on Oil & Gas Agreements: Joint Operations 4-1, 4-13, *Rocky Mtn. Min. L. Found.*, December 2007; D.H. Sweeney, *Oil and Gas Joint Operating Agreements: A Comparative World-wide Analysis*, LexisNexis Matthew Bender & Company, Newark, NJ 2016, §8.03.

4 AAPL 610 §VI.B.1. In agreements with generally applicable voting mechanisms, such as agreements based on the AAPL 810 form, a vote of the parties may be required to authorise the operation; however, the 'pass mark' (termed an 'Election' in the AAPL 810 form) is, in practice, generally fairly low, such that any party with a cost-bearing interest may cause many types of operations to be conducted, subject to obtaining 100% subscription of the relevant costs. AAPL 810 §8.2.2.

process by sending the other parties entitled to participate in the operation an AFE that describes the proposed operation and its estimated costs. The type and amount of information required usually depends to some extent on the context of the agreement. In general, operations of lower cost and complexity are proposed with AFEs containing a relatively small amount of information when compared to AFEs for high-cost or high-complexity operations. AFEs for some onshore wells may include no more information with respect to the proposal than the surface location, target formation and depth, associated gross and net estimated costs, and a general description of the proposed well or operation.[5] Conversely, AFEs for offshore operations generally include significantly more detail, such as a breakdown of costs by operational category, well design details, contingency and emergency response plans, and regulatory filings. For example, Article 2.74 of the AAPL 810 form requires that a well AFE include a 'Well Plan', which must set forth, in addition to the usual contents of a typical onshore AFE, expected time horizons for commencement and conclusion of operations; a drilling plan, 'inclusive of casing and/or liner sizes, anticipated days versus depth graph, estimated depth settings, pore pressure frac gradient curve, estimated mud weights, temperature profile, listing of wells used for pore pressure prediction and well trajectory and directional drilling details' and information regarding the rig to be used.[6] However, in neither case are AFEs generally required to be based on any pre-approved work programme or budget, even where, as described below, operational forecasts are required.

Non-proposing parties generally have a certain period of time to respond to an AFE. This period varies from 24 hours for 'urgent' matters, such as subsequent operations at objective depth when a rig is onsite,[7] to thirty days for a 'normal' operation under an onshore agreement,[8] to more than six months for a proposal to construct a development system under an offshore agreement. The failure of a party to respond to an AFE generally results in a deemed 'non-consent' (except in respect of plugging and abandonment proposals) and a resulting relinquishment of interest in the proposed operation, or, in some cases, a portion (or all) of the

---

5 See, e.g., *ArcadiEnergy, Inc. v McCord Exploration Co.*, 596 So.2d 1334, 1342 (La. Ct. App. 1992) (holding in the context of the 1977 version of the AAPL 610 form that 5 facts must be disclosed in order for an AFE to be valid: (i) a description of the operation, (ii) objective formation, (iii) surface location, (iv) proposed objective formation and (v) estimated cost, and, where a party that sent an AFE did not disclose a change in objective formation the non-proposing parties did not receive notice of the operation and did not elect not to participate); see also *French v Joseph E. Seagram & Sons, Inc.*, 439 S.W.2d 448 (Tex. Civ. App – El Paso 1969, writ ref'd n.r.e.) (upholding an AFE which contained the location, proposed depth, objective formation and costs of a proposed well, even though, due to a non-consent, the interests of the participating parties in the operation changed subsequent to their execution of the AFE).

6 AAPL 810 §2.74.

7 E.g., AAPL 810 §10.2.1 (24 hours); AAPL 610 §VI.B.1 (48 hours).

8 E.g., AAPL 610 §VI.B.1.

contract area. If it does respond, a party may generally (i) elect to participate, (ii) elect not to participate or (iii) propose a 'conflicting' operation. If a party proposes a 'conflicting' operation, either a priority of operations clause (if there is one in the agreement) or a vote by the parties dictates which operation will be conducted. In US offshore agreements and agreements based on the RMMLF and API forms, which contain generally applicable voting procedures (but not operating committees), the proposal that receives the highest vote and attains the required pass mark 'wins.'[9] In contrast, under the AAPL 610 and CAPL forms, the operational proposal that receives the highest vote, without reference to a pass mark, generally 'wins'.[10] If 100% of the costs of a proposed operation are subscribed, whether jointly by all parties, or by some of the parties, and the applicable pass mark (if any) is met, the operation may be conducted.[11]

North American onshore agreements typically do not contain cost overrun provisions. In this type of agreement, an AFE is, in some respects, a 'blank cheque'. Regardless of the level of over-expenditure, the non-operators are bound to pay their respective shares of the costs of operations to which the AFE relates. As one commentator put it, '[c]ontrary to popular lore, AFEs do not limit expenditures – they are only an estimate of the anticipated costs associated with a proposed operation.'[12] Practically, the impact of this is mitigated to some extent by the fact that the operator frequently bears the single largest share of these costs and could presumably at some point be removed for breach of its obligation to conduct operations in a 'good and workmanlike manner', even if it could not be held disproportionately liable under the operator exculpatory clause.[13] Offshore agreements, by contrast, generally do contain expenditure limitations.[14] If the operator exceeds AFE costs by a certain, lower threshold, it must provide an informational notification to the non-operators. Over-expenditures above a higher threshold result in a supplemental AFE. This supplemental AFE is generally treated like any other AFE. So long as a relatively minimal pass mark ('Election' in the language of the AAPL 810 form) is met, the operation continues, and parties that elect not to participate in further costs are treated as though they 'non-consented' to the operation insofar as it relates to the

9 See *supra* n. 5.

10 AAPL §VI.B.6.

11 E.g., AAPL §VI.B.2.(a).

12 M.E. Curry, 'Operations Not Covered or Inadequately Covered by the Joint Operating Agreement and Other Problem Areas', Institute on Oil & Gas Agreements: Joint Operations 8-1, 8-4 – 8-5, *Rocky Mtn. Min. L. Found.*, December 2007; see also CAPL §3.01C ('A Party's approval of an AFE constitutes its approval of all expenditures necessary to conduct the operation described therein').

13 AAPL 610 §V.B.1. ('good cause' includes material breach of the joint operating agreement); CAPL §2.02B.(b) (operator may be removed if it 'defaults in performance of any of its duties' after notice and an opportunity to cure).

14 See, e.g., AAPL 810 §6.2.2; AAPL 710 §8.7.

costs that they did not bear.[15] However, because there is usually no binding work programme and budget, there is no cumulative over-expenditure limitation on an annual basis.

2.2. CONTRACT AWARDS GENERALLY

US onshore agreements generally do not contain specific limitations on an operator's ability to procure goods and services other than common restrictions on self-dealing and a general requirement to drill wells on 'a competitive basis at the usual rates prevailing in the area'.[16] For example, under the AAPL 610 form, an operator may generally award contracts to third parties without any specific procurement procedure or a requirement to seek the approval of the non-operators for contracts above a certain dollar amount, although agreement of the parties may be required for the use by the operator of its own tools and equipment and the procurement by the operator of goods and services from an affiliate.[17] US offshore agreements are generally somewhat more restrictive. In addition to normal limitations on self-dealing, drilling contracts must generally have been entered into fewer than a certain number of years before the relevant operation and must have been on 'market' terms at that time.[18] In contrast to almost every other US form, shallow water offshore agreements based on the AAPL 710 form require that the operator use 'competitive bidding' to procure goods and services 'insofar as possible'.[19] While the use of the phrase 'competitive bidding' implies a tender process, it neither proscribes a specific procedure, nor requires non-operator consent.

The CAPL form takes this a step further. It contains both an express standard by which procurement is judged and a provision requiring the competitive award for contracts above a certain dollar value. Specifically, the operator must award contracts with a value over $50,000 'in accordance with good contracting practices in the oil and gas industry ... [considering] such factors as reliability, safety, environmental protection, technology, cost, quality of service, delivery time and other factors relevant to the contract'.[20] Strategic sourcing

---

15 E.g., AAPL 810 §6.2.2; AAPL 710 §8.7.

16 AAPL 610 §V.D. While the use of the word 'competitive' in this context implies a tender procedure of some sort, the manner in which it is used elsewhere Article V.D. suggests that it is a reference to terms that the operator could readily obtain from another third party. For example, work performed by affiliates must be performed at 'competitive' rates.

17 AAPL 610 §V.D.; see also COPAS (2005) §II.7.

18 AAPL 710 §5.7; AAPL 810 §2.9 (definition of 'Competitive Contract').

19 AAPL 710 §5.7.

20 CAPL §§3.03A, 3.03B.

('alliance arrangements'), preferred supply arrangements and local preference requirements are excluded from these rules in some cases.[21]

2.3. NORTH AMERICAN AGREEMENTS WITH WORK PROGRAMME AND BUDGET PROCEDURES

While pre-planned work programmes and budgets typically do not play a major role in the vast majority of North American joint operating agreements, they are more a part of the operational DNA of North America than most would suspect. Many agreements based on the CAPL, AAPL 810, and API 5UO2 forms provide for annual work programmes and budgets.[22] These operational forecasts are generally for informational purposes only; however, underlying legal and granting instrument requirements may render them meaningful to some degree in practice.[23] Further, agreements that have evolved to deal with high-cost, high-complexity and 'linked' operational contexts may employ work programme and budget procedures much like those found in non-North American joint operating agreements.

2.3.1. RMMLF Forms 1 and 2

In contrast to agreements based on the AAPL 610 form, joint operating agreements based on the RMMLF Forms 1 and 2 provide for 'binding' work programmes. Onshore exploratory units involving US federal governmental leases can be relatively large, encompassing thousands of acres.[24] These units are typically unitised pursuant to a unit agreement based on a statutory form.[25] Unitisation agreements based on this form generally require the conduct of certain minimum operations, such as the drilling of one or more initial wells, as well as the submission of continuing work proposals to an authorised officer of the government (an 'AO'), which become 'binding' to some extent when approved.[26] RMMLF Forms 1 and 2, which were developed to govern operations for this type of unit, reflect these planning requirements. The operator must submit a proposed plan for additional development work to the parties for

---

21 *Ibid.*, §3.03B.

22 AAPL 810 §6.4.1; CAPL §5.04; API 5UO2 §11.2.

23 See 43 C.F.R. 3186.1 §9 (requiring submission of operational plans, approval of which makes them binding on the parties; *cf.* 30 C.F.R. 550.201 (requiring submissions to government of operational plans).

24 S.B. Richardson and L.P. Hendrix, 'The Unit Operating Agreement for Federal Exploratory Units', Institute on Oil & Gas Agreements: Joint Operations 13-1, 13-2, *Rocky Mtn. Min. L. Found.*, December 2007.

25 43 C.F.R. 3186.1.

26 *Ibid.*, §9.

review prior to the submission of this material to the AO. The proposed plan is then subject to non-operator review and comment and ultimately must be approved by a pass mark vote prior to being submitted to the AO. If the plan is not approved, it is revised and resubmitted for a further vote. If the plan is never approved, the operator may submit a 'compromise' plan that '[reflects] as nearly as practicable the views expressed by the parties.'[27] The submitted plan is subject to review and potential rejection or modification by the AO, at which point it is re-submitted to the parties.[28] If approved, a plan becomes binding, subject to proposed amendments, which must be approved by the parties and the AO, and the ability of parties to participate, or not participate, in operations when later proposed via AFE.[29]

2.3.2. *Informational Work Programmes*

Even where not mandated by underlying granting instruments or applicable law, some North American joint operating agreements provide for periodic operational forecasts. US offshore joint operating agreements – especially those governing deepwater projects – generally provide for an 'annual operating plan'.[30] Beginning with the approval of a development plan, the operator must submit a plan of operations for the following year to the parties for their review. This plan is generally broken down into capital expenditures ('capex') and operating expenses ('opex'), and must contain, among other things, a list of proposed wells to be drilled, the details of these wells, and estimated costs; equipment-related capital expenditures with greater than a to-be-negotiated dollar value; an overall estimate for capex; well operations for which the relevant costs would be considered opex and not capex; other non-capex projects with costs over a to-be-negotiated amount; a total opex project budget; and an operations and maintenance budget.[31] In addition, the operator must submit informational

---

27 RMMLF Form 2 §7.1, *et seq.*; RMMLF Form 1 §20.2, *et seq.*

28 *Ibid.* RMMLF Form 1 does not contain provisions allowing non-operators to object to proposed operational plans. In practice, this type of agreement is less frequently encountered than Form 2-based agreements.

29 43 C.F.R. 3186.1 §10; RMMLF Form 2 §§8.1, *et seq.* (development wells); 9.1, *et seq.* (exploratory wells). RMMLF Form 1 does not allow the submission of a plan that contains operations that have not been authorised by the parties chargeable with the costs of those operations. While the ability of a party to 'go non-consent' in an operation that was otherwise included in an approved work programme would potentially be permitted under a non-North American joint operating agreement, depending on the options selected, such an election would generally not be permitted for an operation that is was required by the granting instrument, such as a minimum work obligation.

30 AAPL 810 §6.4.1. In the author's experience, this procedure is frequently included in actual deepwater joint operating agreements with relatively few changes.

31 AAPL 810 §6.4.1.

forecasts relating to, among other things, production, injection, fuel gas, scheduled facility downtime, facility constraints, and 'other areas deemed of significance'.[32] The non-operators have a certain amount of time to review and comment on the revised plan. The operator incorporates any objections and revisions if it deems them necessary and submits the final plan to the parties, at which point it is deemed to have been adopted without a vote. However, this is of relatively small consequence because, as noted in the introductory paragraph to the 'annual operating plan' procedures, the plan is 'for informational and planning purposes and does not obligate any Party to any course of action or expenditures or constitute a Vote, Election or unanimous agreement to participate in any specific activity or operation.'[33]

Similarly, the API forms of unit operating agreement and the CAPL form require periodic operational and budgetary forecasts. Under the API 5UO2 form, the operator must submit an annual budget, broken down by calendar quarter, to the parties soon after the effective date of the agreement and thereafter before a certain date each year. However, these forecasts are 'estimates only, and shall be adjusted by the Unit Operator whenever an adjustment or correction is proper'.[34] The CAPL form likewise provides for 'a written forecast outlining all anticipated Joint Operations during the next 12 month period and their estimated costs'.[35] As with the API and AAPL 810 forms, however, this forecast is information only, and, as noted by the relevant annotations to the CAPL form, '[i]t is seldom used in practice'.[36]

While these informational provisions may lack 'teeth', proponents sometimes argue that they prompt discussions and allow non-operators to anticipate, and budget for, operations and charges that could be problematic before they become issues. In any event, the operational planning provisions of RMMLF Forms 1 and 2 and the underlying requirements of the federal unit agreement do not necessarily impose obligations on parties to actually participate in the operations encompassed by an approved plan, even if those operations are binding to some extent as between the government and the parties. Work programme and budget-like procedures are sometimes encountered in two other situations in North America – coalbed methane operations and 'unconventional' joint ventures. In both of these situations, depending on the specific agreements at issue, work programme and budget requirements may actually have 'teeth' and function in a manner similar to non-North American agreements.

---

32 *Ibid.*, §6.4.1.3.
33 *Ibid.*, §6.4.1.
34 API 5UO2 §11.2.
35 CAPL §5.04.
36 Annotations to CAPL 19.

2.3.3. *Coalbed Methane and 'Unconventional' Joint Ventures*

Individual operations in coalbed methane projects are frequently more interconnected than operations in conventional exploration and production projects. Each development well requires significant infrastructure for disposing of water produced during the 'de-watering' process (allowing the well to produce water in order to reduce the pressure within the coal seam to free the associated natural gas), as well as an existing transportation and compression network, without which individual wells, or even groupings of wells, would generally not be economic. As should be obvious from the discussion above, the AAPL 610 form does not address these particularities, and thus, in 2005, model changes to this form were proposed to accommodate coalbed methane projects.[37]

These changes recognise the interdependence of coalbed methane operations and contain options to group wells and infrastructure together. One option is to conduct operations based on an 'annual development plan'. The suggested provisions to accomplish this are quite similar to work programme and budget provisions in the 2002 version of the AIPN form of joint operating agreement. An initial development plan is agreed to at the same time as the execution of the joint operating agreement. Prior to 1 November of each year thereafter, the operator must propose the annual plan of development for the following calendar year. The parties then meet to discuss the plan. If it is not approved, the operator submits a revised plan. That process continues until an agreement is reached; however, if no plan has been approved by 31 December the latest version of the plan proposed is deemed approved. Each party has the option to participate in the 'approved' plan. If a party does not participate, its interests in all operations encompassed by the plan may be relinquished.[38]

Similarly, decision-making structures adopted by most unconventional joint ventures utilise operational and budgetary forecasts.[39] Large-scale joint venture arrangements for the development of unconventional resources are generally not based on any generally accepted North American form and are frequently not public; however, some generalisations can be made both based on publicly disclosed transactions and the author's experience. In unconventional projects, as in coalbed methane development projects,[40] operations may be

---

37 F.M. MacDonald, 'The AAPL Form 610 JOA Coalbed Methane Checklist', Institute on Oil & Gas Agreements: Joint Operations 11-1, 11-1 – 11-5, *Rocky Mtn. Min. L. Found.*, December 2007.

38 AAPL 610 (CBM) §VI.A., *et seq.*

39 See D.H. Sweeney, P. Cody, S. Lindberg, and M.P. Darden, 'Fracturing Relationships: The Impact of Risk and Risk Allocation on Unconventional Oil and Gas Projects' (2014) 9 *Tex. J. Oil, Gas, and Energy L.* 289, 306.

40 The term 'unconventional' as used in this context refers to projects in which the relevant reservoir requires horizontal drilling and fracturing and is characterised by relatively high initial production with a relatively steep decline rate. Some would call coalbed methane

more interrelated than most suspect. It generally takes many wells to reduce well variability and 'de-risk' an area such that the parties are certain that the area is, or is not, economic, and each progressive well carries with it the lessons of all of the previous attempts.[41] For this reason, some commentators have re-conceptualised operational phases for unconventional projects.[42] The details of this proposal are beyond the scope of this chapter, but the effect is to interlink groups of operations that, under 'traditional' AAPL 610 provisions, would have been proposed as part of a single AFE, without operational forecasting. Although not always defined in these terms, unconventional joint ventures have frequently taken this approach, sometimes using provisions very much like those found in AIPN form agreements.[43] These include operational forecasts and budgeting procedures that are, to some extent, binding on the parties.

Thus, while work programme and budget procedures are not generally considered to be 'common' in North America, they are not completely out of the ordinary. However, North American joint operating agreements do not exist in the same context, and do not have to address the same requirements, as 'international' agreements.

3. 'INTERNATIONAL' OPERATING AGREEMENTS

Depending on the specifics of the relevant jurisdiction and agreement, work programme and budgeting procedures play a major, or the major, role in the operational proposal and selection process outside of North America. AFEs are still widely used, both for internal and external budgeting and approval purposes, but their importance is generally diminished by virtue of the fact that operations usually have been approved in some form through the work programme and budget procedure before an AFE is ever presented. Granting instruments (and frequently laws) underlying most non-North American projects require that the parties conduct certain minimum work obligations and submit, and obtain approval for, operational plans.[44] Failure to comply with these requirements may

operations 'unconventional;' however, for the purposes of this Article, they have been kept separate for the purposes of discussing the different provisions commonly applicable to each.

41 Sweeney, *supra* n. 40, p. 308.

42 P. Cody, 'Shale vs. Big Exploration: What Sorts of Risks Are You Taking?', E&P, 1 January 2013 <http://www.epmag.com/item/Shale-vs-big-exploration_111180>; see also Sweeney, *supra* n. 40, p. 308.

43 See, e.g., Exco Res., Inc. Current Report (Form 8-K) (11 August 2009).

44 F.C. Alexander, Jr. and F. Milber Gasgrain, *Government Petroleum Contract Handbook (for the international petroleum industry)*, 1st edn, 2009, pp. 19–20; C. Duval et al., *International Petroleum Exploration and Exploitation Agreements: Legal, Economic, & Policy Aspects*, 2nd edn, Barrows Company, 2009, p. 125.

result, among other things, in termination of the granting instrument; damages payable to the host government; forfeiture of a bond, letter of credit, or other surety; the inability of the parties to conduct operations that were approved by the operating committee but not the parties; disallowance of cost recovery for all or part of the costs of an operation; fines; debarment from participating in oil and gas activities in the relevant country and even, in extreme cases, criminal charges.

3.1. WORK PROGRAMME AND BUDGET PROCEDURES

A joint operating agreement is generally signed with a work programme and budget for the initial 'stub' year in mind. This work programme must, under most agreements, be presented within a certain number of days after the execution of the agreement. In practice, the initial work programme and budget is frequently either annexed to the joint operating agreement, agreed to in a side letter or heads of joint operating agreement, or incorporated into a farm-out or other acquisition agreement. Every year following this initial 'stub' period, the operator must submit a work programme and budget for the subsequent year a certain period of time before the end of the current year or before the a work programme must be submitted to the government. Dates between 1 September and 30 October seem to be particularly popular when a date certain is used. The contents of a proper work programme and budget proposal are in part a function of the requirements of the underlying granting instrument, applicable laws and the operational phase of the project. Submissions that relate to an exploration period with only data-related work obligations and in which all non-operators are carried parties are likely to be substantially less detailed than if the minimum work obligations include two deepwater exploration wells and the non-operators have a voting interest that is relatively close in quantity to that of the operator. In either case, in general, work programmes and budgets must contain an itemised list and description of the proposed operations for the upcoming year, together with the 'nature, scope, location, timing, and duration', estimated costs, and other supporting information regarding each line item.[45]

Once the draft work programme and budget is submitted, the operating committee meets to discuss the proposal and either accept, reject or modify it. If a work programme is not agreed upon before one must be submitted to the government, most agreements contain a procedure whereby a proposal that meets the minimum work requirements for the applicable period, takes into

45 AIPN (2012) §6.1.C; AIPN (2002) §6.4; OGUK §14.1; AMPLA §8.1. The OGUK form (or, in older agreements, the accounting procedure) generally requires somewhat more information, including, notably, 'an estimate of the timing and value of AFEs' and a breakdown in sufficient detail to 'allow adequate cost allocation and control'.

account previous commitments under a multi-year plan and receives the largest percentage vote (even if not a pass mark) is submitted to the government for approval.[46] The same basic procedure is followed for the appraisal, development and production phases, with some distinction among forms.[47] Thus, for example, in the event of a discovery in a project governed by an agreement based on the AIPN (2012) form, the operator notifies the government and the non-operators and makes a recommendation regarding whether appraisal operations should be conducted. If the operating committee makes a positive determination in this respect, the operator delivers a proposed appraisal work programme and budget to the operating committee, which is evaluated, modified, and ultimately submitted to the government.[48] Upon approval (or deemed approval) both by the parties and the government, the operator generally has the right and obligation to conduct the relevant operations, subject to a few exceptions, including, in some cases, the AFE procedure.[49]

3.2. AFES IN 'INTERNATIONAL' AGREEMENTS

Regardless of their 'official' role in a joint operating agreement, AFEs are ubiquitous in the exploration and production industry, serving, among other things, as an internal budgeting and approval tool and means of judging the performance of, and incentivising, major contractors (for example, by allocating a portion of costs under AFE for a drilling rig to the rig's crew as an incentive payment). However, outside of North America, their importance is generally somewhat diminished by work programme and budget procedures. Most joint operating agreements take one of two general approaches – either AFEs are not required at all (or are for informational purposes only) or an AFE triggers a review and approval process by the parties or the operating committee. Each option has its adherents and detractors,[50] but, as with many joint operating agreement alternatives, the propriety of one or the other option rests in part on

---

46 AIPN (2002) §6.1, *et seq.*; AIPN (2012) §6.1, *et seq.*; OGUK §10.1, *et seq.*; AMPLA §8.2(a).

47 AIPN (2002) §§6.1 (exploration and appraisal), 6.2 (development), 6.3 (production); AIPN (2012) §§6.1 (exploration and generally applicable WPB provisions), 6.2.C. – 6.2.G (appraisal), 6.3 (development), 6.4 (production), 6.5 (decommissioning); OGUK §§10.1.1 (exploration), 10.1.3 (appraisal), 11.1.1 (development), 12.1 (production), 13.1 (decommissioning); AMPLA §§8.1 (exploration and general WPB provisions), 9.2(b) (appraisal), 9.3(d) (development), 17.2(a) (abandonment).

48 AIPN (2012) §§6.2.C – 6.2.G; see also OGUK §10.1.3; AMPLA §9.2(d).

49 E.g., AIPN (2012) §6.1.F.

50 See, e.g., A.B. Derman, *Model Form International Operating Agreement: An Analysis and Interpretation of the 1995 Form*, 1st edn, 1997, p. 55 ('The AFE procedure is used by some companies to take the proverbial second bite at the apple. Why should AFEs be used as approval mechanisms when the operation and the associated expenditures are included in the Work Program and Budget?).

the project, the parties, and their relative bargaining power. Where a company submits highly detailed work programmes and budgets and operations are likely to be relatively predictable (as might be the case, for example, in the latter phases of a multi-year development plan), a 'functional' AFE system may serve less of a purpose.[51] However, where work programmes and budgets contain only general information (which is frequently the case), it is reasonable to believe that parties might vote in favour of a work programme and budget but still have very different ideas regarding the particulars of each expenditure.

In practice, most joint operating agreements seem to utilise a version of the 'functional' AFE procedure.[52] In these systems, a proposal to conduct an operation that is contemplated to cost in excess of an amount certain, which generally varies depending on the phase of operations, triggers an AFE from the operator.[53] The operating committee then votes on the AFE. Whether, and to what extent, a party is permitted to vote against an AFE varies by agreement. AIPN forms contain 'compromise' alternatives whereby a non-operator is permitted to vote against an AFE, but only in certain circumstances, such as: (i) the costs shown in the AFE exceeding the corresponding budget line items; (ii) the AFE containing imprudent or unsupported technical specifications (for example, non-stainless steel wellheads being ordered for a high hydrogen sulphide reservoir); (iii) the AFE being supplemental to allow a cost overrun in excess of the tolerances permitted under the agreement; and/or (iv) the terms of a contract not approximating 'fair market terms'.[54] In addition, in practice, some agreements provide for informational AFEs during some phases of operation, such as exploration and appraisal, and 'live' AFEs during others. In any case, if an AFE is approved, subject to a party's right to 'go non-consent', if

51 *Ibid.*, p. 47 (arguing that one of the major roles of an AFE – that of prompting operating committee discussion – is served just as well by informational AFEs).

52 In fact, the OGUK and AMPLA forms do not contain any other option. AMPLA §8.3(g); OGUK §§10.2, 11.2, 12.2, 13.2.

53 E.g., AIPN (2012) §6.8.A (Alternative 1). Notably, AFEs are not required for operations that fulfill minimum work obligations, workovers of wells, and general and administrative costs that are listed as separate line items in an approved work programme and budget because, among other things, the parties are generally not permitted to conduct exclusive minimum work obligations in any event and there are certain operational matters, such as G&A costs, for which an AFE could probably contain no more information that a work programme and budget line item without resulting in the disclosure of the makeup of these costs, which, if tracked at all, is likely confidential, and, in any event, could potentially be charged as an indirect costs under the accounting procedure regardless of whether it was approved in an AFE.

54 AIPN (2012) §6.8.B (Alternatives 2–4). The 1990 version of the AIPN form contained an option that allowed disapproval of an AFE only if the relevant party could demonstrate that the rejection was 'duly justified'.

applicable,[55] the operator is authorised to conduct the operation. If the AFE is not approved, the operation is rejected and, subject to the ability of a party to conduct it as a sole risk operation, and the consent of the government if the operation formed part of a previously approved work programme and budget, it is not conducted.

The same basic analysis applies to cost overruns. When the operator reasonably anticipates (or, in some operating agreements, is 'certain') that total expenditures under a work programme and budget or any particular line item in a work programme and budget will exceed a certain amount (typically 10% for any individual line item, not to exceed 5% for an entire work programme and budget), it must notify the operating committee and provide a revised estimate of the costs required to carry out the relevant line item(s).[56] In some agreements, this notice is for informational purposes only. In others, it must be submitted to, and revised and approved by, the operating committee or the parties.[57]

3.3. AWARD OF CONTRACTS

North American joint operating agreements generally do not place material restrictions on the award of contracts. Non-North American agreements do. In general, the award of a contract above a certain dollar value is subject to a competitive tender procedure and, in some cases, review and approval by the operating committee. Under these procedures, contracts are typically classified by dollar value. Those below a certain (generally low) threshold may be awarded by the operator without the conduct of a competitive tender, although even in this case, the contract award is subject to some standards. In the AIPN forms, the contractor selected must be the 'best qualified, as determined by cost, quality, and ability to perform'.[58] The OGUK form, by contrast, requires competitive tender, even for low-value contracts, 'except where the Operator considers that it is impractical or inefficient to do so'.[59] Contracts with a dollar value above this threshold, but below a higher threshold, generally must be put out for competitive tender. The operator provides its bidder list to the non-operators and gives them an opportunity to add parties; however, the operator, and not the

55 E.g. AIPN (2012) §5.13.B (optional); see also Oil & Gas UK, *Joint Operating Agreement Guidance Notes*, Oil & Gas UK, 2009, p. 22 (proposing language for a 'non-consent' provision but noting that 'very few of those on the work group [that put together the 2009 version of the OGUK form] had experience of such 'non-consent' clauses …').

56 AIPN (2012) §6.9.B; AIPN (2002) §6.8(B); OGUK §§10.5, 11.4. 12.4, 13.4; AMPLA §8.4(a)(ii).

57 In practice, some joint operating agreements contain provision for long lead items, which may be handled somewhat differently. This type of provision is discussed in the guidance notes to the AIPN (2012) form and is generally present in North American offshore forms.

58 AIPN (2012) §6.7.A (Alternative 2).

59 OGUK §6.5.6.

operating committee, typically selects the winning bid, although the operator must submit a competitive bid analysis.[60] Under the OGUK form, in respect of contracts in this 'middle' category, the operator must obtain the approval of the operating committee if it awards the contract to a party other than the 'lowest priced technically or operationally acceptable bidder', and the operator need not provide the non-operators with the bidder list in advance.[61] For all contracts above the threshold applicable to the 'middle' category, the operator must generally provide the bidder list or tender documentation to the parties in advance, allow them to add bidders, and allow the operating committee to choose the 'winner' based on either a competitive bid analysis prepared by the operator (under the AIPN forms) or the operating committee's evaluation of the bids (under the OGUK form).[62] The thresholds for each 'level' of procurement generally differ based on the phase of operations. Thus, the award of a contract with a $250,000 value in the exploration phase of a project may require competitive tender, while the same contract might not in the development phase. As with North American agreements, most 'international' agreements restrict the ability of an operator to self-deal or contract with an affiliate if the value of the goods or services is above a certain threshold, although if the value falls within the 'middle' or 'high' portion of the joint operating agreement in the procurement procedure the operator will be subject to competitive tender requirements in any event.

These procedures mirror large companies' procurement policies and procedures, albeit on a much smaller (and simpler) scale. Thus, it is entirely possible that a company would apply a similar mechanism for onshore operations in the US, although the resulting contract would likely apply across many joint operating agreement contract areas. However, the contract award procedures in non-North American agreements are products of their respective environments. Among other things, host government granting instruments and applicable laws frequently require competitive tender at a much lower level than the joint operating agreement. For example, a granting instrument could provide that all contracts above a $200,000 value must be put out for bid such that indigenous companies will have the opportunity to be included in the procurement process.[63] Further, procurement procedures may be, to some extent, protective if a party is subject to a law such as the UK Bribery Act 2010 that prohibits 'commercial'

60 AIPN (2012) §6.7; AIPN (2002) §6.6.

61 OGUK §6.5.5.

62 AIPN (2012) §6.7.C; AIPN (2002) §6.6(C); OGUK §6.5.4. The AMPLA form defers contract award procedures to the dictates of the operating committee. AMPLA §7.2(c).

63 See, e.g., Ghana Petroleum (Local Content and Local Participation) Regulations of 2013, L.I. 2204 §11 (providing that a contractor under a petroleum agreement must 'establish and implement a bidding process for the acquisition of goods and services to give preference to indigenous Ghanaian companies').

bribery.[64] At the end of the day, non-US joint operating agreements tend to involve larger amounts of money than their US counterparts (with the possible exception of deepwater agreements), and non-operators are understandably interested in ensuring that they are getting the best value for their money.

4. A COMPARATIVE ANALYSIS

Joint operating agreements are, to a large extent, creatures of the laws that govern them, the underlying granting instruments, and the manner in which business is generally conducted in the jurisdiction in which the land covered by the granting instrument is located. In North America (and particularly, onshore in the US), the widespread private ownership of hydrocarbon rights, and the legal relationships among the owners of these rights, played a significant role in the progression of the exploration and production industry in a general sense toward more wells on smaller tracts with more participants, and thus a greater number of operating agreements governing smaller contract areas and an emphasis on standardisation and predictability over customisation. Relatively small contract areas, in turn, have the effect of 'de-linking' operations because in general, no single joint operating agreement is likely to cover enough acreage to make overall field wide development plans important to the participants in that individual agreement. Thus, operational plans, if any, that extend beyond a few wells are generally internal to a company and not to the parties to a joint operating agreement that is likely to cover something along the lines of 640 acres as opposed to thousands of acres.[65]

Of course, each individual agreement is unique, and it is difficult to make generalisations about a category of contracts that span an entire industry. As noted above, there are instances in which North American agreements – even onshore – utilise work programme and budgeting procedures that are strikingly similar to those commonly found in 'international' agreements. However, it would be difficult to argue that, on the whole, these are not exceptions to the general rule that apply in particular areas or contexts, such as in offshore operations, large-scale federal units, unconventional 'joint ventures,' or coalbed

---

64 Bribery Act 2010, c.23 (Eng.) §1 <http://www.legislation.gov.uk/ukpga/2010/23/contents>.

65 Some would argue that the relatively rapid pace of North American operations dictates a less restrictive procedure for proposing and conducting operations. However, there is no particular reason why the onshore North American AFE-based model would be 'faster' than the non-North American model. In fact, one could argue that a pre-approved annual work programme and budget could result in a faster operational tempo because the operator would potentially not be required to deal with unanticipated non-consents or, in some cases, send out AFEs at all. In any event, the 'speed' of North American operations is arguably a function of the factors discussed below.

methane projects. This is not surprising, as each type of agreement was drafted to deal with problems specific to its respective context. Among the many factors that have played a significant role in the development of the North American system and have perpetuated it as it currently exists, three stand out: (i) the nature of North American law; (ii) the requirements of North American granting instruments; and (iii) the need for standardisation.

4.1. NORTH AMERICAN LAW

In the US and (to some extent) Canada, private individuals can own hydrocarbon rights. Elsewhere, they generally cannot.[66] In many North American jurisdictions, oil and gas lessees inherit the rights and relationships of their lessors.[67] Thus, a joint operating agreement can be thought of as an agreement among property owners that either own interests in separate tracts of land or are co-tenants in the same tract of land. In many jurisdictions, property owners enjoy rights to explore for, develop and sell hydrocarbons without a joint operating agreement, and, in many instances, without the consent of any other co-owner.[68] Common law duties; spacing, density, and other conservation regulations and the myriad of inconsistent, unpredictable and frequently unfortunate results of attempting to operate individually and without an agreement frequently dictate that the parties act in concert to some extent.[69] In fact, attempting to operate without some sort of agreement to serve as the basis for collective action, at least under US law, increases the risk of a remedial measure known in some jurisdictions as a 'mining partnership' under which, among other things, each party can be held jointly and severally liable to third parties for the sins of the other.[70] However, this

---

66 Alexander, *supra* n. 45, §1.10; E.E. Smith et al., *International Petroleum Transactions*, 2nd edn, *Rocky Mtn. Min. L. Found.* 2000, p. 341; see also E.E. Smith and J. Lang Weaver, *Texas Law of Oil and Gas*, §2.3[A][1] ('[a]ny cotenant of the oil and gas in place can explore, drill, and produce them . . . .').

67 E.g., *Wilson v Superior Oil Co.*, 274 S.W.2d 947, 950 (Tex. Civ. App. – Texarkana 1954, writ ref'd n.r.e); R.W. Hemingway, *The Law of Oil and Gas*, 3rd edn, West Publishing Company 1991, §5.1(A).

68 See, e.g., *Cox v Davison*, 397 S.W.2d 200, 202–203 (Tex. 1965); Hemingway, *supra* n. 67 at §5.1(A). Some jurisdictions, such as West Virginia, require unanimity consent of co-tenants as a precondition to the conduct of oil and gas operations, although this is a modification of historical common law and is the minority rule in the US.

69 See, e.g., Sweeney, *supra* n. 4, pp. §2.01 (describing the consequences of operating without an operating agreement); D.E. Pierce, 'Transactional Evolution of Operating Agreements in the Oil and Gas Industry', Institute on Oil & Gas Agreements: Joint Operations 1-1, 1-3 – 1-9, *Rocky Mtn. Min. L. Found.*, December 2007 (describing the property law dimension to joint operating agreements).

70 E.g., *Wagner Supply Co. v Bateman*, 18 S.W. 576 (Tex. 1929); *Blocker Exploration Co. v Frontier Exploration, Inc.*, 740 P.2d 983 (Colo. 1987).

does not necessarily mean that parties would be anxious to abrogate the freedom that they otherwise would have to enjoy their property rights independently. At its core, an AFE is a notice of the intent of one party to conduct an operation (notably without the necessity for any pre-approved annual work programme and budget procedure, as, in most jurisdictions, no such structure is required for a co-owner of property to use the jointly owned property). When signed by the non-proposing party, this notice becomes an agreement to pay a part of the costs of that operation. This is not far removed from what would occur in the absence of a joint operating agreement.[71]

By contrast, outside of North America, the relationship created by a joint operating agreement is fundamentally contractual in nature. The parties generally do not have rights to conduct operations without host government approval. Further, host governments generally require that a single party be named operator and in many cases view the contractor parties as a unitary body, even if they legally are not. It is thus necessary that the parties act in a coordinated manner, under a methodical operational plan and budget, and, to the extent practicable, face the government with a united, consistent front and a single voice.[72] The work programme and budget procedures found in joint operating agreements outside of North America are designed to achieve this.

4.2. NORTH AMERICAN GRANTING INSTRUMENTS

In contrast to North American oil and gas leases, non-North American granting instruments typically require the submission and approval of work programmes and budgets on a periodic basis. Granting instruments and legal requirements are sacrosanct, both inside and outside of North America. A joint operating agreement that does not track the requirements of the granting instruments and laws to which it pertains is likely to lead to termination of hydrocarbon rights, damages, or worse. Thus, it is unsurprising that where operational plans are required in North America, for example in federal exploratory units,[73] the joint operating agreements that have evolved to address these requirements likewise contain provisions for operational plans, albeit with a reluctance to abandon

---

71 See, e.g., Williams and Meyers, *supra* n. 2, p. 31 (citing *G.H.K. Co. v Janco Investments, Inc.*, 748 P.2d 45 (Okla. Ct. App. 1987, cert. denied) for the proposition that, even in the absence of a joint operating agreement, the execution of an AFE by a non-operator resulted in the non-operator being entitled to participate as a working interest owner in the relevant well); AAPL 610 §VI.B.1. (providing that, if the parties elect to participate in an operation proposed in an AFE, they are 'contractually committed' to do so); see also Smith and Weaver, *supra* n. 66 at §2.3[A][1].

72 For this reason, the operator typically has the sole right to represent the parties before the government. See, e.g., AIPN (2012) §4.2.B.12.

73 43 C.F.R. 3186.1 §10.

the AFE-centric worldview common to most North American joint operating agreements.[74]

4.3. THE NEED FOR STANDARDISATION

The fragmented nature of oil and gas ownership in the US has driven the need for standardisation and predictability of operational proposal protocol over customisation. With the exception of offshore agreements and unit operating agreements governing operations on federal lands, US joint operating agreements generally do not cover as much territory as their 'international' counterparts. Although there are certainly counter-examples (including some Canadian joint operating agreements), in the author's experience, a US onshore joint operating agreement typically covers something on the order of 640 acres (one typical survey section under the public land survey system that is used in many states). A moderately sized operator with onshore North American assets is likely to be party to many operating agreements that must be administered. It would likely prove difficult, both from an administrative and an operational perspective, for an operator to ensure compliance with as many work programmes and budgets, and accompanying procedures (which would almost certainly be inconsistent to some degree, even within the same field) as it has joint operating agreements.

While the drive for uniformity, predictability, and thus (presumably) decreased administration costs is at least part of the reason for the existence of both North American and non-North American forms, the sheer number of options and alternatives, especially in respect of work programmes and budgets and AFEs, in most 'international' joint operating agreement forms would likely significantly increase the difficulty and hence cost of administering asset portfolios in North America. Concurrently, the value of, and costs associated with, any individual contract area is likely to be much smaller in an onshore North American joint operating agreement than an 'international' joint operating agreement. Admittedly, this is not the case for all North American joint operating agreements, especially those governing offshore and large-scale projects; however, these projects are generally governed by agreements that do include work programme and budgeting procedures, such as the AAPL 810 form, RMMLF Forms 1 and 2, the API 5UO2 form, and the CAPL form.[75] Indeed, an

---

74 RMMLF Form 2 §7.1, *et seq.*; RMMLF Form 1 §20.2, *et seq.*

75 See A.B. Derman and J. Barnes, 'Autonomy Versus Alliance: An Examination of the Management and Control Provisions of Joint Operating Agreements' (1996) 42 *Rocky Mtn. Min. L. Inst.* 4-1, 4-53 (arguing that the costs of the autonomy typically afforded to an operator under US joint operating agreements outweigh the benefits in agreements covering 'very large contract areas, incredibly sophisticated detection, drilling and development technologies,

'execution AFE' under an offshore joint operating agreement could be thought of as a work programme and budget, in that it is likely to provide operational plans and expenditures spanning multiple years.[76] These agreements generally cover much larger areas, involve much larger amounts of money, and, in the case of the RMMLF forms, reflect the somewhat unique (in North America) requirements of the underlying unit agreement than the 'typical' North American joint operating agreement. For the same reason, it is not surprising that large-scale unconventional joint venture agreements and coalbed methane projects have tended to utilise work programme and budget procedures that frequently are similar in both form and function to analogue provisions in 'international' joint operating agreements. These agreements govern large areas and operations that are more interlinked and complex than they would be with a 'traditional' North American project.

5. SUCCESS AND THE NORTH AMERICAN MODEL

Whether the 'typical' North American model of AFEs without work programmes and budgets can be thought of as a success when compared to the 'international' model depends, somewhat unsurprisingly, on how one defines success. Some commentators, the author among them,[77] have decried the lack of order and the difficulty in budgeting and planning caused by the general ability of a party to submit an AFE and conduct an operation without prior approval of a work programme and without the boundaries of a meaningful budget. Commonly available 'international' forms of joint operating agreement are arguably more up-to-date, better drafted, easier to read, and provide for a greater degree of operational order. However, the North American method of proposing and conducting operations has achieved remarkably wide acceptance, is relatively easy to administer, and has facilitated a remarkably inclusive, fast-paced and innovative industry. From this perspective, the 'North American' model, while not appropriate in every context, has generally been, and will generally continue to be, a resounding success.

---

exploratory wells that routinely cost tens of millions of U.S. dollars, and development projects that cost literally hundreds of millions or even billions of U.S. dollars …').

76 AAPL 810 §12.7, *et seq*. Integrated project team provisions could additionally be thought of as obviating the need for a work programme and budget procedure because non-operator's personnel may be involved during the planning and development stages of the project, and thus it is difficult to say that the execution AFE and the details and costs of the development system, are a surprise.

77 D.H. Sweeney, 'Same Agreement, Different World: It's Time to Revise the AAPL 610-1989 Model Form Operating Agreement', University of Texas Energy Law Symposium, 9 February 2012.

MAKING THE DEFAULT MECHANISM FAIR AND ENFORCEABLE

Peter Roberts

Despite the apparent magnitude of the term 'default', the customary definition of a default in the context of the JOA is limited to apply to a party's failure to honour its obligation to make payment when due of the amounts which are required by the operator in order to finance the performance of the joint operations.

In this narrow context of a default, the JOA will typically define what constitutes a default by a party and will prescribe a regime (by reference to several forms of remedy) for dealing with that default for as long as it remains unremedied. The forfeiture remedy for a default under the JOA requires particular consideration.

1. THE CONSEQUENCE OF DEFAULT

The default by a party in making payment when due of its share of a cashcall or an invoice request which has been issued by the operator can have serious consequences. The business of exploring for and producing petroleum cannot simply stop because a party has decided not to pay its share of the costs of those activities, and ultimately a default might even jeopardise the continued existence of the concession.

The inability of a party to meet its share of the cashcalls or invoice requests, and so the concern about what the most appropriate remedy for a party's default should be, might vary according to when in the lifecycle of the JOA those costs and the particular defaults arise.

During the exploration and appraisal phase of a JOA, there may be a temptation for a party to cease to pay its share of the cashcalls or invoice requests part way through that phase if that party believes that the prospects of finding commercially recoverable deposits of petroleum are not sufficiently compelling.

During the development and production phase, the parties should be able to reap the benefits of producing petroleum and so will arguably be more inclined to fund ongoing development cashcalls or invoice requests (although the point made in the preceding paragraph could apply equally where there are separate exploration and appraisal activities taking place simultaneously during the development and production phase.

It is arguable that during the period when petroleum production begins to tail off and the decommissioning phase comes into view then the incentive for a party to default will arguably be at its greatest. Historically, it has been the case that the scope for mistrust between the parties around this possibility results in the implementation of decommissioning security, so as to mitigate the risks of a party's payment failure.

The risk of a party's failure to meet its share of a cashcall or an invoice request when due is ever present within any JOA relationship. Historically, the greatest mitigant of this risk has been a combination of the operational sociology and the commercial logic of the JOA: that the parties to the JOA have been solvent and able to meet all of their cashcall or invoice request commitments; that the character of each party is such that it would do nothing to incur the reputational risk associated with becoming known as a defaulter; and that the parties have had an obvious commercial interest in maintaining their interest in a concession (and a JOA) which relates to a project which has significant prospectivity associated with it. Because of the existence of these factors, the remedies contained in the JOA which would be applied to a party's default, while important to have in place, have typically played a secondary role in keeping the JOA relationship on track.

It has long been an article of faith in the operation of the JOA that the ultimate threat to a defaulting party of the loss (at least in part, and possibly completely) of its petroleum project interests, and the reputational damage which would accompany the embarrassment of such a loss, would generally be sufficient to prevent the failure of a party to pay its share of a cashcall or invoice request when due. This has not been an unreasonable expectation, but any change for the worse in the character of the parties to the JOA should necessitate a re-evaluation of this assumption. It may be that a potentially defaulting party might be unconcerned by such a risk of loss, especially where the JOA (and particularly the implication of the attendant decommissioning costs liability) is proving to be more of a liability than an asset.

The existence in a JOA relationship of any combination of the presence of a party which has impaired financial ability to meet its payment commitments across its entire portfolio of interests, or which is less troubled by the risk of reputational damage associated with a default and loss (in whole or in part) of its interests, or the transformation of the nature of the petroleum project to which the JOA relates from one which produces commercial volumes of petroleum to one which is focused on decommissioning and end-of-life issues, could see the emergence of an increasing exposure to the risk of a default. Consequently, what the JOA has to say about how a default is dealt with could come to assume a much greater significance.

The trend in drafting default remediation provisions in JOAs has been towards the conservative, which (when read in conjunction with an apparent reluctance to address issues of collateral support for a party's JOA obligations ahead of the decommissioning phase) could leave the JOA lacking when it comes to providing meaningful protection against a party's unremedied payment failure.

2. THE DEFINITION OF DEFAULT

The definition of a default in the context of a JOA is ordinarily quite specific and is not as wide as a layman might expect it to be.

The principal obligation of each party under the JOA is to fund its share of the costs of the joint operations. In respect of each party, that share will be set by reference to that party's participating interest, subject to any modification to the principle which has been agreed between any of the parties.

The operator will issue periodic cashcalls or invoice requests to the parties, for both operational expenditures and capital expenditures, against which each party will be required to make payment by the requisite date. The failure of a party to comply with the terms of this request for payment will be a default – this sets the benchmark, from which the default provisions of the JOA are then applied.

The JOA is typically carefully crafted as a 'pay now, argue later' contract. That a party wishes to contest the principle or the content of a cashcall or an invoice request is subordinated to the necessity for that party to pay up when required. The JOA ordinarily does not say that the default remedies are disapplied in the event of a non-payment resulting from a bona fide dispute between the parties. Consequently the default remedies can be regarded as applying a strict liability. This is perhaps understandable because any latitude on this point could see a payment default under the JOA characterised as a dispute, and an abuse of the agreed principle.

This strict liability ordinarily applies even in respect of a cashcall or an invoice request which is manifestly inconsistent with any underlying work programme and budget or authority for expenditure. The payment obligation is generally absolute and unqualified under the JOA, and withholding payment as a protest is not a realistic option for a dissatisfied party (unless the JOA is modified accordingly to allow this, or an alternative course of conduct has been undertaken between the parties which effects an effective modification of the JOA).

Consequently, a party wishing to dispute the validity of a cashcall or invoice request should try to make its points at the time when the underlying work programme and budget is set and approved at the OpCom, or when an authority for expenditure is submitted to the OpCom for approval.

The principal definition of a default implies the total failure of a party to pay its defined share of a cashcall or an invoice request by a due date, but it might also be that a party's behaviour is characterised by repeatedly making late payments. These late payments will eventually be remedied each time by the defaulting party, but this pattern will inconvenience the non-defaulting parties, which will effectively be required to act as a form of interim funding facility in order to make good the defaulting party's late payments.

Each such late payment will still constitute a default for the purposes of the JOA, since a default is defined as a failure to make a payment by the due date for that payment. However, the consequences to the defaulting party will be less severe where the JOA provides for an increasing range of sanctions in response to the ongoing duration of the defaulting party's default (see below) and the defaulting party remedies its default before the more meaningful of those sanctions really start to bite.

Consequently, the definition of default under the JOA might be written to address both a total failure to make payment and an accumulation of repeated late payments. Thus, for example, in the AIPN JOA there is an option in the default provision whereby a defaulting party which subsequently cures that default will be subject to a defined probationary period, during which the forfeiture remedy (see below section 6) will apply if there is a subsequent default, and in the OGUK JOA the forfeiture remedy will apply in respect of a cumulative period of sixty days of default for multiple defaults over a successive twelve-month period.

The AIPN JOA also defines a default as the unremedied failure of a party to procure any collateral support when it was required to do so in accordance with the terms of the concession or of the JOA, and also a party's failure to perform its indemnity obligations, which relates principally to the indemnity given in respect of the breach of defined anti-corruption legislation. The OGUK JOA additionally defines a default by reference to the decommissioning security agreement.

Some JOAs suggest that a party's default under the terms of the concession will automatically also constitute a default under the JOA, but there is no obvious logic for this if the breach of the concession does not actually result in any loss or liability to the parties in the context of the JOA.

Force majeure relief will not ordinarily be available to a defaulting party so as to obviate the application of the liability which arises under the default mechanism since under most JOAs the force majeure provisions will typically be written so as to exclude force majeure relief for a party's failure to pay amounts which are due for payment. However, this exclusion would not ostensibly apply to any other default under the JOA (such as the failure of a party to procure collateral support), and so an express provision would be required in the JOA if force majeure relief were required to be excluded for any other events of default.

The previous commentary supposes that the defaulting party is a non-operating party. However, it could be that the defaulting party is the party which has been appointed as the operator under the JOA, in its capacity as a party due to make payment. If this is so, then a practical consequence will be that, in the first instance, the fact of the occurrence of that default will not be apparent to the non-operating parties (unless joint account audit rights are exercised).

The reaction of most JOAs to this possibility is simply to suggest that if the operator is the defaulting party, then any of the other parties can serve the requisite default notice and can thereafter apply the default provisions under the JOA. In practical terms, however, those other parties might (unless the operator promptly and voluntarily admits that it is in default, which is perhaps unlikely) come to realise that a default by the operator has occurred only later, at a time when some harm might have been risked to the integrity of the continued performance of the joint operations and even the concession.

To mitigate this risk, therefore, the terms of the JOA might include an obligation of the operator to confirm periodically (and to prove, if required) to the non-operating parties that it is acting (as a party) in accordance with its funding obligations as a party under the JOA. This could require the operator to furnish the parties with periodic proof that the joint account has been funded by all parties (including the party appointed to act as the operator) in response to a cashcall or an invoice request.

3. THE REACTION TO DEFAULT

The fact of the occurrence of a default by a party should be readily known as a matter of fact (at least to the operator – see above for how a default by the operator is treated), and thereafter the provisions of the JOA which address a default will be brought to bear accordingly.

The parties should not suppose that one of the functions of the operator is to fund a party's default. However it is one of the functions of the operator to take steps to protect the joint venture from the consequences of a party's default, and the JOA ordinarily prescribes a series of steps in order to effect this protection.

In the event of a default occurring, the first step under the JOA will be for the operator to issue a formal notice of default to the defaulting party (and a copy of that notice will also be sent to each of the non-defaulting parties). The notice of default which is given in respect of a defaulting party should recite the amount in default, which will principally be the total amount of the payment which the defaulting party has failed to pay when due and the costs of any remediation of that default already incurred by the non-defaulting parties. If the definition of default under the JOA also includes a party's failure to procure collateral support, the amount in default could also include any costs incurred or associated with procuring any replacement collateral support in respect of the defaulting party.

A daily rate of default interest to accrue on the amount in default might also be specified, following an interest rate specified in the JOA (see below).

Once that default notice has been issued, a defined grace period will begin (which is usually after the passage of a relatively small period of time, typically between two and six days, so as to give the defaulting party a short period within which the default can still be remedied). It is possible that the defaulting party will make good the default within a relatively short period of time, and this is typically what happens where the default is accidental.

If the default has not been remedied by the end of that grace period, the default period begins and the programme of remedies for default which the JOA provides (see below) comes into play.

If the joint operations are to be properly funded and undertaken, in order that the obligations required by the concession are performed and the overall relationship between the state and the parties is not jeopardised, then the immediate reaction to a party's default is that each other non-defaulting party will be required (by the default notice which is issued by the operator) to step in and make good the amount of the default, where the amount to be contributed by such a non-defaulting party will be set pro rata to the proportion of that party's participating interest to the aggregate of the participating interests of all the non-defaulting parties.

Any failure by a non-defaulting party to meet the additional payment obligations which have been generated by the notice of default will constitute a separate default by that party.

The JOA might also reserve the right for the operator to make good the default (in whole or in part) through borrowing the necessary funds from a third party and adding the costs of doing so to the amount of the default. Alternatively, the operator can, at its option, finance the amount of the default itself (subject to the payment of a cost-of-financing charge in the operator's favour, but which should not be set at a rate which enables the operator to make a profit, such that the operator's no loss/no gain principle is compromised).

By these various means, the default will hopefully be fully funded and remedied, and the operator can proceed with the joint operations. Then the non-defaulting parties will turn to the provisions of the JOA to see how the continuing failure of the defaulting party is to be addressed. The operator's claim for payment against the defaulting party is effectively subrogated to the non-defaulting parties, which then exercise the rights of recovery which are provided by the JOA against the defaulting party.

4. THE REMEDIES FOR DEFAULT

The parties should be interested to ensure that the JOA does not allow the prospect of a default by a party to become attractive for use as a credible short-term financing option, and to this end the JOA should recite a series of swift and effective sanctions which will apply to a defaulting party. Over the longer term, the aim of the default remedy should be to balance up the proportionately greater level of financings which have been contributed by the non-defaulting parties with a correspondingly greater level of interests under the JOA and the concession for those non-defaulting parties.

The options which will apply to a party's default under a JOA are typically written so that they will begin upon the date when the default period begins, and will thereafter increase in intensity for as long as the default continues to be unremedied.

In the initial period after a party's default, the first range of sanctions to be applied will reflect the fact that, by its very default, the defaulting party has broken the social contract between the parties which the JOA represents, and so the defaulting party should be disenfranchised and rendered unable to enjoy certain of the rights which are associated with the JOA. Thus, for as long as its default continues unremedied, the defaulting party will lose several entitlements:

- the right to access any data or information generated in relation to the joint operations;
- the right to call, attend or vote at any meetings of the OpCom;
- the right to effect a transfer of its interests under the JOA;
- any of the rights which it might otherwise have in respect of any other party's transfer under the JOA; and
- the right to withdraw from the JOA.

These provisions operate so as to defeat any ambition which the defaulting party might have to sell, or to relinquish, its interests under the JOA in order to escape the problem. However, the loss of these rights should be expressed to be in the discretion of the non-defaulting parties rather than of automatic application. It may be, for example, that there could be some advantage to allowing the defaulting party to effect a transfer of its interests under the JOA, if doing so would thereby enable the non-defaulting parties to recover the amount in default through such a transfer and to get rid of the defaulting party.

Where there is a carry, the carry, or any further carry, might also be suspended if the carried party is a defaulting party.

During this first range of sanctions, the defaulting party typically also loses its right to lift its produced petroleum entitlements (if any – this sanction assumes that the relevant default has not occurred prior to, or after the end of, the production phase). Those entitlements will pass to the non-defaulting parties, to be sold by the operator on behalf of the non-defaulting parties and the resultant proceeds of sale will be applied in satisfaction of the amount of the default which they have been required to contribute at the outset in order to make good the defaulting party's default. Those entitlements will be sold by the operator on whatever commercial terms the operator is best able to secure. This mechanism represents a limited departure from the customary reluctance of the JOA to endorse joint sales of petroleum.

If a power of attorney is granted to the operator to enable the defaulting party's interests to be transferred, the terms of that power of attorney might also be extended to include the necessary authority to so sell the defaulting party's petroleum entitlements.

Any surplus which accrues from the sale of the defaulting party's petroleum entitlements could be kept in a reserve account and held on trust for the defaulting party, to be used to meet any future cashcalls or invoice requests for which the defaulting party might also become liable. Only if the default is remedied and the defaulting party is restored to its original position under the JOA will any remainder of the reserve account then become repayable to the defaulting party.

The remedy of sequestration of produced petroleum entitlements obviously has little to recommend it when the default takes place in the phase of the JOA prior to the commencement of, or after the permanent cessation of, petroleum production.

Thereafter, if the default is still unremedied (or even if the particular default is remedied but represents the latest in a series of persistent defaults – see above), the ultimate sanction is that the defaulting party's interest under the concession and the JOA may be sequestrated. The various model form JOAs prescribe a number of options by which all or part of the interests of the defaulting party in the concession and the JOA will be transferred to the non-defaulting parties in satisfaction of the default amount. These options can be summarised as follows:

- compulsory withdrawal – the defaulting party could be compelled to exercise the withdrawal right under the JOA;
- buy-out – the defaulting party could be compelled to sell its project interests (in whole or in part) to the non-defaulting parties, typically with a buy-out price to be agreed between the parties or to be determined by an independent expert;
- mortgage security – the non-defaulting parties could enforce any mortgage and security interests which they have taken over the defaulting party's project interests. A variation on this theme is the exercise of a lien and charge over the defaulting party's interests; or
- forfeiture – the defaulting party could be compelled to assign its project interests (in whole or in part) to the non-defaulting parties.

Whichever remedies for default are provided for in the JOA, the JOA should also provide that the rights of the non-defaulting parties and the obligations of any of the defaulting parties or the non-defaulting parties should continue to survive despite the application of the JOA's default remedies (and even the termination of the JOA interests) in respect of the defaulting party.

The express remedies for default which are recited in the JOA could also be supplemented by the general rights at law of the non-defaulting parties (and indeed, the JOA usually makes clear that the contractual rights of the parties are without prejudice to any wider rights at law and in equity).

Thus, the amount in default will be due as a debt owing from the defaulting party to the non-defaulting parties (where the amount of that debt is determined as the amount of the default which has been made good by the non-defaulting parties), together with accrued interest (see below). The non-defaulting parties could always elect to sue the defaulting party through the courts for the recovery of that debt. This step could be taken in preference to applying the other default remedies which are specified in the JOA.

Furthermore, if any collateral support has been provided by a party in respect of its payment obligations under the JOA then it is also an option for the non-defaulting parties to call in that collateral support.

The JOA will usually specify a default rate of interest which will apply to the amount in default, typically set by reference to a base component (such as the London Interbank Offered Rate (LIBOR)), plus a defined number of percentage points. This rate should be set at a rate which is greater than the potential cost of borrowing of a party, otherwise there could be a temptation for a particularly impecunious party to default under the JOA, to save money for other projects and to make a later correcting payment with interest at a default rate which represents a saving on the commercial cost of alternative borrowings. The guidance notes to the OGUK JOA suggest a default rate of interest of a defined base rate plus 8%. There is also a tendency when negotiating a JOA at the outset to apply a greater rate of interest to a party which is perceived to be at greater risk of future default.

5. INTEREST SALES

In order to apply a remedy for default where there is considerable experience of successful enforcement in an analogue context, the JOA could provide that the project interests of the defaulting party are forcibly sold (whether to the non-defaulting parties or to third parties) at an established fair market value (with recourse to a valuation expert in the event of a dispute) and the balance of the sales proceeds (after deduction of the default amount and associated enforcement costs) are returned to the defaulting party.

The interest sale option remedy applies a measure of proportionality between the default amount and the net loss of interest which the defaulting party is exposed to, which will be helpful in reducing the prospects of the remedy being impugned as a penalty. An assessment of the prospects of success of the interest sale option can borrow heavily from the world of enforcement of secured lending, where the rights of a lender to sell a borrower's secured property interests (subject to accounting to the borrower for any balance of the resultant sales proceeds beyond the default amount) are tried and tested.

The interest sale option also results in the complete removal of the defaulting party from its standing as a party to the JOA and the concession, which could be attractive to the non-defaulting parties.

The interest sale option is recited as a possible option for default in the AIPN JOA, the AMPLA JOA and also in the OGUK JOA. In the OGUK JOA this is done in simple narrative terms. The AIPN JOA tries to be more formulaic about this, using the following algorithm:

***Buy-out price** shall be deemed to be equal to the fair market value of the Defaulting Party's entire Participating Interest, less the following:*

(a) *The Total Amount in Default;*
(b) *All costs, including the costs of the expert, to obtain such valuation; and*
(c) *_percent (_%) of the fair market value of the Defaulting Party's Participating Interest*

A notable feature of this algorithm is the provision for the extra deduction from the sales proceeds in favour of the non-defaulting parties in limb (c). This deduction has the capacity to be problematic.

It has the appearance of introducing an additional element of penalty into the equation, and this will particularly be so if the amount of the deduction cannot be justified. The costs of the non-defaulting parties are covered by the interest sale option, as is the default amount, and so what is the deduction intended to provide for? If the answer to that question is anything like 'an additional amount to penalise the defaulting party by not giving it a full recovery of the surplus' then it places the interest sale option remedy on dangerous ground.

The position improves if the amount of the deduction can be justified. One argument which could be made in its favour is that it represents some fair measure of compensation to the non-defaulting parties for the additional risk that they have had to accommodate through having their participating interests increased because of the default, but there is still no obvious correlation between the amount of the deduction and that risk. After all, that risk is just a perception, and it is a risk which would still have applied if it was undertaken under the forfeiture remedy.

The OGUK JOA also imports the notion of a defined percentage deduction which is to be applied to the value of the defaulting party's interests. In the guidance notes to the OGUK JOA this is described as an option for 'discounting the agreed or determined price to reflect the default', with the warning that 'this option might be challenged as a penalty'. The AMPLA JOA applies no such deduction.

6. FORFEITURE

Under the forfeiture remedy, as it customarily appears in a JOA, if a defaulting party's default has continued beyond a defined period of time, the defaulting party will be required to withdraw from the JOA and the concession, and the defaulting party's interest under the concession and the JOA will be forfeited (in whole or in part – see below) to and distributed between the non-defaulting parties.

The requirement that the defaulting party will so withdraw will usually be expressed to be an option of the non-defaulting parties, which could be exercised (depending on how the JOA is drafted) by any non-defaulting party, by a simple majority of the non-defaulting parties or by an affirmative vote of the OpCom (depending on the pass-mark vote and subject to the recusal of the defaulting party).

The non-defaulting parties will inherit the defaulting party's participating interest, to be allocated to each non-defaulting party pro rata to the proportion that each non-defaulting party's participating interest bears to the aggregate of the participating interests of all the non-defaulting parties. This will apply unless all of the non-defaulting parties agree on a different basis for the allocation of the forfeited interest between themselves (in which case some additional cash adjustment between the non-defaulting parties might be appropriate in order to reconcile the allocation of their respective contributions to the default).

If the non-defaulting parties do not wish to assume the participating interest of the defaulting party however, then that could evidence some wider dissatisfaction with the petroleum project and it would be an option for any non-defaulting party to exercise its rights to withdraw. This might in turn lead to a wider surrender of the petroleum project.

However, in contrast to the conventional withdrawal right there will be no obligation on the defaulting party to remove any encumbrances over its interests or to procure any decommissioning security as a prelude to the forfeiture. This latter point adds weight to the suggestion that decommissioning security should be provided by the parties sooner rather than later in the lifecycle of the JOA.

The forfeiture remedy is popularly assumed not to constitute a registrable security interest which has been granted by the party which commits to that remedy. In the United Kingdom, it is not obviously apparent that the typical forfeiture provision would be regarded as an instrument which would constitute a charge to which the relevant legislative provisions would apply.

Forfeiture of the defaulting party's interests might be expressed to be in full satisfaction of the underlying default, such that the non-defaulting parties cannot apply any other remedy or make a double recovery in respect of a default (that is, to secure a forfeiture of the defaulting party's interests and also to sue for recovery of the default amount as a debt). This is laudable in principle, but it overlooks the practical difficulty of what should happen where the value of the forfeited interest is much less than the extent of the amount in default.

To complete the transfer of interests which the forfeiture remedy envisages, the JOA might prescribe that each party will irrevocably appoint each other party as its attorney for the purpose of concluding such a transfer if the need arises, rather than having to compel the defaulting party to execute the necessary transfer documents at the time of exercise of the forfeiture remedy and taking the risk of the defaulting party's obvious reluctance to do so. That said, however sensible it might appear to be, this sort of provision is not always encountered in JOAs.

One practical consequence of the nervousness around the forfeiture remedy relates to where the remedy has been successfully applied against a defaulting party. If a non-defaulting party then wishes to on-sell the sequestered interests of the defaulting party which it has thereby acquired then a subsequent purchaser of those interests could be concerned as to whether they are tainted in some manner (such as by the prospect of continuing legal challenge by the defaulting party), and the purchaser could require significant indemnification from the selling party.

The customary tone of the various commentaries on the efficacy of the default provisions under the JOA is to suggest that the forfeiture remedy, while providing a fair measure of protection to all the parties to the JOA and at the same time giving a means of ensuring that they are each properly incentivised to pay their way according to their defined shares, is a powerful tool which must be exercised with great care and responsibility. Forfeiture is not a remedy applied without some concerns about its complete effectiveness. There are some areas of legal nervousness about the real usefulness of the forfeiture remedy which should be considered.

Historically, the principal concern regarding the operation of the forfeiture remedy has revolved around whether the remedy might be determined by a court to be a penalty and so potentially unenforceable by the non-defaulting parties against the defaulting party. This is based on the principle that under the rules of equity a provision will be unenforceable if it is imposed '*in terrorem*' (that is, where it is intended to enforce the performance of a contract by a defaulting party rather than to compensate the non-defaulting party for a breach of contract).

In the event of a forfeiture the defaulting party will surrender its interests in the concession and the JOA. This consequence can be contrasted with the application of a conventional penalty obligation, whereby a defaulting party will not give anything up in the same sense but will become the subject of an obligation to make payment of a sum of money. That said, despite the differences of characterisation between giving up an interest and paying out a sum of money, the principles which will arise for consideration in determining whether a provision could be impugned as a penalty will be the same.

The historical principal case under English law on the definition of a penalty, *Dunlop Pneumatic*, adopts a fourfold test. The key issue to note from this definition for the present purposes is that a penalty might be inferred where the sum stipulated for payment (which, in the context of a JOA, could be read as the interest which is stipulated to be surrendered by the defaulting party) is 'extravagant and unconscionable in amount in comparison with the greatest loss that could conceivably be proved to have followed from the breach.'

Following on from this, where a defaulting party is at risk of forfeiting its interests because of a default in respect of a monetary amount which is comparatively much smaller than the value of those interests, the defaulting party might argue that the forfeiture remedy constitutes a penalty and so is unenforceable, because the gravity of the remedy applies irrespective of the size of the default. This principle should especially be considered also if the JOA provides for a multi-interest forfeiture remedy (see below).

Something of a paradox operates here, in that the parties will want the forfeiture remedy to threaten the risk of the loss by a party of an interest which is greater than the amount which that party has failed to pay, such that the forfeiture remedy has some real meaning and will be effective in deterring a default, but not at the risk of suggesting a lack of proportionality between the breach of the JOA and the applicable remedy which might suggest that the remedy is actually a penalty.

However, even if the forfeiture remedy was found to be a penalty that would render the forfeiture provision unenforceable only insofar as it would constitute a penalty, the entire package of default remedies which are afforded to the non-defaulting parties would not be wholly void. Furthermore, even if a court did decide that the forfeiture clause was penal in nature, the remedy awarded by the court might be one of compromise, whereby the court might not treat the clause as void, but rather would defer the application of the clause as it was intended to operate, conditional upon an opportunity being given to the defaulting party to remedy the relevant default.

In *Talal El Makdessi v. Cavendish Square Holdings* the English courts considered whether the common law's antipathy towards penalty clauses would apply where forfeiture of interests against a defaulting party was the prescribed contractual remedy. Although not focused on the oil and gas sector, the principles behind the court's decision could have an impact upon the application of forfeiture clauses in JOAs.

In *Makdessi* the seller of part of its shareholding in a company gave certain covenants to the buyer which were intended to protect the continuing value of the company. These covenants principally obliged the seller not to compete with the business of the company after completion of the sale. The sale and purchase agreement (SPA) between the parties provided a form of forfeiture remedy (in that the seller would forego significant future payments due for the shares which had been sold and would also be obliged to sell its remaining shares in the company to the buyer at a significantly discounted value) in the event of a breach of the covenants by the seller.

The seller later admitted to breaching the covenants and the buyer sought to apply the SPA's forfeiture remedy against the seller. The seller issued proceedings in court, seeking a declaration that the forfeiture remedy was a penalty and so unenforceable. The seller's arguments in favour of the allegation of a penalty related principally to the lack of proportionality between the loss suffered by the buyer because of the seller's breach of covenant and the extent of the seller's exposure under the forfeiture remedy.

The Court of Appeal focused on whether the remedy was commercially justifiable in all the circumstances, rather than on the more traditional English law approach to the analysis of penalties of whether the alleged penalty clause constituted a genuine attempt to pre-estimate loss and concluded that the forfeiture remedy was a penalty. Two particular aspects of the Court of Appeal's judgment were key:

- The magnitude of the degree of forfeiture of interests faced by the seller (relative to the buyer's likely loss, which was negligible) was quite disproportionate. This was based in part on recognition also that the forfeiture remedy would apply entirely despite the extent of the seller's breach. This was not of itself conclusive in determining that the forfeiture clause was penal however.
- The forfeiture remedy so lacked a justifiable commercial or economic function that it must be penal in nature and so would be unenforceable by the buyer against the seller. The Court of Appeal upheld the principle from *Lordsvale Finance v. Bank of Zambia* that a contractual remedy which fails to represent a genuine pre-estimate of loss may nevertheless be enforceable if it has sufficient commercial justification. The forfeiture remedy in the *Makdessi* case was not commercially justifiable since its principal purpose was to deter the seller from breaching the SPA.

The customary reaction in the drafting of the JOA to the concern about the forfeiture provision possibly constituting a penalty has been to reduce the risk of adverse intervention by the courts by moderating the potential impact of the forfeiture remedy through a proportional sale of interests. At this point two options present themselves for consideration: the withering interest forfeiture remedy, and a sale of the defaulting party's project interests to the non-defaulting parties (or to third parties) in consideration of the payment of a price which is set at a fair market value.

Since the principal purpose of the forfeiture remedy is to recompense the non-defaulting parties for the amounts they have had to pay in order to make good the defaulting party's default, there must be some careful consideration around proportionality – the loss of the defaulting party's interests in the concession and the JOA should be effected only to such extent as is necessary to give full recompense to the non-defaulting parties.

Proportionality of the forfeiture remedy could be realised by a mechanism in the JOA whereby the extent of the defaulting party's interests which are forfeited to the non-defaulting parties is directly commensurate with the default amount. This will result in the defaulting party remaining party to the concession but enjoying a reduced level of interest in the petroleum project as expressed through the JOA. This structure leads to a consideration of what is popularly called the withering interest formulation in the JOA.

The AIPN JOA is the only model form JOA which conceives of the withering interest formulation. In contrast, the OGUK JOA's forfeiture provision applies to the full value of the defaulting party's interests.

The proper purpose of a withering interest formulation is to fix an equation between the amounts paid by the non-defaulting parties in making good the default and the defaulting party's interests in the concession and the JOA, such that only a corresponding portion of those interests are sequestered by the non-defaulting parties in satisfaction of what they had to pay out to cover the default. Few withering interest provisions actually achieve this goal however. Most withering interest formulations simply end up with the defaulting party losing something less than 100% of its project interests, in the vague hope that any partial project interest loss would somehow be more defensible.

The JOA might apply a simple narrative to the effect that the forfeiture remedy will apply to whatever proportion of the defaulting party's project interests correspond to the extent of that party's default. The parties will then be left to work it out for themselves, and a formal dispute between them as to the accuracy of the resultant calculation is unlikely to be far away.

The alternative to this purposefully deflective approach is to prescribe a particular algorithm in the JOA, which will be applied mechanistically in order to quantify the extent of the interest to be forfeited. This approach is preferable, but only if it is done properly.

The AIPN JOA's withering interest provision is based around such an algorithm. With all due credit for the intention, the execution is somewhat lacking. The AIPN's withering interest provision is, in its standard form of drafting and without modification, difficult to apply.

The withering interest formulation allows a prospectively defaulting party to calculate the consequences of its default, such that default and forfeiture could be used by that party as a means of managing its interests in the JOA and the concession. A withering interest formulation might be of attraction to the prospectively defaulting party to see its interests (and its share of the potential decommissioning costs liability) so reduced, where the underlying petroleum project is coming to the end of its economic life and the concession is starting to become more of a liability than an asset. Conversely, the non-defaulting parties would be reluctant to see their participating interests (and their share of the potential decommissioning costs liability) starting to increase towards the end of the lifetime of the JOA through the exercise of the forfeiture remedy (although this particular risk would abate if decommissioning security were provided).

As a further refinement of the withering interest mechanism, the JOA might also seek to apply different levels of forfeiture (outright forfeiture or forfeiture of a partial interest) according to when, in the lifecycle of the project, the default and the forfeiture takes place. It is sometimes suggested that the exercise of the forfeiture remedy will be more exposed to the risk of being declared to be penal in nature where that exercise takes place after the defaulting party has made significant payments in respect of cashcalls or invoice requests already and the production of petroleum has commenced, in contrast to the situation where the default and the forfeiture occur at an early stage in the lifetime of the JOA relationship (such as prior to the full commencement of the exploration and appraisal phase and before the defaulting party has made any real investment into the value of its interests). Thus, in the OGUK JOA the provision for forfeiture of the defaulting party's interests is modified to the effect that the non-defaulting parties will pay some compensation to the defaulting party if the forfeiture occurs after the exploration and appraisal activities have concluded and a development plan has been approved.

This formulation does not sit easily with the principle expressed in *Dunlop Pneumatic* that the question of whether a provision amounts to a penalty must be judged at the time the contract was entered into, and not when the breach later occurred and the remedy was applied (and consequently the alleged penalty issue arose), and so is inaccurate. More recent law on how a penalty is to be construed (see above) could offer a different perspective on this, however.

THE RELATIONSHIP AND CHALLENGES BETWEEN A THIRD PARTY OPERATOR, THE JOINT OPERATING COMPANY AND JOA

Syed Marzidy SYED MARZUKI

1. OPERATORSHIP

The oil and gas business, particularly in relation to upstream activities, namely exploration, development and production, has always been regarded as high risk and high reward. The cost of exploration, development and production varies depending whether the activities take place onshore, offshore or in a deepwater region, or in an unconventional landscape, which can run into hundreds of million and even billions of dollars. In this context it is paramount that a capable operator with strong technical expertise, knowledge, experience and financial standing is chosen to undertake the petroleum operations of any such ventures. The operator is expected to ensure that upon the signing of the production sharing contract (PSC), concession or licence with the host government(s), the obligations to achieve certain milestones, such as the minimum work obligations, are fulfilled within an agreed time frame. In addition, it is incumbent upon the operator who acts on behalf of the other joint venture parties ('all of them are regarded as Contractor by the host authorities') to carry out the petroleum operations in a safe, environmentally friendly manner and to comply with the international health and safety standards regarding operations. Thus the operator has a fiduciary duty to perform as the lead partner in the joint venture within the contractual and legal framework of the host country.

There are a few ways that petroleum operations can be managed. It is common for the party who has the highest participating interest in a joint venture to become the operator of the oil and gas block. As mentioned earlier, the main criterion is that the operator is an entity that has good financial standing or backing, knowledge and experience and is technically sound. Unless an entity has the experience and knowledge, the entity may not be able to meet the requirements of a PSC. This will not only jeopardise the venture but may attract penalties and even termination of the PSC by the host authorities. The further consequence is that it will erode shareholders value by attracting close scrutiny by the market analysts and worst if it fails audit exercises by auditors and the host authorities.

Thus in a 40:30:20:10 joint venture, the party that has the 40% share will tend to become the operator. So long as such a party fulfils the criteria, it is natural to expect that it will lead the joint venture as the operator as it will contribute the most funds and would require that its investment is well managed. Therefore it is understandable that that party would like to safeguard their interests in the quest of exploring the hydrocarbons and the development and production if there is commercially viable discovery.

In the current low oil price climate, it is in the company's interest to maintain low operations costs and minimise general and administration expenditures. An imprudent operator may operate in a fashion where their general and administrative expenditure is high due to providing lucrative compensation and fringe benefit packages to their employees, thus increasing the costs of operations. This may not be desired by other non-operators. Furthermore, there is a likelihood that such costs will be subject to the scrutiny of the host authorities and may not be recoverable if they are rejected for cost recovery purposes under a production sharing contract regime. In this situation, even the non-operator is affected as they will have to share additional costs with the operator without receiving reimbursement from cost recovery. Such an amount will escalate if left unchecked over the next 20 or 25 years life of the PSC. This is not healthy for the joint venture. There have been cases where the non-operators questioned the validity of lavish packages given to the operator's employees, including huge bonuses, and this ultimately led to arbitration as the matter could not be resolved amicably.

There are certain instances where a minority partner is appointed as an operator. In this instance the majority partner may have the money to invest but lack the skills and expertise. Some regulators may also 'require' their national oil company to be allowed to run the operation, with the result that the other majority partners have little choice but to accept such an arrangement. This type of arrangement is rarely implemented, as more often than not no majority partners will want to take this risk unless the national oil company has a proven track record or is known to have the expertise. An acceptable compromise is to have a joint operating company (JOC) that consists of members of all the partners.

In a joint venture the operator will be supervised by the non-operators through the establishment of an operating committee. The lead company that becomes the operator owes a fiduciary obligation towards the non-operators in fulfilling the contractual obligations under the PSC.

2. TYPES OF OPERATORSHIP

2.1. THIRD PARTY OPERATOR

If a third party meets the criteria to be an operator – and there indeed currently oil and gas service providers that have the resources, technology and expertise to undertake petroleum operations – it is possible to outsource the petroleum operations to that third party. Under this arrangement the third party may be paid a fee, or even a combination of a fee and success fee (where if they successfully attain or exceed a certain production level they are given an additional bonus payment). In certain instances the commercial arrangement may even include a petroleum sharing formula in order to incentivise the third party operator to manage the operations well and in the most cost-effective way as their remuneration or service fees hinges upon the best execution of the development and production activities.

The arrangement with a third party operator can be any type of commercial arrangement. However, this arrangement should not be confined to a purely commercial arrangement as it is essential to also agree on the risk and liabilities of a third party operator. As it is, the host authority grants the hydrocarbon rights to the joint venture parties and, as far as the PSC instrument is concerned, the joint venture parties are still regarded as the contractor appointed to undertake the oil and gas activities, typically under the joint and several liability principle. Thus the host authorities will still expect the joint venture parties to continue to be accountable to them as regards the management of issues in relation to the operations.

The joint venture parties should also place a greater emphasis on the strict compliance with health, safety and environmental-related matters in ensuring safe operations that meet international standards. In this context, more often than not a third party operator will negotiate for a capping of their liability. Whilst it is understandable that they are operating for the joint venture and thus should not be overly exposed, they need to recognise that a capping of liability cannot be sustained if there is gross negligence on their part. Furthermore, as was seen in the infamous Macondo incident involving the Deepwater Horizon Rig in 2009 in the Gulf of Mexico, the exposure to the operator and joint venture partners in terms of damages and penalties is enormous.

2.2. JOINT OPERATING COMPANIES AS OPERATORS

It is also common for joint venture parties to set up an incorporated entity or a special purpose vehicle (SPV) to carry out exploration and development activities. There are many reasons to set up such an entity, such as to learn from each other where, for example, one is an expert in deepwater exploration and development whereas the other is an expert in shallow water or onshore exploration and development or unconventional oil and gas exploitation. In many instances it is a requirement of the oil and gas framework of the host countries to form such an incorporated entity in order to develop the local national oil company (NOC), local talent and local expertise. In other instances such joint ventures may be set up for the sake of tax advantages. However the organisation of such an incorporated entity and its terms of reference and management may differ from country to country due to the requirements or influence of the legislative framework of each country.

A JOC that includes a NOC may have certain peculiarities pertaining to the participating interest, voting, cost recovery, management, localisation and procurement. Challenges on localisation will be pertaining to the local workforce expertise, acceptance and the requirements of local laws.[1]

The participating interest of an NOC sometimes depends on the country's laws and the aspirations of the government.

1 See S.M. Syed Marzuki, 'The Dynamism of the Joint Operating Agreement' (2013) 4 *OGEL*.

2.2.1. *Africa*

In certain African countries such as Sudan there is a requirement to set up a JOC upon the signing of PSC. In certain instances the host authorities may permit the usage of an existing JOC if for example parties who have signed the new PSC mainly comprise the same parties operating an existing JOC. In this way the parties to both oil blocks are able to optimise their resources and costs and expedite the petroleum operations in the new oil block. Under this model the JOC is entrusted to run the operation to achieve the objective of the PSC. There will be a shareholders' agreement that governs such joint venture parties relationship, including the appointment of office bearers such as the president and management committee, the frequency of board meetings, voting, and so on. Normally the larger shareholder will be given the task of leading the company following a similar principle to that discussed earlier, and he will be assisted by heads of departments of development and production, legal, human resources, information technology, finance, and so on. There will also be an NOC representative who will become the deputy general manager or vice-president, as well as other secondees who will occupy other positions as agreed during the negotiation of the shareholders' agreement. The division of the positions among the joint venture parties is dependent on their participating interests, expertise and technical know-how.

The JOC will typically be run like any other normal company, being subject to the local laws and the law of the company's domicile. But the striking difference is that its finances are based on cash calls and not on shareholder funds. Therefore the authorised and paid up capital will be minimal as the company's activities are funded by monthly or quarterly cash calls to the joint venture parties. Invariably, this mode of managing a company is governed by the terms of the JOA. In this context, rather than having a company which is a subsidiary of the main contributor, an SPV is set up and run based on the terms of the JOA. For the sake of compliance it will also be subject to the minimum requirements of the jurisdiction where the company is domiciled.

2.2.2. *Middle East*

In certain Middle Eastern countries there is also a requirement that an SPV be formed. For example in Egypt, during the exploration stage and from the signing of the exploration agreement, the contractor is normally allowed to manage and lead the operations. However, if there is commercial discovery the contractor will have to obtain a development or exploitation production sharing agreement. At this stage it is a requirement, although there maybe exceptions, that the running of the company or SPV be handed over to the host authorities. The management positions of the SPV during development and production will normally be held by individuals linked with the government or the regulator, although exceptions to this rule can be made. The president and the various key positions will be held by persons nominated and appointed by the Regulator.

2.2.3. Latin America

Venezuela used to use a concession system in awarding an oil block, until it introduced a hybrid PSC regime. The current regime is a hybrid as there is a requirement under the country's hydrocarbon laws that for an oil PSC the government exploration and production arm, i.e. Petroleos de Venezuela SA (PDVSA), must hold a 60% share of the participating interest. The other companies who partner PDVSA, and form part of the consortium in the joint ventures can only own the remaining 40%. Under a typical contractual arrangement in other countries, each party will bear their own share of the cost of development of the oil field. In Venezuela, however, it is usual for the parties that hold the remaining 40% share of the participating interests in the PSC to bear the cost of the exploration and development. In addition, if financing is needed to be able to exploit the hydrocarbon reserves, the other companies in the venture are required to bear the entirety of the risk, including the obligation and the liabilities. Furthermore, the procurement guidelines are stringent, as not only is the SPV required to adhere to the government procurement guidelines, but payment to service providers must also be made in conformity with strict procedures that include obtaining government approval.

2.2.4. South East Asia

In Vietnam, for example, the JOCs are 'created' upon the signing of the PSC. The PSC, JOA, accounting procedures and JOC charter are signed together and form part of the PSC. These JOCs must get investment licences from the Ministry of Investment and Trade ('Ministry') before they can operate – in fact, the PSC itself must be approved by the Ministry. If a party wishes to leave the venture or transfer its assets, it has to get approval from the Ministry before the transfer can be effected.

In Indonesia, however, the requirement to set up a JOC is prescribed under the legislative framework instead of the PSC. No one company is allowed to hold two PSCs. As such, investors are required to incorporate an SPV or set up a separate company to participate in and operate each block.

In Malaysia the PSC requires the companies to either be incorporated in Malaysia or have a branch office in Malaysia. The finalisation and signing of the JOA between joint venture parties are required prior to the signing of the PSC. This will eliminate the prolonged negotiation of a JOA and demonstrate to the regulator that the joint venture parties are able to work together. The appointment of an operator is provided for in the PSC. Sometimes the forms of such operatorship can be joint operatorship or establishment of a consortium that sets up an SPV.

2.2.5. *Canada*

It is quite typical for a company which is involved in an oil and gas exploration to set up an SPV where the shareholders are comprised of a holding company and a limited partnership type of company, to become the operator of their licences. This mode of operation is preferred due to the deferred tax advantage which is permissible for this kind of set-up under the Canadian legislative framework. Under this set-up most employees will be housed under the SPV. Only a handful will be in the holding company.

Under the set-up of an SPV to form a JOC in all the above jurisdictions in the Middle East, Africa, Latin America or even South East Asia, it is essential that the secondees of each respective company work together for the common good of meeting the objective of the PSC. A high degree of compliance with the provisions of the JOA is needed to avoid squabbles. However, this set-up has its own inherent challenges. Parties to this type of joint venture must also be aligned in terms of having a global procurement strategy by bringing the relevant expertise to optimise their costs. It is also vital to send secondees with the right experience to manage the petroleum operations and not treat the joint venture solely as a training ground for employees.

We must bear in mind that the oil and gas landscape differs from continent to continent, country to country and government to government. Therefore, it is essential that a company takes this into consideration in striking a balance between risk and reward and makes cost/benefit analysis to determine whether a particular operating model is acceptable.

3. JOINT OPERATING AGREEMENT

3.1. INTRODUCTION

The JOA perhaps can be regarded as one of the key documents after the award of a PSC, concession or licence, as it is a contractual arrangement that governs the relationship between parties in an incorporated or unincorporated oil and gas joint venture. The JOA prescribes the rights, obligations, means of sharing risk and liabilities, procurement, budgeting and the mechanics of how the joint venture will be managed by the lead party who is appointed as the operator of the oil and gas block. It is usually immediately executed by the joint venture parties after the award of an oil and gas contract – whether a PSC, a concession or a licence – by the host authorities. The JOA, as is well known in the oil and gas industry, has evolved over many decades and its general features cover both offshore and onshore exploration and production activities. The aim of this chapter is to highlight the different aspects of the JOA in managing the rights and obligations, sharing of risk, liabilities and rewards, and how it is implemented in certain parts of the world.

3.2. FUNCTIONS OF A JOA

The JOA serves several functions, governing, for example, the rights and liabilities of the joint venture parties, proportionate investment sharing, sole risk ventures, default, transfers, the mode of operation, budgeting and approvals of activities, and the accounting procedure. As oil and gas ventures require capital-intensive investment, and as participating interests of each joint venture parties may differ, it is paramount that parties to a joint venture agree on the terms of the JOA that will ensure the smooth running of an operation and minimise their exposure in terms of expenditure and liabilities.

The advantage of a JOA is that it may exist and be enforced even if a party is not a shareholder of the company (which can be an SPV) that operates the oil block as it may take the form in an unincorporated or incorporated joint venture. It is typical for the company that operates the block to be a subsidiary of an established oil and gas company or a new company set up to house all the new joint venture parties if the block is to be operated jointly. This model is common in countries where the aspiration of the government is to develop a local NOC and cultivate the skills and expertise of local manpower, such as in Sudan, Egypt, Vietnam, Venezuela and Malaysia.

Another important distinction that needs to be made is that the way a JOC operates under a PSC and JOA framework is not similar to the running of a typical company. This is because the JOC is not typically funded by the injection of funding from shareholders in the form of a payment of paid-up capital, but rather it manages its activities by making cash calls to the respective joint venture parties for funds.

4. OPERATING COMMITTEE VERSUS THE BOARD

It is interesting to note the different practices adopted by JOCs set up under the various jurisdictions around the world. The striking difference is that in a typical company set-up the board of the company will be the decision maker in the majority of important decisions, whereas the management of the company will be in charge of the day-to-day operations and making decisions based on the limits of authorities granted to them by the board. However a JOC set up under the guise of a shareholders agreement which is preceded by a JOA to conduct petroleum operations may have a different mode of operations.

As mentioned earlier the typical JOA consists of an arrangement that demarcates the risks and liabilities of the various partners or parties to the agreement based on the participation interest/equity in the PSC. Normally similar proportions of risks and liabilities are allocated to the same partners or parties in the JOCs. Under this set up it is expected that parties to the JOA will have their rights, risks and liabilities in the same proportion as in the JOC.

Although the board continues to be the highest decision-making body of the JOC, there are specific matters where the operating committee has the power to decide, as the funding of the JOC and the operations is contributed by the joint venture parties based on the decision of the operating committee. As illustrated by the figure below, we might expect that the board of the JOC would be the highest body, but in actual fact the existence of the JOA and operating committee mean that the operating committee under the JOA is the body that decides on or approves certain matters for the purposes of carrying out the obligations under the PSCs, including the budget, drilling of exploration wells, undertaking development activities upon commercial discovery, and production.

Figure 1. The set up of a joint operating company

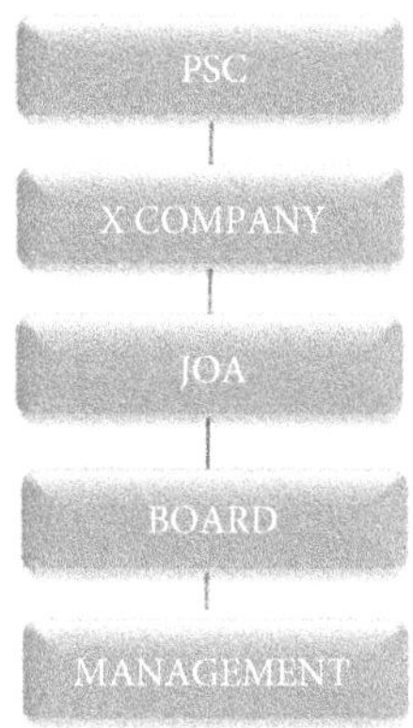

Figure 1 shows that the operating committee set up under the JOA is 'higher' than the board. This shows that the decisions made at the operating committee level should be respected and regarded as final by the board members of the JOC. This does not mean that the board members of the JOC are 'permitted to abdicate' their fiduciary duties as the decisions at the operating committee level only cover certain significant items such as the budget, exploration and development plan, and perhaps a few others. Operational matters such as the execution of the exploration and development programme or activities still fall within the responsibility of the board.

Figure 2. Common misconception of the power of the board within a JOA set up

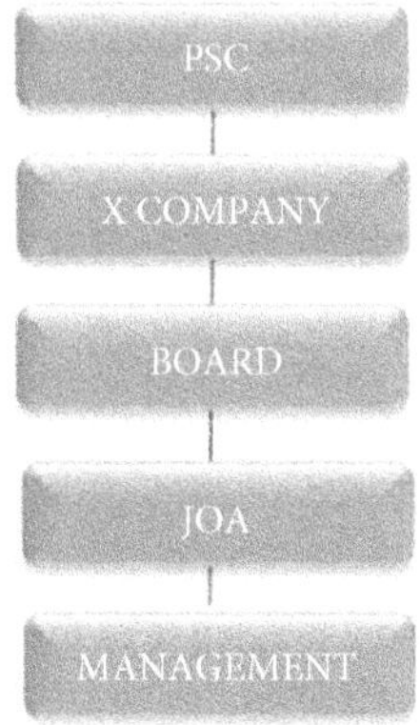

Figure 2 shows the common board hierarchy under the company that is executing the petroleum operations. Although normal companies in many other industries are managed in this way, where the board acts as the ultimate authority in key decision making, it is different under a JOA or JOA set up. Certain parties were of the opinion that even though there is an operating committee that made decisions on the petroleum operations and activities there is avenue for the board members to deviate from the decision or to make a different decision or even reject the operating committee's decision. Although it is true that the board has a fiduciary duty, in reality its oversight role, power and authority to give direction to the company is subjected to the oil and gas joint venture arrangement described by figure 1 above. In short the operating committee's decision takes precedence over the board and should prevail.

5. COMPOSITION OF BOARD MEMBERS

The composition of board members in the SPV or joint venture company normally depends on the participating interest of the parties in the venture, which can be seen in operations in Malaysia, Sudan, Vietnam and Indonesia. However, in certain jurisdictions the legislative framework dictates that the composition of the board members and to a certain extent the members of the management team are comprised of members of the regulatory body. In Venezuela, for example, the hydrocarbon legislation specifies that the joint venture with the government national oil company must be of 60:40 proportion, thus dictating a 60:40 split between the government and the investor in the PSC. A similar proportion of participating interests split is also reflected in the JOA and the JOC. It further dictates that the members of the company's management will be appointed by the government. In this situation the investor's role is somewhat reduced to acting purely as a project manager: the investor only has rights as a minority and thus is unlikely to succeed in situations where voting is necessary under the joint shareholders agreement or where a management decision needs to be made which involves the areas of development, production, procurement, financing, human resources and a whole gamut of other matters that dominate operations.

It is possible to mitigate an investor's exposure to unfavourable decisions by limiting the areas of decision making; this is done by negotiating the areas or items to be unanimously approved by the joint venture parties. However, these areas or items may be limited to, for example, procurement, financing and HSE-related matters.

6. COST SHARING UNDER DIFFERENT PSCs

In Sudan, Vietnam or Indonesia, an investor or contractor may be required to either set up a new JOC for each new PSC or utilise an existing JOC to undertake a new obligation under a new PSC. This is normally done if that particular PSC consists of the same parties or, if not, the parties to the respective PSCs are agreeable to optimise or save costs by utilising the existing JOC to undertake the new tasks under the new PSC. Under this arrangement the parties to the PSCs are agreeable to sharing the costs of the operations, which is typically done or monitored through a cost allocation or time-based calculation made by the JOC.

7. CARRIED COSTS

In some instances the immediate costs of a project are not borne proportionately by all the participants. A non-operator may be required to advance money toward its share of the costs of a work programme before the operator has incurred the costs, or one or more parties may agree to pay the costs of some other participant who is to be 'carried'. The carried party may be the host country state oil company, or in the case of farm-out the farmee may agree to 'carry' the farmor. In all these situations, the payors anticipate that they will recoup their costs out of production but recognise that they bear the risk of unprofitable operations.

In less developed or developing countries it is understandable that some governments aspire to establish their own NOC. In furtherance of this aim, the government will dictate that the NOC must be involved in the joint venture. In certain instances the NOC may be willing to pay its share of exploration costs and hence bear the risks. However, in many instances the NOC may be a party to the venture on a carried basis. This means that the investor parties will undertake to pay the NOC's portion of the costs and recover it later in a formula that is normally agreed during the negotiation of the PSC. In certain other instances the government or NOC may opt to exercise their back-in right if there is a commercial discovery. Under these models the NOC does not take or mitigate its upfront risks. This particular matter and the formula for recovering the costs are negotiated during the negotiation of the PSC.

Under this model it also is normal to negotiate the voting rights, as a party that does not pay – even an NOC – will not normally be allowed to decide on critical matters if they are not taking any risks associated with the result of the vote.

8. DEFAULT

In any joint venture there is a risk of default by a member of the joint venture. The JOA normally prescribed the mode of issuing notices to the defaulting party as a reminder about the effect and consequence of such a default. As default is regarded as a serious omission by a joint venture party it is vital that the JOA specifically prescribes how it is to be managed, whether by the non-defaulting party or by the operator. In a default situation it is essential that a strict procedure is adhered to as the consequences include forfeiture of the interest of the defaulting party in a JOA and PSC. A less efficient operator may not act as swiftly as it should. But from a practical standpoint it is the operator who has the information and 'resources' to strictly enforce the terms of the JOA against the defaulting party. A defaulting party may lose its right to obtain data, information, voting and so on until and unless it settles the defaulted amount within the prescribed time. If it continues to default it will stand to lose even the right to attend meetings and exercise its right to vote on matters that require voting under the JOA or even its participating interest in the PSC.

As forfeiture is the ultimate penalty against a defaulter, it is essential that parties agree at the outset on the mode of forfeiting in order for such consequence to be effective. A possible mode is for parties to grant a power of attorney in advance and upon the default by a party, the non-defaulting party or operator exercises the power of attorney that permits the execution of the instrument of transfer that transfer or forfeits the defaulting party's participating interests. In order to maintain the integrity of such an arrangement the power of attorney and instrument of transfer has to rest with a neutral party such as an external legal firm. If the foregoing method is not applied, it is doubtful whether the forfeiture can be implemented smoothly. The defaulter may resist the forfeiture to the extent that the non-defaulter may need to initiate litigation in order to enforce their contractual rights.

Although forfeiture seems to be the ultimate remedy, it is possible that not all non-defaulters will wish to enforce it. This depends on the stage of the petroleum operations. If the operations are still at exploration stage and the drilling of the first few wells proves to be unsuccessful, the non-defaulter may not be interested in increasing their participating interest in the venture as they will have to incur additional costs of further exploration. Similarly, development costs may increase substantially to the extent that a party may not have the financial standing to continue their participation. Even if the default occurs at the production stage, but the production costs are higher than the revenue or gain, the non-defaulter may still be reluctant to assume the participating interest of the defaulting party because it is not beneficial and could become a liability in the near future. In these circumstances it is possible to exit the joint venture by assigning or farming out to a willing party subject to the procedure governed by the JOA and if applicable, PSC.

9. DISPUTES AND LITIGATION

In carrying out its functions, the operator or the JOC owes a fiduciary duty to other joint venture parties. In the event of litigation, the rights and liabilities of the joint venture parties are normally joint and several. The parties essentially divide their rights and liabilities pro rata based on their respective participating interests. In a normal situation, all joint venture parties will litigate against a third party litigant. However, if the litigant is related to one of the joint venture parties, such as its affiliate, or, in the case of an NOC, if the litigant is even the government, there will be a conflict of interest where the conflicted party is expected to exclude itself from any strategic discussion and litigation. It is essential that the arbitration clause provides an alternative in situations where it is necessary to start proceedings against, for example, a related party or the government without obtaining the agreement of the conflicted party. The related party or NOC is not expected to join the rest of the joint venture parties to litigate against the related party or the government.

10. BUDGET

Each year the operator will table the annual work programme and budget for the approval of the parties to the joint venture, including the non-operator, at the operating committee meeting. The budget, which is prepared yearly with a forecast for the coming three or four years, will provide an overview of the activities that the operator intends to carry out in order to fulfil the minimum work obligations under the PSC, such as seismic acquisition, drilling of an exploration well, implementing the development project, and production. It is normal for the operator to have a detailed review and discussion with the non-operator at the sub-committee level prior to the tabling of the annual budget. The value of the budget required differs as it depends on whether the petroleum operations are at the exploration, development or production stage. Controlling expenditure is one of the ways that an operator can be supervised by the non-operator. It will be ideal if every joint venture parties approve the budget. In the event that there is a disagreement on the approval of the budget, it will be subject to a vote. Disagreements commonly stem from the number of optional exploration wells, the mode of development, or the operating expenditures, particularly if the latter involve the operator's head office expenditure. In the case of a PSC, unlike in a licence regime, the parties must come to a consensus on the annual work programme and budget as these must be approved by the host authority's regulator.

In the event that the necessary threshold of the budget is not met, it is possible in the interim to agree that the operator will carry out activities on a certain budget, such as the previous year's quantum or at most with an increase of, say, 10%, so that the 'non-approval' does not hinder the progress of certain exploration activities and in order to fulfil the obligations under the PSC. When the annual budget is approved, the actual capital and operating expenditure is subject to certain procedures laid down in the JOA and accounting procedure. Certain line items or types of expenditure in relation to exploration and development which exceed certain thresholds may be subjected to an 'approve for expenditure' process. This is to ensure that the particular line item expenditure is within the budgeted amount. In order not to impede the petroleum activities, parties normally allow the procurement of such line items if the cost only exceeds the threshold by 5% or 10%, depending on the overall value of the line items.

11. SOLE RISKS[2]

In the event that the parties cannot reach a consensus on, for example, the exploration programme, i.e. the number of wells to be drilled, their depth and location, the JOA provides for any party and/or the operator to commence sole risk petroleum operations themselves. Any party who does not participate in these operations need not contribute their share of the costs. However, if there is a discovery and the non-participating party thus wishes to participate at a later stage, there is premium that needs to be paid, which can be double or triple the costs incurred because it also acts as a form of penalty to be paid to those who had taken the risks. The common issue that is faced by the parties to a joint venture is determining which option should prevail when the operator wishes to undertake petroleum operations that are different from the operations the non-operator wishes to undertake, such as to deepen an oil well or not, or whether to side track the drilling of an oil well and others. Related to this issue is the

[2] See the Association of International Petroleum Negotiators (AIPN) Model JOA for further information on all matters related to the JOA.

conduct of the petroleum operations should the non-operator insist on carrying out exploration at its chosen drilling site contrary to the operator's choice. Thus the question of who should conduct the exploration drilling for the non-operators can become a thorny issue. This is the tension that may occur that 'motivates' parties to resolve their disagreement amicably. Furthermore, if the oil block is being managed by a JOC, the secondees may be 'fighting' each other in terms of whose interests they should be protecting. In the event that a sole risk operation is undertaken, the procedure of giving the appropriate notices and voting should be followed and recorded to avoid any challenge against the sole risk operations.

12. CONCLUSION

From the above it is quite apparent that oil and gas companies face many challenges in carrying out petroleum operations, as the legislative framework that governs petroleum operations differs from one country to another. In countries where an investor has more than one PSC, and in order to manage an effective and cost-effective operation, it is paramount to always consider using a lead joint venture company or SPV to undertake combined joint operations. This is beneficial not only to the company concerned but also to the host authorities. The cost of operations will be lower and the gains will be higher. However, it is essential to maintain a very good relationship between joint venture parties in order to avoid disagreements that can be costly for the petroleum operations. If all parties work towards a common goal, the differences can be resolved amicably no matter what structure of operations is adopted.

ACCOUNTING PROCEDURE

Can the Operator Make a Profit? How Can a Non-Operator Control the Costs of the Consortium?

Syed Marzidy SYED MARZUKI

1. INTRODUCTION

The accounting procedure is an integral part of a JOA. It provides for the types and categories of expenditure that can be charged to the joint account in the course of carrying out the petroleum operations. It mainly covers the management of billing facilitation of cash calls to the joint venture partners for the payment of costs and expenditures incurred during the prior month, indicating by appropriate classification the nature, the budget category and the apportionment of such costs to each party. It will specify that the accounting treatment will be based on an accrual basis whereby the costs incurred in the current or prior month shall be paid within a certain period (typically thirty days from the date of billing). It will also define the way in which the operator will charge the non-operator, the general and administrative costs that include overheads borne by the operator and possibly its parent company. These are the areas that will be the subject of discussion of this chapter.

2. FUNDAMENTAL PRINCIPLE[1]

In a typical oil and gas joint venture parties will choose one of the parties to become the operator that will carry out the petroleum operations in accordance with the terms and requirements of the production sharing contract, concession or licence. In carrying out the petroleum operations the party that has been chosen as the operator will adhere to the terms and conditions of the JOA and the mode of charging the non-operator based on the agreed accounting procedure.

The fundamental principle is that in carrying out the petroleum operations the operator shall neither make a gain nor suffer a loss by reason of the fact that it acts as the operator. In consideration of this principle parties will mutually agree that in the event that any of the charging methods are proven unfair or inequitable to the parties, the parties will normally meet in good faith and agree on changes in methods deemed necessary to rectify any unfairness or inequity. The accounting procedure will typically provide that there shall be no duplications of charges or revenues in the accounts under the JOA. Further, in the event of a conflict between the provisions of the accounting procedure and the provisions of the JOA, the JOA provisions shall prevail.

1 The reader may wish to refer to the Association of International Petroleum Negotiators (AIPN) Accounting Procedures 2012 Model for examples and further information.

3. EXCLUSIVE OPERATIONS OR SOLE RISK

In the event that the operator or any of the joint venture parties embarks on an exclusive operation (sometimes known as a sole risk operation), the accounting procedure shall apply *mutatis mutandis* in the same manner that it applies to joint operations, provided, however, that revenues, costs and expenditures applicable to the consenting parties shall be distinguished by exclusive operations account.

4. GENERAL PRINCIPLE OF MAINTAINING ACCOUNTING RECORDS

Whenever parties enter into a JOA it is worthwhile thoroughly negotiating the accounting procedure. Parties should agree that the operator shall maintain all accounts and records in accordance with generally accepted and recognised international accounting principles consistent with petroleum industry practices.

This is necessary as each party is responsible for maintaining its own records in order to conform to accounting, tax, legal and other statutory requirements to support all fiscal returns or any other accounting reports required by any governmental authority with regards to the operations.

In all or most instances, the accrual basis of accounting is used in preparing the joint accounts. This means the costs shall be recorded and entered in the joint account when the liability thereto first arises, and revenues shall be recorded and entered in the joint account when the title thereto is acquired.

However, for the purpose of cost recovery as per the contract, the relevant calculations shall be based on cash basis, that is, cost shall be considered only when paid and revenues only when collected.

5. CHARGEABLE EXPENDITURES

There are two types of expenditures that the operator will charge the non-operator. First are the direct charges, which include items such as salaries, wages, material, transportations, licences, permits, employee benefits, royalties, taxes, legal expenses, insurance, third party services, operator's equipment, and decommissioning. Second are the indirect charges, which include the cost of general assistance and support services provided by the operator and its affiliated companies.

6. DIRECT CHARGES

The operator will charge all the costs and expenditures incurred in connection with the joint petroleum operations in accordance with the work programme and budget approved by the parties to the joint account. Although the overall budget has been approved, the non-operator can still control the expenditures by exercising its right in approving items that is required to be approved via the approved for expenditures (AFE) process. In short, the non-operator reserves its right to 'supervise' and sanction exploration and development works that are relevant and directly associated with the agreed petroleum operations and consistent with the work programme and budget. In these circumstances, the operator in certain instances where the expenditure exceeds the threshold may require the non-operator's AFE approval even though the work programme and budget has been approved. If the expenditure threshold is not met then the operator is only required to inform the non-operator. The non-operator should be particular about matters pertaining to employees' salaries, fringe benefits and retirement benefits, as if left unchecked, it may include the operator's employment terms, which at times are beyond the 'acceptable' industry norm/ level.

6.1. LICENCES, PERMITS, ETC.

This type of direct charge pertains to the acquisition, maintenance, renewal or relinquishment of licences, permits, surface rights acquired for joint operations. Such charges are normally acceptable as they are expenditures required by the host authorities, legislative or contractual framework.

6.2. SALARIES, WAGES AND RELATED COSTS

Any party that is chosen as an operator will have its own base or fixed costs, which include salaries, wages, bonuses, vacation, holiday, benefits, sickness, travel time, living and housing allowances, and other related costs. These are among the items that are negotiated by joint venture parties. Although the non-operator understands that the costs that the operator would like to charge is similar to what it incurs, the scope and overall costs must be reasonable. This is also to avoid elements of overcharging and profiteering by charging the non-operator the so-called costs incurred by the operator. For example the non-operator may agree to the payment of bonuses so long as they are not extravagant, for example 12 or 24 month bonuses. In certain instances the operator may attempt to charge retirement bonuses that date from the time its staff join the operator's organisation, which may be long before the start of joint operation. This kind of situation may cause a rift between the joint venture parties and if not resolved amicably can lead to arbitration or litigation.

In addition, if not controlled, items such as housing benefits may even include services such as provisions of maids, drivers and gardeners, which may be acceptable in certain locations, but may not be necessary in other locations.

Although the operator's staff should be accorded comfortable working and living conditions, it is essential that the general and administrative costs are kept to a minimum and if possible optimised, not only so that such expenditures can be recovered, but also to avoid value leakage in terms of unproductive costs.

6.3. OFFICES, CAMPS AND MISCELLANEOUS FACILITIES

Invariably the setting up of a new company or a branch office will require an office space and address in order to fulfil the requirement of the production sharing contract and the host country's company law. In certain instances where the operator has a large operation in a particular country and perhaps has its own head office, it is only 'logical' for the company that becomes the operator of a newly acquired oil and gas block to have its own head office, camps or warehouse premises. In this situation the parties need to ensure that the rent for this space is within the market rate and is not inflated. In addition to that, the charges for the common area should be proportionately divided between other affiliates of the operator if they are renting the same buildings or premises. A proper negotiation of such rent will minimise the operational expenditure and qualify for cost recovery so long as it is seen as reasonable.

6.4. OWNED EQUIPMENT AND FACILITIES OF AFFILIATED COMPANIES

As with renting the operator's affiliates' office space, the new venture of the new block may permit the operator to use the operator's affiliates' equipment and facilities. The non-operator may control expenditure on this item by ensuring that the accounting procedure provides that the rates must not exceed the average commercial rates available. In addition, the non-operator may require the operator to furnish the list of rates and the basis of application, taking into account depreciation, which allows the downwards revision of the rates if the space continues to be used for joint operations.

6.5. SERVICES

If there are services provided by third parties, including the affiliated companies of the respective parties to the joint venture, charges for services by the affiliated companies of the respective parties normally cannot exceed those that would be charged by non-affiliated third parties. This provides some measure of control to ensure that the charges imposed are not exorbitant.

The cost of services performed by the operator's affiliated companies' technical and professional staff not located within the country of operations will normally cover salaries and wages of such technical and professional personnel, fringe benefits, and reasonable expenses, including support costs necessary for personnel to perform such services, such as rent, utilities, communication expenses, computer support and so on.

In order to have an oversight of these charges the non-operator will require the operator to provide proof that these costs or charges are properly allocated and do not get mixed up with other petroleum operations of the operator's affiliates.

In addition the cost of services performed by the operator's affiliated companies' professional and administrative staff located within the country of operations which the operation may use in lieu of having its own staff is normally charged on the basis of a timesheet.

6.6. INSURANCE

In the event that there is a mishap such as flood, theft, storm, fire or accident that damages joint property and that property is insured, all the joint venture parties shall receive the settlement sums received from insurance carried for the benefit of the joint operations for such loss or damage to joint property or materials.

6.7. LITIGATION

Litigation is one of the areas that, if not properly managed, may cause value leakage. Cases that involve multiple and substantial claims, for example in relation to construction during the development phase, require close monitoring and specialised skills. Therefore, it is essential that the parties to the joint venture mutually agreed on the best way to manage such a case in the event the operator lacks that skill. An experienced and knowledgeable joint venture party or non-operator should be chosen to monitor the case in addition to appointing a legal firm that has construction and arbitration expertise. Otherwise, there is the potential that the joint venture may lose an otherwise strong case that they can win, and/or that they may incur significant legal fees. In this respect, if one of the legal staff of one of the parties to the joint venture is chosen to manage the case, a charge commensurate with the reasonable costs of providing and furnishing such services rendered may be made by the party providing the service to the operator for the joint account, but no such charges shall be made until approved by all the parties.

7. INDIRECT CHARGES

There are certain types of services provided by the operator's ultimate parent company that will support the operator in carrying out the petroleum operations, such as meeting administrative overheads. The operator will normally charge the joint account monthly for the cost of indirect services and related office costs of the operator and its affiliated companies unless otherwise specified in the accounting procedure. Indirect costs chargeable represent the cost of general assistance and support services provided by the operator and its Affiliated Companies.

These are costs that it is not practical to identify or associate with specific projects, but are rather for services which provide the joint operations with the necessary resources that the operator requires and which provide a real benefit to the joint operations. These costs and/or expenditures are not subject to audit other than to verify that the overhead percentages are applied correctly according to the reasons the expenditure was made.

The accounting procedure will typically provide that the administrative overhead shall be 2% or 3% of the exploration expenditure, whereas during development and production the administrative overhead is charged at 1.5% or perhaps more.

These charges are subject to negotiation during the finalisation of the JOA and accounting procedure. In some instances the administrative overhead for exploration, development and production is charged at a flat fee of, for example, 2%. In some other instances the charge is subject to negotiation after a period of time if parties find it to be insufficient or excessive.

8. WAYS TO CONTROL EXPENDITURE

Based on the foregoing it is apparent that there are various types of charges and various ways of charging them to the non-operator. Therefore it is incumbent upon the non-operator to first negotiate the types of direct or indirect charges applicable to the joint operations. Furthermore, the non-operator should carefully scrutinise the provisions in the JOA and accounting procedure that will provide the checks and balances sufficient to prevent unnecessary leakage or profiteering, whether directly or indirectly.

8.1. CONTROLLING EXPENDITURE

First the non-operator should be involved in the formulation of the annual work programme and budget, which provides an overview of the proposed activities. This can be achieved by setting up a work programme and budget sub-committee where the non-operator can participate and provide the necessary input on the planned joint operations.

Secondly the non-operator should insist that expenditures that exceed certain thresholds require the non-operator's firm approval for the authorised for expenditure (AFE) items, services or activities before the operator can proceed with the procurement or operation. It is worth noting that there are various categories of AFE. For example, where the cost of the line item is below a certain threshold it is meant for information only, but where the cost of the line item exceeds the threshold then the non-operator's approval is required before purchase.

Thirdly the billings and cash calls are based on an approved work programme and budget and the approved AFE. In instances where there is overpayment, the non-operator can ask for a refund. Normally, the cash is not allowed to be commingled with the operator's other accounts.

8.2. AUDIT

Typically the non-operator will have 24 or 36 months from the end of the calendar year where a statement is submitted for payment to undertake a financial audit of the operation carried out by the operator. If the non-operator fails to audit or challenge the statements, it is usually considered to have been accepted. If it is accepted, it is unlikely that the non-operator will succeed in challenging it, even by bringing legal proceedings, unless it can be shown that there is an element of fraud. The non-operator can carry out the audit independently by engaging a third party or conduct it itself. If more than one party is involved then the parties should conduct the audit jointly. This is necessary to minimise the disruption to the joint operations as the operator needs to allot time and manpower to assist the auditors. If one of the non-operators engages a third party, that non-operator must pay the auditing costs itself, unless the other parties agree to join them and bear the audit costs proportionately, excluding the operator if it decides not to participate.

Lastly, the parties can ask an external auditor to undertake an audit and certify that the operator has neither made any gain nor suffered any loss. This can be regarded as an assurance that the operator is not making any profit from the joint venture.

9. INVENTORIES

The operator is also required to maintain proper records of any stock of materials purchased in accordance with the usual procedures for controlling such materials, as each joint venture party records its portion of the inventories in their respective financial accounts. Thus if the operator incurs any expenses in relation to the periodic check of the inventories, it shall be charged to the joint account. To ensure proper records are being handled, the operator must inventories of all the stocks in the presence of the non-operator representatives. In the event the non-operator is not represented during the taking of the inventory, despite being given adequate notice, it then has to accept the inventory taken by the operator. If there are overages or shortages, it is incumbent upon the operator to make the necessary adjustments with proper explanation. If the adjustments exceed a certain threshold, for example $50,000, they must be approved by the management committee. As a form of control, the operator will be held accountable to the non-operator for shortages due to lack of reasonable diligence.

If at any time any portion of the joint property is categorised as junk and/or obsolete material for which there is no market, the operator is responsible for furnishing details of such material to the parties in order for an adjustment of their respective accounting records to be made, where applicable.

10. ACQUISITION AND DISPOSAL OF MATERIAL

In carrying out the petroleum operations the operator may need to purchase certain materials that will be charged to the joint account. The operator is expected to procure such materials at a competitive price from reputable manufacturers or suppliers. Usually the materials and equipment purchased will be charged at the net cost paid by the operator after deduction of all discounts received which may include but not be limited to insurance, transportation charges, import duties, licence fees and demurrage.

At the end of the petroleum operations, or at the end of the life of the materials or equipment, the operator may decide to dispose of them if they are no longer to be used. As an example, at the end of the exploration stage there may be a surplus of materials like drilling pipes or barite. In undertaking the disposal, and to ensure transparency, the operator is required to set up a disposal committee that will make an assessment regarding the mode of disposal and, if it includes selling, will determine the right reserve price so that joint venture parties will earn the best available price offered by potential bidders or buyers.

11. MARKETING RIGHTS AND FEES

In certain operations the operator may provide marketing services to the non-operator such as off-taking gas production to be distributed to the aggregator or to the market. In this instance it is incumbent upon the non-operator to negotiate the optimum marketing fees to be paid to the operator with adjustments right at the end of the year to cater for over- or underpayment. If need be, both parties should agree on the revision of the formula to pay the marketing fees depending on the gas price at that particular time.

12. CONCLUSION

The JOA and the accounting procedures are documents that will invariably be referred to by both the operator and the non-operator. It is fundamental for the operator to adhere strictly to the terms and conditions of the JOA and the accounting procedure to ensure that the joint operations are carried out in accordance with the mandate given to the operator. It is apparent from the foregoing discussion that there is little room for the operator to manoeuvre and make a profit out of being an operator if the provisions of the JOA and the accounting procedures are strictly followed. In summary the cash calls are made upon obtaining approval from the non-operator as to the kind of expenditures that need to be made. Even if there is an excess of cash calls the operator has the obligation to make a refund. In addition, the fund cannot be commingled with the operator's other funds, leaving no room to obtain interest for the operator's benefit only. Further, there is a provision on adjustments that allows the parties to discuss and reconcile the account so that the principle of just and equitable prevails. However, the parties also need to ensure that there is no unnecessary leakage or wastage during the petroleum operations by ensuring that the operator's general and administrative costs are optimised. In areas where the operator lacks expertise the non-operator should be inclined to offer its expertise to ensure that the petroleum operations can be conducted expeditiously.

The non-operator has ample time to check the veracity of the joint accounts by undertaking an audit, be it jointly or by engaging a third party. In this context the third party can be asked to confirm that the operator is making neither a loss nor a gain. It is crucial that the joint parties, especially non-operators, negotiate the most palatable JOA and accounting procedure terms at the outset to ensure that just terms are agreed for both direct and indirect charges. In conclusion, although it is possible for the operator to take advantage of the situation and 'profiteer', there is little room to do so if the non-operator has negotiated tight JOA and accounting procedure terms.

SENIOR SUPERVISOR, FINANCIAL CAP AND OTHER RESTRICTIONS ON THE OPERATOR'S LIABILITIES AND THEIR IMPLICATIONS

Leslie Weihua ZHANG

1. INTRODUCTION

The JOA entered into by the operator and non-operators always intends to manage the balance of the competing interests and obligations between all the participating parties to the joint petroleum operation. Historically, the oil and gas industry's perspective has been that operators should not be financially responsible to non-operators for the risk of conducting risky or significant operations unless the failure in such operation was caused by the gross negligence or wilful misconduct of the operator.[1] In general, it seems there is a consensus among petroleum industry players that a JOA should include an exculpatory

1 D.G. Mills, C.A. Wright and J.J.M. Inch, 'Exploring the balance of power in the operator/non-operator relationship under the CAPL operating procedure' (2010) 48(2) *Alberta Law Review* 369.

clause limiting the operator's liabilities, absent gross negligence or willful misconduct of the operator. The rationale for such notion is that the operator takes the risk in conducting the petroleum operation not for making any profit. Nevertheless, the 'no loss, no gain' principle that applies to the operator during the performance of its duties is now seemingly being challenged by a number of factors, including stricter penalties for environmental damage, more pressure to comply with regulation, and increasing numbers of stakeholders involved in the process. Properly allocating liabilities between the operator and non-operators is always the most difficult aspect of JOA negotiations. There are at least two reasons why negotiation of the operator's liabilities is so hard: firstly, all the participating parties understand that there are limited options for how liability/risk can be allocated between the operator and non-operators; secondly, the consequences of the allocation are so significant as to have the potential to lead to disastrously adverse damages.

As an in-house counsel often representing NOCs for JOA negotiations over the past ten years, the present author did not find the part of the process focusing on the negotiation of the operator's liabilities a pleasant experience. Especially in the post-Macondo world, it seems to be harder than ever to reach an agreement that is satisfactory to all the participants. Even before BP's oil spill accident in the Gulf of Mexico, it was not an easy task to negotiate a JOA if the participants were big oil companies. As an example, in the JOA agreed between BP, Anadarko and MOEX for Mississippi Canyon Block 252 in the Gulf of Mexico, the reader can see that 'gross negligence' or 'willful misconduct' was not defined in that agreement.[2] After the accident occurred, all the parties argued over whether BP's conduct in petroleum operations constituted gross negligence or wilful misconduct. Although the model JOA which the three parties adopted originated from AAPL Model Offshore Deepwater JOA (in which gross negligence and wilful misconduct are not defined!), I cannot say for certain why these sophisticated oil companies did not include those two definitions in their JOA – however, a possible explanation might be that all the parties could not agree on the specific definitions.

First, this chapter will analyse the relevant parts of the four most widely used model JOAs – those from AAPL, CAPL, OGUK and AIPN[3] – and will summarise the key concepts regarding senior supervisor personnel, the meaning of gross negligence and/or wilful misconduct, and the potential implications of using these phrases under international model JOAs. Then the chapter will further compare the limitation of the operator's liabilities under the international model

---

2 Another explanation might be the model contract all the parties used: unlike other model JOAs issued by some other international institutions, the AAPL Model Offshore Deepwater JOA, which the partners used in Mississippi Canyon Block 252, does not specifically define 'gross negligence' or 'willful misconduct'.

3 For convenience, in the following the AAPL, CAPL, OGUK and AIPN JOAs shall be collectively referred to 'international model JOAs'.

JOAs and provide a practical analysis on this element. Finally, this chapter will examine the possible impact of the phase one trial regarding BP's oil spill in the Gulf of Mexico and the potential influence this has had on the international model JOAs.

2. THE DEFINITIONS OF SENIOR SUPERVISORY PERSONNEL UNDER THE INTERNATIONAL MODEL JOAs

In clause 1.1 of the AIPN 2012 Model JOA, there are five alternatives under the definition of Senior Supervisor Personnel:

(1) Field Supervisor Tier;[4]
(2) Facility Manager Tier;[5]
(3) Functional Manager Tier;[6]
(4) Direct Report Tier;[7] and
(5) Resident Manager Tier.[8]

Previously in the AIPN 2002 Model JOA, there are four alternatives under the definition of Senior Supervisor Personnel.[9] The AIPN Model Contract Draft Committee did not mention the reason why one more alternative was added in the AIPN 2012 Model JOA. The reason may lie in the fact that it is a little bit harder for the negotiating parties (especially with equal negotiation power) to find a mid-point if there are only four alternatives. Five alternatives will be easier to reach a consensus in the event of a stand-off. In practice, the reader may find it somewhat troubling that a negotiation on the senior supervisor personnel usually ends up with the functional manager tier. Initially, the operator always starts from the resident manager tier in negotiating the definition of senior supervisor

4 '[S]uch individual who functions at a management level equivalent or superior to any individual functioning as senior onsite manager or supervisors ... in charge of *the conduct of seismic acquisition, drilling, construction or production...*'.

5 '[S]uch individual who functions at a management level equivalent or superior to any individual functioning as senior onsite manager or supervisors ... in charge of *an onshore or offshore installation or facility...*'.

6 '[S]uch individual who functions at a management level equivalent or superior to any individual functioning as senior manager(s) ... *sufficient to direct the manner in which such operations and activities are conducted...*'.

7 '[S]uch individual who functions at a management level equivalent or superior to any individual functioning as senior manager(s) *reporting directly to the country general manage*'.

8 '[S]uch individual who functions at a management level equivalent or superior to any individual functioning as *country general manager*.'

9 Field Supervisor Tier, Facility Manager Tier, Resident Manager, Direct Managerial Report Tier, and Resident Manager Tier.

personnel; conversely, the non-operators always start from the field supervisor tier. Eventually, the operator and non-operators generally compromise on the functional manager tier. The AIPN Model JOA has simultaneous advantages and disadvantages. On the one hand, it is very convenient for the parties participating in the JOA negotiations and expedites the negotiation process. On the other hand, the options in the AIPN Model JOA are very transparent to all participating parties. In this regard, a compromise is often made by the parties on the mid-point of all the options. The above-described scenario is a general description of the situation in real negotiations. It does not consider the negotiation power and business decision making of the parties during the JOA negotiation and should not be taken to be a one-size-fits-all conclusion.

The OGUK[10] Model JOA contains a similar definition of senior supervisor personnel, in this case called 'Senior Managerial Personnel',[11] to that in the AIPN 2012 Model JOA. There are two categories under the definition of senior managerial personnel in the OGUK Model JOA, one for such personnel from the operator, and the other from the non-operators. Unlike the AIPN 2012 Model JOA, the definition of senior managerial personnel in the OGUK Model JOA does not provide any detailed options. The model contract workgroup explains the reason for this as follows: there was a concern that it was unfair on smaller groups with a flatter management structure in that it might catch persons at a very senior level within the organisation, whereas in the case of a larger organisation with more delegated levels of authority, the definition might catch only the board of directors

10 Oil and Gas UK is the leading representative body for the UK offshore oil and gas industry. It is a not-for-profit organisation, established in April 2007 but with a history stretching back over forty years. See OGUK's official website: <http://www.oilandgasuk.co.uk/aboutus/aboutus.cfm>.

11 Definition of Senior Managerial Personnel, Clause 1.1 OGUK JOA reads: 'Senior Managerial Personnel means in relation to any Participant, any person employed by it or any its Affiliates as a director or other corporate officer or senior manager. For the purposes of this definition, "senior manager" shall mean, only:

(a) in relation to the Operator, [[any member of the management committee comprised of senior managers which has overall responsibility for the management of the assets and interests of [] Limited and its subsidiaries(at the date of this Agreement known as the "[ ] Executive Committee") and/or any person employed by the Operator or its Affiliates who directly reports to any such committee or to the board of directors or to any member of either in his capacity as a member of such committee or board]] OR [[any person of the rank of [] or above]] OR [any person having direct responsibility for the conduct of all Joint Operations]]; and

(b) in relation to any Non-Operator, [[any member of committee or board performing the same or substantially the same or substantially the same function as the board of directors or the management committee referred to in (a) above and any person employed by such Non-Operator or its Affiliates who directly reports to any such committee or board or to any member of either of them in his capacity as a member of such committee or board]] OR [[any person having direct responsibility for the rights and responsibilities of such Non-Operator under this Agreement]]'.

of a local subsidiary.[12] In the end, the work group decided that a title should not be included in the square brackets for the operator.[13]

There is no definition similar to senior supervisory personnel in the CAPL Model JOA 2007[14] and the AAPL Model Offshore Deepwater JOA. Theoretically speaking, an operator that uses JOAs based on the CAPL Model JOA 2007 or the AAPL Model Offshore Deepwater JOA has more risk exposure to non-operators in the event of any breach committed by the operator. In negotiating a CAPL or AAPL based-JOA, negotiators may consider introducing the senior supervisory personnel concept in the section on the operator's liabilities. Whether the negotiators can successfully insert this concept into the CAPL or AAPL based-JOA is subject to the negotiation power of the parties and the resistance for one party due to deviate from the market practice. In some instances, to use the customary wording is preferred by all the parties in negotiation under the international model JOAs[15]

3. WHAT IS THE REAL MEANING OF GROSS NEGLIGENCE OR WILFUL MISCONDUCT?

Traditionally, the definitions of gross negligence and wilful misconduct are not very clearly separately defined in the international model JOAs.

12 The work group debated whether to replace the present definitions of operator and non-operator, which are in effect the board of directors or the management committee with overall responsibility for the management of the assets and interests of the participant and any person reporting directly to a member of that board or committee. See: OGUK Joint Operating Agreement Guidance Notes January 2009 <http://www.oilandgasuk.co.uk/publications/index.cfm>.

13 The reason that the non-operator has options in the bracket part attributes to the reason that the work group think it is rare for the non-operator to commit willful misconduct (where the definition of Senior Managerial Personnel is used) see OGUK Joint Operating Agreement Guidance Notes January 2009 <http://www.oilandgasuk.co.uk/publications/index.cfm>.

14 Clause 4.02 CAPL Model JOA 2007 reads: '4.02 Limit of Operator's Legal Responsibility. The Operator, its Affiliates and their respective directors, officers and employees will not be liable to any of the Non-Operators for any Losses and Liabilities resulting from or in any way attributable to or arising out of any act, omission or failure to act, whether negligent or otherwise, of the Operator or its Affiliates and their respective directors, officers, agents, contractors or employees in the performance of the Operator's duties under this Agreement(including those in planning or conducting any Joint Operation), except insofar as:(a) those Losses and Liabilities are a direct result of, or are directly attributable to the Gross Negligence or Wilful Misconduct of the Operator, its Affiliates or their respective directors, officers, employees, agents or contractors…' The reader can see this clause introduce the wording 'directors, officers, agents, contractors or employees in the performance of the Operator's duties' in the liabilities part, which is much broader than the scope of 'Senior Supervisory Personnel' or 'Senior Managerial Personnel'.

15 The writer himself has participated in a lot of JOA negotiations in various jurisdictions and his experiences confirm that market practice is a very common negotiating basis to reach a mutually accepted JOA.

Gross negligence is not a well-defined term in most jurisdictions and the concept differs between jurisdictions. There are two quotes from two great English judges justifying the above common understanding. Judge Lord Cranworth in 1843 said he 'could see no difference between negligence and gross negligence; that it was the same thing, with the addition of a vituperative epithet.'[16] Lord Justice Millett said: '[b]ut while we regard the difference between fraud on the one hand and mere negligence, however gross, on the other as a difference in kind, we regard the difference between negligence and gross negligence as merely one of degree'.[17] Some states in the United States, however, hold a totally different view from the English courts. For example, under New York law, the court noted that gross negligence 'differs in kind, not only degree, from claims of ordinary negligence' and that gross negligence is 'conduct that evinces a reckless disregard for the rights of others or "smacks" of intentional wrongdoing'.[18]

As regards wilful misconduct, it is in a better situation than gross negligence. The definition of wilful misconduct is at least relatively widely accepted. According to the traditional definition in English law, 'willful misconduct in such a special condition means misconduct to which the will is party as contradistinguished from accident, and is far beyond any negligence, even gross or culpable negligence, and involves that a person willfully misconducts himself who knows and appreciates that it is wrong conduct on his part in the existing circumstances to do, or to fail or omit to do (as the case may be), a particular thing, and yet intentionally does, or fails or omits to do it, or persists in the act, failure, or omission regardless of consequences ... or acts with reckless carelessness, not caring what the results of his carelessness maybe.'[19]

Given the fact that there is not a very clear distinction between 'gross negligence' and 'wilful misconduct', there are three approaches in the international model JOAs: (1) the 'combined approach', (2) the 'separate approach', and (3) the 'no specific definition approach'.

The Model AIPN JOA puts 'gross negligence' alongside 'wilful misconduct' and does not distinguish between them at all.[20] Philip Weems and Michael Bolton explain that the Model AIPN JOA adopts this approach because, 'since willful misconduct is unitized under English law as opposed to gross negligence,

---

[16] See *Wilson v Brett* (1843) 11 M&W 113.

[17] See *Armitage v Nurse* [1997] EWCA Civ 1279.

[18] *Colnaghi, USA Ltd. v Jewelers Protection Services, Ltd.* 81 N.Y.2d 377.

[19] See LJ Alverstone comments in *Forder v Great Western Railway* (1905) 2KB 532.

[20] Clause of 1.1 AIPN 2012 Model JOA defines gross negligence/wilful misconduct as follows: 'Gross Negligence/Willful Misconduct means any act or failure to act (whether sole, joint or concurrent) by any person or entity that was intended to cause, or was in reckless disregard of or wanton indifference to, harmful consequences such person or entity knew, or should have known, such act or failure would have on the safety or property of another person or entity.'

the defined term gross negligence/wilful misconduct was developed in order to ease the document's used under English law.'[21]

The CAPL Model JOA 2007 uses 'or' to connect the definition of gross negligence to wilful misconduct.[22]

The OGUK Model JOA adopts the traditional English law concept that gross negligence is the same kind as negligence by a different degree. The OGUK Model JOA only provides the definition of wilful misconduct,[23] and not gross negligence. The reason for this is quite simple, as explained above: under English law, gross negligence is not a separate kind from negligence; rather it is the same kind[24] but of a different degree. This reflects the fact that English law is traditionally unwilling to make a distinction between negligence and gross negligence.

The AAPL Model Offshore Deepwater JOA does not define 'gross negligence' or 'wilful misconduct', although it connects 'gross negligence' and 'wilful misconduct' with the word 'or'.[25] Oil and gas petroleum activities in the United States are highly competitive and it is not customary for the AAPL Model Offshore Deepwater JOA to offer the parties a lot of freedom to their JOAs.

---

21 See 'Highlights of key revisions-2002 AIPN Model from International Operating Agreement' at http://www.rmmlf.org/Istanbul/ there are a lot of training materials regarding AIPN model contracts.

22 See the CAPL Model JOA 2007, 'Gross Negligence or Willful Misconduct means any act, omission or failure to act (whether sole, joint or concurrent) by a person that was intended to cause, or was in reckless disregard of, or wanton indifference to, the harmful consequences to the safety or property of another person or to the environment which the person acting or failing to act knew (or should have known) would result from such act, omission or failure to act. However, Gross negligence or Willful Misconduct does not include any act, omission or failure to act insofar as it:(i) constitute mere ordinary negligence; or (ii) was done or omitted in accordance with the express instructions or approval of all Parties, insofar as the act, omission or failure to act otherwise constituting Gross Negligence or Willful Misconduct was inherent in those instructions or that approval.' The reader can see that the approach is a 'combined' approach which puts the definition of gross negligence and wilful misconduct together.

23 The OGUK defines 'wilful misconduct' as 'an intentional or reckless disregard by Senior Managerial Personnel of Good Oilfield Practice or any of the terms of this Agreement in utter disregard of avoidable and harmful consequences but shall not include any act, omission, error of judgement or mistake made in the exercise in good faith of any function, authority or discretion vested in or exercisable by such Senior Managerial Personnel and which in the exercise of such good faith is justifiable by special circumstances, including safeguarding of life, property or the environment and other emergencies'.

24 According to Black's Law Dictionary, negligence means 'the failure to exercise the standard of care that a reasonably prudent person would have exercised in a similar situation'.

25 The writer offered some observations to explain the reasons why BP and its partners did not include a detailed definition of 'gross negligence' or 'wilful misconduct' respectively in the beginning of this chapter. The reason why the AAPL Model Offshore Deepwater JOA might be partly attributable to the fact that there are various different jurisdictions and each jurisdiction may hold different views on the interpretation of 'gross negligence' or 'wilful misconduct'.

The way in which 'gross negligence' or 'wilful misconduct' as found in the CAPL Model JOA 2007 and the AAPL Model Offshore Deepwater JOA are understood is very much dependant on the court ruling.[26]

For example, in the CAPL Model JOA 2007, 'it still remains unclear whether either of these definitions do enough to limit an operator's ongoing risk of liability for administrative oversight. What may be missing is the explicit recognition in operating agreements of the conceptual distinction between negligence/gross negligence in the conduct of an operator's administrative duties, versus in the conduct of its operational field duties. In other words, an operator would only be found to be grossly negligent if it takes a less diligent approach to its jointly held properties than it does to its 100% owned properties'.[27] In this regard, the courts in the United States hold the same views on the interpretation of these definitions under the AAPL Model Offshore Deepwater JOA as Canadian courts interpret the two definitions under the CAPL Model JOA 2007.[28]

The difference between gross negligence and wilful misconduct in the AAPL Model Offshore Deepwater JOA remains to be settled via a court ruling.[29]

International Model JOAs	Combined approach	Separate approach	No specific definition approach
AIPN 2012 Model JOA	Yes	No	No
OGUK Model JOA	No	Yes	No
AAPL Model Offshore Deepwater JOA[30]	Yes	No	Yes
CAPL Model JOA 2007	Yes	No	No

26 In the BP Gulf of Mexico Oil Spill Phase One Trial, the judge said, 'a distinction is frequently made between gross negligence and willful, wanton or reckless conduct. While the jurisdictions adopting this distinction consider gross negligence substantially and appreciably higher in magnitude than ordinary negligence, it is still not equivalent to wanton or willful conduct and it does not encompass reckless behavior ... Negative in nature, gross negligence implies an absence of care. Willful misconduct, on the other hand, requires an intentional act or an intentional failure to act, either with knowledge that serious injury is a probable result, or with a positive and active disregard for the consequences.' At n. 180 *In re: Oil Spill by the Oil Rig "Deepwater Horizon" in the Gulf of Mexico*, on April 20, 2010 MDL 2179 Section J 2014 WL 4375933, 44 ELR 20200 (E.D. La. Sept. 4, 2014),<http://www.uscourts.gov/courts/laed/9042014FindingsofFactandConclusionsofLaw.pdf>.

27 <http://www.lawsonlundell.com/media/news/300_EnergyBulletinOperatorLiabilityAdminisrativeGrossNegligence.pdf> See Mills, Wright and Inch, *supra* n. 2, p. 363. More analysis on the case *Adeco Exploration Company Ltd. v. Hunt Oil Company of Canada Inc.* 2008 ABCA 214 can be found at: <http://ablawg.ca/wp-content/uploads/2009/09/blog_nb_adeco_abca_june2008.pdf>.

28 See H.M. Gibson, J.J. Harris and A.V. Henley, 'Protection of Operators under Joint Operating Agreements' <http://www.lexology.com/library/detail.aspx?g=f01091aa-7121-4b5b-bda8-48103693d4a4>.

29 In 2012, the Texas Supreme Court concluded that the exculpatory clause in AAPL Form 610-1989 JOA applied to a breach of contract claim, which expanded the scope of the activities an operator would not be held liable for absent gross negligence or wilful misconduct.

30 Although the AAPL Model Offshore Deepwater JOA put 'gross negligence' or 'wilful misconduct' together, it is not certain that the drafting committee holds that the two concepts

4. LIMITATION OF OPERATOR'S LIABILITIES UNDER INTERNATIONAL MODEL JOAs[31]

As discussed at the beginning of this chapter, the petroleum industry has accepted the concept that the operator shall not be responsible to the non-operator (except to the extent of the operator's participating interest) for the losses, damages or claims caused during the petroleum operation, with the soles exception of gross negligence or wilful misconduct of (the senior supervisory Personnel) of the operator. The use of the concepts of gross negligence, wilful misconduct and senior supervisory personnel is a meaningful way for the operator to further limit its risk exposure during the joint operations.

In petroleum industry, the party who plays the operator role is always trying to limit its risk exposure under the JOA by restricting non-operators' rights to make claims against it. Conversely, the non-operators keep pushing the operator to accept a JOA which entitles the non-operator to have more claims against the operator if things go wrong.

The purpose of liabilities limitation clauses under the international model JOAs is to limit the extent to which the operator is bound to indemnify the non-operator in respect of the consequences of performing its obligations under the JOA.[32]

Under the 'limitations of operator's liabilities' philosophy, there are various ways to limit the operator's liabilities: the first is to use these limitations such as gross negligence, wilful misconduct or senior supervisory personnel as already discussed; the second is to receive the undertaking from the non-operators in which the non-operator needs to defend, hold harmless and indemnify[33] the operator from losses, damages or liabilities on stipulated events; the third is to have a financial cap on the operator's liabilities.

are the same. In the AIPN 2012 Model JOA and CAPL Model JOA 2007, 'gross negligence' and 'wilful misconduct' are not only put together, but also share the same definition.

31 Please note that the liabilities analysis discussed herein is based on common law, not civil law. For example, the indemnity mechanism does not have a corresponding concept in some civil law jurisdictions and the applicability of such mechanism needs be studied or consulted in the context of the specific jurisdiction.

32 According to Judge Donaldson, there are three types of exception clause: 'Protective conditions are of three distinct types, namely, first those which limit or reduce what would otherwise be the defendants' duty, second, those which exclude the defendants' liability for breach of specified aspects of that duty and third, those which limit the extent to which the defendant is about to indemnify the plaintiff in respect of the consequences of breach of that duty.' See *Kenyon, Son & Craven Ltd v Baxten Hoare & Co Ltd* [1971] 1 WLR 519. The operator's liabilities limitation under International Model JOAs belongs to the third category.

33 The OGUK Model JOA follows the traditional English law concept that uses the three words 'defend, indemnify and hold … harmless' in full, in contrast to 'defend and indemnify', which is used in AIPN 2012 Model JOA.

The financial cap sought by the operators can be explored by using different options as follows. One option is the so-called 'no consequential loss[34] or environmental 'oss'.[35] The AIPN 2012 Model JOA provides that 'under no circumstances shall Operator (except as a Party to the extent of its Participating Interest) or any other Operator Indemnitee bear any Consequential Loss or Environmental Loss.' In other international model JOAs, the definition of the consequential loss or environmental loss or similar definitions are used in various ways. Another option is to limit the operator's risk exposure in relation to joint property.[36] A third option is to fix the financial limit at at a certain level.[37]

From the operator's perspective, the latter option is the best. With the financial limit fixed at a certain level,[38] the operator can quantify its maximum exposure even if any losses, claims or damages caused by any senior supervisory personnel of the operator engaging in gross negligence or wilful misconduct. The present author has negotiated quite a lot of JOAs over the past 10 years, but did not see any that successfully put a fixed number on its financial liabilities cap. Theoretically speaking, the financial cap on the operator's liabilities is an excellent option, but it cannot in reality be achieved in most cases.

One another practical issue requiring the reader's attention is that negotiators may wish to revise the section on the limitation of the operator's liabilities to confirm that the limitation provisions do not apply to claims between the parties.

---

34 Only the AIPN 2012 Model JOA and OGUK Model JOA use the term 'Consequential Loss'; but the CAPL Model JOA 2007 and AAPL Model Offshore Deepwater JOA do not use that term but instead use 'Indirect' loss in the agreements. The AAPL Model Offshore Deepwater JOA provides: 'Unless specifically provided otherwise in this Agreement, liability for losses, damages, costs, expenses, or claims involving activities or operations under this Agreement or affecting the Leases or the Contract Area which are not covered by or in excess of the insurance carried for the Joint Account shall be borne by each Party in proportion to its Participating Interest Share in the activity or operation out of which that liability arises, except that when liability results from the gross negligence or willful misconduct of a Party, that Party shall be solely responsible for liability resulting from its gross negligence or willful misconduct. Under no circumstances will a party be liable to another party for punitive damages, consequential, indirect, unforseen, loss of profit, or other indirect or penalty damages either in law or equity.' The CAPL Model JOA 2007 uses the term 'Extraordinary Damages' and states that the operator shall be responsible for any extraordinary damages.

35 Only AIPN 2012 Model JOA uses the term 'Environmental Loss', the other three Model JOAs in International Model JOAs do not use such specific term therein.

36 Alternative #2 Article 4.6.D AIPN 2012 Model JOA: 'Operator shall bear only the actual damage, loss, cost and liability to repair, replace and/or remove Joint Property so damaged or lost, if any.

37 Alternative #3 Article 4.6.D AIPN 2012 Model JOA: 'Operator shall bear only the first [US dollars] of such damages, losses, costs, and liabilities.'

38 The AIPN Model JOA draft committee suggests that the users should consider the amount stated as a financial limitation to be adjusted in accordance with an inflation or other index.

5. POSSIBLE IMPACT OF THE BP GULF OF MEXICO OIL SPILL PHASE ONE TRIAL[39]

The BP Gulf of Mexico Oil Spill Phase One Trial has attracted a lot of attention from international petroleum negotiators as this case is a very important one to watch to see how the court will define relevant definitions under the applicable laws and regulations, and the trial will have a profound impact on the petroleum industry in the future. This chapter will discuss how the judge analysed the concept of gross negligence and wilful misconduct and the possible impact the judgment will have.

The distinction between gross negligence and wilful misconduct under the United States Clean Water Act was thoroughly analysed by the judge.

In his 'findings of fact and conclusions of law: phase one trial', the judge wrote: 'However, because it is unclear that what standard Citgo may have applied, the Court will also assume that "gross negligence" is equivalent to "recklessness"'. Although the judge ruled on the basis of an analysis of 'gross negligence' and 'wilful misconduct' under the Clean Water Act, the emphasis on the different aspects of the two definitions might bring about some changes to the various model JOAs.

Further, the judge states: 'while, in theory, gross negligence and willful and wanton misconduct are distinct concepts with different legal bases, in practice there has been much confusion and unfortunate overlap between the two doctrines. Part of the difficulty stems from the fact that the labels are sometimes used interchangeably, with "gross negligence" defined in "willful and wanton misconduct" terms. The designation of wanton acts as "gross negligence" is a misnomer, because such acts are not negligence at all' and '[m]any jurisdictions consider willful, wanton, or reckless conduct to be conduct of a different kind than negligence. Thus, it has been said that willful, malicious, or intentional misconduct is not properly speaking, within the meaning of "negligence", however gross, when "negligence" is used as a term of art.' These citations prove that the situation regarding the difference between 'gross negligence' and 'willful misconduct' is more complex than the situation in English law governing JOAs. Sometimes gross negligence is deemed to be the same concept as wilful misconduct, and in other instances certain rulings clearly distinguish the two concepts, as already discussed above.

---

39 The full text of the phase one trial regarding the BP oil spill on the oil rig 'Deepwater Horizon' in the Gulf of Mexico can be read at: <http://www.uscourts.gov/courts/laed/9092014RevisedFindingsofFactandConclusionsofLaw.pdf>.

In the trial, BP made the interesting argument that gross negligence has objective and subjective elements.[40] On the contrary, the US government argued that gross negligence, like ordinary negligence, requires only objective, not subjective, proof.

Although it is only the phase one trial, and the non-appealable decision is still a long way off, Changes to the section of the operator's liability in the international model JOAs may be expected. Whether gross negligence and wilful misconduct should be separately defined and how the concept of recklessness will be built into the two concepts needs further investigation.

One observation I made after BP's Gulf of Mexico oil spill is that non-operators prefer to receive a counter-indemnification from the operator under extraordinary circumstances in exchange for the indemnification they give the operator in other scenarios. This may further complicate the JOA negotiation.

The present author thinks the section on the operator's liabilities in the international model JOAs may undergo some changes in the future to better address confrontations between the operator and non-operators in the evolving petroleum industry. Everyone in the petroleum industry is well aware of the fact that the JOA is a beneficial means of allocating costs and risks between different companies so that no single company takes on all the risk.[41] In a world with more unpredictable uncertainties, risks and liabilities, the operator and non-operators are increasingly demanding that their interests be adequately protected in the JOA.[42]

6. A COMPARISON OF KEY ISSUES IN THE INTERNATIONAL MODEL JOAs

Based on all the discussions and analysis on the senior supervisor personnel, financial cap and other restrictions in relation to the limitation of the operator's liabilities, the table below allows the reader to compare the different items under the international model JOAs.

40 In the trial, BP contended that gross negligence requires an extreme departure from the ordinary standard of care (objective element). Furthermore, BP also claimed that the actor must have a 'culpable mental state' (subjective element). According to BP, such subjective element requires that the actor must have actual, subjective awareness of the risk involved, but nevertheless proceed with conscious indifference to the rights, safety, or welfare of others. For details, see *supra* n. 39.

41 P. Murphy, 'Joint Operating Agreements: Should Elements of the AIPN Model Form International Operating Agreement Influence a New AAPL Joint Operating Agreement?' <http://www. aipn.org>.

42 H.L. Boigon, 'Joint Operating Agreements. Part 1' (1987/88) 11 *Oil and Gas Law and Taxation Review* 320.

The petroleum industry has already witnessed a lot of referring among the international model JOAs[43] and more referring will be seen in the future because international players are participating in the North American market and the North Sea market more often than the before.[44]

Key Items	AIPN 2012 Model JOA[45]	AAPL Model Offshore Deepwater JOA[46]	CAPL Model JOA 2007[47]	OP026 JOA for UKCS Licence[48]
Definition of senior supervisory personnel or similar concept	Yes	No	No	Yes
Definition of gross negligence/wilful misconduct	Yes	No	Yes	No gross negligence but wilful misconduct
Good oilfield practice or prudent oilfield practice	Yes	Yes	Yes	Yes
Senior supervisory personnel or senior managerial personnel	Yes	No	No	Yes
Indemnity mechanism to limit the operator's liabilities	Yes	Yes	Yes	Yes
Financial liabilities cap option – fixed number	Yes	No	No	No
Consequential loss	Yes	Yes	Yes	Yes
Environmental loss	Yes	To some extent	To some extent	To some extent

Althoug h there are some conceptual, technical or style differences between the international model JOAs, the reader can come to a preliminary conclusion by

43 In the Guidance notes to AIPN 2012 Model JOA, it clearly refers to the Canadian Association of Petroleum Landmen(CAPL) 2007 model form and the relevant articles published in the CAPL Negotiator magazine. Also, in Partrick Murphy's article, see n. 41 *supra*, he mentions that 'the cooperation principles highlighted in the AIPN 2002 JOA suggest that it is time for the AAPL to revise its JOA'.

44 The international player who used to use the AIPN-based JOA will make references from the AIPN-based JOA and then incorporate some concepts or definition thereto into the North American market JOA, the Canadian market JOA and the North Sea market JOA.

45 AIPN 2012 Model International JOA <www.aipn.org>.

46 AAPL-810 (2007) <http://www.landman.org/>.

47 2007 CAPL Operating Procedure <http://www.landman.ca>.

48 Patrick Murphy makes a very good point on the difference between the AIPN and AAPL Model JOAs: 'The AIPN 2002 JOA differs greatly from the AAPL 1989 JOA. While the AAPL 1989 JOA is characterized by autonomy and standardization, the AIPN 2002 JOA is characterized by cooperation and flexibility'. See Murphy, *supra* n. 41.

reading the above table: the operator's liabilities clause under the international model JOAs is a very delicate mechanism to carefully allocate the risks between the operator and non-operators and, in essence, the international model JOAs more or less provide all the key items to balance rights and obligations of all parties. The differences between the international model JOAs are not huge as they might first appear if a careful comparison is made.

7. CONCLUSION

In the author's view, the three most important types of contract in the petroleum upstream sector are: (1) the production sharing contract; (2) the JOA; and (3) the farm-in/farm-out agreement. However, the importance of the JOA cannot be overstated.

Of all points that need to be negotiated in relation to the JOA, the section on the operator's liabilities is obviously one of the most critical, and also the most difficult part to reach a mutually satisfactory agreement. The international model JOAs adopt various means to balance the rights and obligations between the participants in joint petroleum operations. The comparative table in the previous section illustrates how the operator reduces the extent of its risk exposure by using the key terms or other relevant mechanisms in that table.

International negotiators should realise the pros and cons of using the international model JOAs as the basis for JOA negotiations.[49] Furthermore, international negotiators participating in JOAs negotiations should bear in mind the importance of following the changes and/or the referring of international model JOAs, the judicial review of the claims arising out of the interpretation of key terms in different jurisdictions, and the market practice in negotiating the key terms.

49 As discussed above, on the one hand, the model form JOAs can facilitate the JOA negotiations; on the other hand, the model form JOAs may make some parts of the negotiation harder due to the fact that all the participants are well aware of the options or wording under the model form JOAs.

SECONDMENT AND PROJECT TEAM

A Positive Mechanism to Support the Operator or an Effective Tool to Control the Operator?

Leslie Weihua ZHANG

1. INTRODUCTION

The control and reverse control of petroleum operations is one of the key themes in the terms and conditions of JOA. Traditionally, petroleum operations, especially day-to-day operations, are controlled and managed by the operator. Because of this philosophy, non-operators usually ask for some other mechanisms to be provided in the JOA, to some extent, to exert more influence over the petroleum operations. Secondment and/or project team mechanisms are usually deemed to be effective tools to control the operator or positive mechanisms to support the operator in operator-leading operations.

This chapter will discuss the roles, functions, advantages and disadvantages of the secondment and project team mechanisms. In doing so, it will be concluded that these mechanisms can be used to support or control the operator if used properly, although the secondment mechanism focuses more on the supporting side, while the project team mechanism can be used as an effective supporting and supervisory tool.

There is no straightforward answer to the question whether a secondment arrangement is either a positive mechanism to support operator-led joint petroleum operations or an effective tool to control the operator. In my view, this is not a simple 'either/or' question but rather requires a case-by-case analysis.

As discussed above, either the secondment mechanism or the project team mechanism might be used as a positive mechanism to support the operator and an effective tool to control the operator. But from a practical point of view, a secondment arrangement may not, in reality, be used as an effective tool to control the operator,[1] while the integrated project team mechanism is more suitable as a positive mechanism to support and control operator-led joint operations. This chapter will discuss the relevant issues regarding how the secondment arrangement and project team mechanisms are implemented in joint operations and the relevant functions of the two mechanisms hereinafter. This chapter will also examine the relevant clauses provided in the international model JOAs and compare the differences and similarities between them in order to acquaint the reader with the general practice in the petroleum industry.

2. DEFINITION OF SECONDMENT AND PROJECT TEAM

In the petroleum industry, secondment is an arrangement between the operator and non-operators whereby employees of a non-operator or one of its affiliates are placed in the operator's organisation to provide services under a secondment agreement between the operator and the non-operator or its affiliates.[2] Among the international model JOAs,[3] neither the AAPL Model Offshore Deepwater JOA nor the CAPL Model JOA 2007 provide for a secondment arrangement. The OGUK Model JOA for UKCS Licence (OGUK Model JOA) provides for a

1 This does not mean that the secondment arrangement cannot be used as an effective tool to control the operator. If properly designed, the secondment arrangement can achieve the same goal as the project team arrangement.

2 See Article 1 – Definition and Interpretations, AIPN 2012 Model JOA which can be purchased at <www.aipn.org>.

3 For convenience, in the following the AAPL, CAPL, OGUK and AIPN JOAs shall be collectively referred to 'international model JOAs'.

secondment arrangement that differs slightly from the secondment arrangement provided for in the AIPN 2012 Model JOA.

The AIPN 2012 Model JOA distinguishes between a secondment arrangement and a project team arrangement, and further provides for a different approval procedure for each of the two mechanisms.[4] That is to say, the secondment arrangement and project team arrangement under AIPN 2012 Model JOA are two separate mechanisms. The project team is an organisation which consists of a group of employees and/or contract workers (from the operator and the non-operators) assisting the operator to perform the prescribed work. It is subject to the operating committee's approval or must meet the threshold of aggregate participating interest by the parties set out in the JOA. The OGUK Model JOA, however, does not distinguish between the secondment arrangement and the project team arrangement[5] as fully as the AIPN 2012 Model JOA does. On the contrary, the OGUK Model JOA to some extent combines the two mechanisms.[6] Although the provisions contained in the 20th round OGUK Model JOA regarding joint teams have been removed from the main body of the model JOA, any employee nominated by a non-operator to join the joint team shall be seconded to the operator.[7]

According to BusinessDictionary,[8] project team[9] means 'a group of individuals assembled to perform activities that contribute toward achieving a common task related goal. Many business operators will put together a project team consisting of skilled workers from the same or different function areas to work on an important project.' The BusinessDictionary definition of a project team is primarily from a management perspective. Nevertheless, the definition of project team in the international model JOAs attaches more importance to assisting the implementation of joint operations (or in other words, controlling the joint operations conducted by the operator).

---

4 The AIPN 2014 Model Unconventional Resource Operating Agreement continues to adopt this approach.

5 Under OGUK Model JOA, the project team is called the 'Joint Team'.

6 See Clause 6.11 OGUK Model JOA: 'The Participants agree that in certain circumstances a collaborative effort between them may be beneficial to Joint Operations. Such collaborative effort may include the secondment by a Non-Operator of personnel to the Operator's organisation: (i) to work on a term assignment as a member of a project team, or (ii) to fill organisational positions…'.

7 The work group thinks the joint teams were rarely used and in all likelihood any joint team would be the subject of a separate agreement. See OGUK Joint Operating Agreement Guidance Notes, January 2009.

8 BusinessDictionary is the leading online business resource, featuring over 25,000 definitions spanning across critical business-related topics including management, small business, economics, human resources, entrepreneurship, recruiting, and corporate strategy.

9 See <http://www.businessdictionary.com/definition/project-team.html#ixzz4CH60Et5d>.

The definition of project team[10] in the AAPL Model Offshore Deepwater JOA is quite similar to the definition in the AIPN 2012 Model JOA and OGUK Model JOA. The CAPL Model JOA 2007 does not contain the concept of a project team.

In general, the secondment and project team mechanisms are two common mechanisms frequently used in joint petroleum operations, and their definitions in the international model JOAs are quite familiar, except for some minor differences regarding the relationship of the two mechanisms.

3. FUNCTIONS/ROLES OF SECONDMENT ARRANGEMENT UNDER THE INTERNATIONAL MODEL JOAs

This section will examine the functions of a secondment arrangement under the international model JOAs. There are two types of secondment arrangement: firstly a secondment arrangement between the national oil company (NOC) and the operator, and secondly a secondment arrangement between the operator and non-operators (excluding the NOC or its appointed affiliates partnering with foreign investors).

The main purpose of a secondment arrangement entered into by and between the NOC and the operator is usually to second talented local people from NOC or its affiliates in order to receive training and expertise from operator during the joint petroleum operations. Although local talent seconded by the NOC may make some contribution to the operator in the work assigned to them, the practical reality is that the main purpose of such secondment is training and education, rather than contributions to the joint operations. In reality, the operator often has to agree to accept the inexperienced secondees seconded by the NOC on request.

A secondment arrangement between the operator and non-operators is a totally different story. The operator will carefully study the pros and cons of a secondment arrangement during its operation term to decide whether the non-operators' nominees will bring any expertise or experience which is necessary for the potential secondment positions. Furthermore, it has the discretionary power, to some extent, to decide whether or not to adopt such an arrangement and to select the best qualified persons from the nominees made by the non-operators.

---

[10] Article 2.59 AAPL Model Offshore Deepwater JOA reads: 'A group of employees, contractors, and/or consultants of the Participating Parties or their respective Affiliates, who assists the Operator in carrying out the scope of work for the Selection Stage, Define Stage, and Execution Stage and the scope of work under Articles 12.8 *(Post-Production Project Team AFEs)* and 12.11 *(Enhanced Recovery and/or Pressure Maintenance Program Proposals)*'.

The AIPN Model Secondment Agreement (2002) gives a very good perspective on the prevailing industry view of the functions of secondment.[11] Essentially, the secondee sent by the non-operator remains the employee of the non-operator and all employment-related issues such as remuneration, promotion and career planning will be determined by the non-operator. Usually, the operator will have no authority to terminate employment or to administer any disciplinary actions with respect to the secondee. Although the model secondment agreement provides that the secondee shall receive the supervision and control of the operator and perform his duties according to the instructions and direction of operator, it does not really seem to contain any specific measures[12] which entitle the operator to control/manage the secondee.[13]

There are also two issues in the secondment arrangement that demand the reader's attention. Firstly, it is worth noting the rule in the secondment arrangement that neither the non-operator nor the secondee can act as a servant or employer of the operator, and that the non-operator's role will be an independent contractor engaged by the operator to make the secondee available for the services provided for in the secondment agreement.

The second issue which requires attention is the payment structure under the secondment arrangement. The secondees are paid not by the operator, but by their employer – the non-operator.[14] The operator will not be held responsible for making any compensation related to the secondees unless otherwise provided.

A preliminary conclusion may therefore be drawn that a secondment arrangement between the NOC and operator tends to be a favour done by the operator, whereas and a secondment arrangement between the operator and non-operators (excluding the NOC or its appointed affiliates partnering with foreign investors) tends to be a positive mechanism to support the operator.

---

11 Note that the AIPN 2014 Model Unconventional Resource Operating Agreement also contains a secondment mechanism.

12 Although most secondment arrangements are structured such that the secondee shall be integrated into the operator's organisation and shall be subject to the operator's supervision and direction the operator, however, does not have any concrete measure to control the secondees, except for the assessment made by the operator upon the request from the non-operator.

13 This conclusion could be easily drawn by reading Clause 4.3.C.2 and the Alternatives of the AIPN 2012 Model JOA: Clause 4.3.C.2: 'If a proposed Secondment meets the requirements of Article 4.3.C.1, Operator shall as soon as reasonably practicable'; Alternative #1: 'approve or reject any Secondment proposed by a Non-Operator, in Operator's sole discretion'. During the determination of the secondment, the AIPN 2012 Model JOA usually gives the operator a discretionary power or key role to determine the whole secondment arrangement.

14 The compensation will be eventually be paid by the joint account, which is subject to the right of the operator to conduct an audit operator.

4. FUNCTIONS/ROLES OF PROJECT TEAM ARRANGEMENT UNDER THE INTERNATIONAL MODEL JOAs

The purpose of establishing a project team is slightly different from the purpose of sending secondees to the operator. The main purpose of an integrated project team is to gather the talents and capacities of both the operator and non-operators in performing those functions that constitute part of the joint petroleum operations. Usually, the work to be performed by the integrated project team will have been delegated by the operator and operating committee.[15]

In the past, participants in the petroleum industry usually considered the project team arrangement not to be good because the mechanism tends to distract the operator from the operator-leading operation pattern, but is not a useful tool for expediting the petroleum operations.

This misconception can be found in different versions of the AIPN Model JOA. Vigilant readers will probably have noted that the previous version did not contain the integrated project team concept. According to the explanation given by the members of the Model Contract Drafting Committee, the concept of a 'project team' was discussed before the release of the AIPN 2002 JOA, but was ultimately rejected as the drafting committee thought the concept would fragment the operator's responsibilities and dilute its overall accountability.[16]

Nevertheless, AIPN officially introduced the concept of 'project team' in its 2012 Model JOA (after ten years of discussion by the draft committee) – not, however, in the main body of the JOA, but in the exhibit section.[17]

To put the project team mechanism in the exhibit section, the AIPN draft committee gives the operator the option to choose such mechanism in complex petroleum operations. As a common practice, the operator prefers to use the project team in petroleum operations under the highly complex operating situations. Due to the technical difficulties, such as extremely unusual reservoir

---

15 See N. Etteh, 'Joint Operating Agreements: which issues are likely to be the most sensitive to the parties and how can a good contract design limit the damage from such disputes?' < http://www.dundee.ac.uk/cepmlp/gateway/files.php?file=cepmlp_car14_27_215967689.pdf>. In this article, the author says: 'Although the most important duty of a Non-Operator is to provide a share of funds whenever there is a cash-call. However Non-Operators are active investors and they can have an active say in the managing of the JV though the JOC.' The project team mechanism is clearly an effective way for the non-operator to control the joint operation to some extent.

16 See 'Highlights of key revisions – 2002 AIPN Model Form International Operating Agreement' <http://www.rmmlf.org/Istanbul/>.

17 J.A. Josefson, a partner from King & Spalding, said in an article: 'While the 2012 JOA drafting committee and AIPN Board ultimately decided that IPTs are not recognized standard industry practice, IPTs did evoke enough discussion and interest from the drafters to introduce the concept and suggested text in the Guidance Notes.' See: <http://www.jdsupra.com/legalnews/transactions-2012-aipn-model-internatio-98944/>.

forming accumulation or difficult developing situations, the operator is more willing to involve non-operators' experts in the joint operations if the non-operators also have relevant experience. Otherwise it is not necessary to have a project team to join a powerful and capable operator's petroleum operations. A secondment arrangement may suffice under such circumstances if the non-operators do not have the necessary technical expertise to support the joint operations by the means of a project team.

Of the international model JOAs, the AAPL Model Offshore Deepwater JOA provides a very detailed project team mechanism. The project team is widely used under the AAPL Model Offshore Deepwater JOA in the selection stage,[18] definition stage,[19] and execution stage,[20] and the project team also participates in the scope of work under the Post-Production Project[21] and Enhanced Recovery and/or Pressure Maintenance Program Proposals.

In the PRC,[22] the production sharing contract serves both as a PSC and as the JOA between the NOC and foreign contractors. The 1990s version of China's Model Offshore Production Sharing Contract introduced a Project Management Team (PMT).[23] According to China's Model Offshore PSC, the PMT shall consist of the personnel designated by foreign contractors and the NOC and the NOC's personnel shall comprise no less than one third of the

---

18 According to the AAPL Model Offshore Deepwater JOA, the selection stage means 'the stage of a Development Phase during which the Operator, with the assistance of the Project Team, if applicable, will determine whether to (a) install a Development System on the Contract Area, or (b) tie-back to, and utilize (i) a Development System resulting from a previous Development Phase or (ii) a development system and/or facilities located outside the Contract Area in order to produce Hydrocarbons.'

19 According to the AAPL Model Offshore Deepwater JOA, the definition stage means 'the stage of a Development Phase during which the Operator, with the assistance of the Project Team, if applicable, will (a) commence the implementation of a Development plan, (b) complete enough of the detailed design of the Development System to enable contractors to formulate their bids on the components of the Development System, and (c) submit an Execution AFE to the Parties for their review and approval.'

20 According to the AAPL Model Offshore Deepwater JOA, the execution stage means 'the final stage of a Development Phase during which the Operator, with the assistance of the Project Team, will complete the implementation of the Development Plan, implement the Execution AFE, and commence the first production of Hydrocarbons for that particular Development Phase.'

21 The post-production project deals with the drilling of additional development wells, de-bottlenecking the development system, ramping up hydrocarbon production, maximising the recovery of hydrocarbons during the development phase and activities related thereto and further includes reservoir management and production optimising activities.

22 For the purpose of this chapter, 'PRC' refers to People's Republic of China, which includes Mainland China but excluding Hong Kong and Macau.

23 Article 8.7 of China's Model Offshore PSC provides: 'In any Oil Field and/or Gas Field within the Contract Area where [NOC] has the participating interest in the development of said Field, a project management team (hereafter referred to as "PMT") shall be established in the organization of the Operator at the date of approval of the Overall Development Program for said Field by the competent authorities of the Chinese Government.'

total number of personnel within the PMT. The foreign contactor shall designate the person acting as the manager of the PMT, and the NOC shall designate the person acting as the deputy manager of the PMT. When determining the nature of the PMT provided in China's Model Offshore PSC, a comparison can be made with the relevant clauses from the 2012 AIPN JOA. According to the 2012 AIPN JOA, the Integrated Project Team (IPT) can be established by the parties at any time during the petroleum operation period. Usually, the NOC does not second any of its employees to the operator's organisation during the exploration phase; only upon a commercial discovery and the approval of the overall development plan[24] does the NOC have the right to second its employees to the operator's organisation with the aim of learning techniques and petroleum management. Under the 2012 AIPN JOA, non-operators can participate from the very beginning of the joint operation, even in the exploration phase, subject to the prescribed procedural requirement only under the agreement.[25]

In the integrated project provisions contained in the AIPN 2012 Model JOA, the project team's purpose has an optional provision which reads '… and to provide each Participating Party with an opportunity to help determine, through the work of its IPT members, the method by which the Scope of Work.'[26] This optional provision clearly expands the function of the project team. The project team is not only the 'pool of talents and capacities of all Participating Parties in performance of the Scope of Work',[27] but can also assist the operator to efficiently conduct the petroleum operations.

Regarding the functions of a secondment arrangement or a project team arrangement, those of a project team are much wider than those of secondment.[28] Further, secondment demonstrates that the operator has, to some extent, the right to control the whole process during the secondment arrangement. The AIPN 2012 Model JOA confers on the operator sole discretionary power to decide whether or not to accept the secondees recommended by non-operators and whether or not the secondees recommended by the non-operators are qualified.

---

24 In China's Model Offshore PSC.

25 The operator does not have the right to object to such participation of non-operators in the IPT if the operator does not have solid reasons to reject such request.

26 See Integrated Project Team Provisions, AIPN 2012 Model JOA.

27 Ibid.

28 The project team's function could include preparing the development plan or carrying out a special project during the development phase, such as the planning, design, engineering, fabrication, transportation and installation of a production system and associated facilities, such as: offshore surface structures, subsea structures and any other type of structure to develop and produce hydrocarbons, or facilities located downstream of the wellhead connections installed either within or outside the contract area used to enhance, handle, process or transport hydrocarbons to processing facilities. See Guidance Note to Exhibit [] Section 1: Guidance Notes to AIPN 2012 Model Joint Operating Agreement <www.aipn.org>.

5. THE PROCESS TO ESTABLISH THE SECONDMENT ARRANGEMENT AND/OR PROJECT TEAM

Regarding the establishment of a secondment arrangement under the International Model JOAs, there are two customary approaches.[29] The first is the operator-determined approach, whereby the decision as to whether or not to set up a secondment arrangement and/or how to structure the arrangement is made solely by the operator. The operator has the sole discretionary power to decide to accept the secondees from the non-operator, to approve or reject any secondment proposed by the non-operator,[30] to select the most qualified nominees recommended by the non-operator, and to decide on the termination of the secondment of secondees with or without cause. The second approach is the operator-leading approach, which is slightly more favourable to the non-operator. The non-operator has the right to propose a secondment arrangement and the operator still has the right to approve or reject (with the limitation of the wording 'such approval not to be unreasonably withheld') any secondment proposed by a non-operator. Without prejudice to the operator's right to conduct the joint operations, the operator needs to consider the proposed secondment proposal from three angles: (1) the relevant expertise and experience required for the relevant joint operations; (2) the expertise and experience of operator's personnel; and (3) the potential benefits of such secondment to the conduct of the joint operations.[31]

Regarding the establishment of a project team under the international model JOAs, the customary approach[32] is the Joint Operating Committee (JOC)-determined approach. Usually, any party has the right to propose a project team to the JOC and such proposal will be submitted to the JOC for its decision. In practice, there are two negotiation points: (1) whether any party or a party/parties having a participating interest threshold (say, 25%) has the right to make the proposal to establish the project team; and (2) what threshold the JOC's vote must reach for a decision to establish the project team. The AIPN 2012 Model JOA further provides an option for the operator to have the discretionary right to reject the JOC's decision to establish a project team even if the vote threshold is reached.[33] The optional discretionary right is a pro-operator clause. The AIPN

---

[29] The OGUK Model JOA adopts different approaches, which will be discussed later in this chapter.

[30] See the Article 4.3.C.2 Alternative #1 AIPN 2012 Model JOA.

[31] See the Article 4.3.C.3 AIPN 2012 Model JOA.

[32] The AAPL Model Offshore Deepwater JOA provides a unique mechanism in establishing the project team, which will be discussed later in this chapter.

[33] See (4) Formation (b) Alternative #1: 'The Operator shall as soon as reasonably practicable approve (such approval not to be unreasonably withheld) or reject such IPT, considering the

2012 Model JOA also provides an alternative option such that the project team must be established if the JOC, by the required voting threshold, approves the establishment of the project team, with or without the operator's consent.

The AAPL Model Offshore Deepwater JOA provides for a unique mechanism in the establishment of a project team. The mechanism gives the operator an exclusive period to make a proposal on a feasibility team[34] and a project team, and any other participating party shall have the right to make a proposal on a project team if the operator does not exercise such right within the prescribed period.

The operator has more powers in a feasibility team than it has in a project team.[35] The operator has the right, from time to time, to revise the membership of the feasibility team, at its sole discretion, as long as the revisions are necessary to accomplish the scope of work.[36]

As discussed above, the OGUK Model JOA combines the secondment arrangement and joint team arrangement. The OGUK Model JOA does not provide in detail how the secondment arrangement and/or joint team arrangement will be established. The mechanism in the OGUK Model JOA regarding the establishment of the secondment/joint team can be proposed by either the operator or the non-operator (as the case may be) and is ultimately subject to the decision of the JOC.[37] Further, the remit, number, functions, and selection process of secondees, and other issues, shall be subject to the decision of the JOC. The establishment of a secondment arrangement under the OGUK Model JOA can be considered a 'mutual agreement' approach, and the establishment of a joint team arrangement under the OGUK Model JOA can be considered a 'JOC-determined approach', which is similar to other international model JOAs.

expertise and experience of Operator's and other Participating Parties' personnel and potential benefits of the IPT to the conduct of Joint Operations or Exclusive Operations, as applicable'.

34 The feasibility team is intentionally a separate definition from the project team; in the AAPL Model Offshore Deepwater JOA it is defined as '[a] group of employees, contractors, and/or consultants of the Participating Parties or their respective Affiliates that assists the Operator during the Feasibility Stage.'

35 The AAPL Model Offshore Deepwater JOA does not provide that the operator has a discretionary power to remove the membership of the project team.

36 See Clause 12.2 AAPL Model Offshore Deepwater JOA.

37 The OGUK Model JOA Guidance Notes state: 'If the Operator or a Non-Operator acting reasonably is of the opinion that it would be of material benefit to Joint Operations for any part of Joint Operations to be undertaken by a team comprising personnel from one or more Participant instead of or in addition to personnel from the Operator (a "Joint Team"), the Operator or that Non-Operator, as the case may be, shall be entitled to required the creation of such Joint Team.'

Types	AIPN 2012 Model JOA	CAPL Model JOA 2007	AAPL Model Offshore Deepwater JOA	OGUK Model JOA 2007
Secondment arrangement	Operator-lead plus operator-determined approach	N/A	N/A	JOC-determined approach
Project team arrangement	JOC-determined approach	N/A	Operator-lead plus JOC-determined approach	JOC-determined approach
Feasibility team arrangement	N/A	N/A	Operator-determined approach (subject to restriction)	N/A

6. THE RISKS AND LIABILITIES ALLOCATION

When secondees work in the operator's organisation, they must follow the instructions and receive supervision from the operator during the secondment term. What if the secondees cause any damage or losses during the secondment? Will the operator or the non-operator be held liable for such damage or losses? Some people think that any such responsibility in connection with the secondees' misconduct should fall on the operator, while others argue that the employer, i.e. the non-operator, should be responsible for the secondees' misconduct because the contract of employment is between the non-operator and the secondees.

The AIPN 2012 Model JOA provides for a mechanism whereby the operator shall be held liable for all liabilities or losses caused by the secondee if the secondee acts under the direction of operator. The exception to this is that the non-operator shall be held liable for any liabilities or losses caused as the result of gross negligence on the part of the non-operator's senior supervisory personnel.[38] The OGUK Model JOA provides that the operator shall be held

[38] Article 4.3 AIPN Model Secondment Agreement (2002) reads: 'Subject to Article 4.3(F) of the JOA, so long as and to the extent the Secondee is under Operator's direction in the performance of the Services, Operator shall, subject to the limitation on liability of Operator in accordance with Article 4.6 of the JOA, indemnify and hold the Employer, its Affiliates and its and their directors, officers and employees harmless from any and all costs, expenses (including reasonable attorney's fees) or liabilities incident to claims, demands or causes of action of every kind or character (whether for injury to, illness or death of persons, loss or damage to property, breach of contract, contractual indemnity or otherwise) resulting from the acts or omissions of the Secondee arising out or in connection with the performance of the Services; provided, however, that if such costs, expenses or liabilities arose as a result of the Gross Negligence of Employer's Senior Supervisory Personnel, then Operator shall have no obligation to indemnity Employer under this Section 4.3, and Employer shall indemnify Operator, the other Non-Operators under the JOA, its and their Affiliates, and the directors,

liable for all the liabilities or losses caused by the secondee, subject to the limitation on liabilities provided therein.[39] The OGUK Model JOA's section on liabilities regarding the secondee's performance is quite logical, simple and straightforward: it holds that the party who instructs the personnel during the petroleum operations shall be held liable, regardless of which party he has been seconded by. The provisions in the AIPN 2012 Model JOA catch more scenarios and can be used to meet the needs of various negotiation situations.

Regarding the allocation of risks and liabilities under the project team mechanism, there are no specific model provisions to deal with this issue in the international model JOAs, other than in the AIPN 2012 Model JOA. Given the fact that the project team functions as a supportive organisation or a control tool from the operator's perspective, it may be appropriate not to have a liabilities allocation clause in the project team section of the other international model JOAs because the primary purpose of the project team is not to directly participate in the day-to-day petroleum operations. However, in reality, it might be more straightforward to resolve disputes arising out of damage caused by the member of the project team if the JOA were to clearly allocate the risks and liabilities as part of the project team mechanism. The AIPN 2012 Model JOA also introduces the concept of senior supervisory personnel and gross negligence/ wilful misconduct in it section on liabilities. If a project team member who is one of the non-operator's senior supervisory personnel[40] engages in gross negligence or wilful misconduct that causes all the parties to suffer losses, damage or liability, the AIPN 2012 Model JOA provides three options as to who may be held liable: (1) the joint account; (2) the operator; or (3) the non-operator who nominated such secondees.[41]

---

officers and employees of all of them for such costs, expenses or liabilities. For the purpose of this Section 4.3, Gross Negligence of Secondee as a result of interference of the Employer in the performance of the Services in violation of this Secondment Agreement shall be deemed Gross Negligence of Employer's Senior Supervisory Personnel.'

39 Article 6.11.2(C) OGUK Model JOA reads: 'all work undertaken by such person shall be Joint Operations and accordingly the Operator shall retain overall responsibility for such work and such person (and the Participant which seconded him) shall benefit from all indemnities and limitations of liability applying to the Operation hereunder, including those set forth in clause 6.2.4 in relation to such work.'

40 See the relevant analysis on senior supervisory personnel in the chapter 'Senior Supervisor, Financial Cap and Other Restrictions regarding the Operator Liabilities and their Implications'.

41 The specific wording in Alternative #3 (12: liabilities) – Integrated Project Team Provisions of the AIPN 2012 Model JOA says 'the Non-Operator who nominated such member, to the extent Operator would be liable for such Gross Negligence / Willful Misconduct of its own employees under Article 4.6'.

7. REAL SECONDMENT/PROJECT TEAM CLAUSES IN THE INTERNATIONAL PETROLEUM INDUSTRY CONTEXT[42]

This section will examine some real secondment/project team clauses in the international petroleum industry context and try to expand on the conclusions made at the beginning of this chapter.

In a PSC entered into between a Middle East country and a global national oil company,[43] the secondment provision provides that:

> '[T]he GOVERNMENT may request CONTRACTOR to accept secondment of personnel to participate in its conduct of Petroleum Operations with the goal of imparting to [name of the host county] personnel technical, administrative and management skills necessary for safe and efficient Petroleum Operations. The total number of personnel seconded to CONTRACTOR's Petroleum Operations, the criteria for recruitment and dismissal, the selection of those personnel and their duties and hours of work shall be determined by the GOVERNMENT and CONTRACTOR by mutual consultation. All such personnel seconded to CONTRACTOR shall not be employees of CONTRACTOR and their usual salaries, costs, benefits and salary burdens attributable to the period of secondment shall be paid or cause to be paid by the GOVERNMENT and reimbursed by the CONTRACTOR. Costs associated with the secondment of personnel shall be eligible to be submitted by CONTRACOR as Petroleum Costs.'

By reading the above provisions, we can see that the secondment arrangement between the NOC and the IOC (international oil company) (or INOC, 'international' national oil company) focuses on training and technical skills/ management, but not on assisting the IOC as the operator of the petroleum operations. A thorough reading further reveals that there is no liabilities clause which demonstrates the secondees seconded by the government will not play an important role in the operator's organisation and the liabilities allocation in the secondment arrangement could be disregarded.

---

42 For reasons of confidentiality, all the real clauses regarding the secondment and/or project team will not specifically disclose the signing parties.

43 Seyed Kamran Bagheri and Alberto Di Minin state: 'some NOCs have made substantial progress in enhancing their efficiency and differentiating themselves from the traditional oil and gas state monopolies. These companies, variously referred to as Global NOCs, International NOCs, NOC Tigers, Super NOCs and Leading Group of NOCs are partially state-owned companies that compete globally across multiple sectors much like IOCs': S. Kamran Bagheri and A. Di Minin, 'The changing competitive landscape of the global upstream petroleum industry' (2015) 8(1) Journal of World Energy Law and Business 1-19 <http://jwelb.oxfordjournals.org/content/8/1/1.full>.

Another example comes from a JOA between a major oil company and an INOC. The secondment section of the JOA specifically includes provisions covering the secondment of the INOC's secondees:

> '(a) For so long as the INOC is a Non-Operator under this Agreement and during the term of the Contract, the INOC will be entitled to nominate up to [a fixed number of] Secondees per year from different technical backgrounds to Operator, subject to the provisions of this article 4.3.
>
> (b) Where the INOC Secondees perform primarily a trainee role, the compensation of such Secondees shall be borne by the INOC.
>
> (c) Operator shall use reasonable endeavors to engage [a fixed number of] nominated Secondees from the INOC as per Article 4.3.F.a with a specific trainee role for drilling operations (under rotation roles) during the Exploration and Appraisal operations for such Wells which are "Carried" by the INOC.'

The underlying assets governed by the JOA are located in an offshore deepwater region and the INOC is comparatively lacking in capacity to undertake such deepwater operations. In this regard, the JOA adopts two ways to address the secondment arrangement. If the secondees are seconded by the non-operator for training purposes, the cost of such secondees shall not be paid by the operator and no charges shall be made on the joint account. But if the secondees are seconded by the non-operator for the usual purposes provided under the international model JOAs, the cost of the secondees will be paid by the operator to the non-operator and all these expenditures shall be eventually be paid by the joint account. In this case, the secondment arrangement reveals the two functions: the training function and the function of assisting petroleum operations.

In a JOA entered into by three international oil companies (one is a super major IOC; the other two are important independent exploration and production companies), no secondment arrangement or project team arrangement is provided for. Based on the present author's experience, no secondment arrangement nor project team arrangement is usually provided for in a JOA where the project is led by a super major or a capable IOC (without the NOC's participation). In the event that there is a NOC participating in the project, the secondment arrangement will often be required by the NOC regardless of whether a super major or a capable IOC is part of the project.

Presenting real clauses from different JOAs between different industry players (super majors, independent exploration and production companies, NOCs) demonstrates that the functions, roles and wording of secondment arrangements and project team arrangements will vary in different circumstances.

8. CONCLUSION

Secondment arrangements and the project team agreements are two kinds of mechanism frequently employed by international petroleum players to exercise control over and provide assistance in joint petroleum operations. Although the industry has taken the view in the past that the use of secondment arrangements and project team agreements might have negative consequences (from the operator's perspective) for the operator-leading operations, the petroleum industry is now seeing more participants and projects beginning to use these two mechanisms in some complicated or frontier projects.

Where the projects involve an NOC or less sophisticated industry player, the secondment mechanism is usually used. Where the projects involve some technical difficulties, the project team mechanism is usually used. Both the secondment arrangement and the project team arrangement can be used to assist the operator. Furthermore, the project team mechanism is usually deemed to be an effective tool to control the operator, although a properly devised secondment arrangement may also perform the same function.

www.ingramcontent.com/pod-product-compliance
Ingram Content Group UK Ltd.
Pitfield, Milton Keynes, MK11 3LW, UK
UKHW051846100926
8556IPUK00005B/480

9 781780 684116